SATELLITE IMAGE OF CENTRAL SCOTLAND

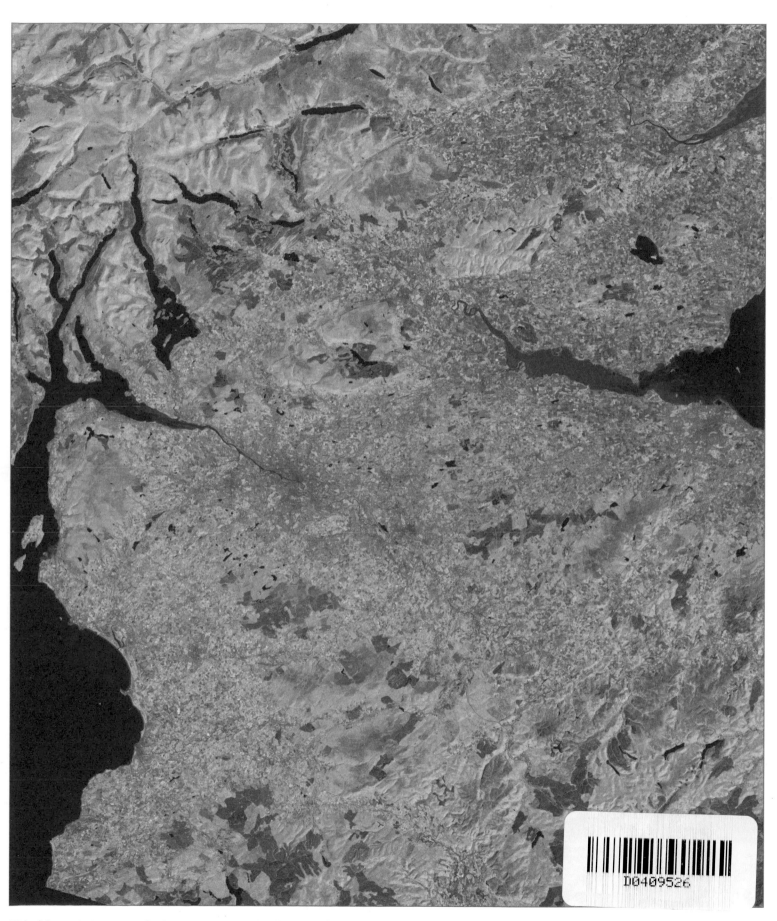

This false-colour composite image was recorded in June. Glasgow and Edinburgh and other settlements in the Forth–Clyde Valley are clearly visible in blue. The bright red areas are fields of healthy crops. Imagery such as this is used to police EU agricultural subsidies. *(EROS)*

PHILIP'S

MODERN SCHOOL ATLAS

93rd edition

IN ASSOCIATION WITH
THE ROYAL GEOGRAPHICAL SOCIETY
WITH THE INSTITUTE OF BRITISH GEOGRAPHERS

CONTENTS

Note: Each section is colour-coded on this contents page and on the heading of each page for ease of reference.

Published in Great Britain in 2000
by George Philip Limited,
a division of Octopus Publishing Group Limited,
2–4 Heron Quays, London E14 4JP

Cartography by Philip's

Ninety-third edition
© 2000 George Philip Limited

ISBN 0–540–07784–4 Paperback edition
ISBN 0–540–07783–6 Hardback edition

BRITISH ISLES MAPS

A separate map key is provided on the first page of the World Maps section.

SETTLEMENTS

■ **LONDON**　　■ **GLASGOW**　　▣ BRADFORD　　▣ Brighton　　◉ Gateshead

◉ Aylesbury　　◎ Sligo　　⊙ Selkirk　　○ Burford　　○ Lampeter

Settlement symbols and type styles vary according to the population and importance of towns

　Built up areas　　　　　　　□ London Boroughs

ADMINISTRATION

—— International boundaries　　**WALES** Country names

—— National boundaries　　　　KENT Administrative area names

—·—·— Administrative boundaries　　*EXMOOR* National park names

COMMUNICATIONS

=== Motorways　　　　　　　　　—— Main passenger railways
=== *under construction*　　　　 —— *under construction*
〕----〔 *in tunnels*　　　　　　　　〕----〔 *in tunnels*

—— Major roads　　　　　　　　—— Other passenger railways
—— *under construction*　　　　 —— *under construction*
〕----〔 *in tunnels*　　　　　　　　〕----〔 *in tunnels*

—— Other important roads　　　　—— Canals
—— *under construction*　　　　 ———— *in tunnels*
〕----〔 *in tunnels*

⊕　Major airports　　　⊕　Other airports

PHYSICAL FEATURES

∿ Perennial rivers　　　　　▲ 444　Elevations in metres

▱ Tidal flats　　　　　　　　▾ 38　Depths below sea level
　　　　　　　　　　　　　　　　　in metres

⬭ Lakes or reservoirs

⬚ Reservoirs under
　construction

ELEVATION AND DEPTH TINTS

Height of Land above Sea Level　　　Land below Sea Level　　　Depth of Sea

in metres	1000	750	500	400	200	100	0							
								150	300	600	1500	3000	6000	in feet
in feet	3000	2250	1500	1200	600	300								
							0	20	50	100	200	500	1000	2000
														in metres

SHETLAND ISLANDS
on same scale

Projection : Conical with two standard parallels

West from Greenwich

ORKNEY ISLANDS on same scale

Pentland Firth

Caithness

Sutherland

Easter Ross

Moray Firth

Black Isle

MORAY

Buchan

ABERDEENSHIRE

Formartine

Garioch

Strathbogie

Mar

Braemar

Badenoch

Grampian Mountains

Cairngorm Mts.

Monadhliath Mts.

Glen More

Kincardine

Braes of Angus

ANGUS

PERTH AND KINROSS

Rannoch

Aberdeen

Fraserburgh

Peterhead

Inverness

1:1 000 000

CARTOGRAPHY BY PHILIP'S.

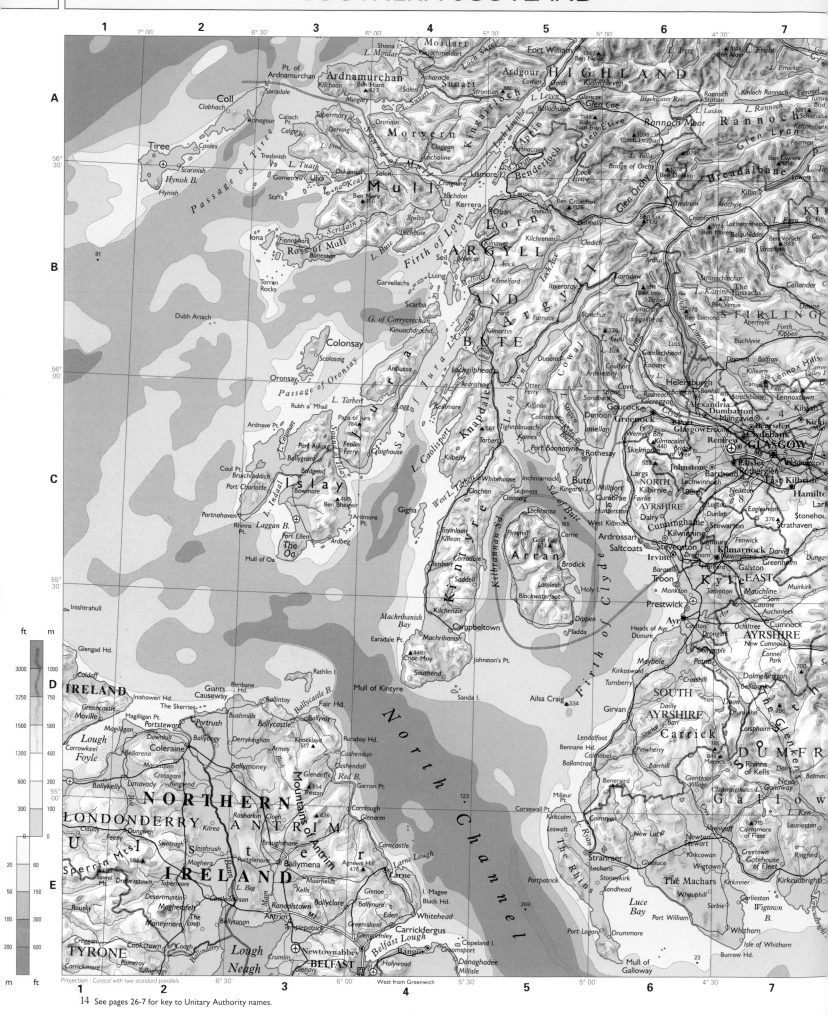

Projection : Conical with two standard parallels

West from Greenwich

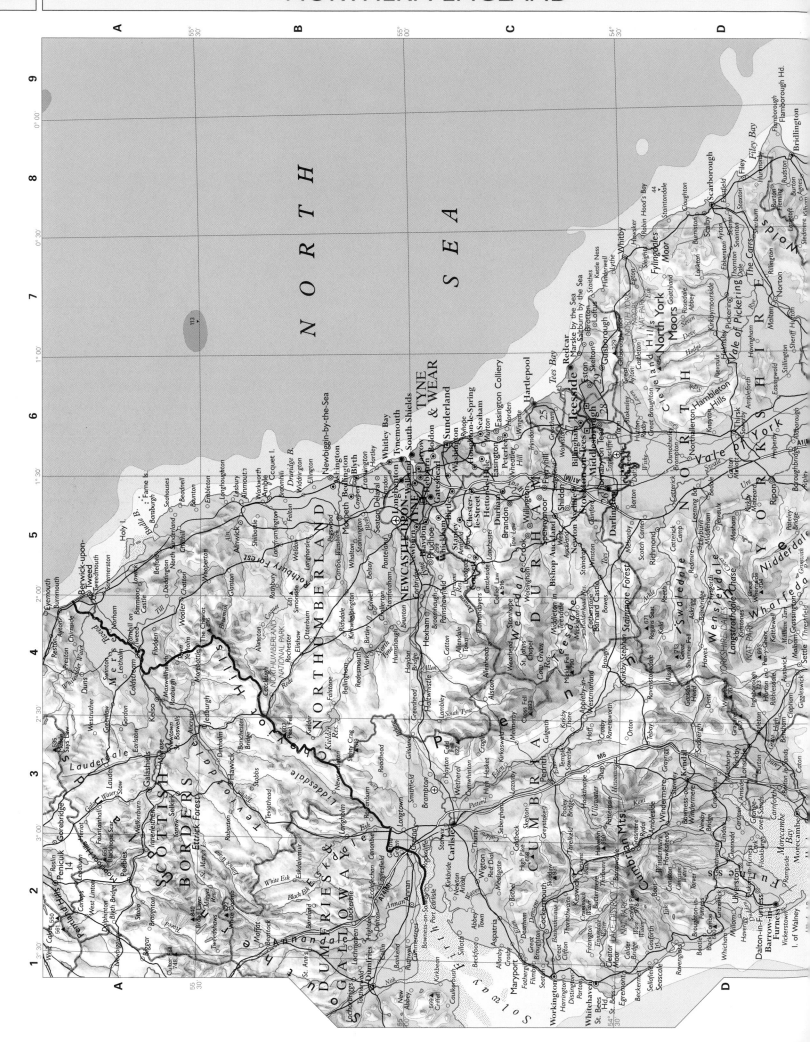

1:1 000 000

COPYRIGHT GEORGE PHILIP LTD.

East from Greenwich

WALES AND

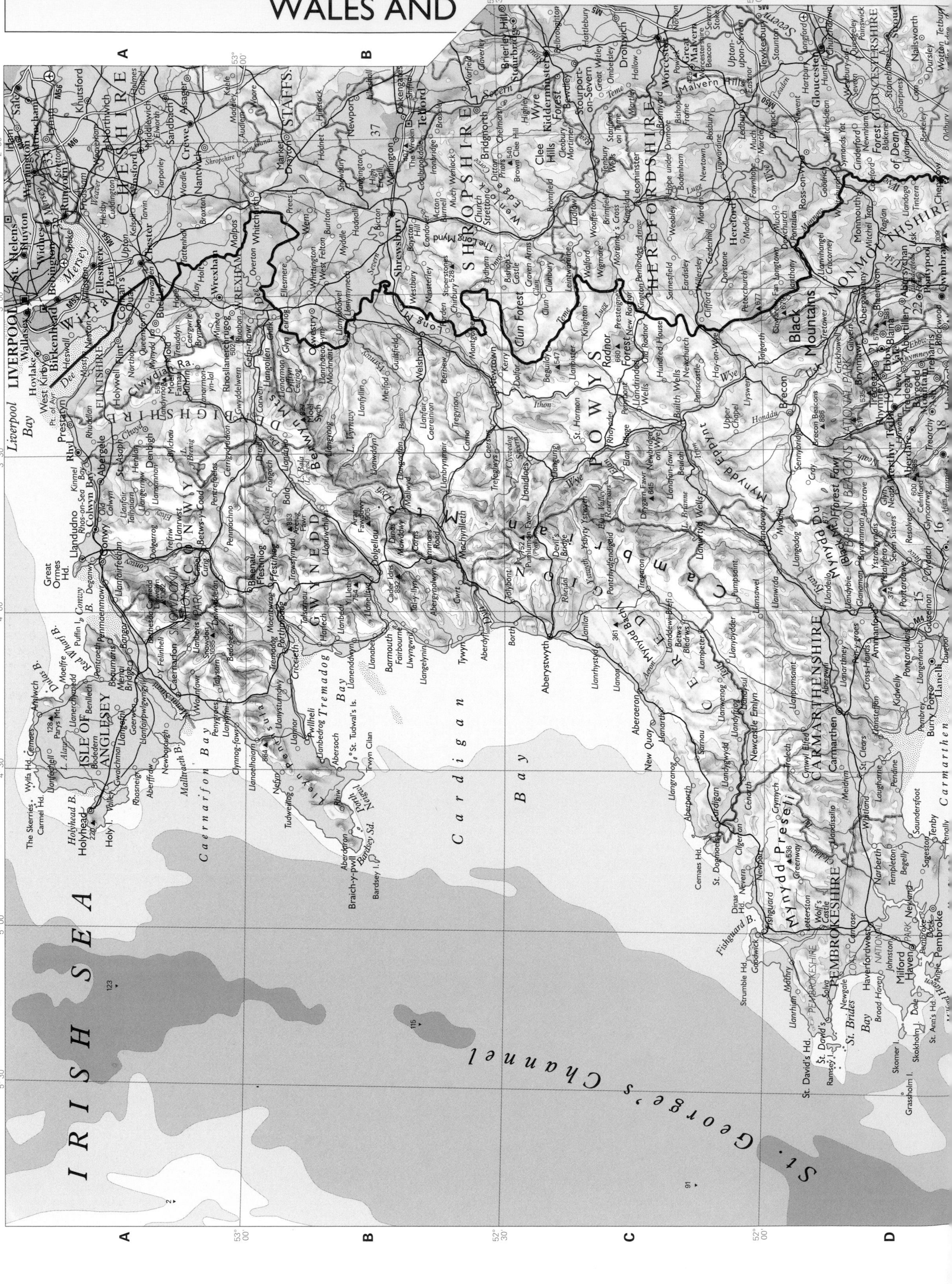
IRISH SEA
St. George's Channel
Cardigan Bay
Caernarfon Bay
Liverpool Bay
Carmarthen
St. Brides Bay
ISLE OF ANGLESEY
GWYNEDD
CONWY
DENBIGHSHIRE
FLINTSHIRE
WREXHAM
CEREDIGION
POWYS
CARMARTHENSHIRE
PEMBROKESHIRE
MONMOUTHSHIRE
CHESHIRE
STAFFS.
SHROPSHIRE
HEREFORDSHIRE
GLOUCESTERSHIRE
Cambrian Mts.
Berwyn Mts.
Black Mountains
Clun Forest
Radnor Forest
Mynydd Preseli
SNOWDONIA NATIONAL PARK
BRECON BEACONS NATIONAL PARK
PEMBROKESHIRE COAST NATIONAL PARK
LIVERPOOL
Birkenhead
Chester
Wrexham
Shrewsbury
Telford
Hereford
Gloucester
Aberystwyth
Cardigan
Carmarthen
Brecon
Holyhead
Caernarfon
Bangor
Llandudno
Rhyl
Wallasey
Fishguard
Milford Haven
Pembroke
Tenby
Llanelli
A
B
C
D
2
3
4
5
6
7
8
9

FRANCE

CHANNEL ISLANDS
on same scale

Passage de la Déroute

Alderney
St. Anne
C. de la Hague
Les Pieux
Barneville-Carteret
Carteret
Jersey
St. Helier
St. Peter Port
Guernsey
Sark
Herm
St. Martin
Grosnez Pt.
St. Ouens Bay
St. Brelade
Gorey
Rozel
Trinity

CHANNEL ISLANDS

COPYRIGHT GEORGE PHILIP LTD.

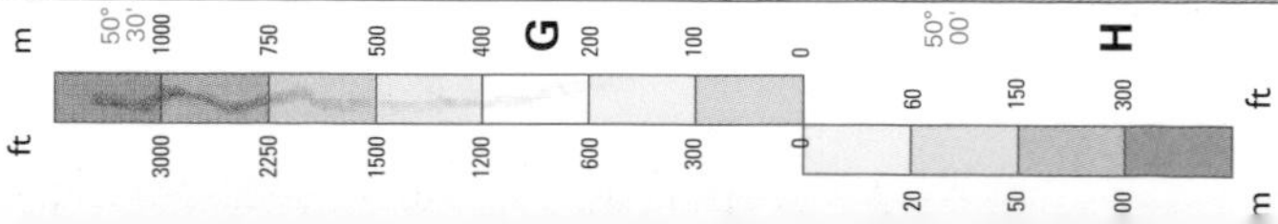

SOMERSET
DEVON
CORNWALL
DORSET

BRISTOL
CARDIFF
Newport
Bath
Weston-super-Mare
Bridgwater
Bay
Bridgwater
Minehead
Exmoor National Park
Barnstaple
Bideford
Ilfracombe
Taunton
Exeter
Tiverton
Dartmoor National Park
Torquay
Torbay
Paignton
Brixham
Dartmouth
Plymouth
Saltash
Bodmin Moor
Bodmin
Truro
Falmouth
Newquay
St. Austell
Redruth
Camborne
Penzance
Land's End
Lizard Pt.

Bristol Channel

Mendip Hills
Quantock Hills
Blackdown Hills
Brendon Hills
North Dorset Downs
South Dorset Downs
Blackmoor Vale
Dorchester
Weymouth
I. of Portland
Portland Bill
Lyme Bay
Sidmouth
Exmouth
Start Pt.
Bolt Head
Start Bay
Mount's Bay
Lundy
Hartland Pt.

Wolf Rock

ISLES OF SCILLY
on same scale

Isles of Scilly
Tresco
St. Martin's
St. Mary's
St. Agnes
Bryher
Gugh
Annet

Gurnard's Hd.
Pendeen
C. Cornwall
St. Just
Sennen
Land's End
St. Buryan
St. Levan
Penzance
Newlyn
Wolf Rock

1:1 000 000

Projection: Conical with two standard parallels
See pages 26-7 for key to Unitary Authority names.

m / ft
3000
2250
1500
1200
600
400
200
0

West from Greenwich

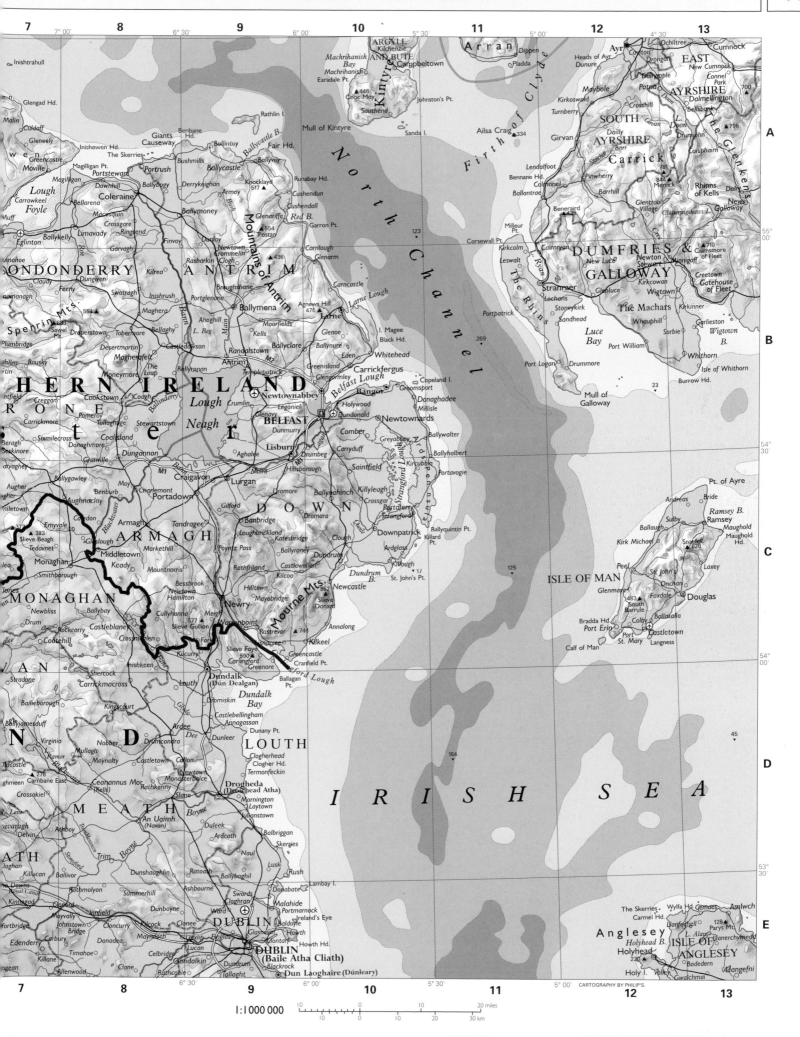

1:1 000 000

CARTOGRAPHY BY PHILIP'S.

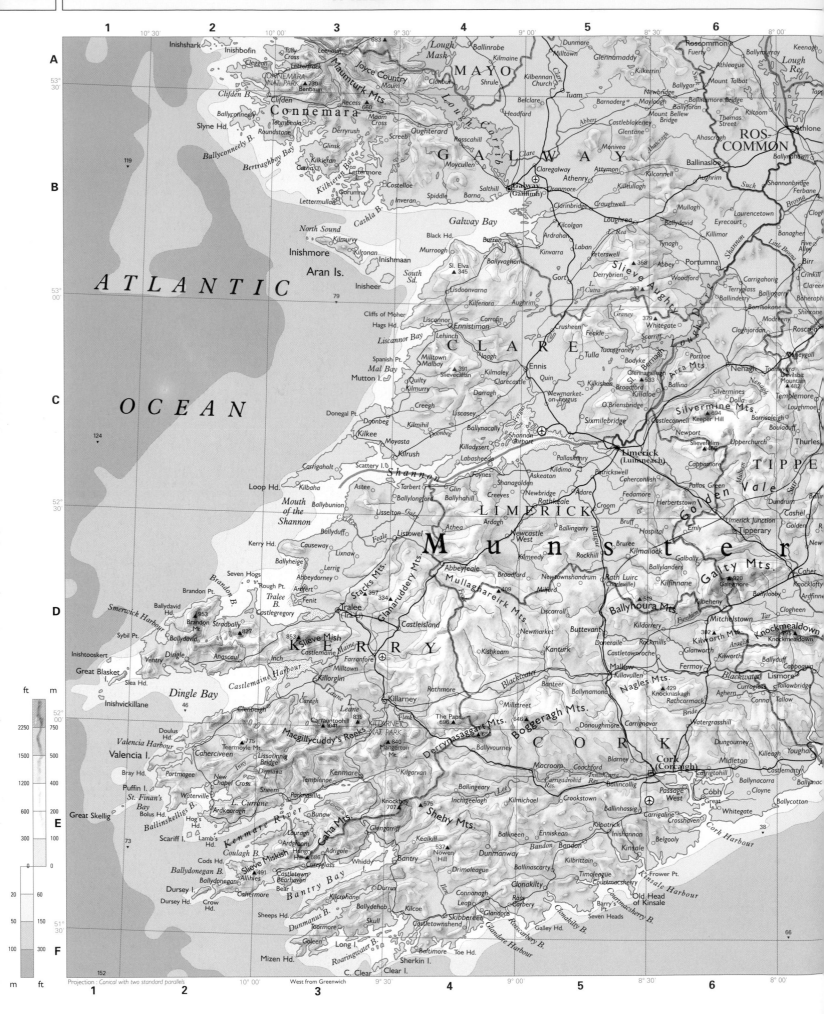

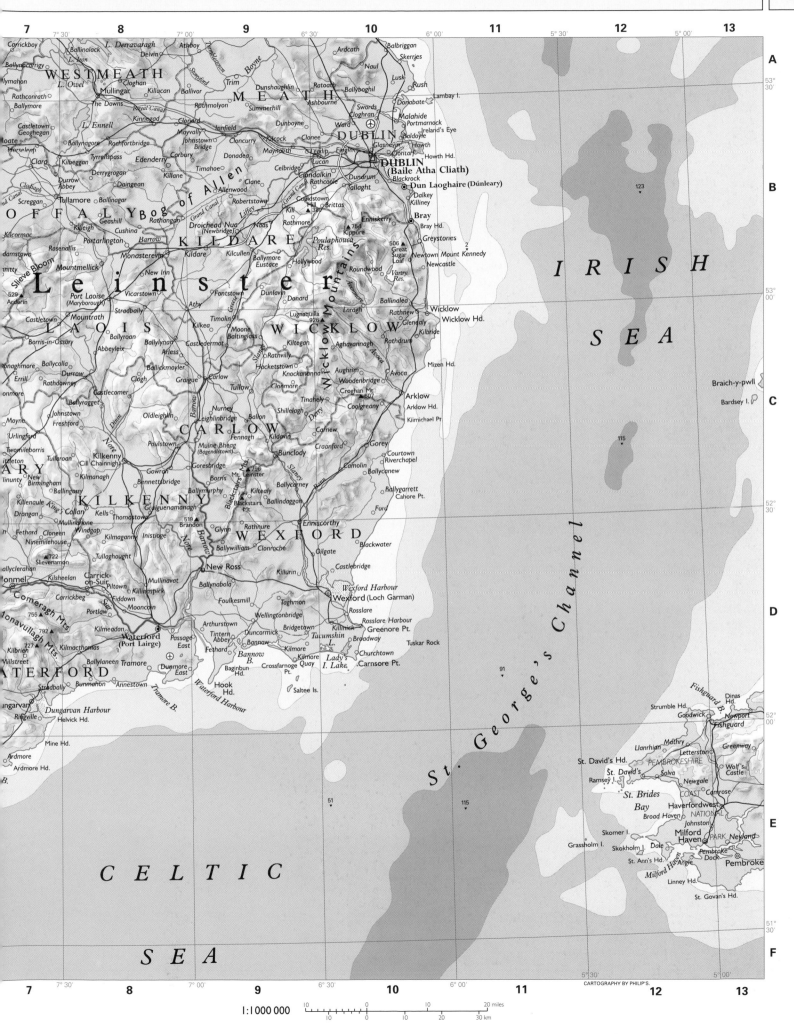

CELTIC

SEA

1:1 000 000

CARTOGRAPHY BY PHILIP'S.

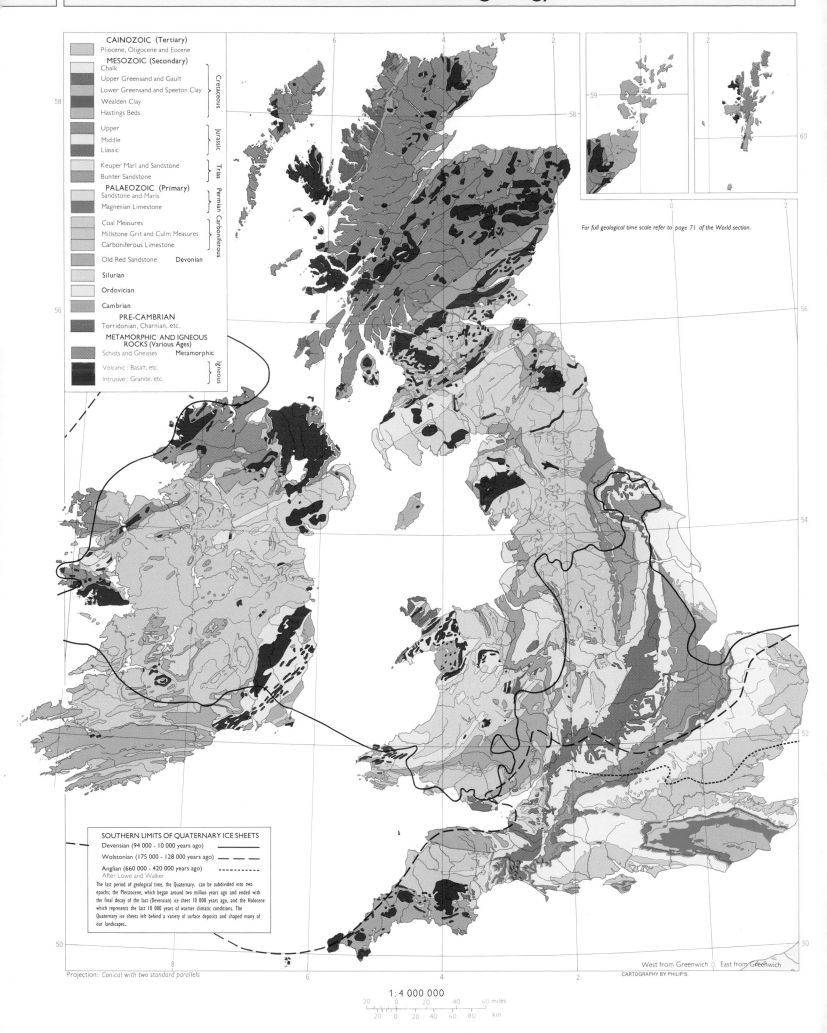

CAINOZOIC (Tertiary)
Pliocene, Oligocene and Eocene

MESOZOIC (Secondary)
Chalk
Upper Greensand and Gault
Lower Greensand and Speeton Clay — Cretaceous
Wealden Clay
Hastings Beds

Upper
Middle — Jurassic
Liassic

Keuper Marl and Sandstone — Trias
Bunter Sandstone

PALAEOZOIC (Primary)
Sandstone and Marls — Permian
Magnesian Limestone

Coal Measures
Millstone Grit and Culm Measures — Carboniferous
Carboniferous Limestone

Old Red Sandstone — Devonian

Silurian

Ordovician

Cambrian

PRE-CAMBRIAN
Torridonian, Charnian, etc.

METAMORPHIC AND IGNEOUS ROCKS (Various Ages)
Schists and Gneisses — Metamorphic

Volcanic : Basalt, etc. — Igneous
Intrusive : Granite, etc.

For full geological time scale refer to page 71 of the World section.

SOUTHERN LIMITS OF QUATERNARY ICE SHEETS
Devensian (94 000 - 10 000 years ago) ————
Wolstonian (175 000 - 128 000 years ago) — — —
Anglian (660 000 - 420 000 years ago) ·············
After Lowe and Walker

The last period of geological time, the Quaternary, can be subdivided into two epochs; the Pleistocene, which began around two million years ago and ended with the final decay of the last (Devensian) ice sheet 10 000 years ago, and the Holocene which represents the last 10 000 years of warmer climatic conditions. The Quaternary ice sheets left behind a variety of surface deposits and shaped many of our landscapes.

Projection: *Conical with two standard parallels*

West from Greenwich 0 East from Greenwich

CARTOGRAPHY BY PHILIP'S.

1 : 4 000 000

20   0   20   40   60 miles

20   0   20   40   60   80 km

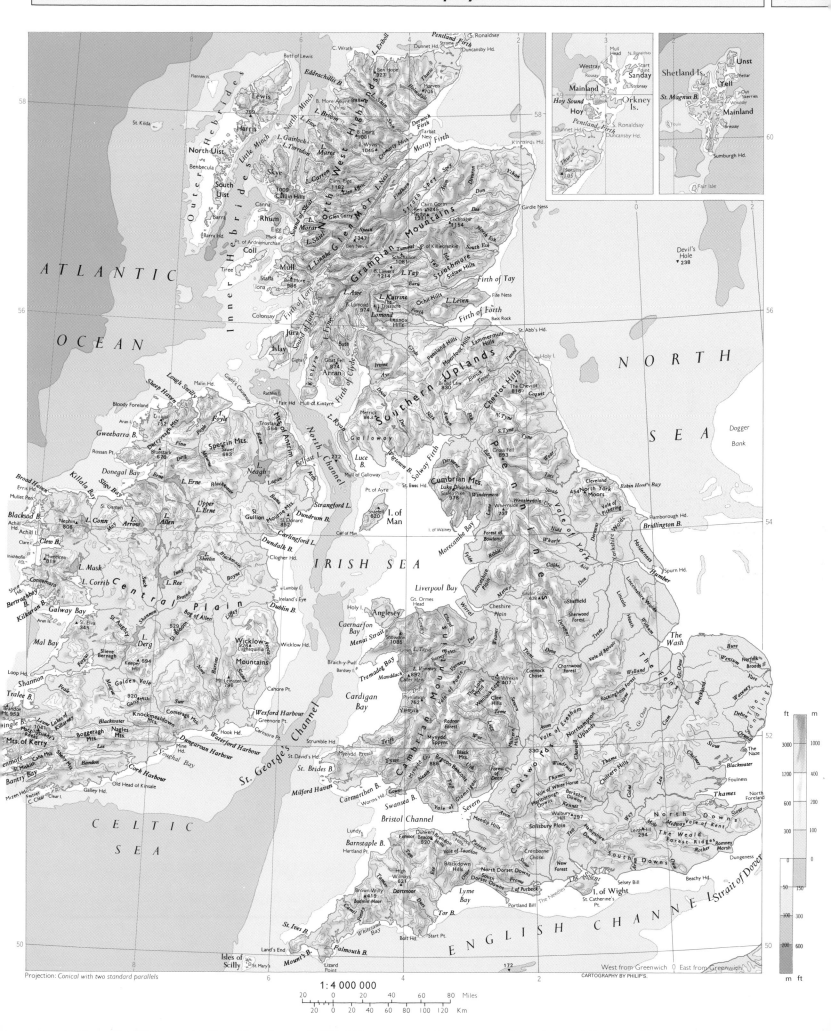

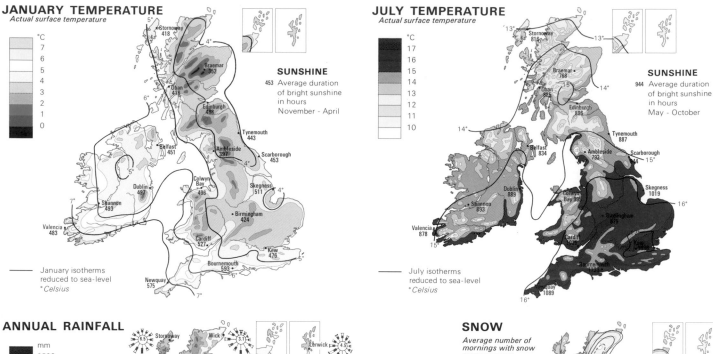

JANUARY TEMPERATURE
Actual surface temperature

°C
7
6
5
4
3
2
1
0

SUNSHINE

453 Average duration of bright sunshine in hours November - April

—— January isotherms reduced to sea-level °Celsius

JULY TEMPERATURE
Actual surface temperature

°C
17
16
15
14
13
12
11
10

SUNSHINE

944 Average duration of bright sunshine in hours May - October

—— July isotherms reduced to sea-level °Celsius

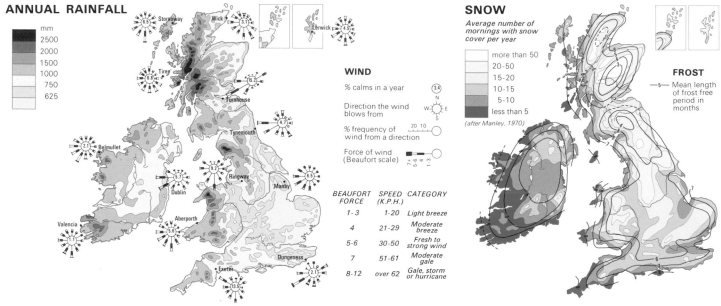

ANNUAL RAINFALL

mm
2500
2000
1500
1000
750
625

WIND

% calms in a year (3.4)

Direction the wind blows from

% frequency of wind from a direction   20 10

Force of wind (Beaufort scale) 7+ 5-6 4 1-3

BEAUFORT FORCE	SPEED (K.P.H.)	CATEGORY
1-3	1-20	Light breeze
4	21-29	Moderate breeze
5-6	30-50	Fresh to strong wind
7	51-61	Moderate gale
8-12	over 62	Gale, storm or hurricane

SNOW

Average number of mornings with snow cover per year

more than 50
20-50
15-20
10-15
5-10
less than 5

(after Manley, 1970)

FROST

—5— Mean length of frost free period in months

VARIABILITY OF RAIN

The percentage frequency with which rainfall varies from the normal rainfall regime in an area: the higher the percentage figure, the more variable the rainfall.

over 20%
18-20%
16-18%
14-16%
12-14%
10-12%
under 10%

(after Gregory, 1955)

CLIMATE STATIONS

• T Climate stations which appear on page 19

Regions of reliably high rainfall (more than 1250mm in at least 70% of the years)

Regions of occasionally low rainfall (less than 750mm in at least 30% of the years)

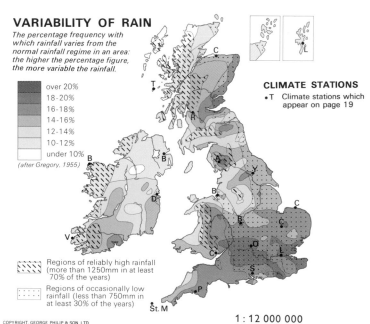

1 : 12 000 000

SYNOPTIC CHART FOR A TYPICAL WINTER DEPRESSION
21st January 1971

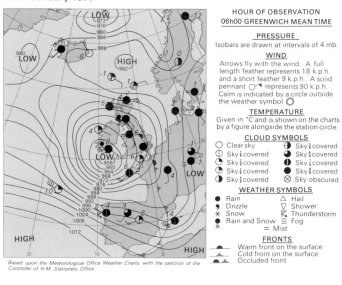

HOUR OF OBSERVATION
06h00 GREENWICH MEAN TIME

PRESSURE
Isobars are drawn at intervals of 4 mb.

WIND
Arrows fly with the wind. A full length feather represents 18 k.p.h. and a short feather 9 k.p.h. A solid pennant represents 90 k.p.h. Calm is indicated by a circle outside the weather symbol ◯

TEMPERATURE
Given in °C and is shown on the charts by a figure alongside the station circle.

CLOUD SYMBOLS

◯ Clear sky	◑ Sky ⅗ covered
◔ Sky ⅛ covered	◕ Sky ⅚ covered
◑ Sky ¼ covered	● Sky ⅞ covered
◑ Sky ⅜ covered	● Sky ⅞ covered
◑ Sky ½ covered	⊗ Sky obscured

WEATHER SYMBOLS

● Rain	△ Hail
🌢 Drizzle	▽ Shower
✳ Snow	⚡ Thunderstorm
✱ Rain and Snow	≡ Fog
	= Mist

FRONTS
Warm front on the surface
Cold front on the surface
Occluded front

Based upon the Meteorological Office Weather Charts, with the sanction of the Controller of H.M. Stationery Office

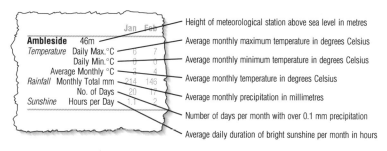

Ambleside 46m — Height of meteorological station above sea level in metres

- *Temperature* Daily Max. °C (6, 7) — Average monthly maximum temperature in degrees Celsius
- Daily Min. °C (0, 0) — Average monthly minimum temperature in degrees Celsius
- Average Monthly °C (3, 4) — Average monthly temperature in degrees Celsius
- *Rainfall* Monthly Total mm (214, 146) — Average monthly precipitation in millimetres
- No. of Days (20, 17) — Number of days per month with over 0.1 mm precipitation
- *Sunshine* Hours per Day (1.1, 2) — Average daily duration of bright sunshine per month in hours

Station		Jan	Feb	Mar	Apr	May	June	July	Aug	Sep	Oct	Nov	Dec	Year
Ambleside 46m														
Temperature	Daily Max. °C	6	7	9	12	16	19	20	19	17	13	9	7	13
	Daily Min. °C	0	0	2	4	6	9	11	11	9	6	3	1	5
	Average Monthly °C	3	4	6	8	11	14	15	15	13	10	6	4	9
Rainfall	Monthly Total mm	214	146	112	101	90	111	134	139	184	196	209	215	1851
	No. of Days	20	17	15	15	14	15	18	17	18	19	19	21	208
Sunshine	Hours per Day	1.1	2	3.2	4.5	6	5.7	4.5	4.2	3.3	2.2	1.4	1	3.3
Belfast 4m														
Temperature	Daily Max. °C	6	7	9	12	15	18	18	18	16	13	9	7	12
	Daily Min. °C	2	2	3	4	6	9	11	11	9	7	4	3	6
	Average Monthly °C	4	4	6	8	11	13	15	15	13	10	7	5	9
Rainfall	Monthly Total mm	80	52	50	48	52	68	94	77	80	83	72	90	845
	No. of Days	20	17	16	16	15	16	19	17	18	19	19	21	213
Sunshine	Hours per Day	1.5	2.3	3.4	5	6.3	6	4.4	4.4	3.6	2.6	1.8	1.1	3.5
Belmullet 9m														
Temperature	Daily Max. °C	8	9	10	12	14	16	17	17	16	14	10	9	12
	Daily Min. °C	3	4	4	6	8	10	11	11	10	8	5	4	7
	Average Monthly °C	5	6	7	9	11	13	14	14	13	11	8	6	10
Rainfall	Monthly Total mm	108	64	82	70	75	80	76	95	108	116	127	131	1132
	No. of Days	18	13	16	15	14	12	14	17	16	18	20	22	195
Sunshine	Hours per Day	1.9	2.5	3.4	5.2	7	6	4.6	5.1	3.9	2.9	1.9	1.3	3.8
Birkenhead 60m														
Temperature	Daily Max. °C	6	6	9	11	15	17	19	19	16	13	9	7	12
	Daily Min. °C	2	2	3	5	8	11	13	13	11	8	5	3	7
	Average Monthly °C	4	4	6	8	11	14	16	16	14	10	7	5	10
Rainfall	Monthly Total mm	64	46	40	41	55	55	67	80	66	71	76	65	726
	No. of Days	18	13	13	13	13	13	15	15	15	17	17	19	181
Sunshine	Hours per Day	1.6	2.4	3.5	5.3	6.3	6.7	5.7	5.4	4.2	2.9	1.8	1.3	3.9
Birmingham 163m														
Temperature	Daily Max. °C	5	6	9	12	16	19	20	20	17	13	9	6	13
	Daily Min. °C	2	2	3	5	7	10	12	12	10	7	5	3	7
	Average Monthly °C	3	4	6	8	11	15	16	16	14	10	7	5	10
Rainfall	Monthly Total mm	74	54	50	53	64	50	69	69	61	69	84	67	764
	No. of Days	17	15	13	13	14	13	15	14	14	15	17	18	178
Sunshine	Hours per Day	1.4	2.1	3.2	4.6	5.4	6	5.4	5.1	3.9	2.8	1.6	1.2	3.6
Cambridge 12m														
Temperature	Daily Max. °C	6	7	11	14	17	21	22	22	19	15	10	7	14
	Daily Min. °C	1	1	2	4	7	10	12	12	10	6	4	2	6
	Average Monthly °C	3	4	6	9	12	15	17	17	14	10	7	5	10
Rainfall	Monthly Total mm	49	35	36	37	45	45	58	55	51	51	54	41	558
	No. of Days	15	13	10	11	11	11	12	12	11	13	14	14	147
Sunshine	Hours per Day	1.7	2.5	3.8	5.1	6.2	6.7	6	5.7	4.6	3.4	1.9	1.4	4.1
Cardiff 62m														
Temperature	Daily Max. °C	7	7	10	13	16	19	20	21	18	14	10	8	14
	Daily Min. °C	2	2	3	5	8	11	12	13	11	8	5	3	7
	Average Monthly °C	4	5	7	9	12	15	16	17	14	11	8	6	10
Rainfall	Monthly Total mm	108	72	63	65	76	63	89	97	99	109	116	108	1065
	No. of Days	18	14	13	13	13	13	14	15	16	16	17	18	180
Sunshine	Hours per Day	1.7	2.7	4	5.6	6.4	6.9	6.2	6	4.7	3.4	1.9	1.5	4.3
Craibstone 91m														
Temperature	Daily Max. °C	5	6	8	10	13	16	18	17	15	12	8	6	11
	Daily Min. °C	0	0	2	3	5	8	10	10	8	6	3	1	5
	Average Monthly °C	3	3	5	7	9	12	14	13	12	9	6	4	8
Rainfall	Monthly Total mm	78	55	53	51	63	54	95	75	67	92	93	80	856
	No. of Days	19	16	15	15	14	14	18	15	16	18	19	18	197
Sunshine	Hours per Day	1.8	2.9	3.5	4.9	5.9	6.1	5.1	4.8	4.3	3.1	2	1.5	3.8
Cromer 54m														
Temperature	Daily Max. °C	6	7	9	12	15	18	21	20	18	14	10	8	13
	Daily Min. °C	1	1	3	5	7	10	12	13	11	8	5	3	7
	Average Monthly °C	4	4	6	8	11	14	16	16	15	11	7	5	10
Rainfall	Monthly Total mm	58	46	37	39	48	39	63	56	54	61	64	53	618
	No. of Days	18	16	13	13	11	11	13	12	14	16	18	18	173
Sunshine	Hours per Day	1.8	2.6	4	5.4	6.4	6.8	6.3	5.8	5	3.6	2	1.9	4.3
Dublin 47m														
Temperature	Daily Max. °C	8	8	10	13	15	18	20	19	17	14	10	8	14
	Daily Min. °C	1	2	3	4	6	9	11	11	9	6	4	3	6
	Average Monthly °C	4	5	7	8	11	14	15	15	13	10	7	6	10
Rainfall	Monthly Total mm	67	55	51	45	60	57	70	74	72	70	67	74	762
	No. of Days	13	10	10	11	10	11	13	12	12	11	12	14	139
Sunshine	Hours per Day	1.9	2.5	3.4	5	6.2	6	4.8	4.9	3.9	3.2	2.1	1.6	3.8
Durham 102m														
Temperature	Daily Max. °C	6	6	9	12	15	18	20	19	17	13	9	7	13
	Daily Min. °C	0	0	1	3	6	9	11	10	9	6	3	2	5
	Average Monthly °C	3	3	5	7	10	13	15	15	13	9	6	4	9
Rainfall	Monthly Total mm	59	51	38	38	51	49	61	67	60	63	66	55	658
	No. of Days	17	15	14	13	13	14	15	14	14	16	17	17	179
Sunshine	Hours per Day	1.7	2.5	3.3	4.6	5.4	6	5.1	4.8	4.1	3	1.9	1.4	3.6
Lerwick 82m														
Temperature	Daily Max. °C	5	5	6	8	11	13	14	14	13	10	8	6	9
	Daily Min. °C	1	1	2	3	5	7	10	10	8	6	4	3	5
	Average Monthly °C	3	3	4	5	8	10	12	12	11	8	6	4	7
Rainfall	Monthly Total mm	109	87	69	68	52	55	72	71	87	104	111	118	1003
	No. of Days	25	22	20	21	15	15	17	17	19	23	24	25	243
Sunshine	Hours per Day	0.8	1.8	2.9	4.4	5.3	5.3	4	3.8	3.5	2.2	2.2	0.5	3
London (Kew) 5m														
Temperature	Daily Max. °C	6	7	10	13	17	20	22	21	19	14	10	7	14
	Daily Min. °C	2	2	3	6	8	12	14	13	11	8	5	4	7
	Average Monthly °C	4	5	7	9	12	16	18	17	15	11	8	5	11
Rainfall	Monthly Total mm	54	40	37	37	46	45	57	59	49	57	64	48	593
	No. of Days	15	13	11	12	12	11	12	11	13	13	15	15	153
Sunshine	Hours per Day	1.5	2.3	3.6	5.3	6.4	7.1	6.4	6.1	4.7	3.2	1.8	1.3	4.1
Oxford 63m														
Temperature	Daily Max. °C	7	7	11	14	17	20	22	22	19	14	10	8	14
	Daily Min. °C	1	1	2	5	7	10	12	12	10	7	4	2	6
	Average Monthly °C	4	4	6	9	12	15	17	17	14	11	7	5	10
Rainfall	Monthly Total mm	61	44	43	41	55	52	55	60	59	64	69	57	660
	No. of Days	13	10	9	9	10	9	10	10	10	11	12	13	126
Sunshine	Hours per Day	1.7	2.6	3.9	5.3	6.1	6.6	5.9	5.7	4.4	3.2	2.1	1.6	4.1
Plymouth 27m														
Temperature	Daily Max. °C	8	8	10	12	15	18	19	19	18	15	11	9	14
	Daily Min. °C	4	4	5	6	8	11	13	13	12	9	7	5	8
	Average Monthly °C	6	6	7	9	12	15	16	16	15	12	9	7	11
Rainfall	Monthly Total mm	99	74	69	53	63	53	70	77	78	91	113	110	950
	No. of Days	19	15	14	12	12	12	14	14	15	16	17	18	178
Sunshine	Hours per Day	1.9	2.9	4.3	6.1	7.1	7.4	6.4	6.4	5.1	3.7	2.2	1.7	4.6
Renfrew 6m														
Temperature	Daily Max. °C	5	7	9	12	15	18	19	19	16	13	9	7	12
	Daily Min. °C	1	1	2	4	6	9	11	11	9	6	4	2	6
	Average Monthly °C	3	4	6	8	11	14	15	15	13	9	7	4	9
Rainfall	Monthly Total mm	111	85	69	67	63	70	97	93	102	119	106	127	1109
	No. of Days	19	16	15	15	14	15	17	17	17	18	18	20	201
Sunshine	Hours per Day	1.1	2.1	2.9	4.7	6	6.1	5.1	4.4	3.7	2.3	1.4	0.8	3.4
St Helier 9m														
Temperature	Daily Max. °C	9	8	11	13	16	19	21	21	19	16	12	10	15
	Daily Min. °C	5	4	6	7	10	13	15	15	14	11	8	6	9
	Average Monthly °C	7	6	8	10	13	16	18	18	17	13	10	8	12
Rainfall	Monthly Total mm	89	68	57	43	44	39	48	67	69	77	101	99	801
	No. of Days	19	15	13	12	11	10	11	12	15	15	17	19	169
Sunshine	Hours per Day	2.3	3.1	5	6.7	7.8	8.5	7.8	7.6	5.6	4.1	2.5	1.8	5.3
St Mary's 50m														
Temperature	Daily Max. °C	9	9	11	12	14	17	19	19	18	15	12	10	14
	Daily Min. °C	6	6	7	7	9	12	13	14	13	11	9	7	9
	Average Monthly °C	8	7	9	10	12	14	16	16	15	13	10	9	12
Rainfall	Monthly Total mm	91	71	69	46	56	49	61	64	67	80	96	94	844
	No. of Days	22	17	16	13	14	14	16	15	16	17	19	21	200
Sunshine	Hours per Day	2	2.9	4.2	6.4	7.6	7.6	6.7	6.7	5.2	3.9	2.5	1.8	4.8
Southampton 20m														
Temperature	Daily Max. °C	7	8	11	14	17	20	22	22	19	15	11	8	15
	Daily Min. °C	2	2	3	5	8	11	13	13	11	7	5	3	7
	Average Monthly °C	5	5	7	10	13	16	17	17	15	11	8	6	11
Rainfall	Monthly Total mm	83	56	52	45	56	49	60	69	70	86	94	84	804
	No. of Days	17	13	13	12	12	12	13	13	14	14	16	17	166
Sunshine	Hours per Day	1.8	2.6	4	5.7	6.7	7.2	6.5	6.4	4.9	3.6	2.2	1.6	4.5
Tiree 9m														
Temperature	Daily Max. °C	7	7	9	10	13	15	16	16	15	12	10	8	12
	Daily Min. °C	4	3	4	5	7	10	11	11	10	8	6	5	7
	Average Monthly °C	5	5	6	8	10	12	14	14	13	10	8	6	9
Rainfall	Monthly Total mm	117	77	67	64	55	70	91	90	118	129	122	128	1128
	No. of Days	23	19	17	17	15	16	20	18	20	23	22	24	234
Sunshine	Hours per Day	1.3	2.6	3.7	5.7	7.5	6.8	5.2	5.3	4.2	2.6	1.6	0.9	4
Valencia 9m														
Temperature	Daily Max. °C	9	9	11	13	15	17	18	18	17	14	12	10	14
	Daily Min. °C	5	4	5	6	8	11	12	13	11	9	7	6	8
	Average Monthly °C	7	7	8	9	11	0	15	15	14	12	9	8	11
Rainfall	Monthly Total mm	165	107	103	75	86	81	107	95	122	140	151	168	1400
	No. of Days	20	15	14	13	13	13	15	15	16	17	18	21	190
Sunshine	Hours per Day	1.6	2.5	3.5	5.2	6.5	5.9	4.7	4.9	3.8	2.8	2	1.3	3.7
York 17m														
Temperature	Daily Max. °C	6	7	10	13	16	19	21	21	18	14	10	7	13
	Daily Min. °C	1	1	2	4	7	10	12	12	10	7	4	2	6
	Average Monthly °C	3	4	6	9	12	15	17	16	14	10	7	5	10
Rainfall	Monthly Total mm	59	46	37	41	50	50	62	68	55	56	65	50	639
	No. of Days	17	15	13	13	13	14	15	14	14	15	17	17	177
Sunshine	Hours per Day	1.3	2.1	3.2	4.7	6.1	6.4	5.6	5.1	4.1	2.8	1.6	1.1	3.7

WATER SUPPLY

- Regions of reliably high rainfall (more than 1250 mm in at least 70% of the years)
- ③ Major reservoirs (capacity over 20 million cubic metres, see list opposite for details)
- → Existing inter-regional transfers of water (by pipeline and river)
- → Proposed inter-regional transfers of water (by pipeline and river)
- □ Proposed estuary storage site
- ▽ Proposed groundwater storage site
- Principal sources of groundwater (porous and jointed aquifers)

1 : 7 000 000

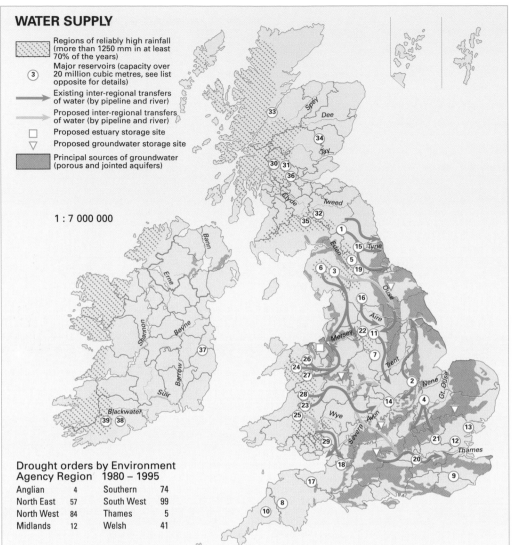

Drought orders by Environment Agency Region 1980 – 1995

Anglian	4	Southern	74
North East	57	South West	99
North West	84	Thames	5
Midlands	12	Welsh	41

Major reservoirs (with capacity in million m³)

England		Wales	
1 Kielder Res.	198	23 Elan Valley	99
2 Rutland Water	123	24 Llyn Celyn	74
3 Haweswater	85	25 Llyn Brianne	62
4 Grafham Water	59	26 Llyn Brenig	60
5 Cow Green Res.	41	27 Llyn Vyrnwy	60
6 Thirlmere	41	28 Llyn Clywedog	48
7 Carsington Res.	36	29 Llandegfedd Res.	22
8 Roadford Res.	35		
9 Bewl Water Res.	31	**Scotland**	
10 Colliford Lake	29	30 Loch Lomond	86
11 Ladybower Res.	28	31 Loch Katrine	64
12 Hanningfield Res.	27	32 Megget Res.	64
13 Abberton Res.	25	33 Loch Ness	26
14 Draycote Water	23	34 Blackwater Res.	25
15 Derwent Res.	22	35 Daer Res.	23
16 Grimwith Res.	22	36 Carron Valley Res.	21
17 Wimbleball Lake	21		
18 Chew Valley Lake	20	**Ireland**	
19 Balderhead Res.	20	37 Poulaphouca Res.	168
20 Thames Valley (linked reservoirs)		38 Inishcarra Res.	57
21 Lea Valley (linked reservoirs)		39 Carrigadrohid Res.	33
22 Longendale (linked reservoirs)			

Average daily domestic water use in England and Wales

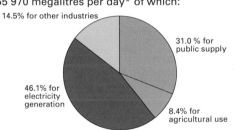

W.C. flushing	Bath/shower	Washing machine	Other uses (e.g. dishwashers, drinking water, washing, cleaning, outside, etc.)
32%	17%	12%	39%

Water abstractions in England and Wales (1995) 55 970 megalitres per day* of which:

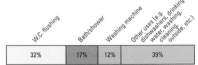

- 14.5% for other industries
- 31.0 % for public supply
- 46.1% for electricity generation
- 8.4% for agricultural use

*average daily domestic consumption per head 380 litres.

WATER ABSTRACTIONS   1 : 12 000 000

THAMES — Environment Agency Region

1883 (16%) — Water supply* in megalitres per day (with percentage of total abstraction from groundwater in brackets)

*Piped mains water, excluding water abstracted for agricultural and industrial use

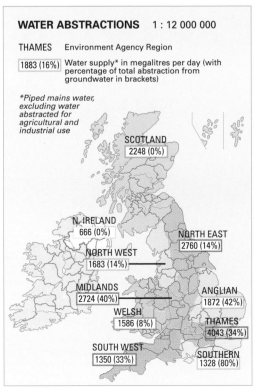

- SCOTLAND 2248 (0%)
- N. IRELAND 666 (0%)
- NORTH EAST 2760 (14%)
- NORTH WEST 1683 (14%)
- MIDLANDS 2724 (40%)
- ANGLIAN 1872 (42%)
- WELSH 1586 (8%)
- THAMES 4043 (34%)
- SOUTH WEST 1350 (33%)
- SOUTHERN 1328 (80%)

WATER QUALITY   1 : 12 000 000

The percentage of all rivers and canals of poor or bad quality within each Environment Agency Region 1993 – 1995

- Over 15%
- 10% – 15%
- 5% – 10%
- Under 5%

The percentage of bathing beaches complying with E.C. standards in 1996

- Over 95%
- 75% – 95%
- Under 75%

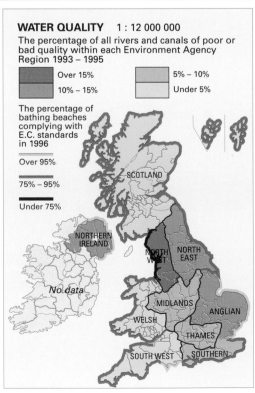

- SCOTLAND
- NORTHERN IRELAND
- NORTH WEST
- NORTH EAST
- No data
- MIDLANDS
- WELSH
- ANGLIAN
- THAMES
- SOUTH WEST
- SOUTHERN

SOILS   1 : 12 000 000

- Calcareous brown earth
- Brown earth
- Acid brown earth
- Podsol
- Peaty podsol
- Grey-brown podso[l]
- Gley
- Basin peat and alluvial gleys
- Peaty gley and blanket peat

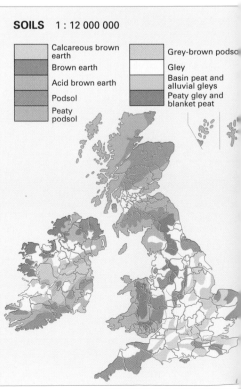

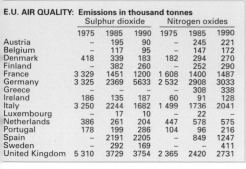

E.U. AIR QUALITY: Emissions in thousand tonnes

	Sulphur dioxide			Nitrogen oxides		
	1975	1985	1990	1975	1985	1990
Austria	–	195	90	–	245	221
Belgium	–	117	95	–	147	172
Denmark	418	339	183	182	294	270
Finland	–	382	260	–	252	290
France	3 329	1451	1200	1 608	1400	1487
Germany	3 325	2369	5633	2 532	2908	3033
Greece	–	–	–	–	308	338
Ireland	186	135	187	60	91	128
Italy	3 250	2244	1682	1 499	1736	2041
Luxembourg	–	17	10	–	22	–
Netherlands	386	261	204	447	578	575
Portugal	178	199	286	104	96	216
Spain	–	2191	2205	–	849	1247
Sweden	–	292	169	–	–	411
United Kingdom	5 310	3729	3754	2 365	2420	2731

FORESTRY 1 : 12 000 000

The percentage of the total area covered by woodland and forest

- Over 20%
- 15% – 20%
- 10% – 15%
- 5% – 10%
- Under 5%
- △ 50%-80% coniferous
- △ Over 80% coniferous

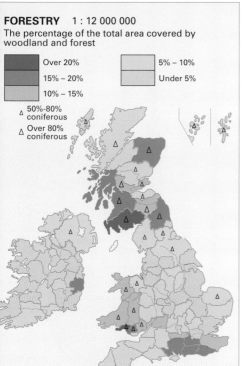

NATURAL VEGETATION 1 : 12 000 000

The plant cover associated with a particular environment if it is unaffected by human activity

- Oak
- Beech and Oak
- Ash and Oak
- Birch and Oakwood
- Scots Pine
- Heath, moorland, water meadows, fen, bog and marsh

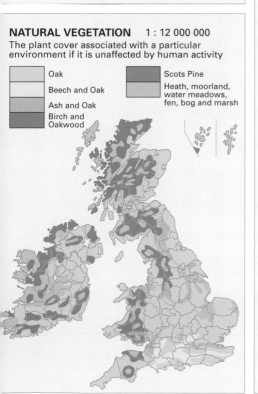

ACID RAIN 1 : 12 000 000

Average acidity of precipitation in the U.K. (pH scale)

- 4.29 and under (most acidic)
- 4.30 – 4.39
- 4.40 – 4.49
- 4.50 – 4.59
- 4.60 – 4.69
- 4.70 – 4.79
- 4.80 and over (least acidic)

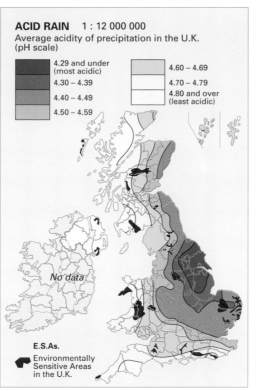

No data

E.S.As.

▬ Environmentally Sensitive Areas in the U.K.

AIR QUALITY 1 : 12 000 000

Hourly average of tropospheric ozone (O₃) exceeding 100 parts per billion (summer 1990)*

- Over 45
- 30 – 45
- 15 – 30
- Under 15

Ground-level concentrations of smoke in the U.K., by region
U.K. average: 12 micrograms per m³

- Less than the U.K. average
- More than the U.K. average
- Over 3x the U.K. average

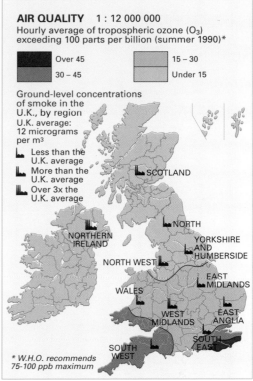

SCOTLAND
NORTH
NORTHERN IRELAND
YORKSHIRE AND HUMBERSIDE
NORTH WEST
EAST MIDLANDS
WALES
WEST MIDLANDS
EAST ANGLIA
SOUTH WEST
SOUTH EAST

* W.H.O. recommends 75-100 ppb maximum

CONSERVATION

- National Parks
- Areas of Outstanding Natural Beauty
- National Scenic Areas
- Forest Parks and Special Protected Areas
- Green Belts (and the urban areas they surround)
- Heritage Coast (England and Wales)/Coastal Conservation Zones (Scotland)

1 : 7 000 000

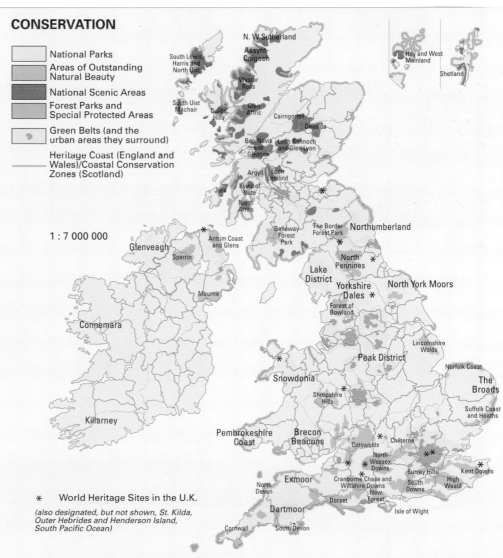

N. W Sutherland
South Lewis, Harris and North Uist
Assynt-Coigach
Hoy and West Mainland
Shetland
Wester Ross
South Uist Machair
Cuillin Hills
Glen Affric
Cairngorms
Deeside
Ben Nevis and Glencoe
Loch Bannoch and Glen Lyon
Argyll
Loch Lomond
Jura
Kyles of Bute
North Arran
Galloway Forest Park
The Border Forest Park
Northumberland
Glenveagh
Antrim Coast and Glens
Sperrin
North Pennines
Lake District
Mourne
Yorkshire Dales
North York Moors
Forest of Bowland
Connemara
Lincolnshire Wolds
Peak District
Norfolk Coast
Snowdonia
The Broads
Shropshire Hills
Suffolk Coast and Heaths
Killarney
Pembrokeshire Coast
Brecon Beacons
Cotswolds
Chilterns
North Wessex Downs
Surrey Hills
Kent Downs
Exmoor
Cranborne Chase and Wiltshire Downs
South Downs
High Weald
North Devon
New Forest
Dorset
Isle of Wight
Dartmoor
Cornwall
South Devon

✳ World Heritage Sites in the U.K.

(also designated, but not shown, St. Kilda, Outer Hebrides and Henderson Island, South Pacific Ocean)

TYPES OF FARM

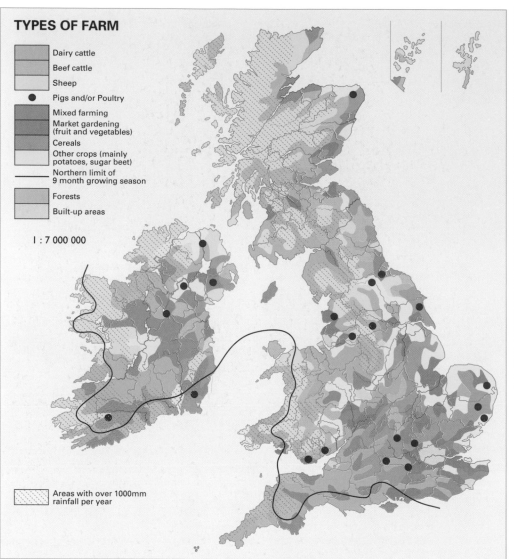

- Dairy cattle
- Beef cattle
- Sheep
- ● Pigs and/or Poultry
- Mixed farming
- Market gardening (fruit and vegetables)
- Cereals
- Other crops (mainly potatoes, sugar beet)
- —— Northern limit of 9 month growing season
- Forests
- Built-up areas

1 : 7 000 000

Areas with over 1000mm rainfall per year

LAND UNDER AGRICULTURE 1 : 12 000 000

The percentage of the total land area used for farming in 1995

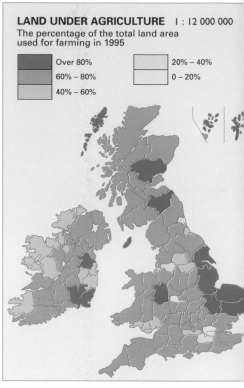

- Over 80%
- 60% – 80%
- 40% – 60%
- 20% – 40%
- 0 – 20%

AGRICULTURAL LAND USE 1995 (U.K. only)

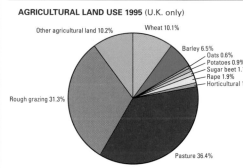

- Other agricultural land 10.2%
- Wheat 10.1%
- Barley 6.5%
- Oats 0.6%
- Potatoes 0.9%
- Sugar beet 1.1%
- Rape 1.9%
- Horticultural 1.0
- Rough grazing 31.3%
- Pasture 36.4%

WHEAT 1 : 12 000 000

The percentage of the total farmland used for growing wheat in 1995

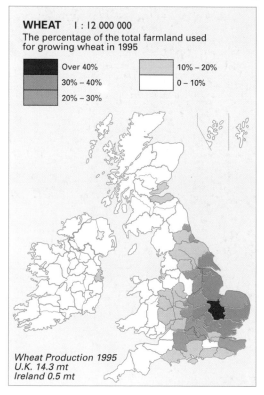

- Over 40%
- 30% – 40%
- 20% – 30%
- 10% – 20%
- 0 – 10%

Wheat Production 1995
U.K. 14.3 mt
Ireland 0.5 mt

BARLEY 1 : 12 000 000

The percentage of the total farmland used for growing barley in 1995

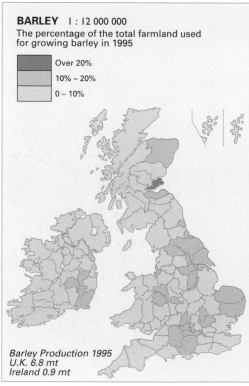

- Over 20%
- 10% – 20%
- 0 – 10%

Barley Production 1995
U.K. 6.8 mt
Ireland 0.9 mt

PASTURE 1 : 12 000 000

The percentage of the total farmland used for grazing livestock in 1995

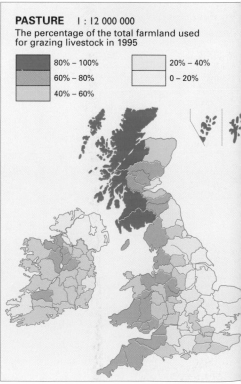

- 80% – 100%
- 60% – 80%
- 40% – 60%
- 20% – 40%
- 0 – 20%

NUMBER AND SIZE OF AGRICULTURAL HOLDINGS IN THE U.K.

Average size of holdings (hectares)

	1940	1980	1995
England & Wales	33.8	60.2	61.7
Scotland	81.8	96.2	160.2
Northern Ireland	13.7	24.2	35.9

Over 100 hectares
50 – 100 hectares
40 – 50 hectares
20 – 40 hectares
5 – 20 hectares
2 – 5 hectares
Under 2 hectares

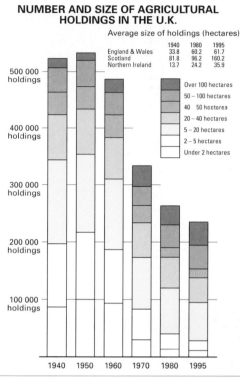

500 000 holdings
400 000 holdings
300 000 holdings
200 000 holdings
100 000 holdings

1940 1950 1960 1970 1980 1995

POTATOES 1 : 12 000 000
The percentage of the total farmland used for growing potatoes in 1995

Over 3%
2% – 3%
1% – 2%
Under 1%

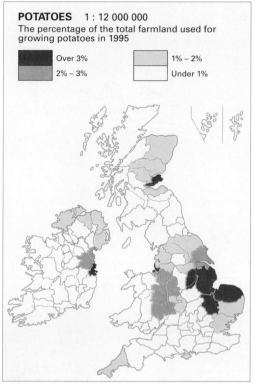

MARKET GARDENING 1 : 12 000 000
The percentage of the total farmland used for market gardening in 1995

Over 4%
3% – 4%
2% – 3%
1% – 2%
Under 1%

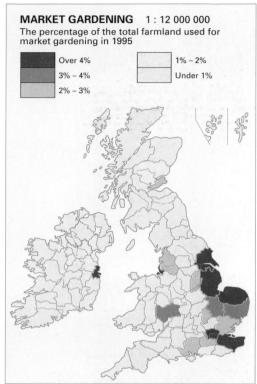

FISHING

Quantities of fish landed at major ports (port districts in Scotland) in 1995

('000 tonnes)
100
50
25
10
5

Type of fish landed

Demersal (Deep Sea Fish)
Pelagic (Shallow Water Fish)
Shellfish

Fishing Regions

IV	North Sea
VIa	West Scotland
VIIa	Irish Sea
VIIb/h/j	W. Ireland & Sole Bank
VIId/e	English Channel
VIIf/g	Bristol Ch. & S. E. Ireland

Region boundary

Fish landed according to region of capture (1995)

Demersal
Pelagic

1 fish represents 10 000 tonnes caught

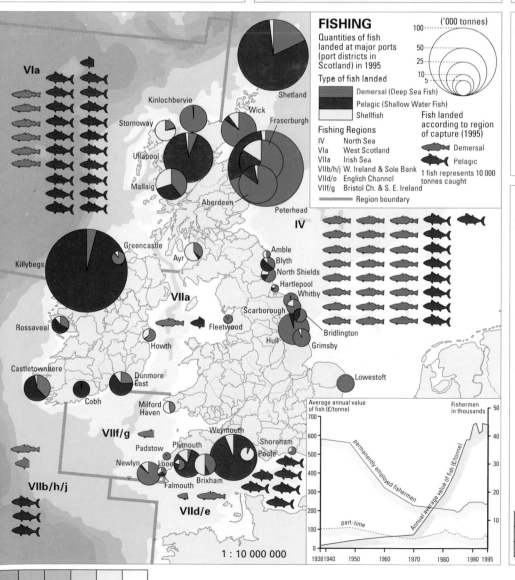

Vla
Kinlochbervie
Shetland
Stornoway
Wick
Fraserburgh
Ullapool
Mallaig
Aberdeen
Peterhead
IV
Greencastle
Amble
Blyth
Killybegs
Ayr
North Shields
Hartlepool
Whitby
VIIa
Scarborough
Rossaveal
Fleetwood
Bridlington
Howth
Hull
Grimsby
Castletownbere
Dunmore East
Lowestoft
Cobh
Milford Haven
VIIf/g
Weymouth
Padstow
Plymouth
Shoreham
Newlyn
Looe
Poole
Falmouth
Brixham
VIIb/h/j
VIId/e

1 : 10 000 000

1000 500 200 100 50 m

Average annual value of fish (£/tonne)
Fishermen in thousands
700
600
500
400
300
200
100
50
40
30
20
10

permanently employed fishermen
Annual average value of fish (£/tonne)
part-time

1938 1940 1950 1960 1970 1980 1990 1995

VALUE OF AGRICULTURAL OUTPUT (U.K. only)

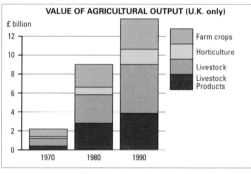

£ billion
12
10
8
6
4
2
0

1970 1980 1990

Farm crops
Horticulture
Livestock
Livestock Products

AGRICULTURAL LAND & LIVESTOCK, 1970-90 (U.K. only)

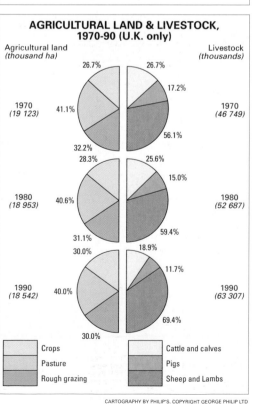

Agricultural land (thousand ha)
Livestock (thousands)

1970 (19 123)
26.7%
41.1%
32.2%

1970 (46 749)
26.7%
17.2%
56.1%

1980 (18 953)
28.3%
40.6%
31.1%

1980 (52 687)
25.6%
15.0%
59.4%

1990 (18 542)
30.0%
40.0%
30.0%

1990 (63 307)
18.9%
11.7%
69.4%

Crops
Pasture
Rough grazing
Cattle and calves
Pigs
Sheep and Lambs

EMPLOYMENT IN MANUFACTURING
The percentage of the workforce employed in manufacturing in 1996

- Over 30%
- 25% – 30%
- 20% – 25%
- 15% – 20%
- 12.5% – 15%
- Under 12.5%

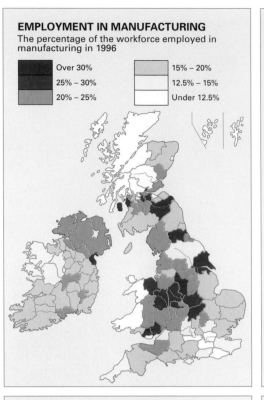

CHANGE IN MANUFACTURING EMPLOYMENT
The percentage change in the number of people employed in manufacturing 1980-89*

- Over 10% gain
- 0 – 10% gain
- 0 – 10% loss
- 10% – 20% loss
- 20% – 30% loss
- Over 30% loss

*Ireland 1979-88. Includes energy and water supply industries

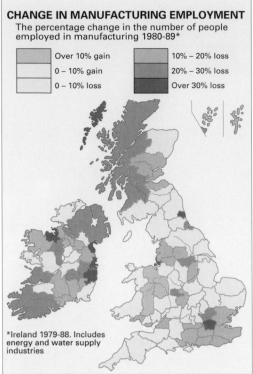

LOCATION OF MANUFACTURING INDUSTRY

Heavy Industry
- ▲ Chemicals
- ■ Iron and Steel
- ● Motor vehicles

Light Industry
- ◆ Electrical Engineering

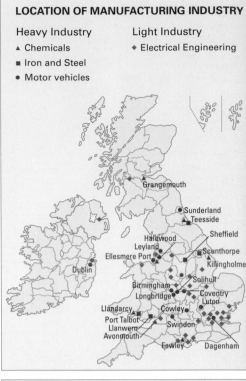

EMPLOYMENT IN AGRICULTURE
The percentage of the workforce employed in agriculture in 1996

- Over 25%
- 10% – 25%
- 2.5% – 10%
- 1% – 2.5%
- 0 – 1%

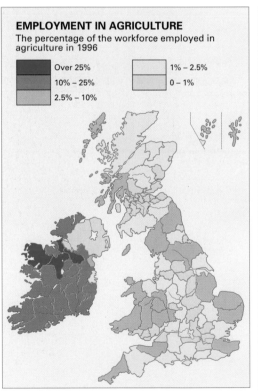

EMPLOYMENT IN SERVICES
The percentage of the workforce employed in the service industry in 1996

- Over 80%
- 70% – 80%
- 60% – 70%
- 50% – 60%
- Less than 50%

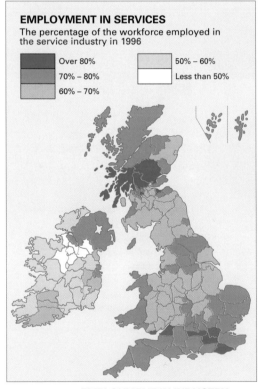

ASSISTED AREAS
These are areas in which extra financial support is focused to encourage economic growth

- Development areas in the U.K.
- Intermediate areas in the U.K.

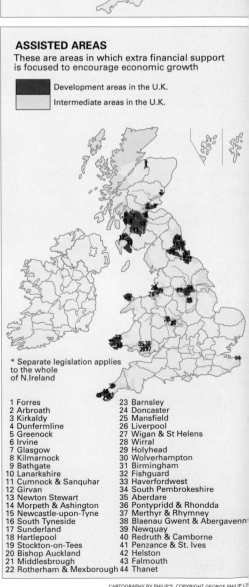

* Separate legislation applies to the whole of N.Ireland

1 Forres	23 Barnsley
2 Arbroath	24 Doncaster
3 Kirkaldy	25 Mansfield
4 Dunfermline	26 Liverpool
5 Greenock	27 Wigan & St Helens
6 Irvine	28 Wirral
7 Glasgow	29 Holyhead
8 Kilmarnock	30 Wolverhampton
9 Bathgate	31 Birmingham
10 Lanarkshire	32 Fishguard
11 Cumnock & Sanquhar	33 Haverfordwest
12 Girvan	34 South Pembrokeshire
13 Newton Stewart	35 Aberdare
14 Morpeth & Ashington	36 Pontypridd & Rhondda
15 Newcastle-upon-Tyne	37 Merthyr & Rhymney
16 South Tyneside	38 Blaenau Gwent & Abergavenny
17 Sunderland	39 Newquay
18 Hartlepool	40 Redruth & Camborne
19 Stockton-on-Tees	41 Penzance & St. Ives
20 Bishop Auckland	42 Helston
21 Middlesbrough	43 Falmouth
22 Rotherham & Mexborough	44 Thanet

EMPLOYMENT IN INDUSTRY

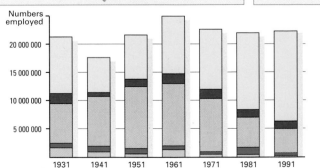

Numbers employed

- 20 000 000
- 15 000 000
- 10 000 000
- 5 000 000

1931 1941 1951 1961 1971 1981 1991

Employment in the U.K. by industry
- Services
- Transport
- Manufacturing
- Mining & energy supply
- Agriculture, forestry and fishing

1 : 12 000 000

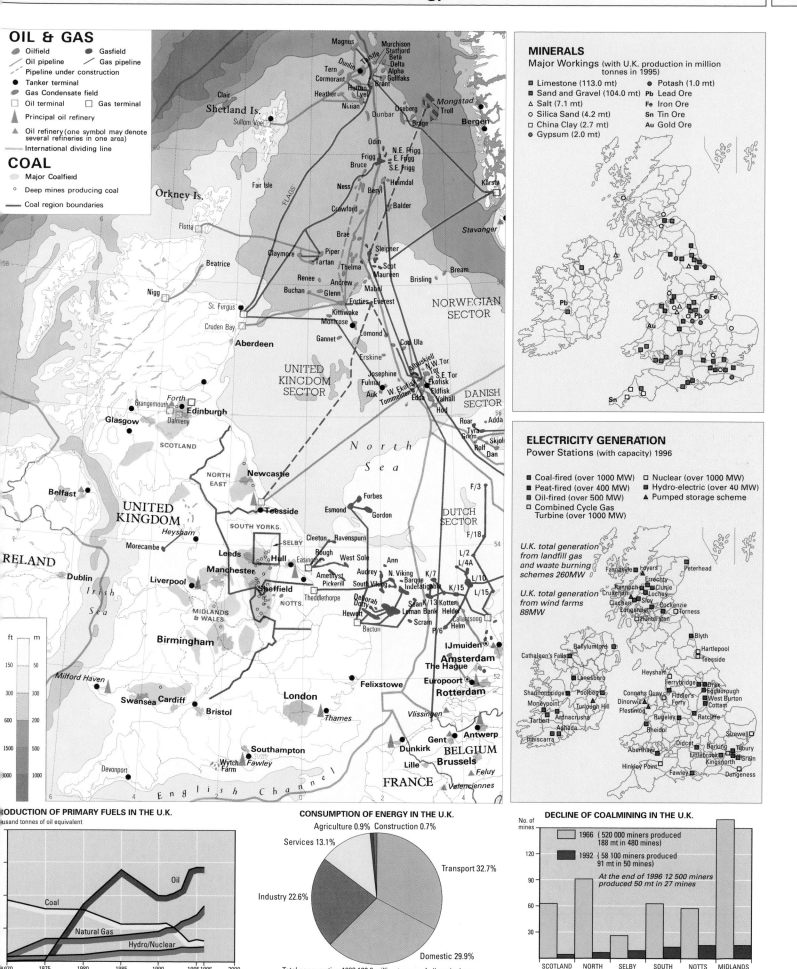

OIL & GAS

- ⬭ Oilfield ⬤ Gasfield
- Oil pipeline — Gas pipeline
- Pipeline under construction
- ● Tanker terminal
- ▢ Gas Condensate field
- ▢ Oil terminal ▢ Gas terminal
- ▲ Principal oil refinery
- ▲ Oil refinery (one symbol may denote several refineries in one area)
- International dividing line

COAL

- Major Coalfield
- ○ Deep mines producing coal
- Coal region boundaries

MINERALS

Major Workings (with U.K. production in million tonnes in 1995)

- ■ Limestone (113.0 mt)
- ■ Sand and Gravel (104.0 mt)
- △ Salt (7.1 mt)
- ○ Silica Sand (4.2 mt)
- ▢ China Clay (2.7 mt)
- ● Gypsum (2.0 mt)
- ■ Potash (1.0 mt)
- Pb Lead Ore
- Fe Iron Ore
- Sn Tin Ore
- Au Gold Ore

ELECTRICITY GENERATION

Power Stations (with capacity) 1996

- ■ Coal-fired (over 1000 MW)
- ■ Peat-fired (over 400 MW)
- ■ Oil-fired (over 500 MW)
- ▢ Combined Cycle Gas Turbine (over 1000 MW)
- ▢ Nuclear (over 1000 MW)
- ■ Hydro-electric (over 40 MW)
- ▲ Pumped storage scheme

U.K. total generation from landfill gas and waste burning schemes 260MW

U.K. total generation from wind farms 88MW

PRODUCTION OF PRIMARY FUELS IN THE U.K.
thousand tonnes of oil equivalent

(Graph: Oil, Coal, Natural Gas, Hydro/Nuclear; years 1970, 1975, 1980, 1985, 1990, 1995 1996, 2000)

CONSUMPTION OF ENERGY IN THE U.K.

- Agriculture 0.9%
- Construction 0.7%
- Services 13.1%
- Industry 22.6%
- Transport 32.7%
- Domestic 29.9%

Total consumption 1996 160.8 million tonnes of oil equivalent

DECLINE OF COALMINING IN THE U.K.

- ☐ 1966 (520 000 miners produced 188 mt in 480 mines)
- ■ 1992 (58 100 miners produced 91 mt in 50 mines)

At the end of 1996 12 500 miners produced 50 mt in 27 mines

(Regions: SCOTLAND, NORTH EAST, SELBY, SOUTH YORKSHIRE, NOTTS, MIDLANDS AND WALES)

CARTOGRAPHY BY PHILIP'S. COPYRIGHT GEORGE PHILIP LTD

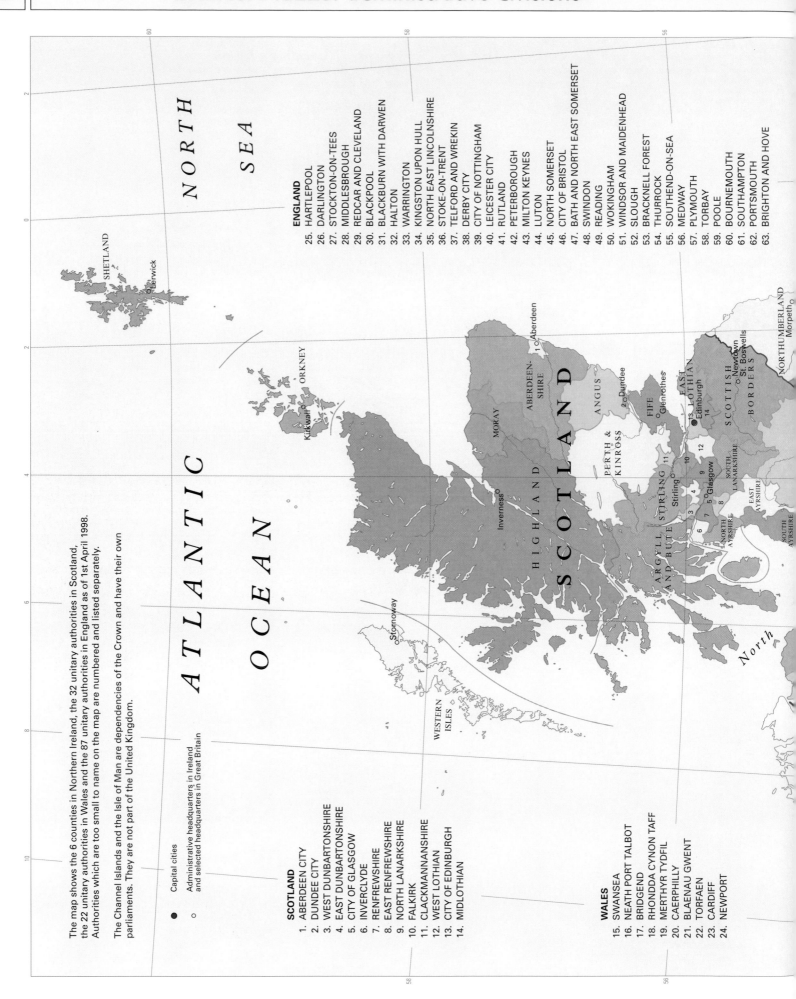

The map shows the 6 counties in Northern Ireland, the 32 unitary authorities in Scotland, the 22 unitary authorities in Wales and the 87 unitary authorities in England as of 1st April 1998. Authorities which are too small to name on the map are numbered and listed separately.

The Channel Islands and the Isle of Man are dependencies of the Crown and have their own parliaments. They are not part of the United Kingdom.

● Capital cities

○ Administrative headquarters in Ireland
  and selected headquarters in Great Britain

SCOTLAND
1. ABERDEEN CITY
2. DUNDEE CITY
3. WEST DUNBARTONSHIRE
4. EAST DUNBARTONSHIRE
5. CITY OF GLASGOW
6. INVERCLYDE
7. RENFREWSHIRE
8. EAST RENFREWSHIRE
9. NORTH LANARKSHIRE
10. FALKIRK
11. CLACKMANNANSHIRE
12. WEST LOTHIAN
13. CITY OF EDINBURGH
14. MIDLOTHIAN

WALES
15. SWANSEA
16. NEATH PORT TALBOT
17. BRIDGEND
18. RHONDDA CYNON TAFF
19. MERTHYR TYDFIL
20. CAERPHILLY
21. BLAENAU GWENT
22. TORFAEN
23. CARDIFF
24. NEWPORT

ENGLAND
25. HARTLEPOOL
26. DARLINGTON
27. STOCKTON-ON-TEES
28. MIDDLESBROUGH
29. REDCAR AND CLEVELAND
30. BLACKPOOL
31. BLACKBURN WITH DARWEN
32. HALTON
33. WARRINGTON
34. KINGSTON UPON HULL
35. NORTH EAST LINCOLNSHIRE
36. STOKE-ON-TRENT
37. TELFORD AND WREKIN
38. DERBY CITY
39. CITY OF NOTTINGHAM
40. LEICESTER CITY
41. RUTLAND
42. PETERBOROUGH
43. MILTON KEYNES
44. LUTON
45. NORTH SOMERSET
46. CITY OF BRISTOL
47. BATH AND NORTH EAST SOMERSET
48. SWINDON
49. READING
50. WOKINGHAM
51. WINDSOR AND MAIDENHEAD
52. SLOUGH
53. BRACKNELL FOREST
54. THURROCK
55. SOUTHEND-ON-SEA
56. MEDWAY
57. PLYMOUTH
58. TORBAY
59. POOLE
60. BOURNEMOUTH
61. SOUTHAMPTON
62. PORTSMOUTH
63. BRIGHTON AND HOVE

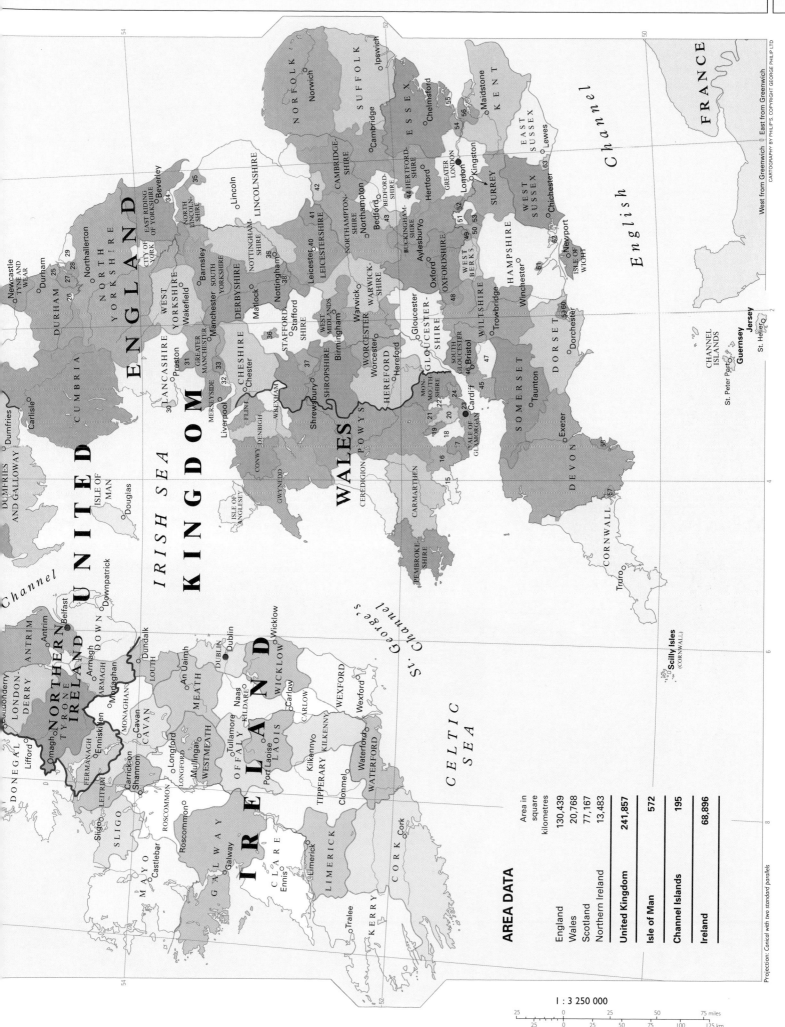

FRANCE

English Channel

West from Greenwich 0 East from Greenwich
CARTOGRAPHY BY PHILIP'S. COPYRIGHT GEORGE PHILIP LTD

ENGLAND

UNITED

KINGDOM

WALES

IRISH SEA

Channel

NORTHERN IRELAND

George's Channel

IRELAND

CELTIC SEA

CHANNEL ISLANDS
Guernsey
St. Peter Port
Jersey
St. Helier

Scilly Isles
(CORNWALL)

NORFOLK
Norwich
SUFFOLK
Ipswich
Cambridge
ESSEX
Chelmsford
Maidstone
KENT
EAST SUSSEX
Lewes
WEST SUSSEX
Chichester
Newport
ISLE OF WIGHT
HAMPSHIRE
Winchester
Trowbridge
WILTSHIRE
DORSET
Dorchester
SOMERSET
Taunton
Exeter
DEVON
CORNWALL
Truro

GREATER LONDON
London
Kingston
SURREY
HERTFORD-SHIRE
Hertford
BEDFORD-SHIRE
Bedford
BUCKINGHAM-SHIRE
Aylesbury
OXFORDSHIRE
Oxford
WEST BERKS
Northampton
NORTHAMPTON-SHIRE
LEICESTERSHIRE
Leicester
WARWICK-SHIRE
Warwick
WEST MIDLANDS
Birmingham
WORCESTER
Worcester
HEREFORD
Hereford
GLOUCESTER-SHIRE
Gloucester
SOUTH GLOUCESTER
Bristol
Cardiff
VALE OF GLAMORGAN
MONMOUTH-SHIRE

CAMBRIDGE-SHIRE
LINCOLNSHIRE
Lincoln
NORTH LINCOLN SHIRE
NOTTINGHAM-SHIRE
Nottingham
DERBYSHIRE
Matlock
SOUTH YORKSHIRE
Barnsley
WEST YORKSHIRE
Wakefield
CITY OF YORK
York
EAST RIDING OF YORKSHIRE
Beverley
NORTH YORKSHIRE
Northallerton
GREATER MANCHESTER
Manchester
CHESHIRE
Chester
MERSEYSIDE
Liverpool
LANCASHIRE
Preston
STAFFORD-SHIRE
Stafford
SHROPSHIRE
Shrewsbury

DURHAM
Durham
Newcastle
TYNE AND WEAR
CUMBRIA
Carlisle
DUMFRIES AND GALLOWAY
Dumfries
ISLE OF MAN
Douglas

DENBIGH
FLINT
WREXHAM
CONWY
GWYNEDD
ISLE OF ANGLESEY
POWYS
CEREDIGION
CARMARTHEN
PEMBROKE-SHIRE

Belfast
Antrim
ANTRIM
DERRY
LONDON-DERRY
Coleraine
Londonderry
TYRONE
Omagh
FERMANAGH
Enniskillen
Lifford
DONEGAL
ARMAGH
Armagh
DOWN
Downpatrick
Dundalk
LOUTH
MONAGHAN
Monaghan
Lifford

An Uaimh
MEATH
CAVAN
Cavan
Longford
LONGFORD
WESTMEATH
Mullingar
Tullamore
OFFALY
LAOIS
Port Laoise
KILDARE
Naas
Dublin
DUBLIN
WICKLOW
Wicklow
Carlow
CARLOW
WEXFORD
Wexford
KILKENNY
Kilkenny
TIPPERARY
Clonmel
WATERFORD
Waterford
LEITRIM
Carrick on Shannon
SLIGO
Sligo
ROSCOMMON
Roscommon
MAYO
Castlebar
GALWAY
Galway
CLARE
Ennis
LIMERICK
Limerick
KERRY
Tralee
CORK
Cork

AREA DATA

	Area in square kilometres
England	130,439
Wales	20,768
Scotland	77,167
Northern Ireland	13,483
United Kingdom	**241,857**
Isle of Man	572
Channel Islands	195
Ireland	68,896

Projection: Conical with two standard parallels

1 : 3 250 000

25 0 25 50 75 miles
25 0 25 50 75 100 125 km

POPULATION DENSITY 1891

See map at right for reference to colours

Density in 1891 by country :
U.K. 142 people per km²
Ireland 49 people per km²

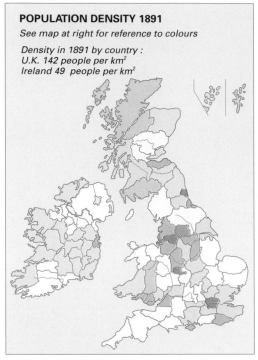

POPULATION DENSITY 1995

Persons per km²

	Over 1000
	500 – 1000
	200 – 500
	100 – 200
	50 – 100
	25 – 50
	Under 25

The density for the whole of the U.K. is 241 people per km², the density for Ireland is 53.

1 : 7 000 000

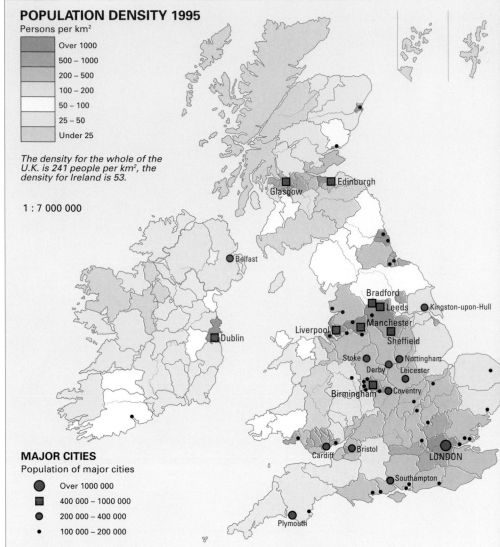

MAJOR CITIES
Population of major cities

⬤	Over 1000 000
⬛	400 000 – 1000 000
●	200 000 – 400 000
•	100 000 – 200 000

AGE STRUCTURE OF THE U.K.

The bars represent the percentage of males and the percentage of females in the age group shown

◻ 1901   ◻ 1990   ─ Projected 2150

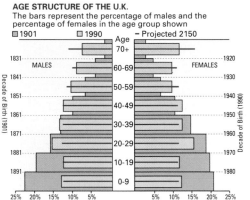

YOUNG PEOPLE 1 : 12 000 000

The percentage of the population under 15 years old in 1995 (Ireland 1991)

	Over 30%		19% – 20%
	25% – 30%		18% – 19%
	20% – 25%		Under 18%

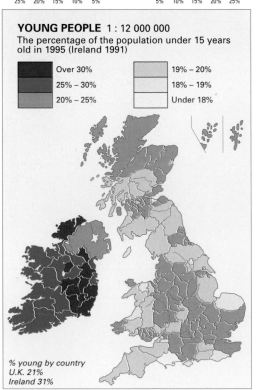

% young by country
U.K. 21%
Ireland 31%

OLD PEOPLE 1 : 12 000 000

The percentage of the population over pensionable age* in 1995 (Ireland 1991)

	Over 20%		12.5% – 15%
	17.5% – 20%		10% – 12.5%
	15% – 17.5%		Under 10%

Pensionable age is 65 for males, 60 for females

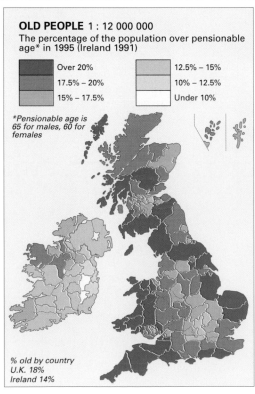

% old by country
U.K. 18%
Ireland 14%

URBANIZATION 1 : 12 000 000

The percentage of the population living in towns and cities (latest available year)

	Over 90%		60% – 70%
	80% – 90%		50% – 60%
	70% – 80%		Under 50%

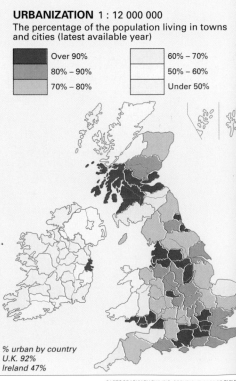

% urban by country
U.K. 92%
Ireland 47%

NATURAL POPULATION CHANGE

The difference between the number of births and the number of deaths per thousand inhabitants in 1995

Over 10 more births
5 – 10 more births
2.5 – 5 more births
0 – 2.5 more births
0 – 2.5 more deaths
Over 2.5 more deaths

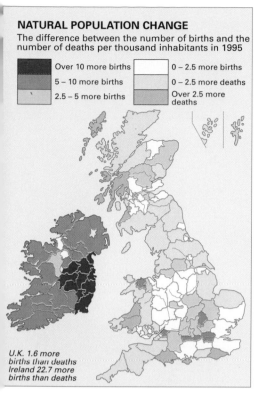

U.K. 1.6 more
births than deaths
Ireland 22.7 more
births than deaths

ETHNIC GROUP

Ethnic minorities as a % of total population in 1995/1996

Over 6%
4% – 6%
2% – 4%
0 – 2%

Ethnic minority groups

Indian/ Pakistani/ Bangladeshi
W. Indian/ African
Other

77 000 Total number of ethnic minority people in each region

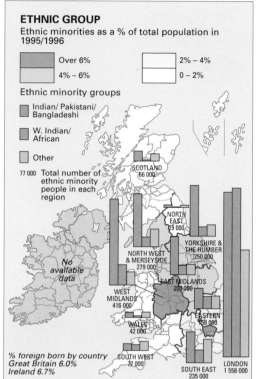

No available data

SCOTLAND 66 000
NORTH EAST 49 000
YORKSHIRE & THE HUMBER 250 000
NORTH WEST & MERSEYSIDE 279 000
EAST MIDLANDS 200 000
WEST MIDLANDS 416 000
EASTERN 158 000
WALES 42 000
SOUTH WEST 77 000
SOUTH EAST 235 000
LONDON 1 558 000

% foreign born by country
Great Britain 6.0%
Ireland 6.7%

MIGRATION 1 : 12 000 000

The difference between the number moving in and the number moving away (per 1000 inhabitants)*

Over 15 moved in
10 – 15 moved in
5 – 10 moved in
0 – 5 moved in
0 – 5 moved away
5 – 10 moved away

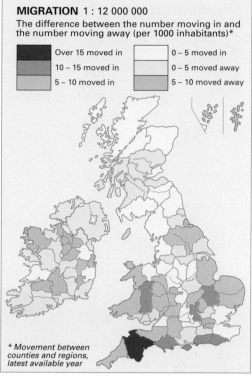

* Movement between counties and regions, latest available year

U.K. VITAL STATISTICS, 1900-2000

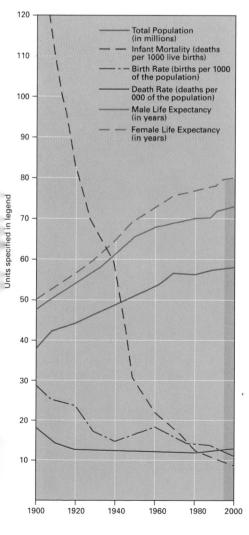

Units specified in legend

Total Population (in millions)
Infant Mortality (deaths per 1000 live births)
Birth Rate (births per 1000 of the population)
Death Rate (deaths per 000 of the population)
Male Life Expectancy (in years)
Female Life Expectancy (in years)

POPULATION CHANGE 1961-1991

The percentage change in the number of people between 1961 and 1991

Over 30% gain
25% – 30% gain
20% – 25% gain
15% – 20% gain
10% – 15% gain
5% – 10% gain
0 – 5% gain

0 – 5% loss
5% – 10% loss
Over 10% loss

1 : 7 000 000

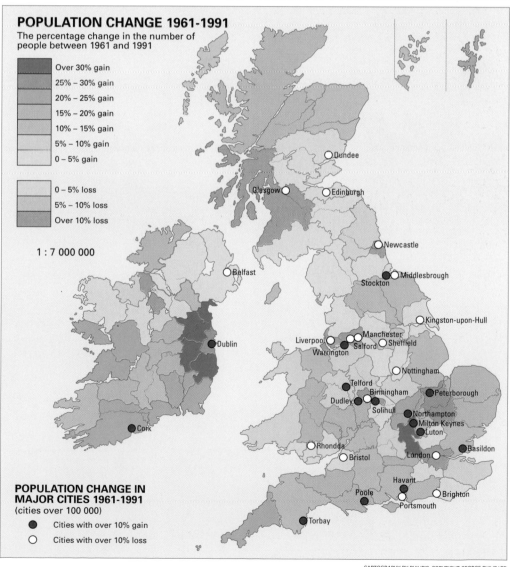

Dundee
Glasgow
Edinburgh
Newcastle
Belfast
Middlesbrough
Stockton
Kingston-upon-Hull
Dublin
Liverpool
Manchester
Salford
Sheffield
Warrington
Nottingham
Telford
Birmingham
Peterborough
Dudley
Solihull
Northampton
Milton Keynes
Luton
Cork
Rhondda
Basildon
Bristol
London
Havant
Poole
Brighton
Portsmouth
Torbay

POPULATION CHANGE IN MAJOR CITIES 1961-1991
(cities over 100 000)

● Cities with over 10% gain
○ Cities with over 10% loss

CARTOGRAPHY BY PHILIP'S. COPYRIGHT GEORGE PHILIP LTD

HOUSE OWNERSHIP

The percentage of dwellings which are owner-occupied in 1990 (Ireland 1985)

- Over 80%
- 70% – 80%
- 60% – 70%
- 50% – 60%
- Under 50%

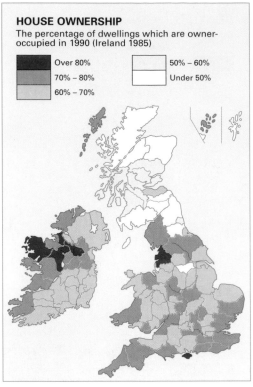

CAR OWNERSHIP

The number of new* cars per thousand people in 1990

- Over 50
- 40 – 50
- 30 – 40
- 20 – 30
- 10 – 20

No data

*First year of registration

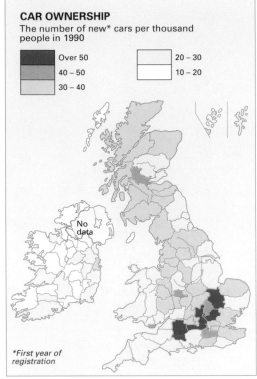

INCOME

The average gross weekly earnings of males and females in full employment in 1996 (U.K. only)*

- Over £400
- £375 – £400
- £350 – £375
- £325 – £350
- £300 – £325
- Under £300

*No data available for Ireland, Borders, Islands or Hartlepool

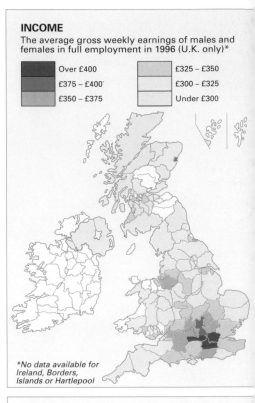

HEALTH

The number of doctors per 100 000 people (by health authority, latest available year)

- Over 90
- 80 – 90
- 70 – 80
- 60 – 70
- 50 – 60
- Under 50

Regional health authority boundaries

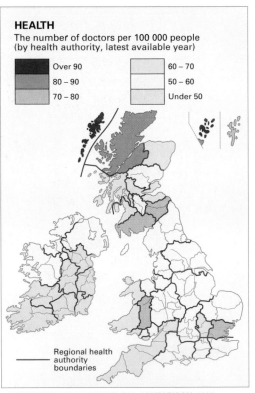

EDUCATION

The percentage of pupils aged 16 staying on in education in 1994/1995 (U.K. only)

- Over 90%
- 85% – 90%
- 80% – 85%
- 75% – 80%
- 70% – 75%
- Under 70%

No comparable data

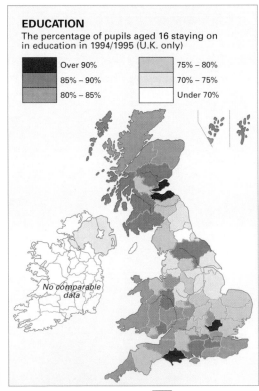

UNEMPLOYMENT

The percentage of the workforce unemployed in 1995 (Ireland 1992)

- Over 15.0%
- 12.5% – 15.0%
- 10.0% – 12.5%
- 7.5% – 10.0%
- 5% – 7.5%
- Under 5.0%

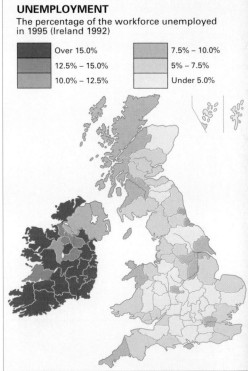

HOUSEHOLD EXPENDITURE: E.U. COMPARISON, 1992

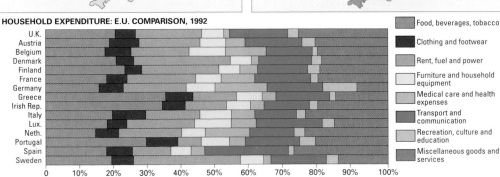

U.K.
Austria
Belgium
Denmark
Finland
France
Germany
Greece
Irish Rep.
Italy
Lux.
Neth.
Portugal
Spain
Sweden

0 10% 20% 30% 40% 50% 60% 70% 80% 90% 100%

* Medical expenses are provided free in the U.K. and Denmark

- Food, beverages, tobacco
- Clothing and footwear
- Rent, fuel and power
- Furniture and household equipment
- Medical care and health expenses
- Transport and communication
- Recreation, culture and education
- Miscellaneous goods and services

% OF U.K. HOUSEHOLDS OWNING DOMESTIC APPLIANCES

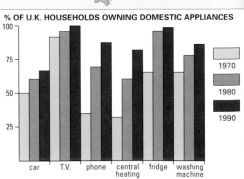

car   T.V.   phone   central heating   fridge   washing machine

- 1970
- 1980
- 1990

U.K. TRADE
TOP TEN TRADING PARTNERS 1996

One container represents 1% of the total value of imports or 1% of the total value of exports

IMPORTS

Germany £27.2b

Total Imports 1996 £184billion

Total Exports 1996 £167billion

U.S.A. £22.8b

France £17.7b

Netherlands £12.4b

Japan £9.0b

Italy £8.8b

Belgium/Lux. £8.6b

Irish Republic £7.2b

Switzerland £5.4b

Norway £5.0b

EXPORTS

Germany £20.8b

U.S.A. £19.8b

France £17.1b

Netherlands £13.5b

Irish Republic £8.7b

Belgium/Lux. £8.5b

Italy £8.0b

Spain £6.7b

Sweden £4.4b

Japan £4.3b

TYPE OF GOODS

- Machinery and Transport Equipment
- • Road Vehicles
- Other manufactured Goods
- Chemicals
- Food and Live Animals
- Mineral fuels, Lubricants, etc.
- Other Goods

U.K. TOTAL FOREIGN TRADE 1970-1996 (£ million)

	Imports	Exports		Imports	Exports
1970	£9 051m	£8 063m	**1986**	£84 790m	£78 331m
1974	£23 117m	£16 494m	**1990**	£126 165m	£103 655m
1978	£40 969m	£37 368m	**1994**	£149 468m	£134 663m
1982	£56 940m	£55 538m	**1996**	£183 893m	£167 413m

TOURISM
TOP 20 TOURIST ATTRACTIONS (U.K. 1996)

- ● Theme Park
- ● Museum
- ○ Country Park
- ● Historic Property

	Visitors
● Blackpool Pleasure Beach	7 500 000
● British Museum, London	6 228 275
○ Strathclyde Country Park	5 500 000
● National Gallery, London	5 000 000
● Palace Pier, Brighton	4 250 000
● Alton Towers, Staffs.	2 749 000
● Madame Tussauds, London	2 715 000
● Tower of London	2 539 000
● Westminster Abbey, London	2 500 000
● Eastbourne Pier	2 200 000
● York Minster	2 200 000
● Tate Gallery, London	2 002 000
● St. Pauls Cathedral, London	2 000 000
● Pleasureland, Southport	2 000 000
● Canterbury Cathedral	1 700 000
● Chessington World of Adventures, Surrey	1 700 000
● Natural History Museum, London	1 607 255
● Science Museum, London	1 548 286
○ Sandwell Valley Country Park	1 500 000
● Legoland, Windsor	1 420 511

FOREIGN VISITORS TO THE U.K.

Nature of visit
- Business
- Leisure

Country of origin
- North America
- Western Europe
- Other

No. of visits (millions)

18
15
12
9
6
3
0

1970 1980 1990

INCOME FROM TOURISM

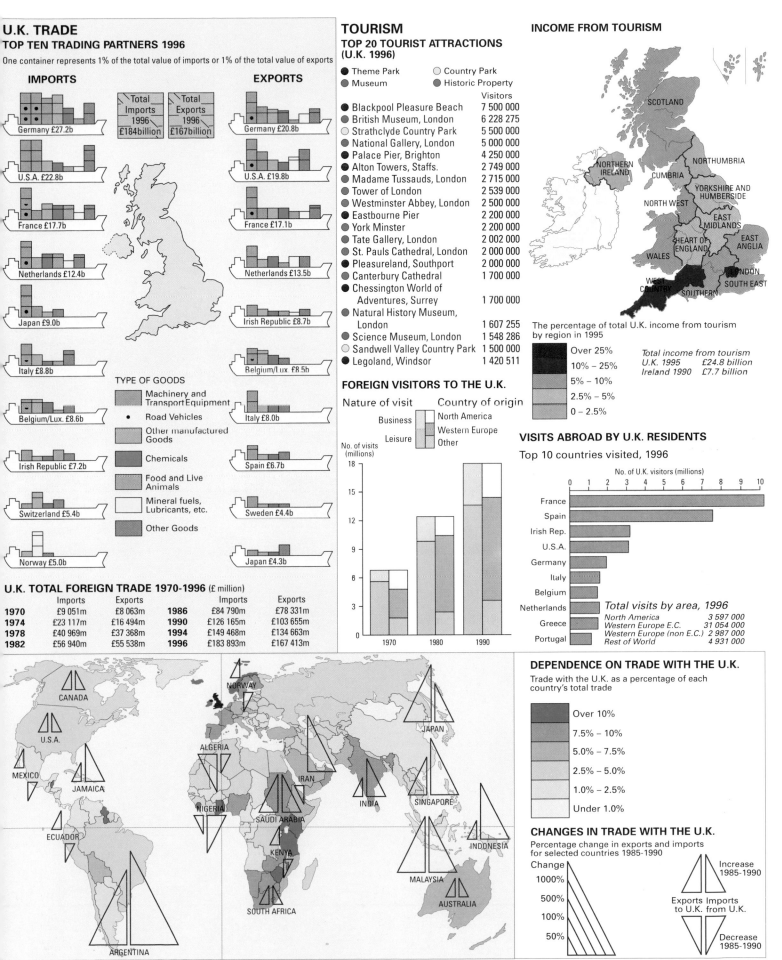

The percentage of total U.K. income from tourism by region in 1995

- Over 25%
- 10% – 25%
- 5% – 10%
- 2.5% – 5%
- 0 – 2.5%

Total income from tourism
U.K. 1995   £24.8 billion
Ireland 1990   £7.7 billion

VISITS ABROAD BY U.K. RESIDENTS

Top 10 countries visited, 1996

No. of U.K. visitors (millions)
0 1 2 3 4 5 6 7 8 9 10

- France
- Spain
- Irish Rep.
- U.S.A.
- Germany
- Italy
- Belgium
- Netherlands
- Greece
- Portugal

Total visits by area, 1996
North America   3 597 000
Western Europe E.C.   31 054 000
Western Europe (non E.C.) 2 987 000
Rest of World   4 931 000

DEPENDENCE ON TRADE WITH THE U.K.

Trade with the U.K. as a percentage of each country's total trade

- Over 10%
- 7.5% – 10%
- 5.0% – 7.5%
- 2.5% – 5.0%
- 1.0% – 2.5%
- Under 1.0%

CHANGES IN TRADE WITH THE U.K.

Percentage change in exports and imports for selected countries 1985-1990

Change
1000%
500%
100%
50%

Increase 1985-1990

Exports Imports to U.K. from U.K.

Decrease 1985-1990

CARTOGRAPHY BY PHILIP'S. COPYRIGHT GEORGE PHILIP LTD

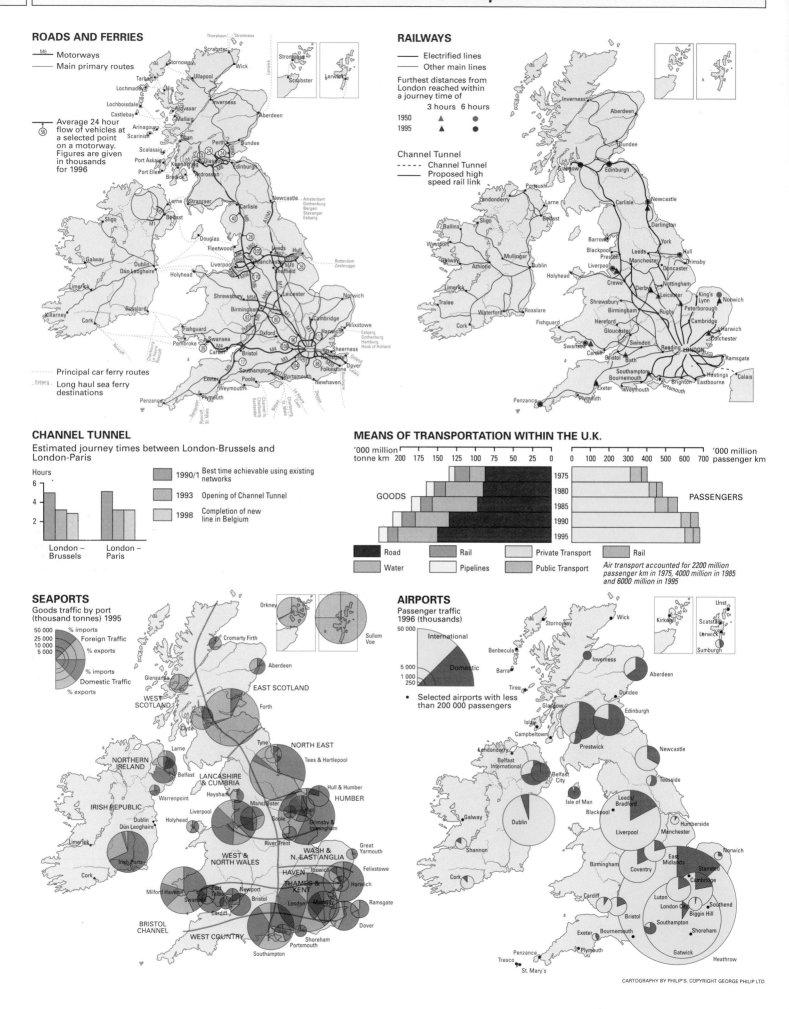

ROADS AND FERRIES

— M6 — Motorways
—— Main primary routes

⬭ 56 Average 24 hour flow of vehicles at a selected point on a motorway. Figures are given in thousands for 1996

···· Principal car ferry routes

— Esbjerg — Long haul sea ferry destinations

RAILWAYS

—— Electrified lines
—— Other main lines

Furthest distances from London reached within a journey time of

	3 hours	6 hours
1950	▲	●
1995	▲	●

Channel Tunnel
- - - - Channel Tunnel
—— Proposed high speed rail link

CHANNEL TUNNEL

Estimated journey times between London-Brussels and London-Paris

Hours

▓ 1990/1 Best time achievable using existing networks
▓ 1993 Opening of Channel Tunnel
▓ 1998 Completion of new line in Belgium

London – Brussels
London – Paris

MEANS OF TRANSPORTATION WITHIN THE U.K.

'000 million tonne km   200 175 150 125 100 75 50 25 0   0 100 200 300 400 500 600 700   '000 million passenger km

GOODS

PASSENGERS

1975
1980
1985
1990
1995

■ Road   ▓ Rail   ▢ Private Transport   ▨ Rail
▓ Water   □ Pipelines   ▨ Public Transport

Air transport accounted for 2200 million passenger km in 1975, 4000 million in 1985 and 6000 million in 1995

SEAPORTS

Goods traffic by port (thousand tonnes) 1995

50 000
25 000
10 000
5 000

% imports — Foreign Traffic
% exports
% imports — Domestic Traffic
% exports

AIRPORTS

Passenger traffic 1996 (thousands)

50 000
International
5 000
1 000
Domestic
250

• Selected airports with less than 200 000 passengers

CARTOGRAPHY BY PHILIP'S. COPYRIGHT GEORGE PHILIP LTD

INDEX TO

BRITISH ISLES MAPS

This index lists the major placenames which appear on the large-scale maps of the British Isles (pages *2–15* with the yellow band). Placenames for the rest of the world can be found in the World Index, with the turquoise band.

The first number beside each name in the index gives the map page on which that feature or place will be found. The letter and figure immediately after the page number give the grid square within which the feature is situated. The letter represents the latitude and the figure the longitude. In some cases the feature may fall within the specified square, while the name is outside. This is usually the case only with very large features. Rivers are indexed to their mouths or confluence.

The 'geographical co-ordinates' which follow the letter-figure references give the latitude and longitude of each place. The first co-ordinate indicates latitude – the distance north of the Equator. The second co-ordinate indicates longitude – the distance east or west of the Greenwich Meridian. Both latitude and longitude are measured in degrees and minutes (there are 60 minutes in a degree).

Thus the entry in the index for Runcorn reads:

Runcorn **7 F3** 53 20N 2 44W

This indicates that Runcorn appears on map page 7 in grid square F3 at latitude 53 degrees, 20 minutes north and at longitude 2 degrees, 44 minutes west. To find Runcorn by using the geographical co-ordinates, look at the edges of the map. The degrees of latitude are indicated by blue figures on the left-hand edge of the map and the degrees of longitude are marked on the bottom edge of the map. Runcorn will be found where lines extended from the two points on the map edge would cross on the map.

An open square □ indicates that the name refers to an administrative unit such as a county or region; rivers are indicated by an arrow →. Names composed of a proper name (Wight) and a description (Isle of) are positioned alphabetically by the proper name. All names beginning St. are alphabetized under Saint. A list of abbreviations used can be found in the World Index at the end of the atlas.

A

Abberton Res. **9 C10** 51 50N 0 52 E
Abbeyfeale **14 D4** 52 23N 9 20W
Aberaeron **10 C5** 52 15N 4 16W
Aberayron = Aberaeron **10 C5** 52 15N 4 16W
Abercarn **10 D7** 51 39N 3 9W
Aberchirder **3 G12** 57 34N 2 40W
Aberdare **10 D7** 51 43N 3 27W
Aberdeen **3 H13** 57 9N 2 6W
Aberdeenshire □ **3 H12** 57 17N 2 36W
Aberdovey = Aberdyfi **10 B5** 52 33N 4 3W
Aberdyfi **10 B5** 52 33N 4 3W
Aberfeldy **5 A8** 56 37N 3 50W
Abergavenny **10 D7** 51 49N 3 1W
Abergele **10 A6** 53 17N 3 35W
Abersychan **10 D7** 51 44N 3 3W
Abertillery **10 D7** 51 44N 3 9W
Aberystwyth **10 C5** 52 25N 4 6W
Abingdon **8 C6** 51 40N 1 17W
Aboyne **3 H12** 57 4N 2 48W
Accrington **7 E4** 53 46N 2 22W
Achill Hd. **12 D1** 53 59N 10 15W
Achill I. **12 D1** 53 58N 10 5W
A'Chralaig **2 H7** 57 11N 5 10W
Adlington **7 E3** 53 36N 2 36W
Adwick le Street **7 E6** 53 35N 1 12W
Agnews Hill **13 B10** 54 51N 5 55W
Ailsa Craig **4 D5** 55 15N 5 7W
Ainsdale **7 E2** 53 37N 3 2W
Aird Brenish **2 F3** 58 8N 7 8W
Airdrie **5 C8** 55 53N 3 57W
Aire → **7 E7** 53 42N 0 55W
Alcester **8 B5** 52 13N 1 52W
Aldbrough **7 E8** 53 50N 0 7W
Aldeburgh **9 B12** 52 9N 1 35 E
Alderley Edge **7 F4** 53 18N 2 15W
Alderney **11 H9** 49 42N 2 12W
Aldershot **9 D7** 51 15N 0 43W
Aldridge **7 G5** 52 36N 1 55W
Alexandria **4 C6** 55 59N 4 40W
Alford, *Aberds.* **3 H12** 57 13N 2 42W
Alford, *Lincs.* **7 F9** 53 16N 0 10 E
Alfreton **7 F6** 53 6N 1 22W
Allen, Bog of **15 B9** 53 15N 7 0W
Allen, L. **12 C5** 54 12N 8 5W
Alloa **5 B8** 56 7N 3 49W
Alness **3 G9** 57 41N 4 15W
Alnmouth **6 B5** 55 24N 1 37W
Alnwick **6 B5** 55 25N 1 42W
Alsager **7 F4** 53 7N 2 20W
Alsh, L. **2 H6** 57 15N 5 39W
Alston **6 C4** 54 48N 2 26W
Alton **9 D7** 51 8N 0 59W
Altrincham **7 F4** 53 25N 2 21W
Alva **5 B8** 56 9N 3 49W
Alyth **5 A9** 56 38N 3 15W
Amble **6 B5** 55 20N 1 36W
Ambleside **6 D3** 54 26N 2 58W
Amersham **9 C7** 51 40N 0 38W
Amesbury **8 D5** 51 10N 1 46W
Amlwch **10 A5** 53 24N 4 21W
Ammanford **10 D5** 51 48N 4 0W
Ampthill **9 B8** 52 3N 0 30W
An Teallach **2 G7** 57 49N 5 18W
An Uaimh **13 D8** 53 39N 6 40W
Andover **8 D6** 51 13N 1 29W
Anglesey, Isle of □ **10 A5** 53 16N 4 18W
Angus □ **5 A10** 56 46N 2 56W
Angus, Braes of **3 J11** 56 51N 3 10W
Annagh Hd. **12 C1** 54 15N 10 5W
Annalee → **13 C7** 54 3N 7 15W
Annan **5 E9** 54 57N 3 17W
Annan → **5 E9** 54 58N 3 18W
Annandale **5 D9** 55 10N 3 25W
Anstey **7 G6** 52 41N 1 14W
Anstruther **5 B10** 56 14N 2 40W
Antrim **13 B9** 54 43N 6 13W
Antrim □ **13 B9** 54 55N 6 20W
Antrim, Mts. of **13 B9** 54 57N 6 8W
Appin **4 A5** 56 37N 5 20W
Appleby-in-Westmorland **6 C4** 54 35N 2 29W
Appledore **11 E5** 51 3N 4 12W
Aran Fawddwy **10 B6** 52 48N 3 40W
Aran I. **12 B4** 55 0N 8 30W
Aran Is. **14 B3** 53 5N 9 42W
Arbroath **5 A10** 56 34N 2 35W
Arbury Hill **8 B6** 52 13N 1 12W
Ardee **13 D8** 53 51N 6 32W
Arderin **15 B7** 53 3N 7 40W
Ardgour **4 A5** 56 45N 5 25W
Ardivachar Pt. **2 H3** 57 23N 7 25W
Ardmore Hd. **15 E7** 51 58N 7 43W
Ardmore Pt. **4 C3** 55 40N 6 2W
Ardnamurchan **4 A4** 56 43N 6 0W
Ardnamurchan, Pt. of **4 A3** 56 44N 6 14W
Ardnave Pt. **4 C3** 55 54N 6 20W
Ardrossan **4 C6** 55 39N 4 50W
Ards Pen. **13 B10** 54 30N 5 30W
Arenig Fawr **10 B6** 52 56N 3 45W
Argyll **4 B5** 56 14N 5 10W
Argyll & Bute □ **4 B5** 56 13N 5 28W
Arisaig **2 J6** 56 55N 5 50W
Arisaig, Sd. of **2 J6** 56 50N 5 50W
Arkaig, L. **2 J7** 56 58N 5 10W
Arklow **15 C10** 52 48N 6 10W
Arklow Hd. **15 C10** 52 46N 6 10W
Armadale **5 C8** 55 54N 3 42W
Armagh **13 C8** 54 22N 6 40W
Armagh □ **13 C8** 54 18N 6 37W
Armthorpe **7 E6** 53 32N 1 3W
Arnold **7 F6** 53 2N 1 8W
Arran **4 C5** 55 34N 5 12W
Arrow, L. **12 C5** 54 3N 8 20W
Arun → **9 E7** 50 48N 0 33W
Arundel **9 E7** 50 52N 0 32W
Ascot **9 D7** 51 24N 0 41W
Ash **9 D7** 51 14N 0 43W
Ashbourne **7 F5** 53 2N 1 44W
Ashburton **11 F6** 50 31N 3 45W
Ashby de la Zouch **7 G6** 52 45N 1 29W
Ashdown Forest **9 D9** 51 4N 0 2 E
Ashford **9 D10** 51 8N 0 53 E
Ashington **6 B5** 55 12N 1 35W
Ashton-in-Makerfield **7 F3** 53 29N 2 39W
Ashton under Lyne **7 F4** 53 30N 2 8W
Aspatria **6 C2** 54 45N 3 20W
Assynt **2 F7** 58 20N 5 10W
Athboy **13 D8** 53 37N 6 55W
Athenry **14 B5** 53 18N 8 45W
Atherstone **7 G5** 52 35N 1 32W
Atherton **7 E3** 53 32N 2 30W
Athlone **14 B7** 53 26N 7 57W
Atholl, Forest of **3 J10** 56 51N 3 50W
Athy **15 C9** 53 0N 7 0W
Attleborough **9 A11** 52 32N 1 1 E
Auchterarder **5 B8** 56 18N 3 43W
Auchtermuchty **5 B9** 56 18N 3 15W
Aughnacloy **13 C8** 54 25N 6 58W
Aviemore **3 H10** 57 11N 3 50W
Avoca **15 C10** 52 52N 6 13W
Avoca → **15 C10** 52 48N 6 9W
Avon →, *Bristol* **8 D3** 51 30N 2 43W
Avon →, *Hants.* **8 E5** 50 44N 1 45W
Avon →, *Warks.* **8 C4** 51 57N 2 9W
Avonmouth **8 C3** 51 30N 2 42W
Awe, L. **4 B5** 56 15N 5 15W
Axe Edge **7 F5** 53 14N 1 59W
Axminster **11 F7** 50 47N 3 1W
Aylesbury **9 C7** 51 48N 0 49W
Aylsham **9 A11** 52 48N 1 16 E
Ayr **4 D6** 55 28N 4 37W
Ayr → **4 D6** 55 29N 4 40W
Ayr, Heads of **4 D6** 55 25N 4 43W
Ayr, Pt. of **10 A7** 53 21N 3 19W
Ayre, Pt. of **3 E12** 58 55N 2 43W

B

Bacton **9 A11** 52 50N 1 29 E
Bacup **7 E4** 53 42N 2 12W
Badenoch **3 J9** 56 59N 4 15W
Bagenalstown = Muine Bheag **15 C9** 52 42N 6 57W
Baggy Pt. **11 E5** 51 11N 4 12W
Bagh nam Faoileann **2 H3** 57 22N 7 13W
Baginbun Hd. **15 D9** 52 10N 6 50W
Bagshot **9 D7** 51 22N 0 41W
Baildon **7 E5** 53 52N 1 46W
Baile Atha Cliath = Dublin **15 B10** 53 20N 6 18W
Bakewell **7 F5** 53 13N 1 40W
Bala **10 B6** 52 54N 3 36W
Bala, L. **10 B6** 52 53N 3 38W
Balbriggan **13 D9** 53 35N 6 10W
Baldock **9 C8** 51 59N 0 11W
Ballachulish **4 A5** 56 40N 5 10W
Ballagan Pt. **13 D9** 54 0N 6 6W
Ballaghaderreen **12 D4** 53 55N 8 35W
Ballater **3 H11** 57 2N 3 2W
Ballina, *Mayo,* **12 C3** 54 7N 9 10W
Ballina, *Tipp.,* **14 C6** 52 49N 8 27W
Ballinasloe **14 B6** 53 20N 8 12W
Ballinderry → **13 B8** 54 40N 6 32W
Ballinrobe **12 D3** 53 36N 9 13W
Ballinskelligs B. **14 E2** 51 46N 10 11W
Ballybunion **14 C3** 52 30N 9 40W
Ballycastle **13 A9** 55 12N 6 15W
Ballyclare **13 B10** 54 46N 6 0W
Ballyconneely B. **14 B2** 53 23N 10 8W
Ballydavid Hd. **14 D2** 52 15N 10 20W
Ballydonegan B. **14 E2** 51 38N 10 6W
Ballyhaunis **12 D4** 53 47N 8 47W
Ballyhoura Mts. **14 D5** 52 18N 8 33W
Ballymena **13 B9** 54 53N 6 18W
Ballymoney **13 A8** 55 5N 6 30W
Ballymote **12 C4** 54 5N 8 31W
Ballynahinch **13 C10** 54 24N 5 55W
Ballyquintin Pt. **13 C11** 54 20N 5 30W
Ballyshannon **12 B5** 54 30N 8 10W
Balmoral Forest **3 J11** 57 0N 3 15W
Baltimore **14 F4** 51 29N 9 22W
Bamber Bridge **7 E3** 53 44N 2 39W
Bamburgh **6 A5** 55 36N 1 42W
Banbridge **13 C9** 54 21N 6 17W
Banbury **8 B6** 52 4N 1 21W
Banchory **3 H13** 57 3N 2 30W
Bandon **14 E5** 51 44N 8 45W
Bandon → **14 E5** 51 40N 8 41W
Banff **3 G12** 57 40N 2 32W
Bangor, *Down* **13 B10** 54 40N 5 40W
Bangor, *Gwynedd* **10 A5** 53 13N 4 9W
Bann →, *Down* **13 C8** 54 30N 6 31W
Bann →, *L'derry.* **13 A8** 55 10N 6 40W
Bannockburn **5 B8** 56 5N 3 55W
Bannow B. **15 D9** 52 13N 6 48W
Banstead **9 D8** 51 19N 0 10W
Bantry **14 E4** 51 40N 9 28W
Bantry B. **14 E3** 51 35N 9 50W
Bard Hd. **2 B15** 60 6N 1 5W
Bardsey Sd. **10 B4** 52 47N 4 46W
Bargoed **10 D7** 51 42N 3 22W
Barking and Dagenham **9 C9** 51 31N 0 10 E
Barmouth **10 B5** 52 44N 4 3W
Barnard Castle **6 C5** 54 33N 1 55W
Barnet **9 C8** 51 37N 0 15W
Barnoldswick **7 E4** 53 55N 2 11W
Barns Ness **5 C11** 55 59N 2 27W
Barnsley **7 E6** 53 33N 1 29W
Barnstaple **11 E5** 51 5N 4 3W
Barnstaple B. **11 E5** 51 5N 4 20W
Barra **2 J3** 57 0N 7 30W
Barra Hd. **2 J2** 56 47N 7 40W
Barrhead **4 C7** 55 48N 4 23W
Barrow → **15 D9** 52 14N 6 58W
Barrow-in-Furness **6 D2** 54 8N 3 15W
Barrow upon Humber **7 E8** 53 41N 0 22W
Barrowford **7 E4** 53 51N 2 14W
Barry **11 E7** 51 23N 3 19W
Barry I. **11 E7** 51 23N 3 17W
Barry's Pt. **14 E5** 51 36N 8 40W
Barton upon Humber **7 E8** 53 41N 0 27W
Basildon **9 C9** 51 34N 0 29 E
Basingstoke **8 D6** 51 15N 1 5W
Bass Rock **5 B10** 56 5N 2 40W
Bath **8 D4** 51 22N 2 22W
Bathgate **5 C8** 55 54N 3 38W
Batley **7 E5** 53 43N 1 38W
Battle **9 E9** 50 55N 0 30 E
Beachy Hd. **9 E9** 50 44N 0 16 E
Beaconsfield **9 C7** 51 36N 0 39W
Beaminster **8 E3** 50 48N 2 44W
Bearsden **4 C7** 55 55N 4 21W
Beauly **3 H9** 57 29N 4 27W
Beauly → **3 H9** 57 26N 4 28W
Beauly Firth **3 H9** 57 30N 4 20W
Beaumaris **10 A5** 53 16N 4 7W
Bebington **7 F2** 53 23N 3 1W
Beccles **9 B12** 52 27N 1 33 E
Bedford **9 B8** 52 8N 0 29W
Bedford Level **9 A8** 52 35N 0 15W
Bedfordshire □ **9 B8** 52 4N 0 28W
Bedlington **6 B5** 55 8N 1 35W
Bedwas **11 D7** 51 36N 3 10W
Bedworth **8 B6** 52 28N 1 29W
Bee, L. **2 H3** 57 22N 7 21W
Beeston **7 G6** 52 55N 1 11W
Beighton **7 F6** 53 21N 1 21W
Beinn a' Ghlo **3 J10** 56 51N 3 42W
Beinn Mhor **2 G4** 57 59N 6 39W
Beith **4 C6** 55 45N 4 38W
Belfast **13 B10** 54 35N 5 56W
Belfast L. **13 B10** 54 40N 5 50W
Belmullet **12 C2** 54 13N 9 58W
Belper **7 F6** 53 2N 1 29W
Belturbet **12 C7** 54 6N 7 28W
Bembridge **8 E6** 50 41N 1 4W
Ben Alder **3 J9** 56 50N 4 30W
Ben Avon **3 H11** 57 6N 3 28W
Ben Bheigeir **4 C3** 55 43N 6 6W
Ben Chonzie **5 B8** 56 27N 4 0W
Ben Cruachan **4 B5** 56 26N 5 8W
Ben Dearg, *Highl.* **3 G8** 57 47N 4 58W
Ben Dearg, *Perth & Kinr.* **3 J10** 56 52N 3 52W
Ben Dhorain **3 F10** 58 7N 3 50W
Ben Dorain **4 A6** 56 32N 4 42W
Ben Eighie **2 G7** 57 37N 5 30W
Ben Hee **3 F8** 58 16N 4 43W
Ben Hiant **4 A3** 56 42N 6 1W
Ben Hope **3 F8** 58 24N 4 36W
Ben Ime **4 B6** 56 14N 4 49W

Place names on the turquoise-coded World Map section are to be found in the index at the rear of the book.

Ben Klibreck   **Darton**

Darvel **4 C7** 55 37N 4 20W
Darwen **7 E4** 53 42N 2 29W
Daventry **8 B6** 52 16N 1 10W
Dawlish **11 F7** 50 34N 3 28W
Dawros Hd. **12 B4** 54 48N 8 32W
Deal **9 D11** 51 13N 1 25 E
Dean, Forest of **8 C3** 51 50N 2 35W
Dearne **7 E6** 53 32N 1 17W
Dee →, *Aberds.* **3 H13** 57 4N 2 7W
Dee →, *Flints.* **10 A7** 53 15N 3 7W
Deer Sd. **3 E12** 58 58N 2 50W
Denbigh **10 A7** 53 12N 3 26W
Denbighshire □ **10 A7** 53 8N 3 22W
Denby Dale **7 E5** 53 35N 1 40W
Dennis Hd. **3 D13** 59 23N 2 26W
Denny **5 B8** 56 1N 3 55W
Denton **7 F4** 53 26N 2 10W
Derby **7 G6** 52 27N 1 28W
Derbyshire □ **7 F5** 53 0N 1 30W
Derg, L. **14 C6** 53 0N 8 20W
Derravaragh, L. **12 D7** 53 38N 7 22W
Derry = Londonderry **12 B7** 55 0N 7 23W
Derry → **15 C9** 52 43N 6 35W
Derrynsaggart Mts. **14 E4** 51 58N 9 15W
Derwent →, *Derby* **7 G6** 52 53N 1 17W
Derwent →, *N. Yorks.* **7 E7** 53 45N 0 57W
Desborough **9 B7** 52 27N 0 50W
Deveron → **3 G12** 57 40N 2 31W
Devilsbit **14 C7** 52 50N 7 58W
Devizes **8 D5** 51 21N 2 0W
Devon □ **11 F6** 50 50N 3 40W
Devonport **11 G5** 50 23N 4 11W
Dewsbury **7 E5** 53 42N 1 38W
Didcot **8 C6** 51 36N 1 14W
Dinas Hd. **10 C4** 52 2N 4 56W
Dingle **14 D2** 52 9N 10 17W
Dingle B. **14 D2** 52 3N 10 20W
Dingwall **3 G9** 57 36N 4 26W
Dinnington **7 F6** 53 21N 1 12W
Diss **9 B11** 52 23N 1 6 E
Ditchling Beacon **9 E8** 50 49N 0 7W
Dizzard Pt. **11 F4** 50 46N 4 38W
Dodman Pt. **11 G4** 50 13N 4 49W
Dolgellau **10 B6** 52 44N 3 53W
Dolgelley = Dolgellau **10 B6** 52 44N 3 53W
Dollar **5 B8** 56 9N 3 41W
Don →, *Aberds.* **3 H13** 57 14N 2 5W
Don →, *S. Yorks.* **7 E7** 53 41N 0 51W
Donaghadee **13 B10** 54 38N 5 32W
Doncaster **7 E6** 53 31N 1 9W
Donegal **12 B5** 54 39N 8 8W
Donegal □ **12 B6** 54 53N 8 0W
Donegal B. **12 B4** 54 30N 8 35W
Donegal Harbour **12 B5** 54 35N 8 15W
Donna Nook **7 F9** 53 29N 0 9 E
Dooega Hd. **12 D1** 53 54N 10 3W
Doon, L. **4 D7** 55 15N 4 22W
Dorchester **8 E4** 50 42N 2 28W
Dorking **9 D8** 51 14N 0 20W
Dornoch **3 G9** 57 52N 4 5W
Dornoch Firth **3 G10** 57 52N 4 0W
Dorridge **8 B5** 52 22N 1 45W
Dorset □ **8 E4** 50 48N 2 25W
Douglas **13 C13** 54 9N 4 29W
Doulus Hd. **14 E2** 51 57N 10 19W
Doune **4 B7** 56 12N 4 3W
Dounreay **3 E10** 58 34N 3 44W
Dove → **7 G5** 52 51N 1 36W
Dover **9 D11** 51 7N 1 19 E
Dovey = Dyfi → **10 B6** 52 32N 4 0W
Down □ **13 C10** 54 20N 5 47W
Downham Market **9 A9** 52 36N 0 22 E
Downpatrick **13 C10** 54 20N 5 43W
Downpatrick Hd. **12 C3** 54 20N 9 21W
Driffield **7 D8** 54 1N 0 25W
Drogheda **13 D9** 53 45N 6 20W
Droichead Atha = Drogheda **13 D9** 53 45N 6 20W
Droichead Nua **15 B9** 53 11N 6 50W
Droitwich **8 B4** 52 16N 2 10W
Dromore **12 B7** 54 31N 7 28W
Dronfield **7 F6** 53 18N 1 29W
Druridge B. **6 B5** 55 16N 1 32W
Drygarn Fawr **10 C6** 52 13N 3 39W
Dublin **15 B10** 53 20N 6 18W
Dublin □ **15 B10** 53 24N 6 20W
Dudley **8 A4** 52 30N 2 5W
Dufftown **3 H11** 57 26N 3 9W
Dukinfield **7 F4** 53 29N 2 5W
Dulas B. **10 A5** 53 22N 4 16W
Dumbarton **4 C6** 55 58N 4 35W
Dumfries **5 D8** 55 4N 3 37W
Dumfries & Galloway □ **5 D8** 55 5N 4 0W
Dún Dealgan = Dundalk **13 C9** 54 1N 6 25W
Dun Laoghaire **15 B10** 53 17N 6 9W
Dunaff Hd. **12 A6** 55 18N 7 30W
Dunany Pt. **13 D9** 53 51N 6 15W
Dunbar **5 C10** 56 0N 2 32W
Dunblane **5 B8** 56 10N 3 58W
Duncansby Hd. **3 E12** 58 39N 3 0W
Dundalk **13 C9** 54 1N 6 25W
Dundalk B. **13 D9** 53 55N 6 15W
Dundee **5 B10** 56 29N 3 0W
Dundrum **13 C10** 54 17N 5 50W
Dunfermline **5 B9** 56 5N 3 28W
Dungannon **13 B8** 54 30N 6 47W
Dungarvan **15 D7** 52 6N 7 40W
Dungarvan Harbour **15 D7** 52 5N 7 35W
Dungeness **9 E10** 50 54N 0 59 E
Dunipace **5 B8** 56 4N 3 55W
Dunkeld **5 A8** 56 34N 3 36W
Dunkery Beacon **8 D1** 51 15N 3 37W
Dúnleary = Dun Laoghaire **15 B10** 53 17N 6 9W
Dunmanway **14 E4** 51 43N 9 8W
Dunnet B. **3 E11** 58 37N 3 23W
Dunoon **4 C6** 55 57N 4 56W
Duns **5 C11** 55 47N 2 20W
Dunstable **9 C7** 51 53N 0 31W
Dunster **8 D2** 51 11N 3 28W
Dunvegan Hd. **2 G4** 57 30N 6 42W
Durham **6 C5** 54 47N 1 34W
Durham □ **6 C5** 54 42N 1 45W
Durlston Hd. **8 E5** 50 35N 1 58W
Durness **3 E8** 58 34N 4 45W
Dursley **8 C4** 51 41N 2 21W
Dury Voe **2 B15** 60 20N 1 8W
Dyce **3 H13** 57 12N 2 11W
Dyfi → **10 B6** 52 32N 4 0W
Dymchurch **9 D11** 51 2N 1 0 E

E

Ealing **9 C8** 51 30N 0 19W
Earadale Pt. **4 D4** 55 24N 5 50W
Earby **7 E4** 53 55N 2 8W
Earl Shilton **7 G6** 52 35N 1 20W
Earlsferry **5 B10** 56 11N 2 50W
Earn → **5 B9** 56 20N 3 19W
Earn, L. **4 B7** 56 23N 4 14W
Easington **6 C6** 54 50N 1 24W
Easington Colliery **6 C6** 54 49N 1 19W
East Ayrshire □ **4 D7** 55 26N 4 11W
East Cowes **8 E6** 50 45N 1 17W
East Dereham **9 A10** 52 40N 0 57 E
East Dunbartonshire □ **4 C7** 55 57N 4 20W
East Grinstead **9 D9** 51 8N 0 0 E
East Kilbride **4 C7** 55 46N 4 10W
East Linton **5 C10** 56 0N 2 40W
East Lothian □ **5 C10** 55 57N 2 48W
East Renfrewshire □ **4 C7** 55 48N 4 23W
East Retford = Retford **7 F7** 53 19N 0 55W
East Riding of Yorkshire □ **7 E8** 53 52N 0 26W
East Sussex □ **9 E9** 51 0N 0 20 E
East Wittering **9 E7** 50 46N 0 53W
Eastbourne **9 E9** 50 46N 0 18 E
Easter Ross **3 G8** 57 50N 4 35W
Eastleigh **8 E6** 50 58N 1 21W
Eastwood **7 F6** 53 2N 1 17W
Eaval **2 G3** 57 33N 7 12W
Ebbw Vale **10 D7** 51 47N 3 12W
Eccleshall **7 G4** 52 52N 2 14W
Eckington **7 F6** 53 19N 1 21W
Eday Sd. **3 D12** 59 12N 2 45W
Eddrachillis B. **2 F7** 58 16N 5 10W
Eddystone **11 G5** 50 11N 4 16W
Eden → **6 C2** 54 57N 3 2W
Edenbridge **9 D9** 51 12N 0 4 E
Edenderry **15 B8** 53 21N 7 3W
Edge Hill **8 B6** 52 7N 1 28W
Edinburgh **5 C9** 55 57N 3 12W
Egham **9 D7** 51 25N 0 33W
Egremont **6 D1** 54 28N 3 33W
Eigg **2 J5** 56 54N 6 10W
Eil, L. **2 J7** 56 50N 5 15W
Eishort, L. **2 H6** 57 9N 6 0W
Elan → **10 C6** 52 17N 3 30W
Elan Valley Reservoirs **10 C6** 52 12N 3 42W
Elgin **3 G11** 57 39N 3 20W
Elie **5 B10** 56 11N 2 50W
Elland **7 E5** 53 41N 1 49W
Ellesmere Port **7 F3** 53 17N 2 55W
Ellon **3 H13** 57 21N 2 5W
Ely **9 B9** 52 24N 0 16 E
Emsworth **9 E7** 50 51N 0 56W
Enard B. **2 F7** 58 5N 5 20W
Enfield **9 C8** 51 39N 0 4W
Ennell, L. **12 E7** 53 29N 7 25W
Ennis **14 C5** 52 51N 8 59W
Enniscorthy **15 D9** 52 30N 6 35W
Enniskillen **12 C6** 54 20N 7 40W
Ennistimon **14 C4** 52 56N 9 18W
Eport, L. **2 G3** 57 33N 7 10W
Epping **9 C9** 51 42N 0 8 E
Epsom **9 D8** 51 19N 0 16W
Eriboll, L. **3 F8** 58 28N 4 41W
Ericht, L. **3 J9** 56 50N 4 25W
Eriskay, Sd. of **2 H3** 57 5N 7 20W
Erisort L. **2 F4** 58 5N 6 30W
Erne → **12 C5** 54 30N 8 16W
Erne, Lower L. **12 C6** 54 26N 7 46W
Erne, Upper L. **12 C7** 54 14N 7 22W
Errigal **12 A5** 55 2N 8 8W
Erris Hd. **12 C2** 54 19N 10 0W
Erskine **4 C7** 55 52N 4 27W
Esha Ness **2 A14** 60 30N 1 36W
Esher **9 D8** 51 21N 0 22W
Esk → **5 E9** 54 58N 3 4W
Eskdale **5 D9** 55 12N 3 4W
Essex □ **9 C9** 51 55N 0 30 E
Eston **6 C6** 54 33N 1 6W
Etive, L. **4 A5** 56 30N 5 12W
Ettrick Water → **5 C10** 55 31N 2 55W
Evesham **8 B5** 52 6N 1 57W
Ewe, L. **2 G6** 57 49N 5 38W
Ewell **9 D8** 51 20N 0 15W
Exe → **11 F7** 50 38N 3 27W
Exeter **11 F6** 50 43N 3 31W
Exmoor **11 E6** 51 10N 3 59W
Exmouth **11 F7** 50 37N 3 26W
Eye, *Cambs.* **7 G8** 52 36N 0 11W
Eye, *Suffolk* **9 B11** 52 19N 1 9 E
Eye Pen. **2 F5** 58 13N 6 10W
Eyemouth **5 C11** 55 53N 2 5W
Eynhallow Sd. **3 D11** 59 8N 3 7W
Eynort, L. **2 H3** 57 13N 7 18W

F

Fair Hd. **13 A9** 55 14N 6 10W
Fair Isle **2 C14** 59 32N 1 36W
Fairford **8 C5** 51 42N 1 48W
Fakenham **9 A10** 52 50N 0 51 E
Faldingworth **7 F8** 53 21N 0 22W
Falkirk **5 B8** 56 1N 3 47W
Falkland **5 B9** 56 15N 3 13W
Falmouth **11 G3** 50 9N 5 5W
Fanad Hd. **12 A6** 55 17N 7 40W
Faraid Hd. **3 E8** 58 35N 4 48W
Fareham **8 E6** 50 52N 1 11W
Faringdon **8 C5** 51 39N 1 34W
Farnborough **9 D7** 51 17N 0 46W
Farne Is. **6 A5** 55 38N 1 37W
Farnham **9 D7** 51 13N 0 49W
Farnworth **7 E4** 53 33N 2 24W
Fauldhouse **5 C8** 55 50N 3 44W
Faversham **9 D10** 51 18N 0 54 E
Fawley **8 E6** 50 49N 1 20W
Feale → **14 D3** 52 26N 9 40W
Featherbed Moss **7 E5** 53 31N 1 56W
Felixstowe **9 C11** 51 58N 1 22 E
Felton **6 B5** 55 18N 1 42W
Fergus → **14 C5** 52 45N 9 0W
Fermanagh □ **12 C6** 54 21N 7 40W
Fermoy **14 D6** 52 4N 8 18W
Ferndown **8 E5** 50 48N 1 53W
Ferryhill **6 C5** 54 42N 1 32W
Fethaland, Pt. of **2 A15** 60 39N 1 20W
Ffestiniog **10 B6** 52 58N 3 56W
Fife □ **5 B9** 56 13N 3 2W
Fife Ness **5 B10** 56 17N 2 35W
Filey **6 D8** 54 13N 0 18W
Filton **8 C3** 51 30N 2 34W
Findhorn → **3 G10** 57 38N 3 38W
Findochty **3 G12** 57 42N 2 53W
Finn → **12 B6** 54 50N 7 55W
Fionn L. **2 G6** 57 46N 5 30W
Fishguard **10 D4** 51 59N 4 59W
Fitful Hd. **2 C15** 59 54N 1 20W
Five Sisters **2 H7** 57 11N 5 21W
Flamborough Hd. **6 D8** 54 8N 0 4W
Fleet **9 D7** 51 16N 0 50W
Fleet, L. **3 G9** 57 57N 4 2W
Fleetwood **7 E3** 53 55N 3 1W
Flint **10 A7** 53 15N 3 7W
Flintshire □ **10 A7** 53 15N 3 10W
Flitwick **9 C8** 51 59N 0 30W
Flodden **6 A4** 55 37N 2 8W
Foinaven **3 F8** 58 30N 4 53W
Folkestone **9 D11** 51 5N 1 11 E
Fordingbridge **8 E5** 50 56N 1 48W
Foreland Pt. **11 E6** 51 14N 3 47W
Forfar **5 A10** 56 40N 2 53W
Formartine **3 H13** 57 20N 2 15W
Formby **7 E2** 53 33N 3 3W
Forres **3 G10** 57 37N 3 38W
Fort Augustus **3 H8** 57 9N 4 40W
Fort William **2 J7** 56 48N 5 8W
Forth **5 B8** 56 8N 3 48W
Forth, Firth of **5 B10** 56 5N 2 55W
Fortrose **3 G9** 57 35N 4 10W
Fortuneswell **11 F9** 50 33N 2 26W
Foulness I. **9 C10** 51 36N 0 55 E
Fowey **11 G4** 50 20N 4 39W
Fowey → **11 G4** 50 20N 4 39W
Foyle → **13 B7** 55 0N 7 13W
Foyle, L. **13 A7** 55 6N 7 8W
Foynes **14 C4** 52 37N 9 5W
Framlingham **9 B11** 52 14N 1 20 E
Fraserburgh **3 G13** 57 41N 2 3W
Frimley **9 D7** 51 18N 0 43W
Frinton-on-Sea **9 C11** 51 50N 1 16 E
Frodsham **7 F3** 53 17N 2 45W
Frome **8 D4** 51 16N 2 17W
Frome → **8 E4** 50 44N 2 5W
Frower Pt. **14 E6** 51 40N 8 30W
Fulwood **7 E3** 53 47N 2 41W
Furness **6 D2** 54 14N 3 8W
Fyne, L. **4 C5** 56 0N 5 20W

G

Gaillimh = Galway **14 B4** 53 16N 9 4W
Gainsborough **7 F7** 53 23N 0 46W
Gairloch **2 G6** 57 42N 5 40W
Gairloch, L. **2 G6** 57 43N 5 45W
Galashiels **5 C10** 55 37N 2 50W
Gallan Hd. **2 F3** 58 14N 7 2W
Galley Hd. **14 E5** 51 32N 8 56W
Galloway **4 D7** 55 1N 4 25W
Galloway, Mull of **4 E6** 54 38N 4 50W
Galston **4 C7** 55 36N 4 22W
Galty Mts. **14 D6** 52 22N 8 10W
Galtymore **14 D6** 52 22N 8 12W
Galway **14 B4** 53 16N 9 4W
Galway □ **14 B4** 53 16N 9 3W
Galway B. **14 B4** 53 10N 9 20W
Gamlingay **9 B8** 52 9N 0 11W
Gara, L. **12 D5** 53 57N 8 26W
Garforth **7 E6** 53 48N 1 22W
Garioch **3 H12** 57 18N 2 40W
Garron Pt. **13 A10** 55 3N 6 0W
Garry, L. **3 H8** 57 5N 4 52W
Garstang **7 E3** 53 53N 2 47W
Gatehouse of Fleet **4 E7** 54 53N 4 10W
Gateshead **6 C5** 54 57N 1 37W
Gatley **7 F4** 53 25N 2 15W
Gerrans B. **11 G4** 50 12N 4 57W
Gerrards Cross **9 C7** 51 35N 0 32W
Giants Causeway **13 A8** 55 15N 6 30W
Gibraltar Pt. **7 F9** 53 6N 0 20 E
Gill, L. **12 C5** 54 15N 8 25W
Gillingham, *Dorset,* **8 D4** 51 2N 2 15W
Gillingham, *Kent,* **9 D10** 51 23N 0 34 E
Girdle Ness **3 H13** 57 9N 2 2W
Girvan **4 D6** 55 15N 4 50W
Gisborough Moor **6 D7** 54 30N 1 2W
Glanaruddery Mts. **14 D4** 52 20N 9 27W
Glandore Harbour **14 E4** 51 33N 9 8W
Glas Maol **3 J11** 56 52N 3 20W
Glasgow **4 C7** 55 52N 4 14W
Glastonbury **8 D3** 51 9N 2 42W
Glen Affric **3 H8** 57 15N 5 0W
Glen B. **12 B4** 54 43N 8 45W
Glen Garry, *Highl.* **2 H7** 57 3N 5 7W
Glen Garry, *Perth & Kinr.* **3 J9** 56 47N 4 5W
Glen Mor **3 H8** 57 12N 4 37W
Glen Shiel **2 H7** 57 8N 5 20W
Glencoe **4 A5** 56 40N 5 6W
Gleneagles **5 B8** 56 16N 3 44W
Glengad Hd. **13 A7** 55 19N 7 11W
Glengarriff **14 E3** 51 45N 9 33W
Glennamaddy **12 D4** 53 37N 8 33W
Glenrothes **5 B9** 56 12N 3 11W
Glenties **12 B5** 54 48N 8 18W
Glossop **7 F5** 53 27N 1 56W
Gloucester **8 C4** 51 52N 2 15W
Gloucestershire □ **8 C4** 51 44N 2 10W
Goat Fell **4 C5** 55 37N 5 11W
Godalming **9 D7** 51 12N 0 37W
Goil, L. **4 B6** 56 8N 4 52W
Golden Vale **14 C6** 52 33N 8 17W
Golspie **3 G10** 57 58N 3 58W
Goodwick **10 C3** 52 1N 5 0W
Goole **7 E7** 53 42N 0 52W
Gorebridge **5 C9** 55 51N 3 2W
Gorey **15 C10** 52 41N 6 18W
Goring-by-Sea **9 E8** 50 49N 0 26W
Gorleston **9 A12** 52 35N 1 44 E
Gorseinon **10 D5** 51 40N 4 2W
Gort **14 B5** 53 4N 8 50W
Gosport **8 E6** 50 48N 1 8W
Gourock **4 C6** 55 58N 4 49W
Gower **11 D5** 51 35N 4 10W
Grafham Water **9 B8** 52 18N 0 17W
Gragareth **6 D4** 54 12N 2 29W
Grampian Highlands = Grampian Mts. **3 J10** 56 50N 4 0W
Grampian Mts. **3 J10** 56 50N 4 0W
Granard **12 D6** 53 47N 7 30W
Grand Union Canal **9 B7** 52 5N 0 52W
Grange-over-Sands **6 D3** 54 12N 2 55W
Grangemouth **5 B8** 56 1N 3 43W
Grantham **7 G7** 52 55N 0 39W
Grantown-on-Spey **3 H10** 57 19N 3 36W
Grassington **6 D5** 54 5N 2 0W
Gravesend **9 D9** 51 25N 0 22 E
Grays **9 D9** 51 28N 0 23 E
Great Blasket I. **14 D1** 52 5N 10 30W
Great Driffield = Driffield **7 D8** 54 1N 0 25W
Great Dunmow **9 C9** 51 52N 0 22 E
Great Harwood **7 E4** 53 47N 2 25W
Great I. **14 E6** 51 52N 8 15W
Great Malvern **8 B4** 52 7N 2 19W
Great Ormes Hd. **10 A6** 53 20N 3 52W
Great Ouse → **9 A9** 52 47N 0 22 E
Great Shunner Fell **6 D4** 54 22N 2 16W
Great Stour = Stour → **9 D11** 51 15N 1 20 E
Great Sugar Loaf **15 B10** 53 10N 6 10W
Great Torrington **11 F5** 50 57N 4 9W
Great Whernside **6 D5** 54 9N 1 59W
Great Yarmouth **9 A12** 52 40N 1 45 E
Greater London □ **9 C8** 51 30N 0 5W
Greater Manchester □ **7 E4** 53 30N 2 15W
Green Lowther **5 D8** 55 22N 3 44W
Greenholm **4 C7** 55 40N 4 20W
Greenock **4 C6** 55 57N 4 46W
Greenore **13 C9** 54 2N 6 8W
Greenore Pt. **15 D10** 52 15N 6 20W
Greenstone Pt. **2 G6** 57 55N 5 38W
Greenwich **9 D9** 51 28N 0 0 E
Greian Hd. **2 H2** 57 1N 7 30W
Gretna **5 E9** 54 59N 3 4W
Gretna Green **5 E9** 55 0N 3 3W
Greystones **15 B10** 53 9N 6 4W
Griminish Pt. **2 G3** 57 40N 7 29W
Grimsby **7 E8** 53 35N 0 5W
Gruinard B. **2 G6** 57 56N 5 35W
Gruinart, L. **4 C3** 55 50N 6 20W
Gruting Voe **2 B14** 60 12N 1 32W
Guernsey **11 J8** 49 30N 2 35W
Guildford **9 D7** 51 14N 0 34W
Guisborough **6 C6** 54 32N 1 2W
Guiseley **7 E5** 53 52N 1 43W
Gullane **5 B10** 56 2N 2 50W
Gurnard's Hd. **11 G2** 50 12N 5 37W
Gweebarra B. **12 B5** 54 52N 8 21W
Gweedore **12 A5** 55 4N 8 15W
Gwynedd □ **10 B6** 52 52N 3 59W

H

Hackley Hd. **3 H14** 57 19N 1 58W
Hackney **9 C8** 51 33N 0 2W
Haddington **5 C10** 55 57N 2 48W
Hadleigh, *Essex,* **9 C10** 51 33N 0 37 E
Hadleigh, *Suffolk,* **9 B10** 52 3N 0 58 E
Hags Hd. **14 C4** 52 57N 9 28W
Hailsham **9 E9** 50 52N 0 17 E
Halberry Hd. **3 F11** 58 20N 3 11W
Halesowen **8 B4** 52 27N 2 2W
Halesworth **9 B12** 52 21N 1 31 E
Halifax **7 E5** 53 43N 1 51W
Halkirk **3 E11** 58 30N 3 30W
Halstead **9 C10** 51 59N 0 39 E
Halton □ **7 F3** 53 22N 2 44W
Haltwhistle **6 C4** 54 58N 2 27W
Hambleton Hills **6 D6** 54 17N 1 12W
Hamilton **4 C7** 55 47N 4 2W
Hammersmith and Fulham **9 D8** 51 30N 0 15W
Hampshire □ **8 D6** 51 3N 1 20W
Hampshire Downs **8 D6** 51 10N 1 10W
Handa I. **2 F7** 58 23N 5 10W
Haringey **9 C8** 51 35N 0 7W
Harlech **10 B5** 52 52N 4 7W
Harleston **9 B11** 52 25N 1 18 E
Harlow **9 C9** 51 47N 0 9 E
Harpenden **9 C8** 51 48N 0 20W
Harris **2 G4** 57 50N 6 55W
Harris, Sd. of **2 G3** 57 44N 7 6W
Harrogate **7 E5** 53 59N 1 32W
Harrow **9 C8** 51 35N 0 15W
Hartland Pt. **11 E4** 51 2N 4 32W
Hartlepool **6 C6** 54 42N 1 11W
Harwich **9 C11** 51 56N 1 18 E
Haslemere **9 D7** 51 5N 0 41W
Haslingden **7 E4** 53 43N 2 20W
Hastings **9 E10** 50 51N 0 36 E
Hatfield, *Herts.* **9 C8** 51 46N 0 11W
Hatfield, *S. Yorks.* **7 E7** 53 34N 0 59W
Havant **9 E7** 50 51N 0 59W
Haverfordwest **10 D4** 51 48N 4 59W
Haverhill **9 B9** 52 6N 0 27 E
Havering **9 C9** 51 33N 0 20 E
Haweswater **6 C3** 54 32N 2 48W
Hawick **5 D10** 55 25N 2 48W
Hawkhurst **9 D10** 51 2N 0 31 E
Hay-on-Wye **10 C7** 52 4N 3 9W
Hayle **11 G3** 50 12N 5 25W
Haywards Heath **9 D8** 51 0N 0 6W
Hazel Grove **7 F4** 53 23N 2 7W
Healaval Bheag **2 H4** 57 24N 6 41W
Heanor **7 F6** 53 1N 1 20W
Heathfield **9 E9** 50 58N 0 18 E
Heaval **2 J3** 56 58N 7 30W
Hebburn **6 C5** 54 59N 1 30W
Hebden Bridge **7 E5** 53 45N 2 0W
Hecla **2 H3** 57 18N 7 15W
Hednesford **7 G5** 52 43N 2 0W
Hedon **7 E8** 53 44N 0 11W
Helensburgh **4 B6** 56 1N 4 44W
Helli Ness **2 B15** 60 3N 1 10W
Helmsdale **3 F10** 58 8N 3 43W
Helmsley **6 D6** 54 15N 1 2W
Helston **11 G3** 50 7N 5 17W
Helvellyn **6 C2** 54 31N 3 1W
Helvick Hd. **15 D7** 52 3N 7 33W
Hemel Hempstead **9 C8** 51 45N 0 28W
Hemsworth **7 E6** 53 37N 1 21W
Henfield **9 E8** 50 56N 0 17W
Hengoed **10 D7** 51 39N 3 14W
Henley-on-Thames **9 C7** 51 32N 0 53W
Hereford **8 B3** 52 4N 2 42W
Herefordshire □ **8 B3** 52 10N 2 30W
Herma Ness **2 A16** 60 50N 0 54W
Herne Bay **9 D11** 51 22N 1 8 E
Hertford **9 C8** 51 47N 0 4W
Hertfordshire □ **9 C8** 51 51N 0 5W
Hessle **7 E8** 53 44N 0 28W
Heswall **7 F2** 53 19N 3 6W
Hetton-le-Hole **6 C6** 54 49N 1 26W
Hexham **6 C4** 54 58N 2 7W
Heysham **6 D3** 54 5N 2 53W
Heywood **7 E4** 53 35N 2 13W
High Pike **6 C2** 54 43N 3 4W
High Willhays **11 F6** 50 41N 3 59W
High Wycombe **9 C7** 51 37N 0 45W
Higham Ferrers **9 B7** 52 18N 0 36W
Highbridge **8 D3** 51 13N 2 59W
Highland □ **3 H7** 57 30N 5 0W
Highworth **8 C5** 51 38N 1 42W
Hillingdon **9 C8** 51 33N 0 29W
Hilpsford Pt. **6 D2** 54 4N 3 12W
Hinckley **7 G6** 52 33N 1 21W
Hindley **7 E3** 53 32N 2 35W
Hinkley Pt. **8 D2** 51 13N 3 9W
Hitchin **9 C8** 51 57N 0 16W
Hockley **9 C10** 51 35N 0 39 E
Hoddesdon **9 C8** 51 45N 0 1W
Hog's Back **9 D7** 51 13N 0 40W
Hogs Hd. **14 E2** 51 46N 10 13W
Holbeach **7 G9** 52 48N 0 1 E
Holborn Hd. **3 E10** 58 37N 3 30W
Holderness **7 E8** 53 45N 0 5W
Holmfirth **7 E5** 53 34N 1 48W
Holsworthy **11 F5** 50 48N 4 21W
Holt **9 A11** 52 55N 1 4 E
Holy I., *Angl.* **10 A4** 53 17N 4 37W
Holy I., *Northumb.* **6 A5** 55 42N 1 48W
Holyhead **10 A4** 53 18N 4 38W
Holywell **10 A7** 53 16N 3 14W
Honiton **11 F7** 50 48N 3 11W
Hook **9 D7** 51 17N 0 55W
Hook Hd. **15 D9** 52 8N 6 57W
Horden **6 C6** 54 45N 1 17W
Horley **9 D8** 51 10N 0 10W
Horn Hd. **12 A6** 55 13N 8 0W
Horncastle **7 F8** 53 13N 0 8W
Horndean **8 E6** 50 50N 1 0W
Hornsea **7 E8** 53 55N 0 10W
Horsforth **7 E5** 53 50N 1 39W
Horsham **9 D8** 51 4N 0 20W
Horwich **7 E3** 53 37N 2 33W
Houghton-le-Spring **6 C6** 54 51N 1 28W
Houghton Regis **9 C7** 51 54N 0 32W
Hounslow **9 D8** 51 29N 0 20W
Hourn, L. **2 H6** 57 7N 5 35W
Hove **9 E8** 50 50N 0 10W
Howden **7 E7** 53 45N 0 52W
Howth Hd. **15 B10** 53 21N 6 3W
Hoy Sd. **3 E11** 58 57N 3 20W
Hoylake **7 F2** 53 24N 3 11W
Hucknall **7 F6** 53 3N 1 12W
Huddersfield **7 E5** 53 38N 1 49W
Hull = Kingston upon Hull **7 E8** 53 45N 0 20W
Humber → **7 E8** 53 40N 0 10W
Hungerford **8 D5** 51 25N 1 30W
Hungry Hill **14 E3** 51 41N 9 48W
Hunstanton **9 A9** 52 57N 0 30 E
Hunterston **4 C6** 55 43N 4 55W

Place names on the turquoise-coded World Map section are to be found in the index at the rear of the book.

Place names on the turquoise-coded World Map section are to be found in the index at the rear of the book.

Narrows   **Slieve Elva**

Place names on the turquoise-coded World Map section are to be found in the index at the rear of the book.

Slieve Foye   **Youghal**

Place names on the turquoise-coded World Map section are to be found in the index at the rear of the book.

WORLD MAPS

SETTLEMENTS

⬠ **PARIS**   ■ **Berne**   ◉ **Livorno**   ◎ Brugge   ◎ *Algeciras*   ○ *Frejus*   ○ *Oberammergau*   ○ *Thira*

Settlement symbols and type styles vary according to the scale of each map and indicate the importance of towns on the map rather than specific population figures

∴   Ruins or Archæological Sites   ᴗ   Wells in Desert

ADMINISTRATION

——— International Boundaries

– – – International Boundaries (Undefined or Disputed)

········· Internal Boundaries

⬡ National Parks

Country Names

NICARAGUA

Administrative Area Names

KENT

CALABRIA

International boundaries show the *de facto* situation where there are rival claims to territory

COMMUNICATIONS

——— Principal Roads

⌒ Other Roads

–·–·– Trails and Seasonal Roads

⋈ Passes

✧ Airfields

⌒ Principal Railways

–··– Railways Under Construction

⌒ Other Railways

⌐---⌐ Railway Tunnels

⸽⸽⸽ Principal Canals

PHYSICAL FEATURES

≈ Perennial Streams

······ Intermittent Streams

⬯ Perennial Lakes

⬭ Intermittent Lakes

Swamps and Marshes

Permanent Ice and Glaciers

▲ 8848 Elevations in metres

▼ 8050 Sea Depths in metres

1134 Height of Lake Surface Above Sea Level in metres

ELEVATION AND DEPTH TINTS

Height of Land Above Sea Level   Land Below Sea Level   Depth of Sea

| in metres | 6000 | 4000 | 3000 | 2000 | 1500 | 1000 | 400 | 200 | 0 |

| in feet | 18 000 | 12 000 | 9000 | 6000 | 4500 | 3000 | 1200 | 600 |

| 6000 | 12 000 | 15 000 | 18 000 | 24 000 | in feet |
| 0 | 200 | 2000 | 4000 | 5000 | 6000 | 8000 | in metres |

Some of the maps have different contours to highlight and clarify the principal relief features

Projection: *Hammer Equal Area*

10 20 **11** 40 **12** 60 **13** 80 **14** 100 **15** **16** 140 **17** 160 **18** 180 80

ARCTIC OCEAN

Svalbard (Norw.)

A

Barents Sea
Novaya Zemlya
Kara Sea
Severnaya Zemlya
Laptev Sea
New Siberian Is.
East Siberian Sea
Wrangel I.
Arctic Circle

gian

Murmansk
Norilsk
Verkhoyansk
Yakutsk
Magadan
Okhotsk
Bering Sea

Sea

B

NORWAY SWEDEN FINLAND Helsinki
Oslo
Stockholm EST.
Copenhagen LATVIA ST. PETERSBURG
DENMARK LITH.
Amsterdam POLAND MINSK
Hamburg Berlin BELARUS
Brussels GERMANY Prague
LUX. Vienna CZECH.
PARIS AUSTRIA HUNG.
Milan ITALY SLVN. Budapest
Marseilles YUG. ROMANIA Bucharest
Rome ALB. BULGARIA
Barcelona GREECE ISTANBUL
Naples Sardinia
Algiers TUNISIA MALTA Athens
Tripoli Izmir

Arkhangelsk
Salekhard
Ob
Perm
Yekaterinburg
Tomsk
Krasnoyarsk
Moscow
Kazan
L. Baikal
Irkutsk
Ulan Ude
Samara
Chelyabinsk
Omsk
Novosibirsk
Barnaul
Volga
Kiev
UKRAINE
Odessa
Saratov
Astana
Karaganda
KAZAKSTAN
Volgograd
Astrakhan
Aral Sea
L. Balkhash

Sea of Okhotsk
Sakhalin
Komsomolsk
Khabarovsk
Petropavlovsk-Kamchatskiy
International Date Line

Sappo
Vladivostok
Harbin
Changchun
SHENYANG
NORTH KOREA
Pyongyang
SEOUL
SOUTH KOREA
Dalian

40

MONGOLIA
Ulan Bator

JAPAN
TŌKYŌ
Ōsaka
Kitakyūshū

PACIFIC

C

Caspian Sea
Black Sea
GEORGIA
Tbilisi
Baku
AZER.
ARMENIA Yerevan
TURKEY
Ankara
CYPRUS
SYRIA
Beirut Damascus
Jerusalem ISR.
JORDAN
Baghdād
IRAQ
KUWAIT
Riyadh BAHRAIN QATAR
Mecca
SAUDI
ARABIA

UZBEKISTAN
Samarkand
Tashkent
KYRGYZSTAN
Bishkek
TURKMENISTAN
Ashkhabad
TAJIKISTAN
Dushanbe
Mashhad
TEHRAN
Tabriz
Esfahān
IRAN
Shīrāz
Abu Dhabi
U.A.E.
OMAN
Muscat

Ürümqi
CHINA
Lanzhou Taiyuan
Xi'an
Chengdu
CHONGQING
Kunming
GUANGZHOU
TIBET
Lhasa
NEPAL
Katmandu
BHU.

Beijing TIANJIN
Hwang Ho
Nanjing
Wuhan
SHANGHAI
East China Sea
Fuzhou
Taipei
TAIWAN
HONG KONG
Ryukyu Is.

OCEAN

Bonin Is. (Japan)
Volcano Is. (Japan)
Marcus I. (Japan)
Tropic of Cancer
Wake I. (U.S.A.)

20

LIBYA
EGYPT
Aswân

AFGHANISTAN
Kābul
Islamabad
Lahore
PAKISTAN
KARACHI
Ahmadabad
DELHI
New Delhi
Kanpur
Ganges
BANGLA-DESH
DACCA
CALCUTTA (Kolkata)
Nagpur

BURMA MYANMAR
Hanoi
Mandalay
Rangoon
South
China
Sea
Hainan

NORTHERN MARIANAS (U.S.A.)
GUAM (U.S.A.)

D

NIGER CHAD SUDAN
Omdurmân
Khartoum
Ndjamena
L. Chad
Sana
YEMEN
Aden
G. of Aden
Socotra (Yemen)
DJIBOUTI
ERITREA
Asmara

Nile
MUMBAI (Bombay)
Hyderabad
INDIA
Bangalore
CHENNAI (Madras)
Lakshadweep Is. (India)
Arabian Sea
Bay of Bengal
Andaman Is. (India)
Nicobar Is. (India)
SRI LANKA
Colombo

THAILAND
Vientiane
VIET-NAM
BANGKOK
CAMBODIA
Phnom Penh
Ho Chi Minh City
MANILA
PHILIPPINES

FEDERATED STATES
Yap
Truk
Caroline Is.
OF MICRONESIA
PALAU

MARSHALL IS.
Pohnpei

NIGERIA
Abuja
Kano
Niamey
Ibadan
Lagos
BENIN
CAMEROON
Douala
Yaounde
CENTRAL AFRICAN REP.
Bangui
ETHIOPIA
Addis Ababa
SOMALI REP.
Mogadishu
MALDIVES
Equator

MALAYSIA
Kuala Lumpur
PEN. MALAYSIA
Medan
SINGAPORE
SABAH
BRUNEI
Borneo

IRIAN JAYA
Gilbert Is.
NAURU KIRIBATI

EQUATORIAL GUINEA
SAO TOME & PRINCIPE
GABON
Libreville
CONGO
Brazzaville
CONGO (DEM. REP. OF THE)
Kinshasa
Kisangani
UGANDA
Kampala
RWANDA Kigali
BURUNDI Bujumbura
Kananga
L. Turkana
L. Victoria
KENYA
Nairobi
L. Tanganyika
SEYCHELLES
Amirante Is.
Diego Garcia
Chagos Arch. (U.K.)
INDIAN
Palembang
Sumatra
Banjarmasin
INDONESIA
JAKARTA
Bandung Java
Surabaya
Ujung Pandang
PAPUA NEW GUINEA
Port Moresby
C. York
New Ireland
New Britain
SOLOMON IS.
Santa Cruz Is.

E

TANZANIA
Dodoma
Mombasa
Zanzibar
Dar es Salaam
Kanaka
ANGOLA
Luanda
Benguela
Lubumbashi
CABINDA (Angola)
L. Malawi
Aldabra Is.
Agalega Is. (Fr.)
OCEAN
Cocos Is. (Austral.)
Christmas I. (Austral.)
Timor
Arafura Sea
Darwin

NAURU KIRIBATI
TUVALU

ZAMBIA
Lusaka
MALAWI
Lilongwe
NAMIBIA
Windhoek
BOTSWANA
ZIMBABWE
Harare
Bulawayo
MOZAMBIQUE
Mozambique Channel
MADAGASCAR
Antananarivo
COMOROS
Mayotte (Fr.)
Cargados Carajos
Rodriguez
MAURITIUS
RÉUNION (Fr.)
Tropic of Capricorn

Cairns
Townsville
Port Hedland
Alice Springs
AUSTRALIA
Rockhampton
Brisbane

VANUATU
NEW CALEDONIA (Fr.)
FIJI
Suva

20

SOUTH AFRICA
Johannesburg
Pretoria
Caborone
SWAZILAND
Maputo
LESOTHO
Durban
Cape Town
C. of Good Hope
Port Elizabeth

Prince Edward Is. (S.Africa)
Crozet Is. (Fr.)
Amsterdam I. (Fr.)
St.Paul (Fr.)
Kerguelen (Fr.)
McDonald Is. Heard I. (Austral.) (Austral.)

Geraldton
Perth
Fremantle
Kalgoorlie-Boulder
Great Australian Bight
Adelaide
Melbourne
Tasmania
Darling
Newcastle
Sydney
Canberra
Hobart
Lord Howe I. (Austral.)
Norfolk I. (Austral.)
Tasman Sea
NEW ZEALAND
Auckland
North I.
Wellington
Christchurch
South I.
Dunedin
Stewart I.
Bounty Is. (N.Z.)
Antipodes Is. (N.Z.)

F

40

SOUTHERN OCEAN

Bouvet I. (Norw.)
East from Greenwich

Antarctic Circle

Campbell I. (N.Z.)
Auckland Is. (N.Z.)
Macquarie I. (Austral.)
Ross Sea

G

60

Antarctica
c   t   i   c   a

H

10 20 **11** 40 **12** 60 **13** 80 **14** 100 **15** 120 **16** 140 **17** 160 **18** 180 80

Hanoi ● Capital Cities

CARTOGRAPHY BY PHILIP'S.

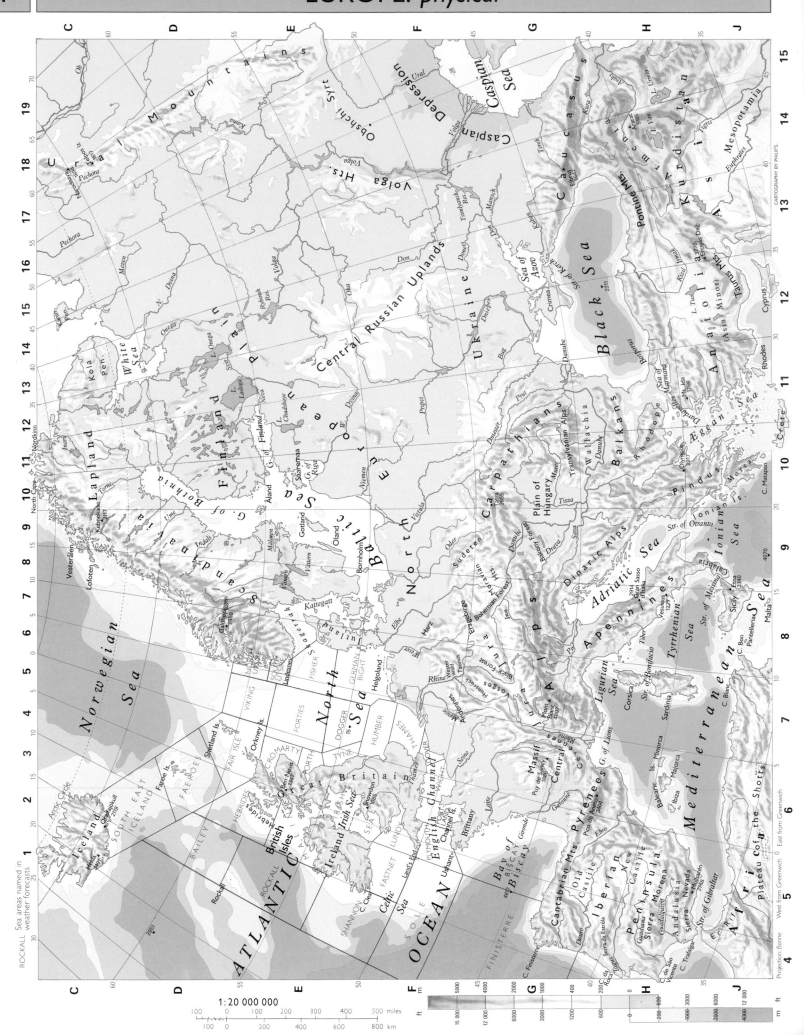

ATLANTIC OCEAN

Norwegian Sea

Mediterranean Sea

Black Sea

Caspian Sea

North Sea

Baltic Sea

Adriatic Sea

Tyrrhenian Sea

Ligurian Sea

Ionian Sea

Ægean Sea

White Sea

Iceland

British Isles

Great Britain

Ireland

Scandinavia

Alps

Carpathians

Pyrenees

Apennines

Caucasus

Ural Mountains

Iberian Peninsula

Russian Plain

Central Russian Uplands

Ukraine

Lapland

Finland

Plain of Hungary

Anatolia (Asia Minor)

Kurdistan

Armenia

Mesopotamia

Caspian Depression

ROCKALL Sea areas named in weather forecasts

1:20 000 000

CARTOGRAPHY BY PHILIP'S

Projection: Borne   West from Greenwich 0 East from Greenwich

100   0   100   200   300   400   500 miles

100   0   200   400   600   800 km

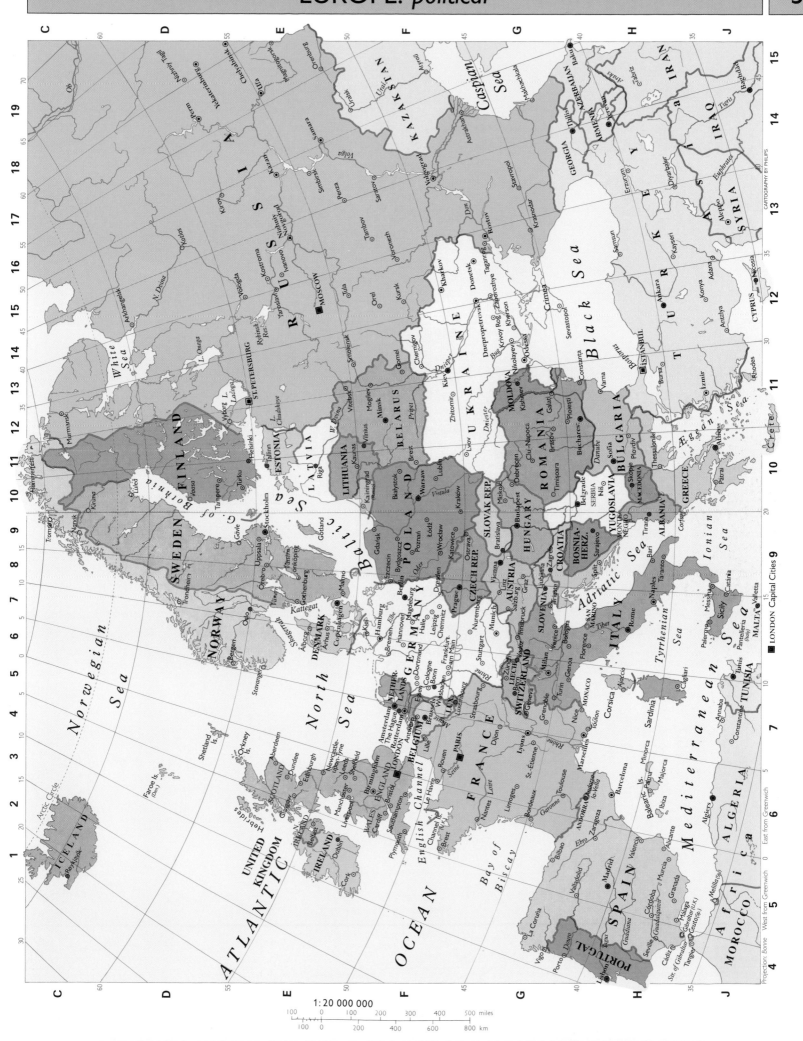

1:20 000 000

100   0   100   200   300   400   500 miles

100   0   200   400   600   800 km

Projection: Bonne   West from Greenwich   0   East from Greenwich

CARTOGRAPHY BY PHILIPS

■ LONDON Capital Cities 9

ICELAND
On the same scale West from Greenwich

Projection: Conical with two standard parallels

East from Greenwich

1:10 000 000

COPYRIGHT. GEORGE PHILIP & SON, LTD.

ATLANTIC OCEAN

NORWAY
Bergen
Askøy
Osøyri
Stord
Bømlo
Leirvik
Haugesund
Kopervik
Åkrahamn
Bokn
Stavanger
Sandnes
Bryne
Nærbø

Shetland Is.
Yell
Unst
Fetlar
Mainland
Lerwick
Foula
Fair Isle

1224
316

Orkney Is.
Westray
Sanday
Stronsay
Mainland
Kirkwall
Hoy
South
Ronaldsay

C. Wrath
Pentland Firth
Thurso
Wick
Helmsdale

Lewis
Stornoway
North Minch
Outer Hebrides
Harris
St. Kilda
North Uist
Benbecula
South Uist

Ullapool
Laing
Golspie
Moray Firth
Buckie
Banff
Fraserburgh
Peterhead

789

Skye
Portree
Nairn
Elgin
Huntly
Inverurie
Dingwall
Inverness
L. Ness
Aviemore
Don
Aberdeen

North West Highlands

Mallaig
Rhum
Eigg
1182
Ben Nevis
1342
Fort William
Dee
311
Ballater
Stonehaven

Inner Hebrides
Coll
Tobermory
1214
Forfar
Montrose
Arbroath

Tiree
Mull
Oban
Perth
Dundee
St. Andrews

SCOTLAND
Grampian Mts.

Colonsay
973
Stirling
Glenrothes
Kirkcaldy
Dunbar

L. Lomond
Dunfermline

Jura
Greenock
Glasgow
Edinburgh
Berwick-upon-Tweed

Islay
Paisley
Hamilton
Galashiels
640
816
Cheviot Hills
Alnwick

Arran
East Kilbride
Jedburgh
Campbeltown
Kilmarnock
Southern Uplands
Hawick

NORTH
SEA

238

Malin Hd.
Buncrana
Ayr
Girvan
Dumfries
Hexham
Newcastle-upon-Tyne

Aran I.
Letterkenny
Coleraine
Kirkcudbright
Annan
South Shields
Sunderland

Londonderry
Ballymena
Larne
Stranraer
Carlisle
Gateshead
Durham

Donegal
Lifford
Omagh
Antrim
Bangor
Workington
893
Hartlepool
Redcar

NORTHERN IRELAND
Lough Neagh
Belfast
Whitehaven
Cumbrian Mts.
Darlington
Middlesbrough

Bundoran
Ulster
Portadown
Lisburn
Lurgan
978
Barrow-in-Furness
Stockton-on-Tees

L. Erne
Enniskillen
Armagh
Newry
Douglas
I. of Man
Lancaster
16
Scarborough

Ballina
Sligo
Leitrim
Cavan
Clones
Castleblaney
Dundalk
Harrogate
Bridlington

Achill
L. Gara
Castlebar
Roscommon
Longford
Mullingar
Boyne
Drogheda
York
Beverley

UNITED KINGDOM

Lough Mask
Westport
Lough Corrib
Athlone
Lough Ree
Blackpool
Burnley
Keighley
Leeds
Kingston upon Hull

Connemara
Galway
Ballinasloe
Tullamore
Preston
Blackburn
Halifax
Bradford
Huddersfield
Scunthorpe
Grimsby

Galway B.
Aran Is.
Dublin
Anglesey
Holyhead
Bolton
Manchester
Oldham
Doncaster
Rotherham
Lincoln
Louth

IRELAND
Ennis
Lough Derg
Birr
Dun Laoghaire
Bray
Bangor
Colwyn Bay
Liverpool
Warrington
Stockport
636
Sheffield
Skegness

IRISH
SEA

Kilrush
Nenagh
Thurles
Carlow
Kilkenny
Snowdon
1085
Chester
Chesterfield
Mansfield
Boston
The Wash
Cromer

Shannon
Limerick
Tipperary
Wexford
Wrexham
Stoke-on-Trent
Derby
Nottingham
King's Lynn

953
Listowel
Clonmel
926
Arklow
Pwllheli
Shrewsbury
Stafford
Trent
Granthorn
Norwich
Great Yarmouth

Tralee
Mallow
Carrick-on-Suir
Waterford
Cambrian Mts.
Telford
ENGLAND
Leicester
Peterborough
Thetford
Lowestoft

Dingle
Killarney
Dungarvan
Cardigan Bay
Welshpool
Wolverhampton
Nuneaton
Corby
Ely
Bury St. Edmunds
Ipswich

Carrantuohill
1041
Macgillycuddy's Reeks
Blackwater
Youghal
Aberystwyth
WALES
BIRMINGHAM
Redditch
Coventry
Rugby
Bedford
Cambridge
Felixstowe

valencia I.
Bantry
Cork
Cobh
Fishguard
Carmarthen
886
Worcester
Hereford
Royal Leamington Spa
Northampton
Milton Keynes
Stevenage
Colchester

99
Bandon
Kinsale
St. George's Channel
Haverfordwest
Milford Haven
Pembroke
Llanelli
Neath
Brecon
Cheltenham
Gloucester
Cotswold Hills
Oxford
High Wycombe
Hemel Hempstead
Luton
Harlow
Chelmsford

NETHERLANDS
Texel
Den Helder
Alkmaar
Haarlem
The Hague
Hoek van Holland
ROTTERDAM
Dordrecht

C. Clear
Swansea
Port Talbot
Rhondda
Newport
Cardiff
Bristol
Bath
Newbury
Reading
LONDON
Slough
Watford
Basildon
Southend-on-Sea
36

Barry
Weston-super-Mare
Swindon
Thames
Chatham
Margate
Vlissingen
Zeebrugge
Oostende
Brugge
Gent
Antwerp
Mechelen

Bristol Channel
Exmoor
Taunton
Basingstoke
Guildford
Reigate
Crawley
Maidstone
Canterbury
Dover
Dunkerque
BELGIUM
BRUSSELS

CELTIC
SEA

Barnstaple
Bude
Yeovil
Salisbury
Winchester
Fareham
Havant
Hastings
Folkestone
Str. of Dover
Calais
Gris Nez
Boulogne-sur-Mer
St-Omer
Béthune
Lille
d'Ascq

618
Dartmoor
Exmouth
Southampton
Bournemouth
Poole
Portsmouth
Brighton
Eastbourne
Le Touquet-Paris-Plage
33
Bruay-en-Artois
Lens
Valenciennes

Newquay
Truro
St. Austell
Torbay
Weymouth
Newport
Isle of Wight
Worthing
Le Tréport
Abbeville
Picardie
Cambrai
St-Quentin

Plymouth
Land's End
Penzance
Falmouth
English Channel
Dieppe
Fécamp
Amiens
FRANCE

Isles of Scilly

C. de la Hague
Alderney
Pte. de Barfleur
Pays de Caux
Rouen
Seine
Elbeuf

Guernsey
St. Peter Port
Sark
Cherbourg
Valognes
Le Havre
Bolbec
Trouville-sur-Mer
Lisieux

Channel Is.
(U.K.)
St. Helier
Jersey
Cotentin
Bayeux
Caen

Projection: Conical with two standard parallels
West from Greenwich
East from Greenwich
CARTOGRAPHY BY PHILIP'S.

1 : 5 000 000

ft m
3000 1000
1500 500
600 200
0
50 150
100 300
500 1500
1000 3000
2000 6000
m ft

FRANCE

1 : 5 000 000

CARTOGRAPHY BY PHILIP'S

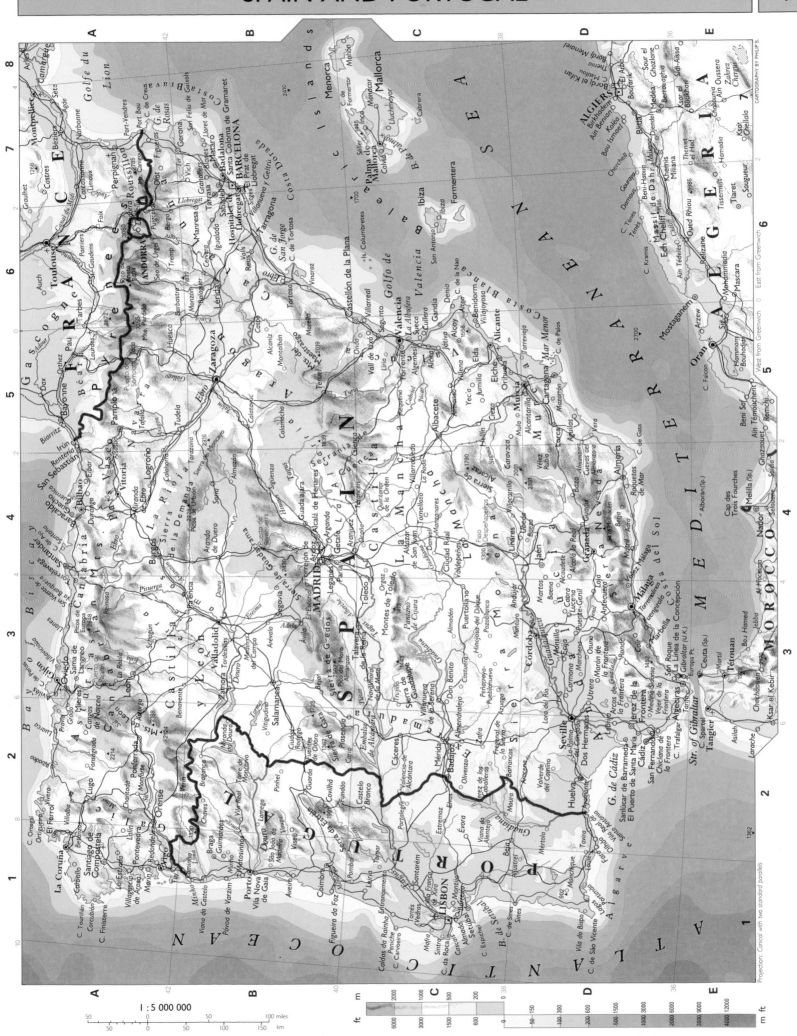

1 : 5 000 000

Projection: Conical with two standard parallels

East from Greenwich

CARTOGRAPHY BY PHILIP'S.

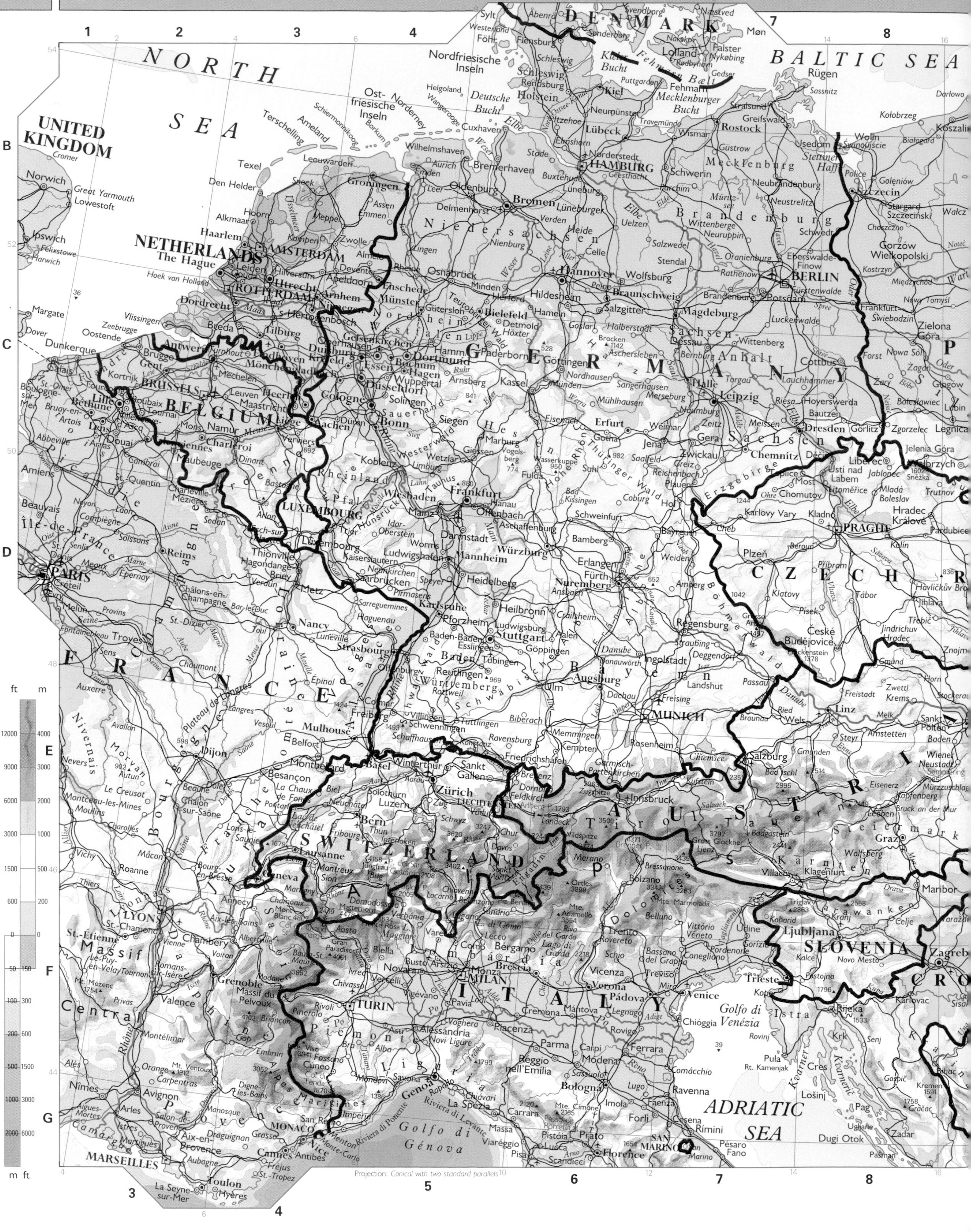

NORTH SEA

BALTIC SEA

UNITED KINGDOM

NETHERLANDS

BELGIUM

LUXEMBOURG

GERMANY

DENMARK

FRANCE

SWITZERLAND

AUSTRIA

ITALY

SLOVENIA

CZECH

MARSEILLES

ADRIATIC SEA

Projection: Conical with two standard parallels

9   10   11   12   13   14   15   16

LITHUANIA

BELARUS

POLAND

UKRAINE

C Z E C H R E P.

SLOVAK REP.

HUNGARY

ROMANIA

MOLDOVA

YUGOSLAVIA

BOSNIA-HERZEGOVINA

BULGARIA

East from Greenwich

1 : 5 000 000

CARTOGRAPHY BY PHILIP'S.

9   10   11   12   13   14   15

SWITZERLAND

AUSTRIA

SLOVENIA

CROAT

FRANCE

I T A L Y

TURIN

MONACO

MARSEILLES

MILAN

Venice

Trieste

Ljubljana

Zagréb

Maribor

Nagykanizsa

Koprivnica

Varaždin

Bjelovar

Virovitica

Graz

Klagenfurt

Wolfsberg

Villach

Bolzano

Merano

Bréssanone

Belluno

Trento

Rovereto

Schio

Vicenza

Verona

Pádova

Treviso

Conegliano

Udine

Gorízia

Pordenone

Koper

Postojna

Novo Mesto

Celje

Kranj

Kobarid

Rijeka

Pula

Krk

Cres

Lošinj

Pag

Zadar

Dugi Otok

Sibenik

Split

Solta

Brač

Hvar

Vis

Korčula

Lastovo

Mljet

Peljesac

Banja Luka

Bosanska Gradiška

Bihać

HER

Annecy

Aix-les-Bains

Chambéry

Albertville

Grenoble

Massif du Pelvoux

Briançon

Valence

Montélimar

Orange

Avignon

Carpentras

Aix-en-Provence

Salon-de-Provence

Toulon

La Seyne-sur-Mer

Hyères

Îles d' Hyères

Cannes

Antibes

Nice

Monte-Carlo

San Remo

Impéria

Savona

Genoa

Rapallo

Chiavari

La Spézia

Massa

Carrara

Viaréggio

Pisa

Livorno

Golfo di Génova

LIGURIAN SEA

C. Corse

Calvi

Bastia

Corte

Ajaccio

Corsica

Porto-Vecchio

Bonifácio

Maddalena

Asinara

C. Falcone

Porto Tórres

Alghero

Sássari

Bosa

Nuoro

Oristano

Sardinia

Iglésias

San Pietro

Sant' Antíoco

Carbonia

Portoscuso

Cágliari

Quartu Sant' Elena

C. Carbonara

C. Spartivento

TYRRHENIAN SEA

Turin

Piémonte

Cuneo

Mondovi

Asti

Alessandria

Novi Ligure

Pavia

Lodi

Crema

Brescia

Bérgamo

Como

Lecco

Monza

Cremona

Mántova

Piacenza

Parma

Carpi

Módena

Ferrara

Bologna

Imola

Faenza

Forlì

Cesena

Rimini

Ravenna

Comácchio

Lugo

Florence

Prato

Pistoia

Lucca

Arno

Cascina

Scandicci

SAN MARINO

San Marino

Urbino

Pésaro

Fano

Senigállia

Falconara Maríttima

Ancona

Civitanova Marche

Fermo

Ascoli Piceno

Teramo

San Benedetto del Tronto

Macerata

Perúgia

Assisi

Fabriano

Iesi

Città di Castello

Arezzo

Siena

Volterra

Rosignano Maríttimo

Grosseto

Elba

Pianosa

Montecristo

Giglio

Orbetello

C. Argentario

Piombino

Portoferráio

Capraia

Viterbo

Orvieto

Terni

Spoleto

Fóligno

Rieti

Gran Sasso d'Italia

L'Áquila

Avezzano

Montesilvano Marina

Pescara

Chieti

Lanciano

Vasto

Térmoli

San Severo

Campobasso

Manfredónia

Fóggia

Cerignola

Barletta

Trani

Andria

Corato

Molfetta

Bari

Monópoli

Altamura

Putignano

Matera

Potenza

Fasano

Martina Franca

Táranto

VATICAN CITY

ROME

Tívoli

Guidónia Montecélio

Frosinone

Isérnia

Pomézia

Velletri

Aprília

Latina

Fondi

Cassino

Terracina

Fórmia

Ánzio

Ísole Ponziane

Ventotene

Gaeta

Caserta

Benevento

Avellino

Ischia

NAPLES

Pozzuoli

Aversa

Torre del Greco

Castellammare di Stábia

Capri

Salerno

Nocera Inferiore

Battipáglia

Sala Consilina

Ágri

Lauria

Pisciotta

Sinni

Coriglíano Cálabro

Rossano Cálabro

Cetraro

Cosenza

Crotone

Catanzaro

Vibo Valéntia

Nicastro

Sambiase

Palmi

Taurianova

C. Spartivento

Réggio di Calábria

Messina

Str. di Messina

Calábria

Golfo di Táranto

Strómboli

Ístole Eólie

Salina

Lípari

Vulcano

C. Peloro

Milazzo

Barcellona Pozzo di Gotto

Cefalù

Palermo

Bagheria

Termini Imerese

Trápani

Érice

Ísole Égadi

Favignana

Marsala

Mazara del Vallo

Castelvetrano

Partinico

Alcamo

Sciacca

Agrigento

Porto Empédocle

Favara

Licata

Caltanissetta

Canicattì

Enna

Adrano

Paternò

Catánia

Acireale

Giarre

Etna

Lentini

Augusta

Siracusa

Caltagirone

Gela

Ragusa

Módica

Vittória

Ávola

 Íspica

C. Passero

SICILY

Monti Nébrodi

Ustica (Italy)

Pantelleria (Italy)

ALGERIA

El Milia

Collo

Skikda

Annaba

Azzaba

El Kala

Constantine

El Khroub

Guelma

Souk-Ahras

Aïn M'lila

Aïn Beïda

Oum-el-Bouaghi

Tébessa

Khenchela

Chéria

Babar

TUNISIA

Bizerte

Menzel-Bourguiba

Mateur

Tabarka

Jendouba

Béja

Bou Salem

Ghardimaou

Souk el Arba

El Kef

Maktar

Kasserine

Sbeitla

Thala

Kalaa-Kebira

Sousse

Monastir

Moknine

Mahdia

Kairouan

Akouda

Hammam Sousse

El Djem

Sbikha

Tunis

Ariana

La Marsa

Bardo

Manouba

Ben Arous

Soliman

Nabeul

Hammamet

Korba

Kelibia

Rass Mostefa

Menzel-Temime

C. Bon

Zaghouan

 Ísole Pelagie (Italy)

I. Linosa

Lampione

Lampedusa

MALTA

Valletta

Gozo

Rabat

MEDITER

Projection: Conical with two standard parallels

ADRIATIC SEA

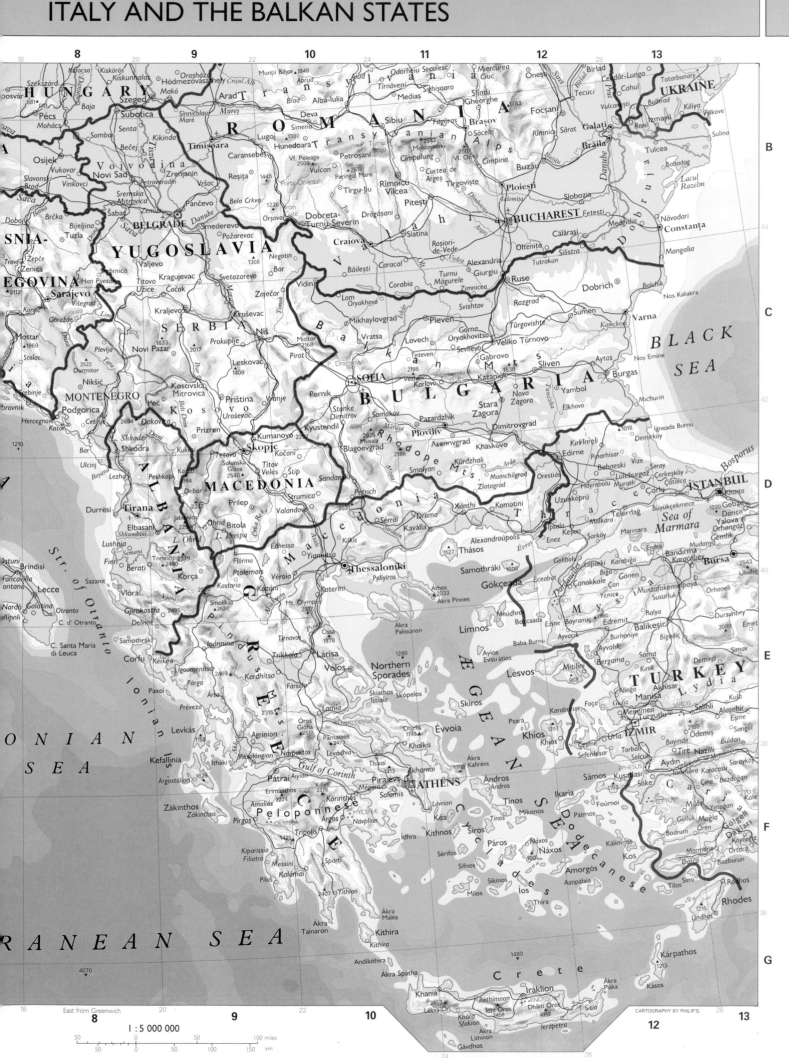

1. Crimea (Ukr.)
2. Adygea (Russ.)
3. Karachey-Cherkessia (Russ.)
4. Kabardino-Balkaria (Russ.)
5. North Ossetia (Russ.)
6. Ingushetia (Russ.)
7. Chechenia (Russ.)
8. Nakhichevan (Azer.)

Projection: Conical with two standard parallels

1:10 000 000

Division between Greeks and Turks
in Cyprus, Turks to the North

East from Greenwich

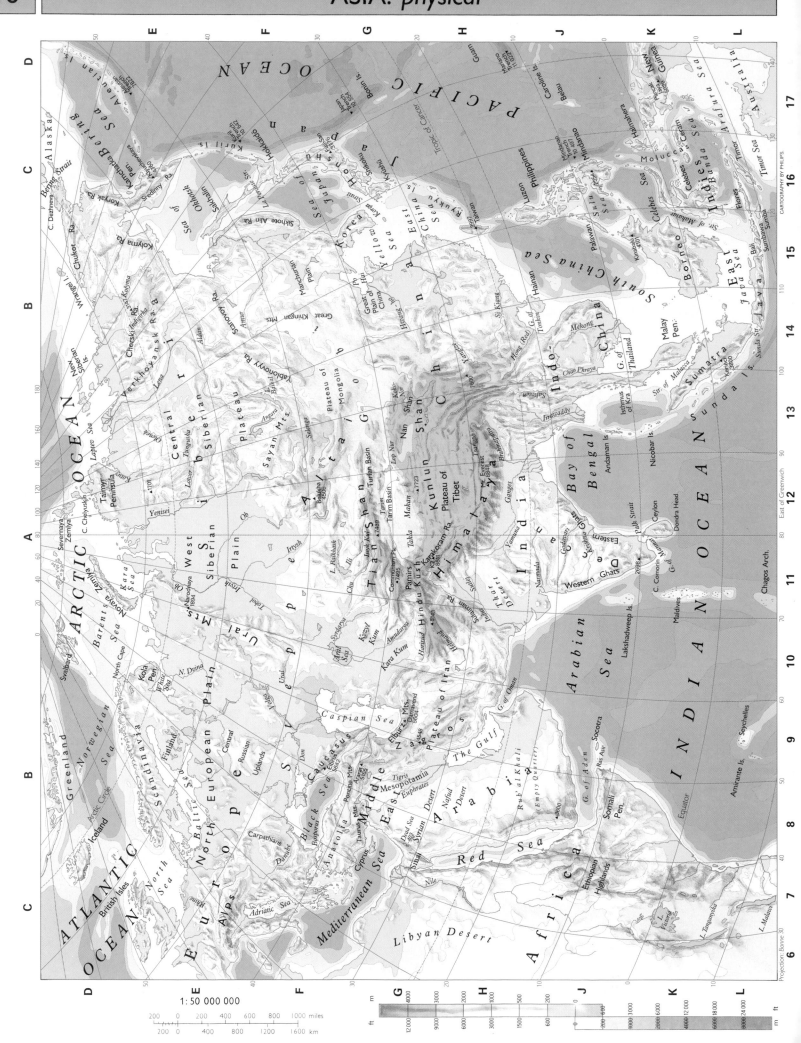

CARTOGRAPHY BY PHILIPS

1:50 000 000

200   0   200 400   600   800   1000 miles

200 0   400   800   1200   1600 km

Projection: Bonne 30

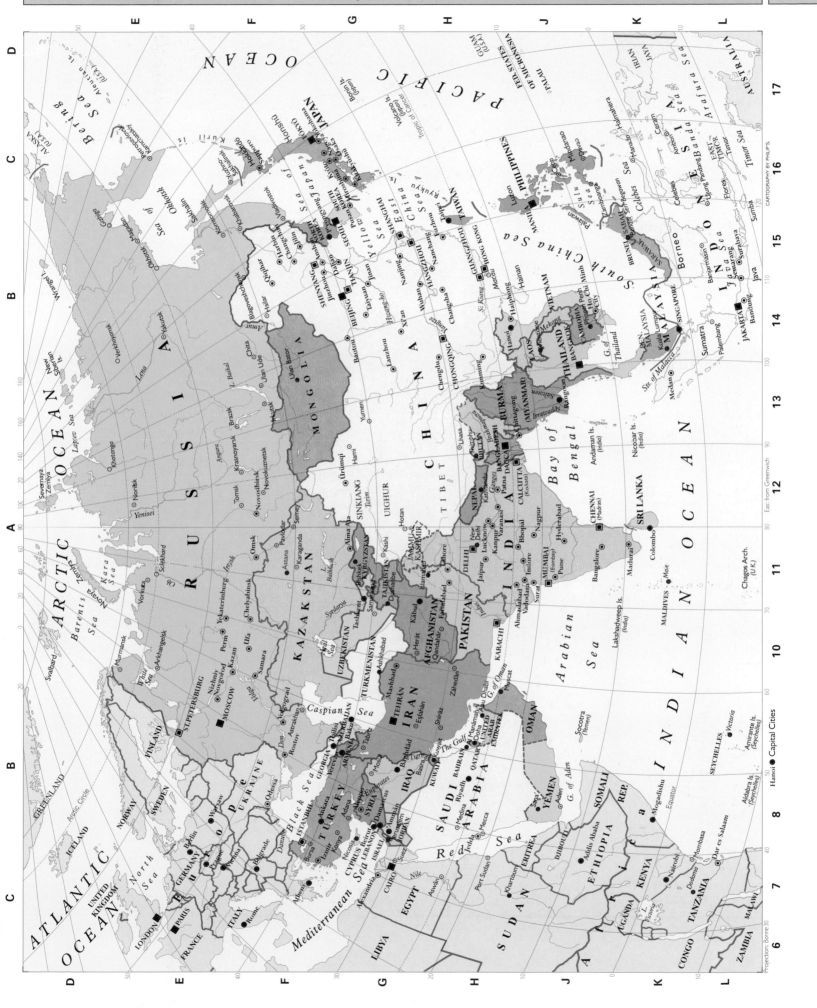

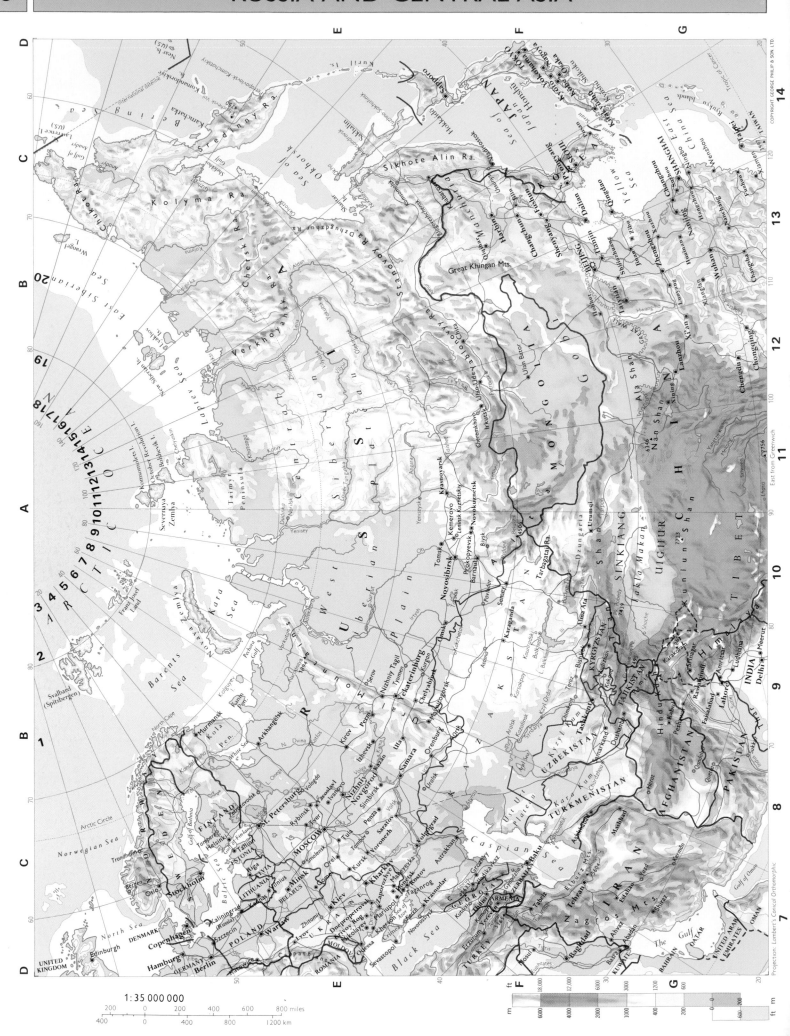

1 : 35 000 000

Projection: Lambert's Conical Orthomorphic

COPYRIGHT GEORGE PHILIP & SON LTD

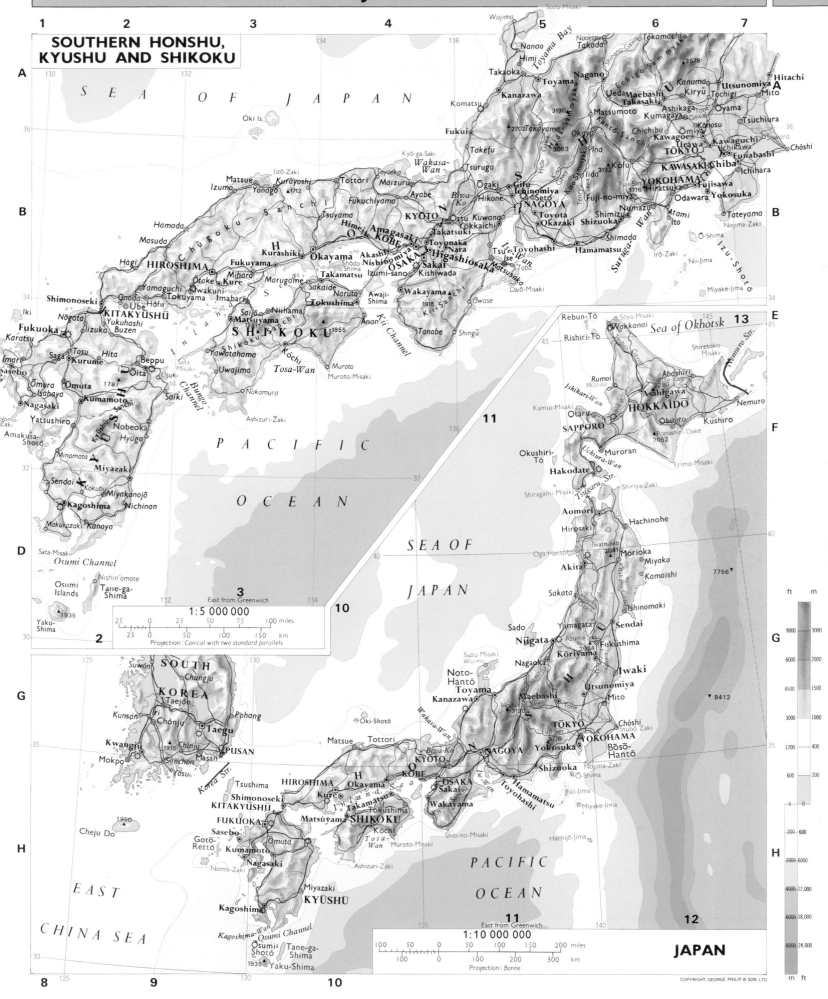

SOUTHERN HONSHU, KYUSHU AND SHIKOKU

1:5 000 000

Projection: Conical with two standard parallels

1:10 000 000

Projection: Bonne

JAPAN

COPYRIGHT. GEORGE PHILIP & SON, LTD.

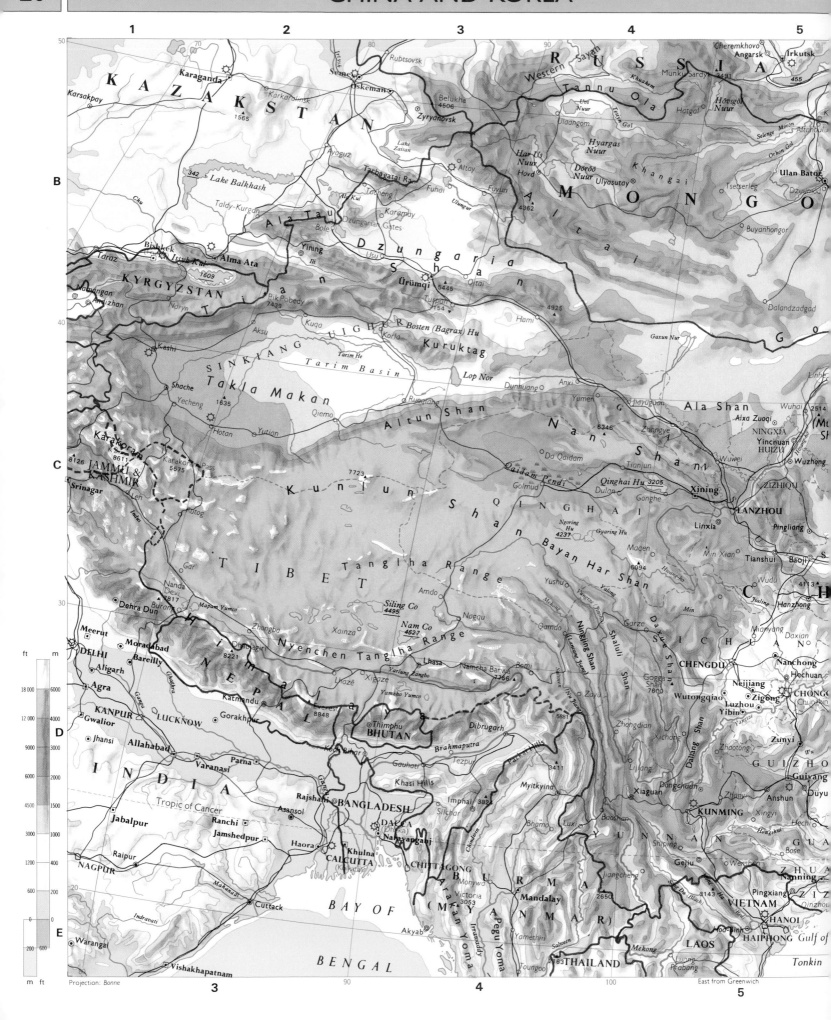

Projection: Bonne

East from Greenwich

SEA OF JAPAN

JAPAN

YELLOW SEA

EAST CHINA SEA

PACIFIC OCEAN

SOUTH CHINA SEA

Ryukyu Islands

Sakhalin

Hokkaido

Korea Bay

G. of Chihli (Bo Hai)

Tropic of Cancer

1 : 15 000 000

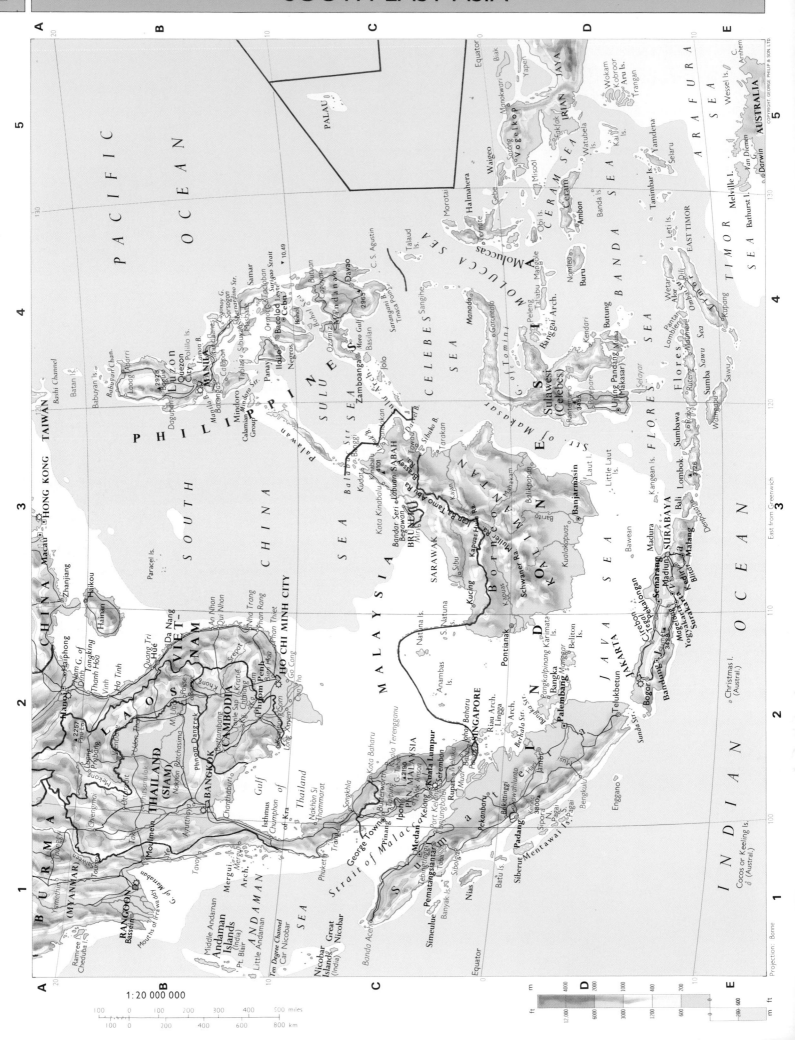

1:20 000 000

Projection: Bonne

East from Greenwich

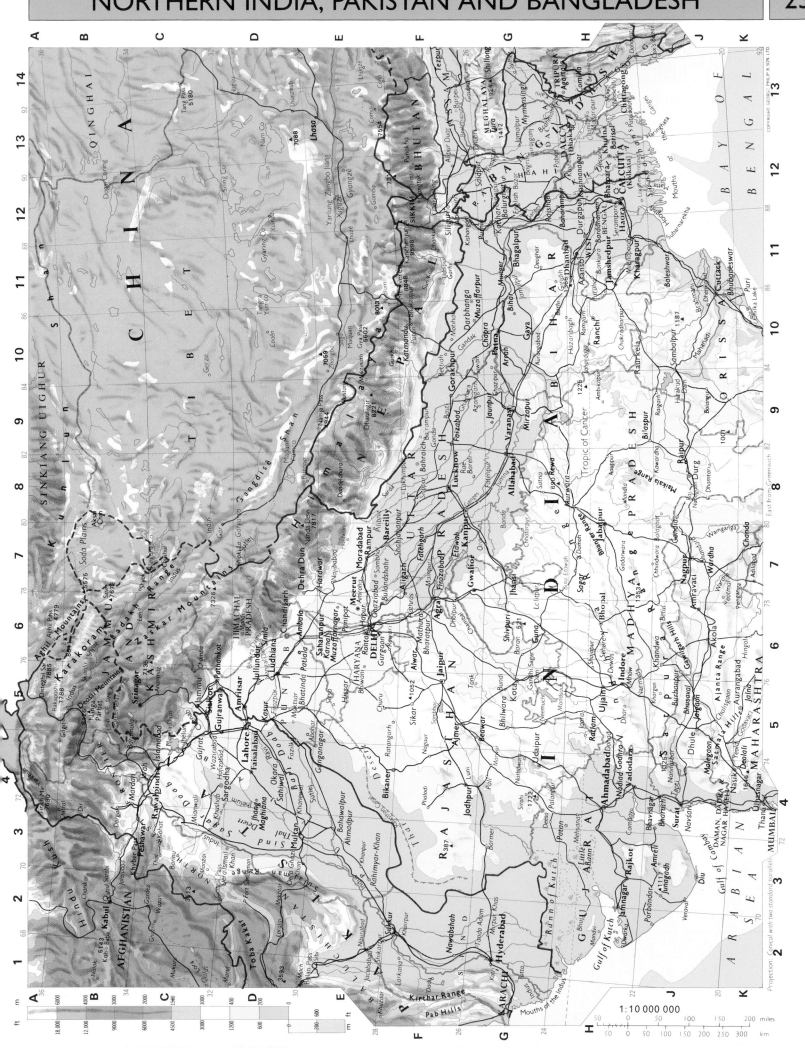

Projection: Conical with two standard parallels

1:10 000 000

COPYRIGHT GEORGE PHILIP & SON, LTD.

Projection : Alber's Equal Area with two standard parallels

East from Greenwich

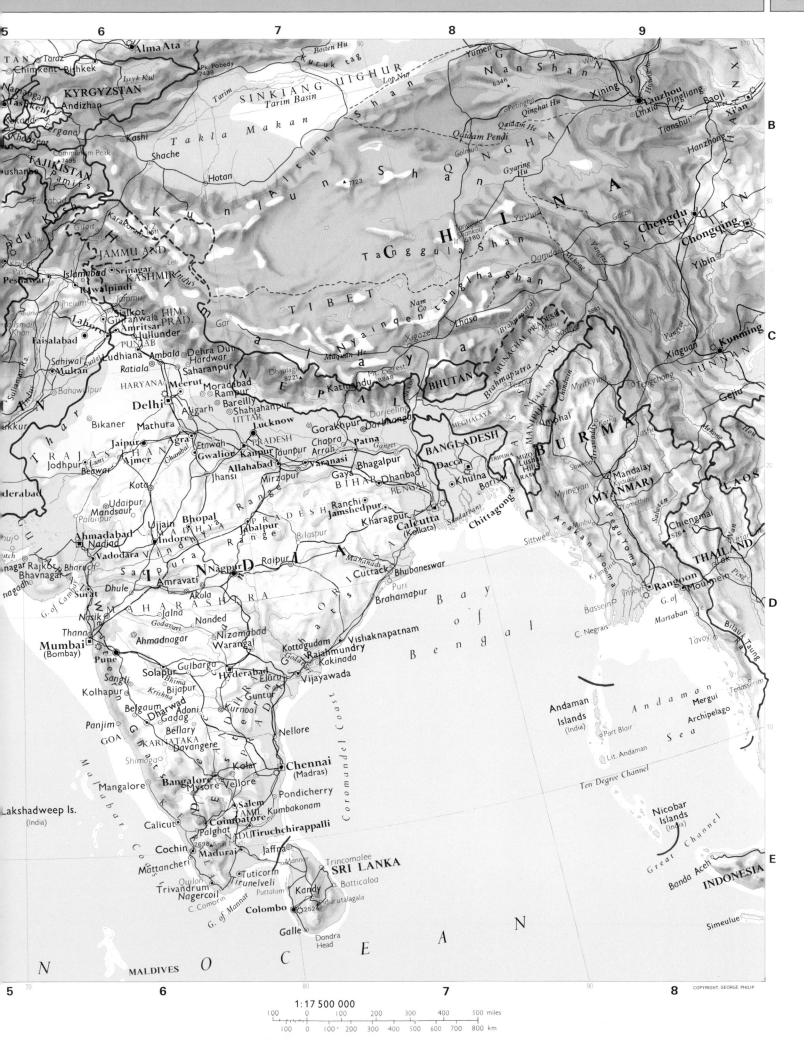

1:17 500 000

100 0 100 200 300 400 500 miles

100 0 100 200 300 400 500 600 700 800 km

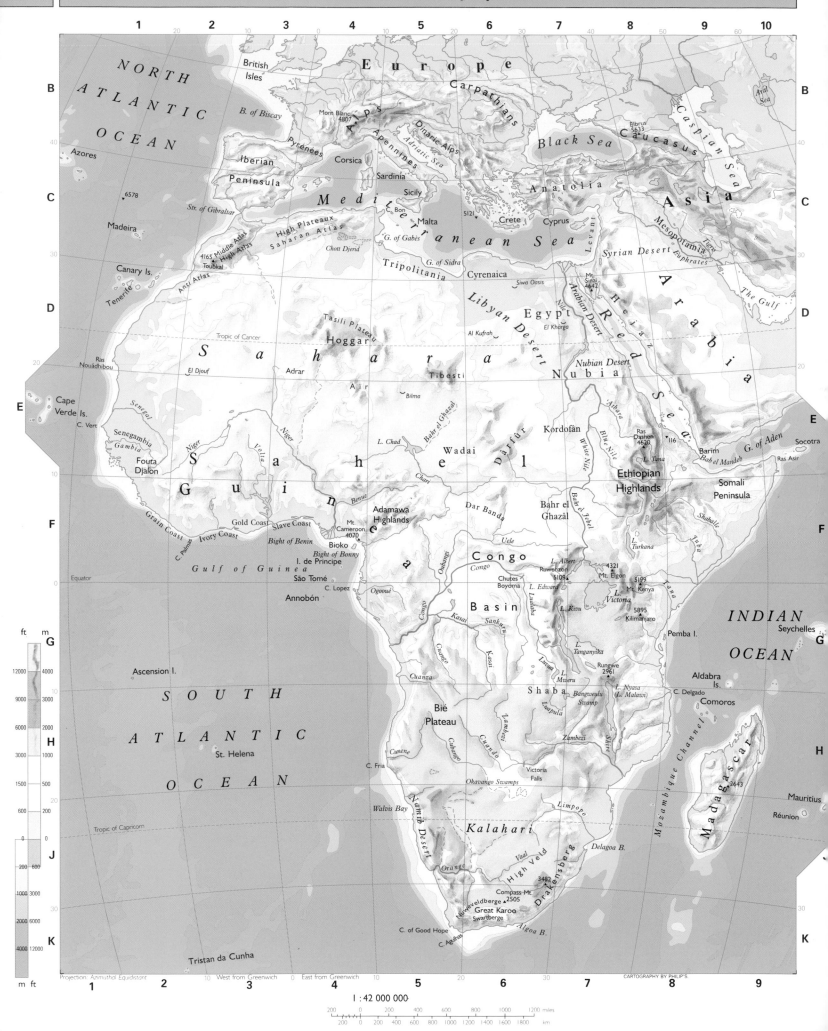

1 : 42 000 000

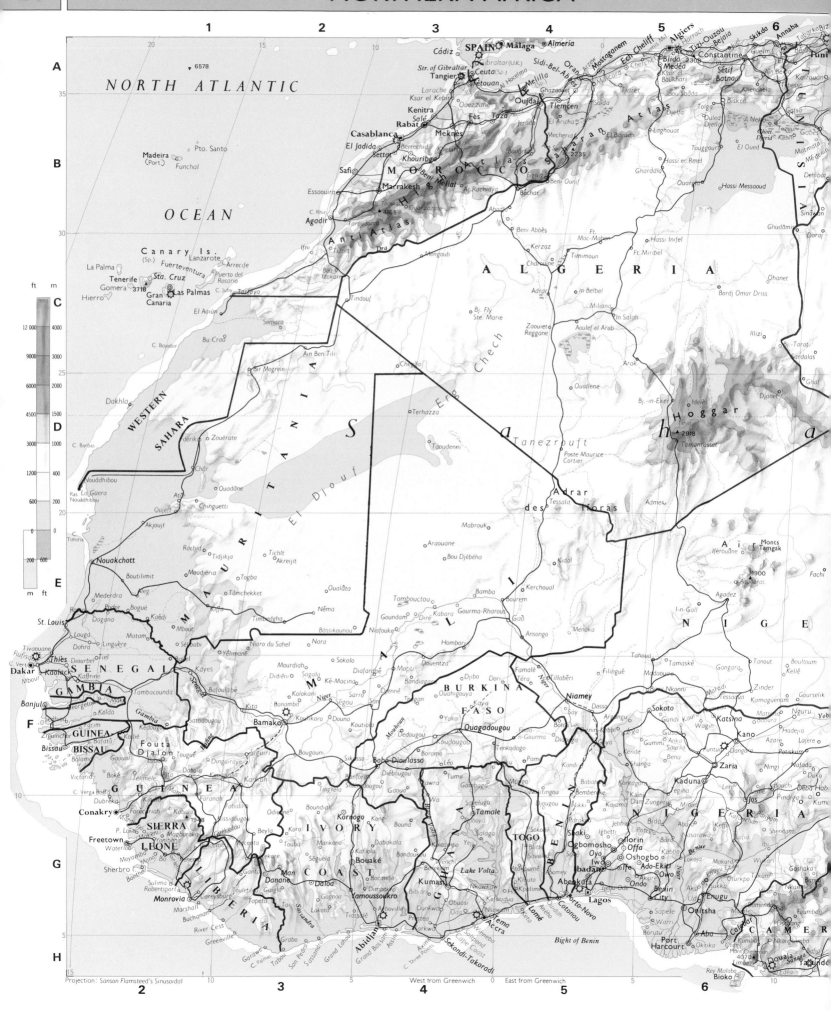

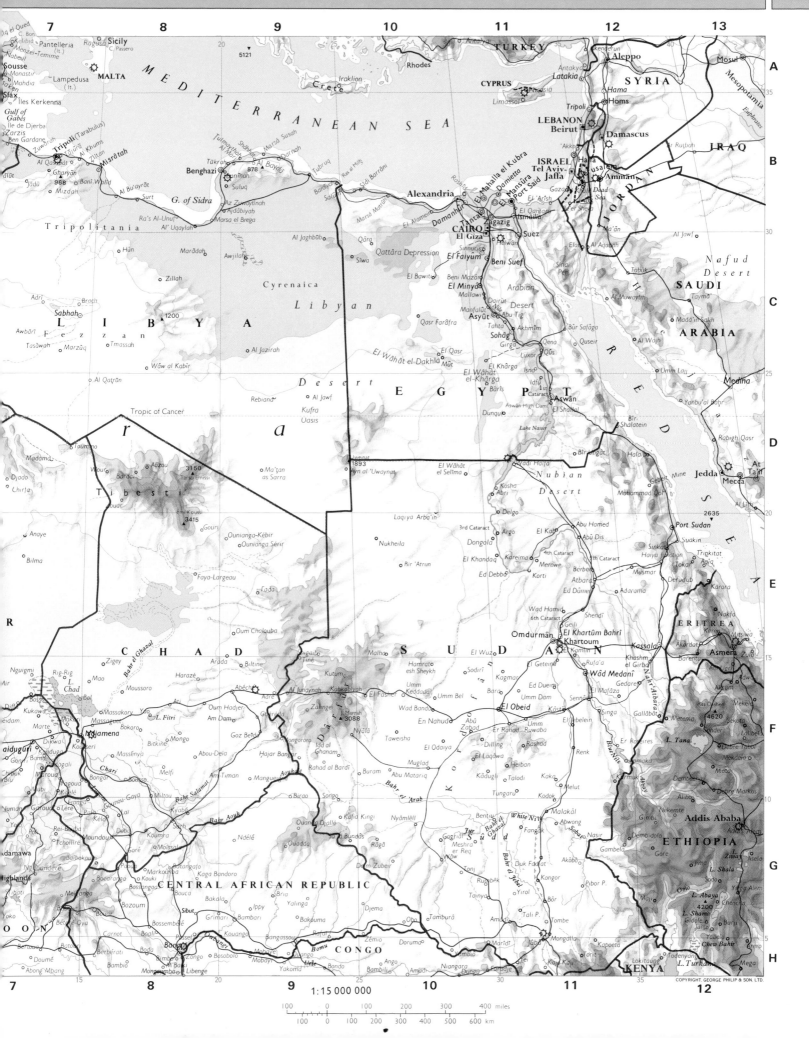

1:15 000 000

100   0   100   200   300   400 miles

100   0   100   200   300   400   500   600 km

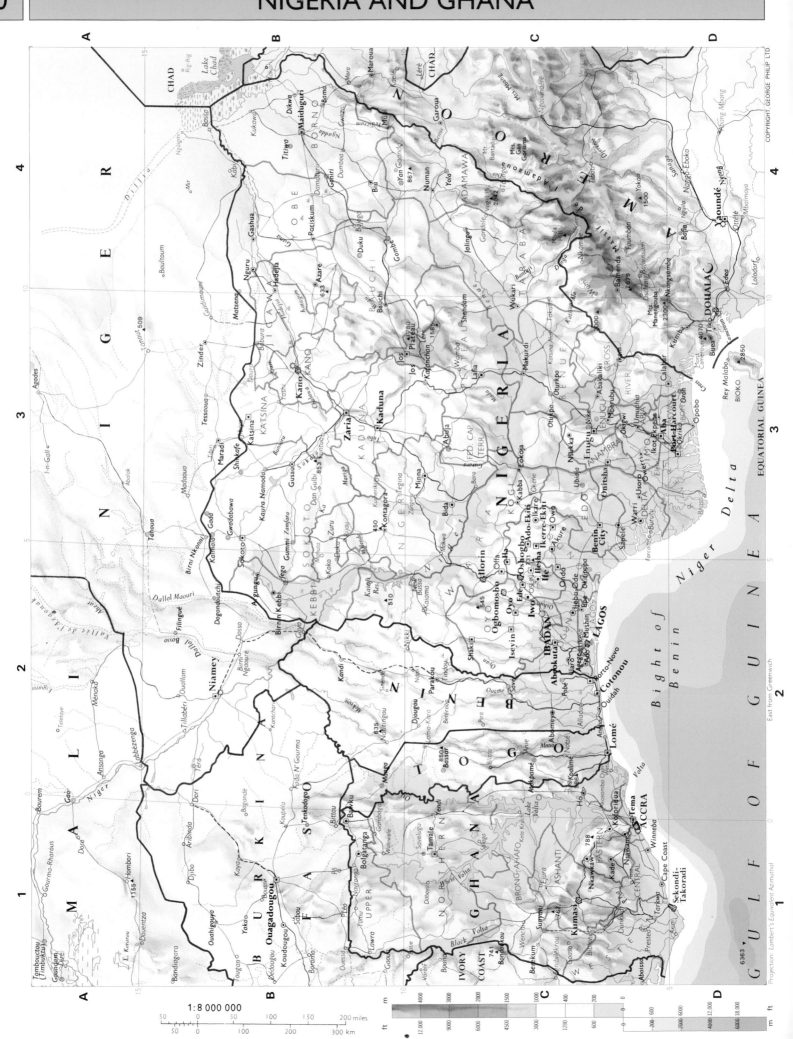

1:8 000 000

Projection: Lambert's Equivalent Azimuthal

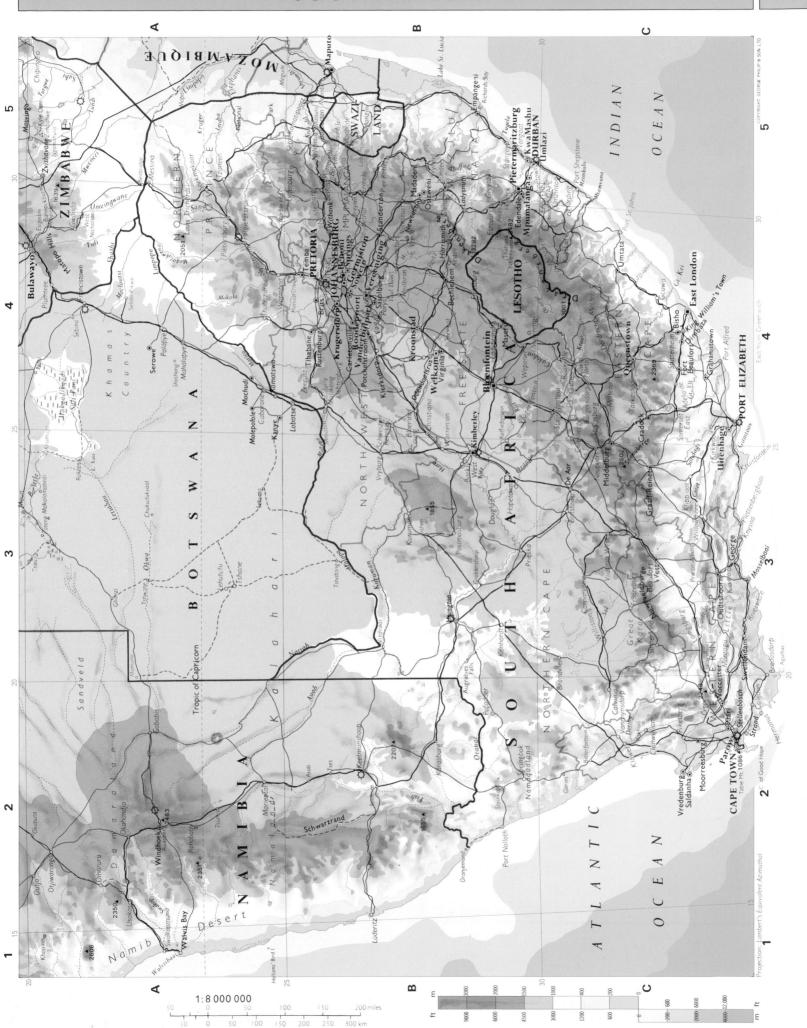

1:8 000 000

Projection: Lambert's Equivalent Azimuthal

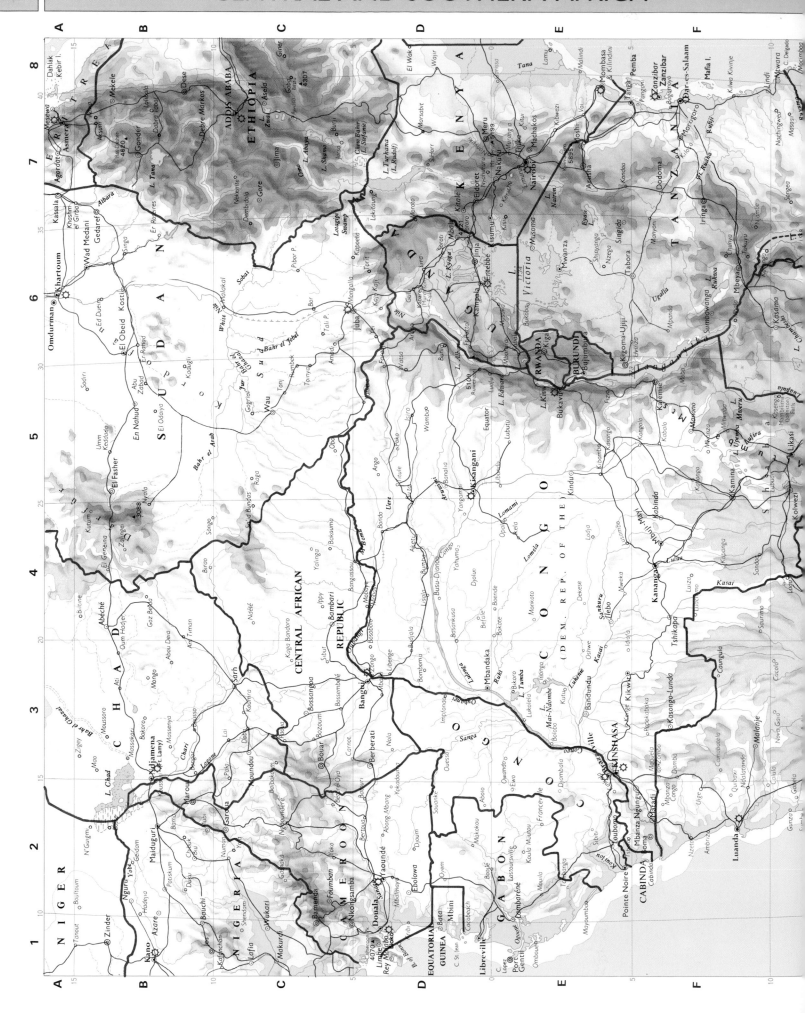

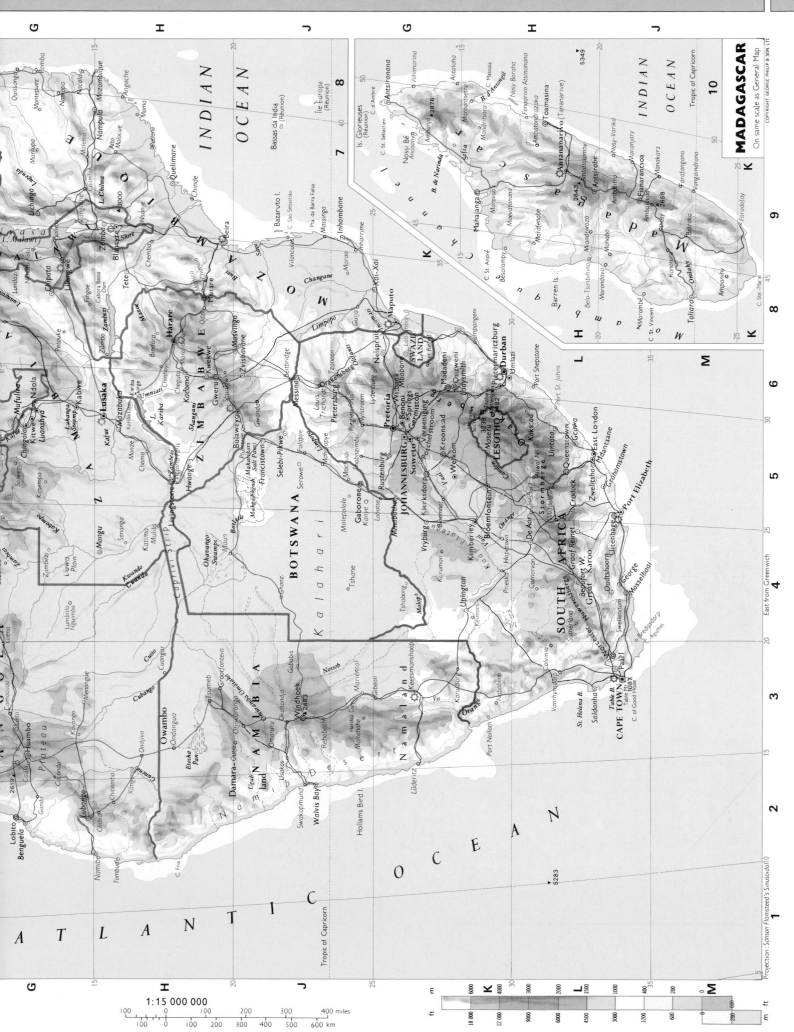

INDIAN OCEAN

ATLANTIC OCEAN

MADAGASCAR
On same scale as General Map
COPYRIGHT GEORGE PHILIP & SON, LTD.

Projection: Sanson Flamsteed's Sinusoidal

1:15 000 000

100   0   100   200   300   400 miles
100   0   100   200   300   400   500   600 km

INDONESIA

Sulawesi (Celebes)
Kendari
Butung
5300
Buru
Ceram
Ambon
Banda Sea
7260
Misool
Sorong
Vogelkop
Fakfak
Kai Is.
3350
Aru Is.
Ujung Pandang (Makasar)
Wetar
Flores Sea
Alor
Leti
Babar
Tanimbar Is.
3310
Sumbawa
Flores
Ende
Dili
Kupang
Timor
Timor Sea
Sumba
6204

Biak
Jayapura
Irian Jaya
Pegunungan Maoke
Puncak Jaya
5029
New Guinea
Wewak
PAPUA NEW GUINEA
Bismarck Archipelago
Kavieng
New Ireland
Madang
Mount Hagen
4508
Mt. Wilhelm
Lae
9140
New Britain
Rabaul
Solomon Sea
Owen Stanley Range
Fly
Gulf of Papua
Port Moresby
D'Entrecasteaux
Louisiade Archipelago

Pulau Yos Sudarso
Arafura Sea
Torres Strait
C. York

C. Croker
C. Arnhem
Melville I.
C. Londonderry
Cambridge G.
Darwin
Arnhem Land
Cape York Peninsula
Weipa
Cape York
Gulf of Carpentaria
Coral Sea

Wyndham
Kimberley Plateau
Derby
Broome
Daly Waters
Larrimah
Wellesley I.
Mitchell
Cooktown
Cairns
1611
Bartle Frere
NORTHERN
Tennant Creek
Barkly Tableland
Kajaabi
Normanton
Forsayth
Coral Sea Islands Territory
Townsville
Charters Towers
Great Sandy Desert
Tanami Desert
TERRITORY
Mount Isa
Hughenden
Mackay

Great Barrier Reef

Port Hedland
Dampier
L. Mackay
MacDonnell Ranges
1510 Mt. Ziel
Alice Springs
Winton
QUEENSLAND
Rockhampton
Gladstone
N.W. Cape
Mt. Bruce 1226
Hamersley Range
Newman
Gibson Desert
Lake Disappointment
Ayers Rock
Mt. Woodroffe 1440
Simpson Desert
Longreach
Diamantina
Bundaberg
Maryborough
Carnarvon
WESTERN
Musgrave Ranges
SOUTH
Lake Eyre
Yaraka
Grey Range
Charleville
Roma
Gympie
Meekatharra
L. Carnegie
Great Victoria Desert
Marree
Cooper Creek
Quilpie
Cunnamulla
Toowoomba
BRISBANE
Leonora
AUSTRALIA
AUSTRALIA
Thargomindah
Dirrabandi
Ipswich
Go Coa
Lismor
Tarcoola
Flinders Range
Bourke
Walgett
1615
Round Mt.
Carnarvon
Deakin
Broken Hill
Darling
Cobar
NEW SOUTH
Tamworth
Murchison
Lake Barlee
Kalgoorlie-Boulder
Penong
Port Augusta
Whyalla
Port Pirie
Marree
WALES
Orange
Taree
Geraldton
Nullarbor Plain
Whyalla
Murray
Dubbo
Newcastle
Bathurst
Meekatharra
Norseman
Great Australian Bight
Port Lincoln
Adelaide
Wagga Wagga
Murray
SYDNEY
Wollongong
Shellharbour
Perth
Northam
5632
Kangaroo I.
Encounter B.
Shepparton
Albury
Mt. Kosciuszko 2237
Canberra
CAPITAL TERRITORY
Bombala
Bunbury
Esperance
Mildura
Horsham
Goulburn
C. Leeuwin
Augusta
Albany
Mount Gambier
VICTORIA
Bendigo
MELBOURNE
Geelong
C. Howe
Ballarat
Warrnambool
Bass Strait
Furneaux Group
King I.
Burnie
Launceston
1617
Mt. Ossa
TASMANIA
Hobart
S.E. Cape

INDIAN OCEAN

Darling Range
Murchison

Projection : Lambert's Equivalent Azimuthal

East from Greenwich

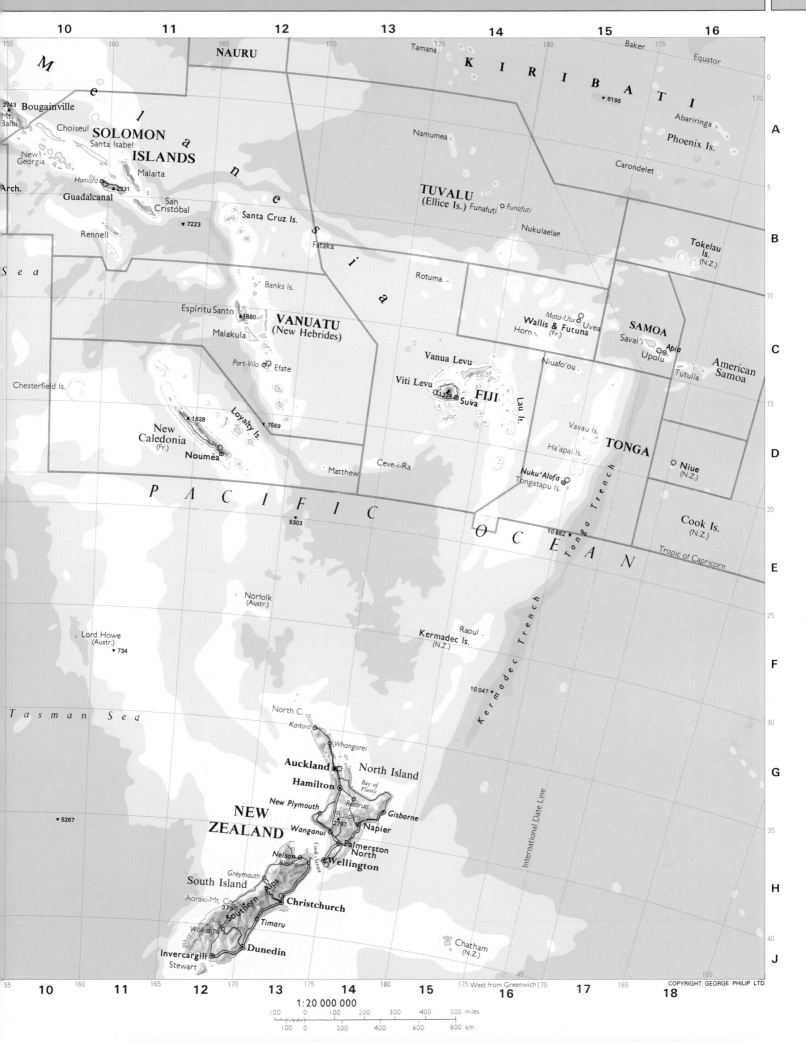

10   11   12   13   14   15   16

NAURU

M e *l* a *n* e *s* i a

Tamana   K I R I B A T I   Baker   Equator

▲2743 Mt. Balbi Bougainville
Choiseul   SOLOMON   ▼6195   Abariringa
Santa Isabel   ISLANDS
New Georgia   Malaita   Namumea   Phoenix Is.   A
Arch.   Honiara   Carondelet
Guadalcanal   ▲2331
Sea   San Cristóbal   TUVALU   B
▼7223   Santa Cruz Is.   (Ellice Is.) Funafuti ○Funafuti
Rennell   Nukulaelae   Tokelau Is. (N.Z.)
Fataka   Rotuma   10

Banks Is.   Mata-Utu ⚙ Uvea
Espíritu Santo   ▲1880   VANUATU   Wallis & Futuna   SAMOA
Chesterfield Is.   Malakula   (New Hebrides)   Horn   (Fr.)   Savai'i ⚙Apia   C
Port-Vila ⚙ Efate   Vanua Levu   Upolu   American
Niuafo'ou   Tutuila   Samoa
Viti Levu   15
New   ▲1628   Loyalty Is.   ▲1324   FIJI   Lau Is.   Vavau Is.
Caledonia (Fr.)   ▼7569   Suva   Ha'apai Is.   TONGA   ⚙ Niue (N.Z.)   D
Nouméa   Ceve-i-Ra   Nuku'Alofa ⚙
Matthew   Tongatapu Is.

P A C I F I C   20
▼5303   ▼10 882   Cook Is. (N.Z.)
O C E A N   Tropic of Capricorn   E

Norfolk (Austr.)   25

Lord Howe (Austr.)   Raoul
▼734   Kermadec Is. (N.Z.)   F
▼10 047

Tasman Sea   30

North C.
Kaitaia
Whangarei   G
Auckland   North Island
Hamilton   Bay of Plenty
New Plymouth   Rotorua
▼5267   NEW   Ruapehu   Gisborne
ZEALAND   Wanganui   ▲2797   Napier   35
Palmerston North
Nelson   Cook Strait   Wellington
Blenheim
Greymouth   South Island   H
Southern Alps
Aoraki-Mt. Cook   Christchurch
▲3753   Timaru
Wakatipu   40
Invercargill   Dunedin   Chatham (N.Z.)
Stewart   J

55   10   160   11   165   12   170   13   175   14   180   15 175 West from Greenwich 170 16   17   165   18   160

1:20 000 000

100 0 100 200 300 400 500 miles
100 0 200 400 600 800 km

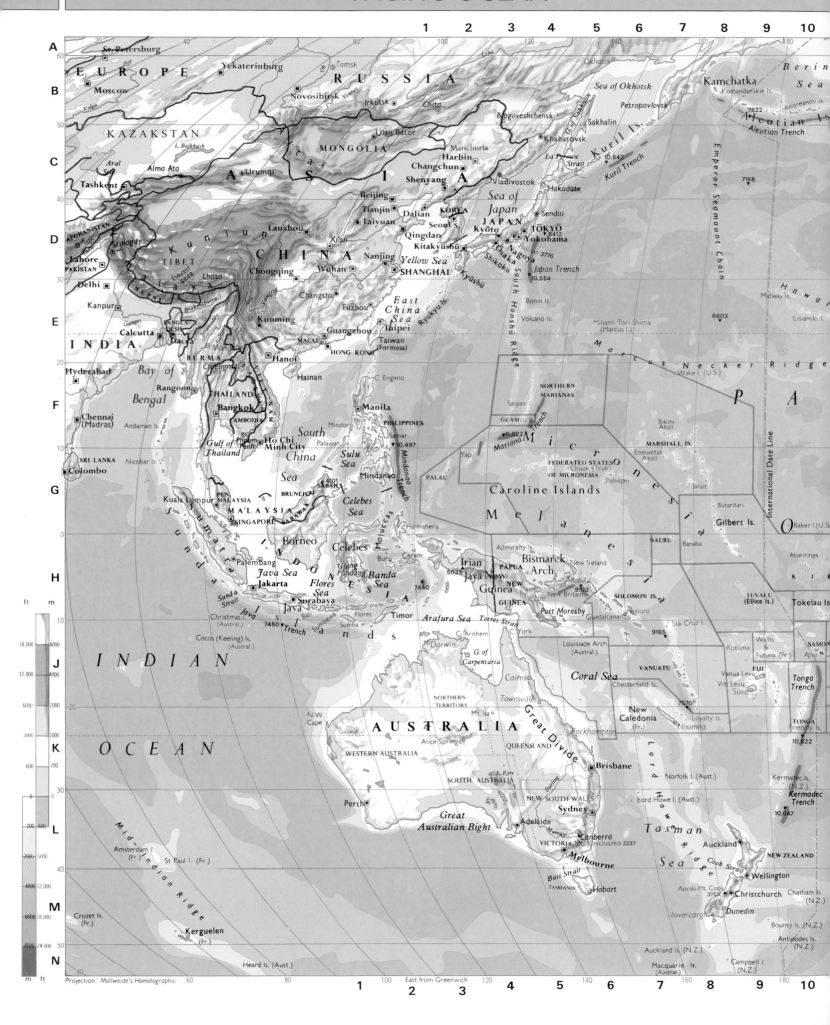

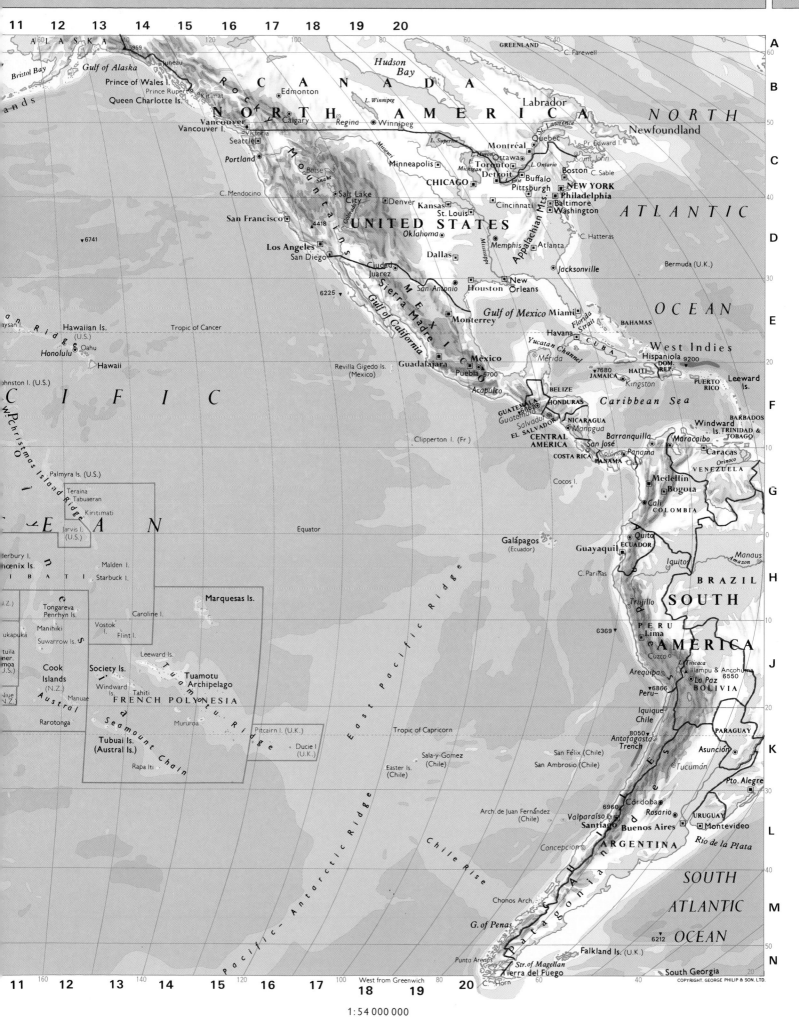

ALASKA

Bristol Bay

Gulf of Alaska

Prince of Wales I.

Prince Rupert

Queen Charlotte Is.

Kitimat

Juneau

GREENLAND

C. Farewell

NORTH

5959

R O C A N A D A

Edmonton

Hudson Bay

NORTH AMERICA

Labrador

Newfoundland

Vancouver

Vancouver I.

Victoria

Seattle

Calgary

Regina

Winnipeg

L. Winnipeg

St. Lawrence

Montréal

Québec

Pr. Edward I.

Saint John

Portland

Mountains

Boise

Missouri

L. Superior

Minneapolis

L. Michigan

Toronto

Ottawa

Detroit

L. Ontario

Buffalo

Boston

C. Sable

ATLANTIC

C. Mendocino

Salt Lake City

Denver

Kansas

CHICAGO

Erie

Pittsburgh

NEW YORK

Philadelphia

Baltimore

Washington

San Francisco

4418

UNITED STATES

Oklahoma

St. Louis

Cincinnati

Memphis

Appalachian Mts.

Atlanta

C. Hatteras

OCEAN

6741

Los Angeles

San Diego

Colorado

Ciudad Juárez

Dallas

San Antonio

Mississippi

Houston

New Orleans

Jacksonville

Bermuda (U.K.)

Hawaiian Is. (U.S.)

Tropic of Cancer

6225

Sierra Madre

M E X I C O

Gulf of California

Monterrey

Gulf of Mexico

Miami

Florida

Havana

Florida Strait

CUBA

BAHAMAS

OCEAN

Laysan I.

Ridge

Oahu

Honolulu

Hawaii

Revilla Gigedo Is. (Mexico)

Guadalajara

México

Puebla

7680

6700

Yucatán Channel

Mérida

West Indies

Hispaniola

DOM. REP.

9200

Johnston I. (U.S.)

Acapulco

BELIZE

GUATEMALA

Guatemala

8562

Salvador

EL SALVADOR

HONDURAS

JAMAICA

Kingston

HAITI

PUERTO RICO

Leeward Is.

P A C I F I C

Clipperton I. (Fr.)

CENTRAL AMERICA

NICARAGUA

Managua

Caribbean Sea

Barranquilla

Maracaibo

BARBADOS

Windward Is.

TRINIDAD & TOBAGO

Christmas Island Ridge

Palmyra Is. (U.S.)

Cocos I.

COSTA RICA

San José

Colón

PANAMA

Panama

Medellín

Orinoco

Caracas

VENEZUELA

Teraina

Tabuaeran

Kiritimati

E A N

Bogotá

Cali

COLOMBIA

Jarvis I. (U.S.)

Equator

Galápagos (Ecuador)

Quito

ECUADOR

Guayaquil

Iquitos

Manaus

Amazon

N.Z.

Tongareva

Penrhyn Is.

Malden I.

Starbuck I.

C. Pariñas

BRAZIL

SOUTH

Manihiki

Suwarrow Is.

Vostok I.

Flint I.

Marquesas Is.

Trujillo

ukapuka

Caroline I.

Leeward Is.

6369

PERU

Lima

AMERICA

tuila

ner.

.S.

Cook Islands (N.Z.)

Society Is.

Windward Is.

Tahiti

Tuamotu Archipelago

Cuzco

L. Titicaca

Illampu & Ancohuma

6550

Niue

N.Z.

Austral

FRENCH POLYNESIA

Manuae

Arequipa

6866

Peru–

La Paz

BOLIVIA

Rarotonga

Seamount Chain

Mururoa

Tropic of Capricorn

Iquique

Chile

PARAGUAY

Tubuai Is. (Austral Is.)

Pitcairn I. (U.K.)

Ducie I. (U.K.)

8050

Antofagasta

Trench

Asunción

Rapa Iti

East Pacific Ridge

Sala-y-Gomez (Chile)

San Félix (Chile)

San Ambrosio (Chile)

Tucumán

Easter Is. (Chile)

Pto. Alegre

Arch. de Juan Fernández (Chile)

6960

Córdoba

Rosario

URUGUAY

Pacific – Antarctic Ridge

Valparaíso

Santiago

Buenos Aires

Montevideo

Concepción

ARGENTINA

Río de la Plata

Chile Rise

SOUTH

ATLANTIC

Chonos Arch.

Patagonia

OCEAN

G. of Penas

6212

Punta Arenas

Str. of Magellan

Falkland Is. (U.K.)

Tierra del Fuego

South Georgia

C. Horn

West from Greenwich

COPYRIGHT GEORGE PHILIP & SON, LTD.

1:54 000 000

CANADA

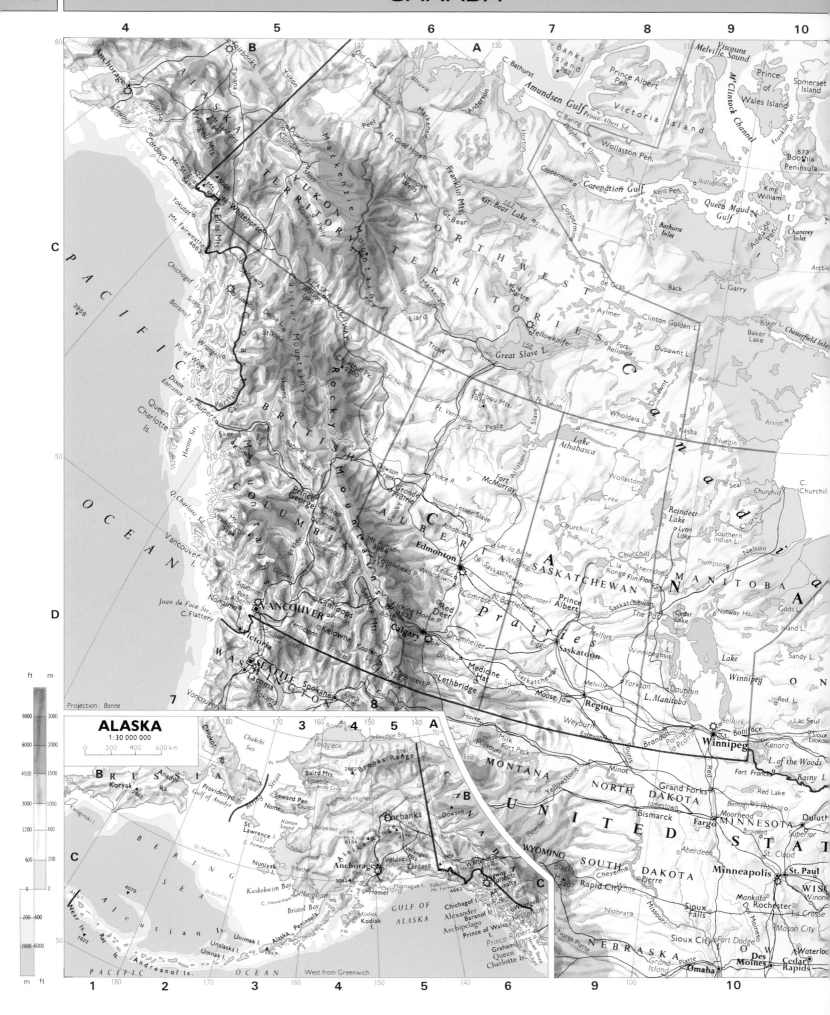

1:15 000 000

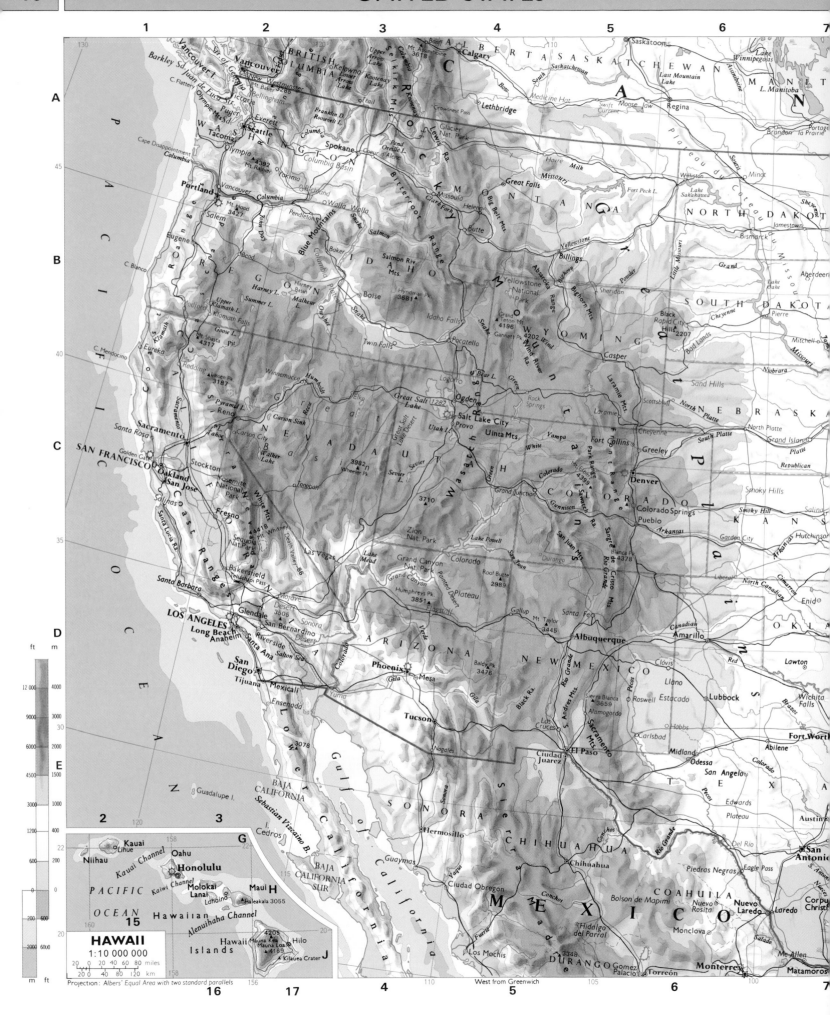

HAWAII
1:10 000 000

Projection: Albers' Equal Area with two standard parallels

1:12 000 000

50 0 50 100 150 200 250 300 miles

50 0 50 100 150 200 250 300 350 400 500 km

COPYRIGHT. GEORGE PHILIP & SON. LTD.

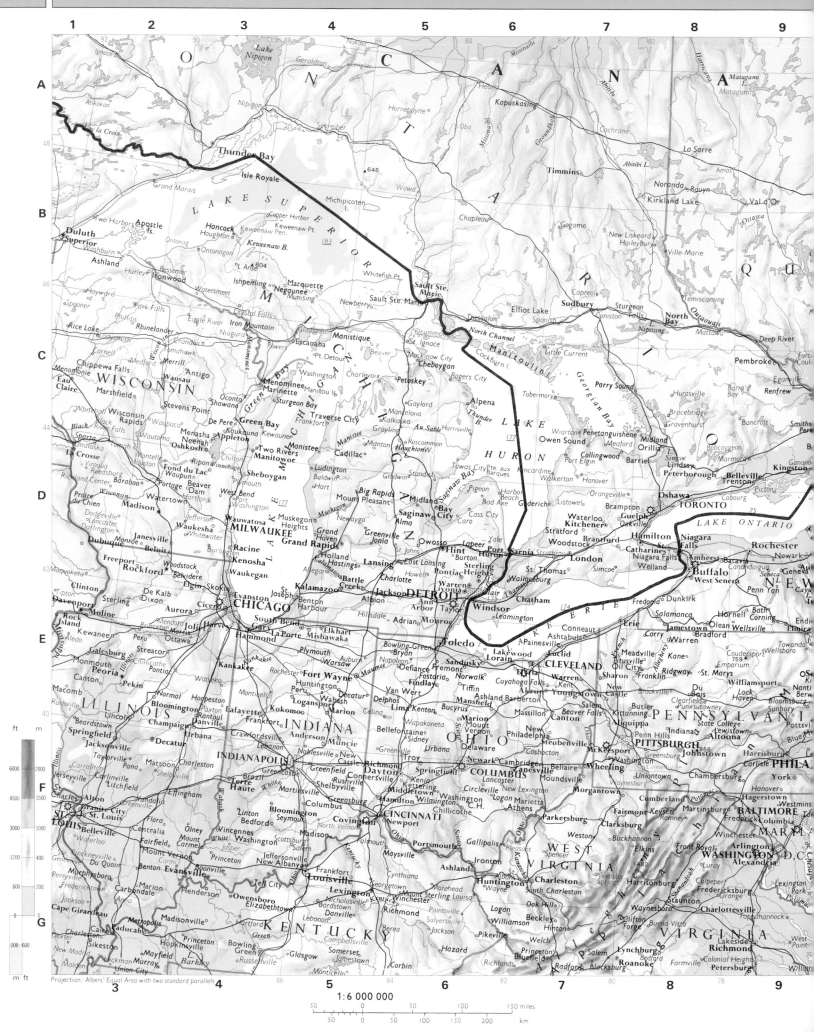

10 **11** **12** **13** **14** **15** **16** **17**

Anticosti I.
Jupiter
Port-Cartier   West Pt.   Heath Pt.

D A
556   Chibougamau
Chibougamau L.
Pipmuacan L.
Cap-Chat   C. Gaspé
Matane   Shickshock Mts.   Gaspé
1310   Gaspé Peninsula
572

GULF OF
ST. LAWRENCE   48

St. Félicien   Roberval   Chicoutimi
Dolbeau   Jonquière   Saguenay   Rimouski
Gouin
Res.
Lac
St. Jean

Magdalen
Is.
(Quebec)
C. North

Rivière du Loup   Campbellton
Edmundston   819   Dalhousie   Chaleur Bay
Bathurst   N E W   Miramichi B.   North Pt.   Tignish
Newcastle   Chatham   PRINCE EDWARD
ISLAND

La Tuque   Baie St. Paul
Fort
Kent Van
Buren   Grand
Falls   B R U N S W I C K   Summerside   Charlottetown   532   Cape Breton
Island
Glace Bay
Sydney

Q U E B E C
Gatineau   Res
Baskatong
Laurier
L'Annonciation   968
Grand-Mère
Shawinigan
Cap-de-la-Madeleine
Trois-Rivières
Louiseville
Plessisville
St-George
Quebec
Lévis
Île d'Orléans
Montmagny
Eagle
Lake
Caribou
Presque Isle
Eagle L.   Chamberlain
Chesuncook   Patten
1605
Mt. Katahdin
Chiputneticook
Lakes
Fredericton
Moncton
Grand L.
Chipman
Springhill
Stellarton   New Glasgow
Truro   Chébucto B.
Canso
Bras d'Or
N O V A

Joliette
St-Jérôme
Victoriaville
Thetford
Mines
Drummondville
Asbestos
Lac-
Mégantic
Mooshead
L.
Greenville
Millinocket
Old Town
Saint
John
Sussex
Kentville
Dartmouth
S C O T I A

Hawkesbury
Ottawa
Lachine
MONTREAL
Granby
St-Hyacinthe
Sorel
Sherbrooke
Magog
Coaticook
Richardson
Lakes
M
A
I
N
E
Foxcroft
Dover
Lincoln
Mattawamkeag
St. Stephen
Bay of Fundy
Halifax

kingham
Cornwall
St-Jean
Beauharnois
Cowansville
Colebrook
Island Pond
Rangeley
Kennebec R
Skowhegan
Bangor
Brewer
Machias
Eastport
Grand Manan I.
Digby
Bridgewater

Prescott
ville
Ottawa
arleton
lace
Massena
Malone
Newport
St. Albans
Winooski
Farmington
Waterville
Ellsworth
Rossignol Res.
44

Ogdensburg
Plattsburgh
Champlain
L.
Johnson
Barre
Rumford
Augusta
Belfast
Bar
Harbor
Mt. Desert
Shelburne
Yarmouth
C. Sable

Potsdam
Canton
Burlington
Montpelier
Berlin
Mt.
Washington
1917
Gardiner
Penobscot B.

Watertown
Lowville
Saranac Lakes
Gouverneur
Adirondack Mts
1629
Middlebury
V E R M O N T
Lancaster
White Mts.
N E W   H A M P S H I R E
Lewiston
Auburn
Bath
Brunswick
Rockland

on
go
Lake Pleasant
Ticonderoga
L.
George
Rutland
Lebanon
Conway
Westbrook
Portland

Rome
Utica
Gloversville
Glens
Falls
Hudson
Saratoga Springs
Claremont
Concord
Laconia
Rochester
Biddeford
Saco

yracuse
oneida
Schenectady
Amsterdam
Brattleboro
Keene
Manchester
Dover
Franklin
Portsmouth
38

Albany
Troy
Greenfield
Fitchburg
Nashua
Lowell
Lawrence
Newburyport
C. Ann

Y O R K
Pittsfield
Northampton
Leominster
Haverhill

rtland
Norwich
Oneonta
Catskill
Catskill Mts
1281
Springfield
M A S S.
Worcester
Cambridge
BOSTON
Quincy
Cape Cod

Johnson City
Binghamton
Kingston
Hudson
Hartford
Chicopee
Woonsocket
Pawtucket
Providence
Brockton
Taunton
Fall River

ton
Carbondale
Poughkeepsie
Newburgh
Beacon
New Britain
Waterbury
Meriden
C O N N.
R. I.
Warwick
New
Bedford

Wilkes
Barre
Hazelton
enandoah
Dunmore
Middletown
Danbury
New
Haven
New
London
Martha's
Vineyard
Nantucket

Easton
Paterson
Jersey City
Mount
Vernon
Yonkers
Bridgeport
Stamford
Block I.

Bethlehem
ntown
Reading
Pottstown
Newark
Elizabeth
NEW YORK
Long Island
Riverhead

PHIA
aster
Norristown
Camden
Chester
Wilmington
New Brunswick
Long Branch
Asbury Park
Trenton
NEW
JERSEY   40

D
Bridgeton
Millville
Vineland
Hammonton
Atlantic City
Ocean City

Milford
Cape May
Henlopen
DELAWARE
Dover

A   T   L   A   N   T   I   C

bury
Cambridge
Seaford
Snow Hill
Accomac   O   C   E   A   N   38

Cape Charles
C. Charles   G

West from Greenwich
10   **11**   **12**   **13**

---

14   **15**   **16**   **17**

GREENLAND
(Denmark)
ICELAND
60

ALASKA
(U.S.A.)   Arctic Circle

Anchorage
C A N A D A   Godthåb

50

Vancouver
Edmonton
Seattle
Winnipeg
Ottawa   Montreal
Toronto   Boston
SAN FRANCISCO
CHICAGO
Detroit
NEW YORK
PHILADELPHIA
Washington D.C.
40

LOS ANGELES
Denver
St. Louis
U N I T E D   S T A T E S
Atlanta
Bermuda
(U.K.)

Houston
New
Orleans
Miami
BAHAMAS
30

Tropic of Cancer
M E X I C O
Monterrey
Havana
CUBA
DOMINICAN
REP.
PUERTO
RICO

Guadalajara
JAMAICA
Kingston
HAITI

MEXICO
BELIZE
GUATEMALA
Guatemala
HONDURAS
EL SALVADOR   NICARAGUA

COSTA RICA
Panamá

NORTH AMERICA
Political 1 : 70 000 000

120   110   100   90   80

8   9   10   11   12   13

A

Atlanta
Columbus
Macon
Augusta
Columbus
Charleston
Savannah
Albany
Tallahassee

C. Fear

Bermuda (U.K.)
Hamilton

ATLANTIC OCEAN

B

Jacksonville
Daytona Beach
Orlando
C. Canaveral
Tampa
St. Petersburg
West Palm Beach
L. Okeechobee
Grand Bahama I.
Freeport
Gt. Abaco I.
Miami
Fort Lauderdale
New Providence I.
C. Sable
Nassau
Eleuthera I.
Key West
BAHAMAS
Cat I.
Andros I.
S. Salvador
Tropic of Cancer

C

Havana
Rio
Matanzas
Cárdenas
Sagua la Grande
Sta. Clara
Morón
Long I.
Mayaguana
Acklins I.
Turks & Caicos Is. (U.K.)
Gt. Inagua

I. de Juventud
Cienfuegos
Sancti Spiritus
Ciego de Avila
Camagüey
Holguin
CUBA
Bayamo
Manzanillo
2000
Santiago de Cuba
Guantánamo
Cap Haïtien
Santiago
San Francisco de Macoris
PUERTO RICO (U.S.A.)
St. Thomas (U.S.A.)
San Juan
Charlotte Amalie
Virgin Is. (U.K.)
Anguilla
St. Martin (Fr. & Neth.)
ST. KITTS-NEVIS

D

Grand Cayman (U.K.)
GREATER
Windward Passage
Gonaives
HAITI
DOMINICAN REP.
2280
La Romana
Mona Passage
Mayagüez
1338
Ponce
Caguas
St. Croix (U.S.A.)
ANTIGUA & BARBUDA
St. John's
Montserrat (U.K.)
Guadeloupe (Fr.)
Pointe à Pitre

Montego Bay
JAMAICA
Kingston
Les Cayes
ANTILLES
Port au Prince
Hispaniola
Barahona
Bani
Santo Domingo
Leeward Islands
LESSER
DOMINICA

Caratasca Lagoon
C. Gracias á Dios
CARIBBEAN SEA
ANTILLES
Windward
ST. VINCENT
THE GRENADINES
Islands
Fort de France
Martinique (Fr.)
ST. LUCIA
BARBADOS
Bridgetown

E

Mosquito Coast
Providencia (Col.)
San Andrés (Col.)
Bluefields
Juan
Pta. Gallinas
Gulf of Venezuela
Aruba (Neth.)
Curaçao
Willemstad
Bonaire
Pen. de NETH.
Paraguaná
ANTILLES
La Blanquilla (Ven.)
GRENADA
Margarita
La Tortuga (Ven.)
Tobago
Port of Spain
TRINIDAD & TOBAGO

Pen. de la Guajira
Santa Marta
Punto Fijo
Coro
Carúpano
G. Paria
San Fernando

F

Limón
Colón
PANAMA
Panama
Vol. Barú
3374
David
Coiba
Azuero Pen.
G. of Panama
G. of Darién
Barranquilla
Cartagena
5800
Sierra Nevada de Santa Marta
Sincelejo
Cauca
COSTA RICA
3857

Maracaibo
Cabimas
L. de Maracaibo
Valera
Mérida
5007
Cord. de Mérida
Barquisimeto
Maracay
Valencia
Caracas
Barcelona
2596
Cumana
Maturin
El Tigre
Orinoco
Ciudad Guayana
Ciudad Bolívar
Delta of the Orinoco
GUYANA
Georgetown
New Amsterdam
SURINAM

Cúcuta
4100
San Cristóbal
Bucaramanga
3960
Barrancabermeja
Barinas
Arauca
Apure
San Fernando de Apure
VENEZUELA
2285
Pto. Ayacucho
Angel Falls
2560
Caroni
Roraima
2810
Cuyuni
Essequibo
Corentyne
280

G

Quibdó
Medellín
Manizales
Pereira
Armenia
COLOMBIA
Tolima 5215
Girardot
Tunja
Bogotá
Meta
Guaviare
Casiquiare
Sierra Pacaraima
BRAZIL

Buenaventura
Cali
4750
Popayán
4646
Magdalena
Guaviare

West from Greenwich   80

COPYRIGHT. GEORGE PHILIP & SON, LTD.

1:15 000 000

100 0 100 200 300 400 miles
100 0 100 200 300 400 500 600 km

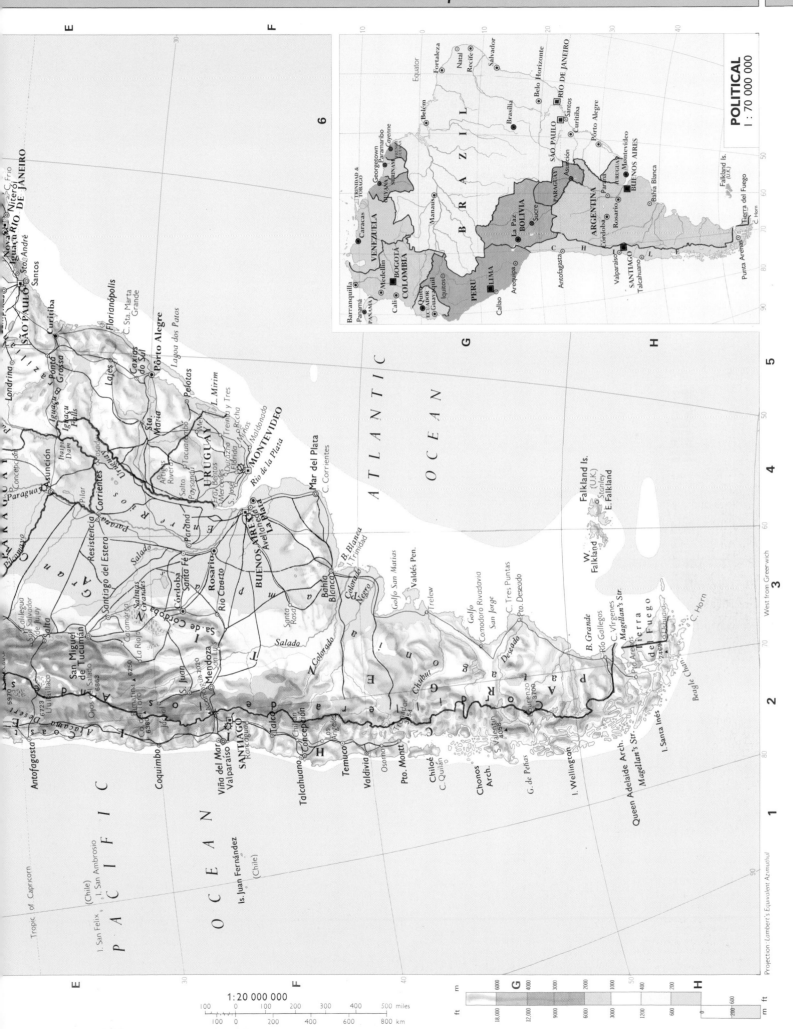

POLITICAL
1 : 70 000 000

1:20 000 000

100 0   100   200   300   400   500 miles

100 0   200   400   600   800 km

Projection: Lambert's Equivalent Azimuthal

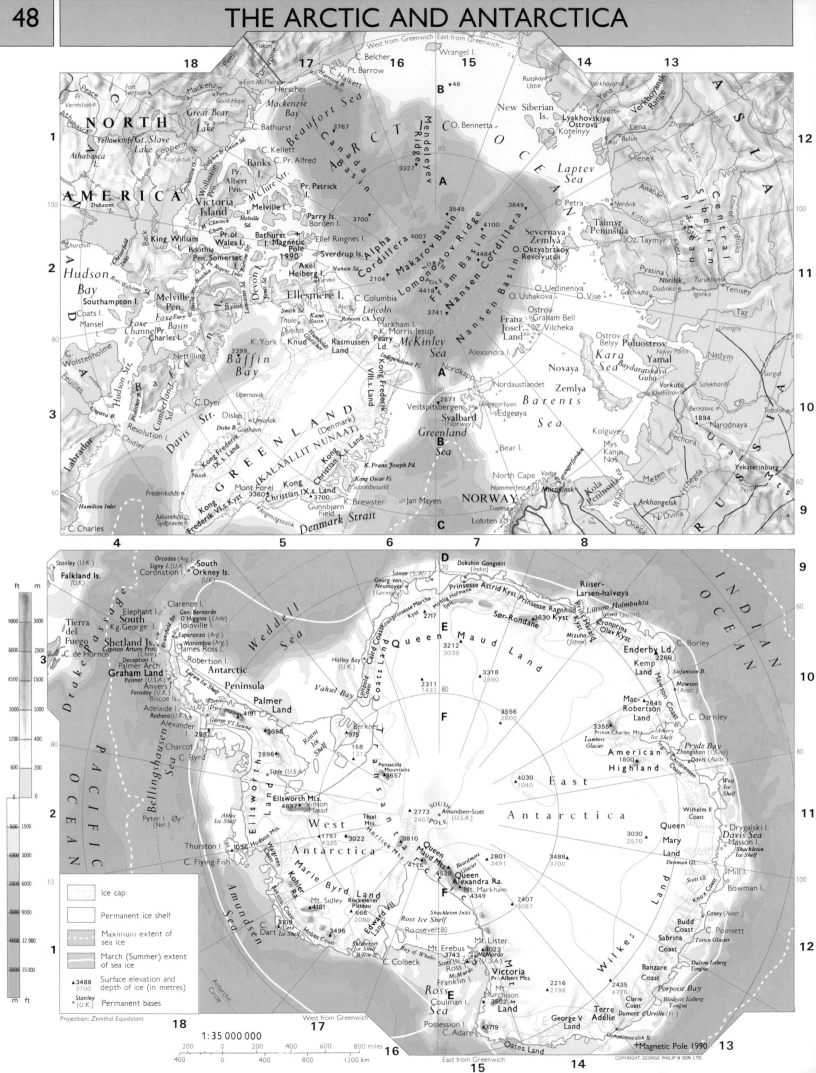

WORLD THEMATIC MAPS

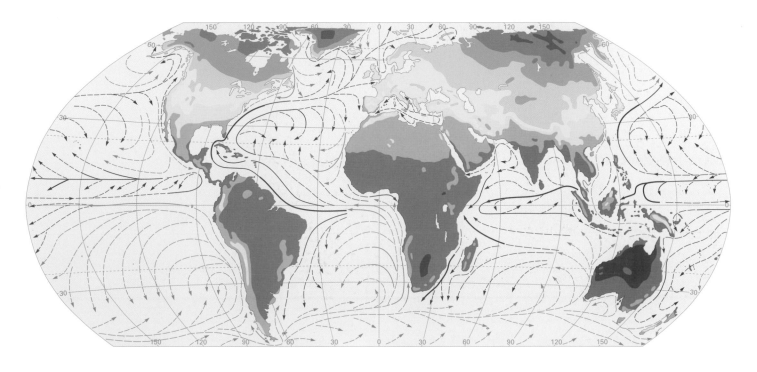

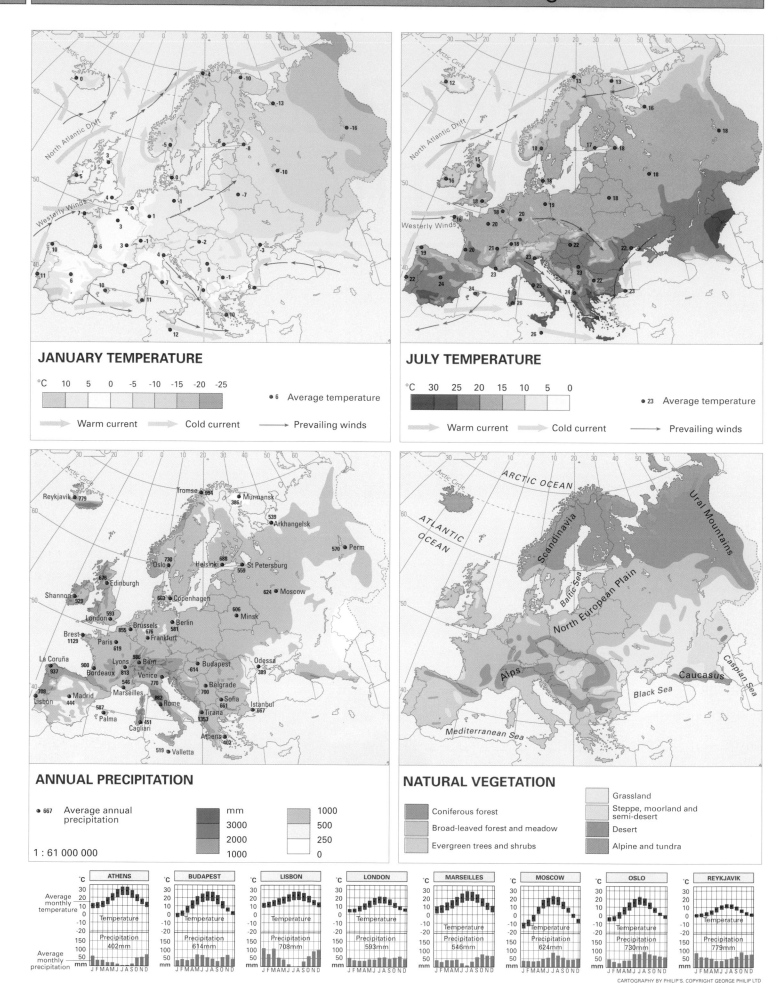

JANUARY TEMPERATURE

°C 10 5 0 -5 -10 -15 -20 -25

● 6 Average temperature

➡ Warm current   ➡ Cold current   → Prevailing winds

JULY TEMPERATURE

°C 30 25 20 15 10 5 0

● 23 Average temperature

➡ Warm current   ➡ Cold current   → Prevailing winds

ANNUAL PRECIPITATION

● 667 Average annual precipitation

mm		1000
3000		500
2000		250
1000		0

1 : 61 000 000

NATURAL VEGETATION

- Coniferous forest
- Broad-leaved forest and meadow
- Evergreen trees and shrubs
- Grassland
- Steppe, moorland and semi-desert
- Desert
- Alpine and tundra

Labels on vegetation map: ARCTIC OCEAN, ATLANTIC OCEAN, Scandinavia, Ural Mountains, Baltic Sea, North European Plain, Alps, Caucasus, Caspian Sea, Black Sea, Mediterranean Sea

Climate graphs (Average monthly temperature / Average monthly precipitation):

ATHENS — Temperature — Precipitation 402mm
BUDAPEST — Temperature — Precipitation 614mm
LISBON — Temperature — Precipitation 708mm
LONDON — Temperature — Precipitation 593mm
MARSEILLES — Temperature — Precipitation 546mm
MOSCOW — Temperature — Precipitation 624mm
OSLO — Temperature — Precipitation 730mm
REYKJAVIK — Temperature — Precipitation 779mm

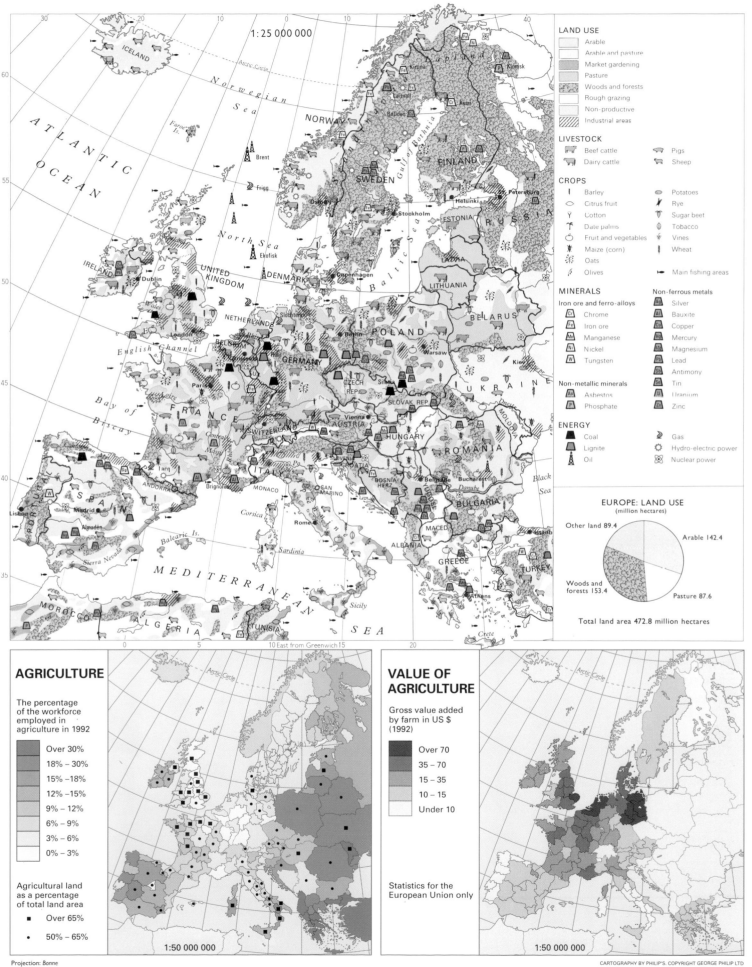

1:25 000 000

LAND USE
- Arable
- Arable and pasture
- Market gardening
- Pasture
- Woods and forests
- Rough grazing
- Non-productive
- Industrial areas

LIVESTOCK
- Beef cattle
- Dairy cattle
- Pigs
- Sheep

CROPS
- Barley
- Citrus fruit
- Cotton
- Date palms
- Fruit and vegetables
- Maize (corn)
- Oats
- Olives
- Potatoes
- Rye
- Sugar beet
- Tobacco
- Vines
- Wheat
- Main fishing areas

MINERALS

Iron ore and ferro-alloys
- Cr Chrome
- Fe Iron ore
- Mn Manganese
- Ni Nickel
- W Tungsten

Non-metallic minerals
- As Asbestos
- P Phosphate

Non-ferrous metals
- Ag Silver
- Al Bauxite
- Cu Copper
- Hg Mercury
- Mg Magnesium
- Pb Lead
- Sb Antimony
- Sn Tin
- U Uranium
- Zn Zinc

ENERGY
- Coal
- Lignite
- Oil
- Gas
- Hydro-electric power
- Nuclear power

EUROPE: LAND USE
(million hectares)

Other land 89.4
Arable 142.4
Woods and forests 153.4
Pasture 87.6

Total land area 472.8 million hectares

AGRICULTURE

The percentage of the workforce employed in agriculture in 1992

- Over 30%
- 18% – 30%
- 15% –18%
- 12% –15%
- 9% – 12%
- 6% – 9%
- 3% – 6%
- 0% – 3%

Agricultural land as a percentage of total land area
- ■ Over 65%
- • 50% – 65%

1:50 000 000

VALUE OF AGRICULTURE

Gross value added by farm in US $ (1992)

- Over 70
- 35 – 70
- 15 – 35
- 10 – 15
- Under 10

Statistics for the European Union only

1:50 000 000

Projection: *Bonne*

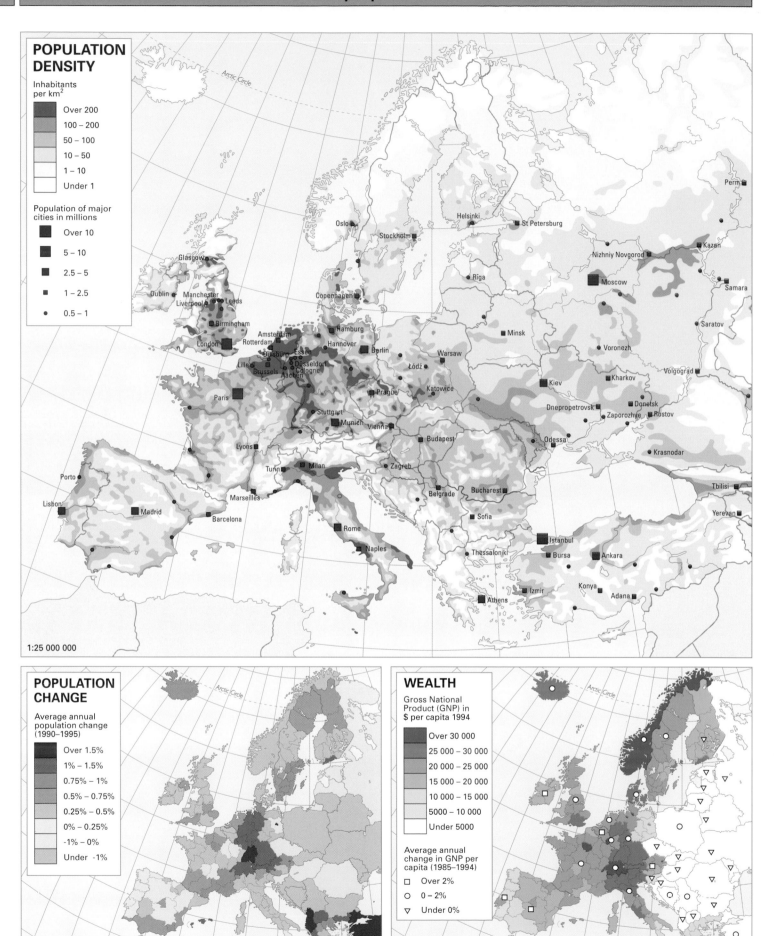

POPULATION DENSITY

Inhabitants per km²

- Over 200
- 100 – 200
- 50 – 100
- 10 – 50
- 1 – 10
- Under 1

Population of major cities in millions

- Over 10
- 5 – 10
- 2.5 – 5
- 1 – 2.5
- 0.5 – 1

1:25 000 000

POPULATION CHANGE

Average annual population change (1990–1995)

- Over 1.5%
- 1% – 1.5%
- 0.75% – 1%
- 0.5% – 0.75%
- 0.25% – 0.5%
- 0% – 0.25%
- -1% – 0%
- Under -1%

1:50 000 000

WEALTH

Gross National Product (GNP) in $ per capita 1994

- Over 30 000
- 25 000 – 30 000
- 20 000 – 25 000
- 15 000 – 20 000
- 10 000 – 15 000
- 5000 – 10 000
- Under 5000

Average annual change in GNP per capita (1985–1994)

- □ Over 2%
- ○ 0 – 2%
- ▽ Under 0%

1 : 50 000 000

Projection: *Bonne*

CARTOGRAPHY BY PHILIP'S. COPYRIGHT GEORGE PHILIP LTD

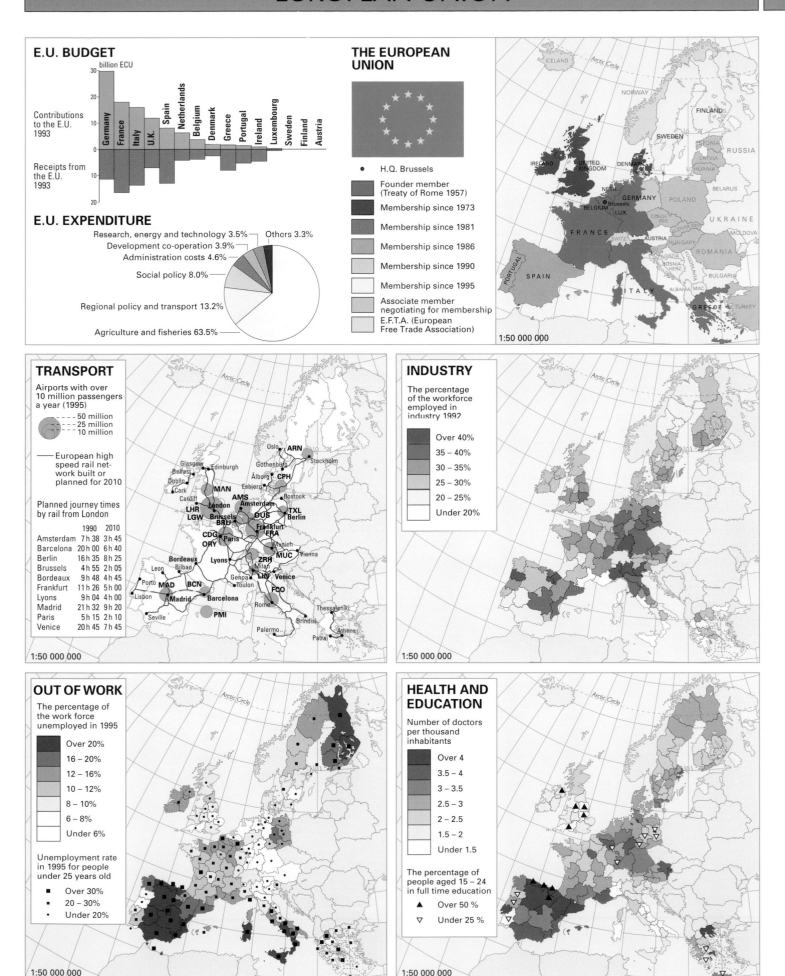

E.U. BUDGET

billion ECU

Contributions to the E.U. 1993

Receipts from the E.U. 1993

Germany
France
Italy
U.K.
Spain
Netherlands
Belgium
Denmark
Greece
Portugal
Ireland
Luxembourg
Sweden
Finland
Austria

E.U. EXPENDITURE

Research, energy and technology 3.5%
Development co-operation 3.9%
Administration costs 4.6%
Social policy 8.0%
Regional policy and transport 13.2%
Agriculture and fisheries 63.5%
Others 3.3%

THE EUROPEAN UNION

- ● H.Q. Brussels
- Founder member (Treaty of Rome 1957)
- Membership since 1973
- Membership since 1981
- Membership since 1986
- Membership since 1990
- Membership since 1995
- Associate member negotiating for membership
- E.F.T.A. (European Free Trade Association)

1:50 000 000

TRANSPORT

Airports with over 10 million passengers a year (1995)
- 50 million
- 25 million
- 10 million

European high speed rail network built or planned for 2010

Planned journey times by rail from London

	1990	2010
Amsterdam	7 h 38	3 h 45
Barcelona	20 h 00	6 h 40
Berlin	16 h 35	8 h 25
Brussels	4 h 55	2 h 05
Bordeaux	9 h 48	4 h 45
Frankfurt	11 h 26	5 h 00
Lyons	9 h 04	4 h 00
Madrid	21 h 32	9 h 20
Paris	5 h 15	2 h 10
Venice	20 h 45	7 h 45

1:50 000 000

INDUSTRY

The percentage of the workforce employed in industry 1992

- Over 40%
- 35 – 40%
- 30 – 35%
- 25 – 30%
- 20 – 25%
- Under 20%

1:50 000 000

OUT OF WORK

The percentage of the work force unemployed in 1995

- Over 20%
- 16 – 20%
- 12 – 16%
- 10 – 12%
- 8 – 10%
- 6 – 8%
- Under 6%

Unemployment rate in 1995 for people under 25 years old

- ■ Over 30%
- ▪ 20 – 30%
- • Under 20%

1:50 000 000

HEALTH AND EDUCATION

Number of doctors per thousand inhabitants

- Over 4
- 3.5 – 4
- 3 – 3.5
- 2.5 – 3
- 2 – 2.5
- 1.5 – 2
- Under 1.5

The percentage of people aged 15 – 24 in full time education

- ▲ Over 50 %
- ▽ Under 25 %

1:50 000 000

Projection: Bonne

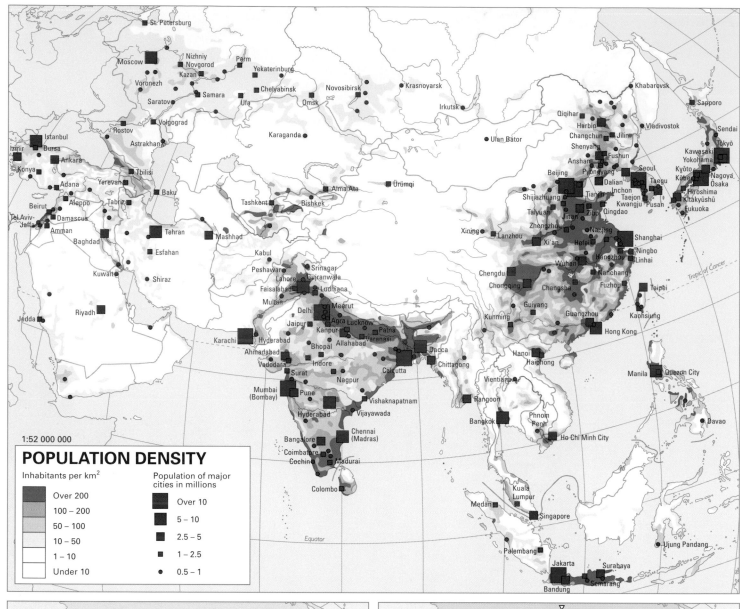

1:52 000 000

POPULATION DENSITY

Inhabitants per km²

	Over 200
	100 – 200
	50 – 100
	10 – 50
	1 – 10
	Under 10

Population of major cities in millions

	Over 10
	5 – 10
	2.5 – 5
	1 – 2.5
	0.5 – 1

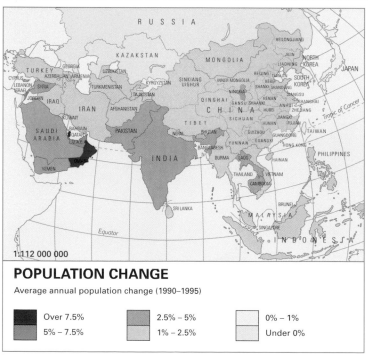

1:112 000 000

POPULATION CHANGE

Average annual population change (1990–1995)

Over 7.5%	2.5% – 5%	0% – 1%
5% – 7.5%	1% – 2.5%	Under 0%

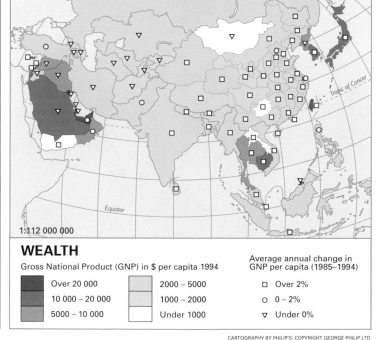

1:112 000 000

WEALTH

Gross National Product (GNP) in $ per capita 1994

Over 20 000	2000 – 5000
10 000 – 20 000	1000 – 2000
5000 – 10 000	Under 1000

Average annual change in GNP per capita (1985–1994)

□	Over 2%
○	0 – 2%
▽	Under 0%

Projection: *Bonne*

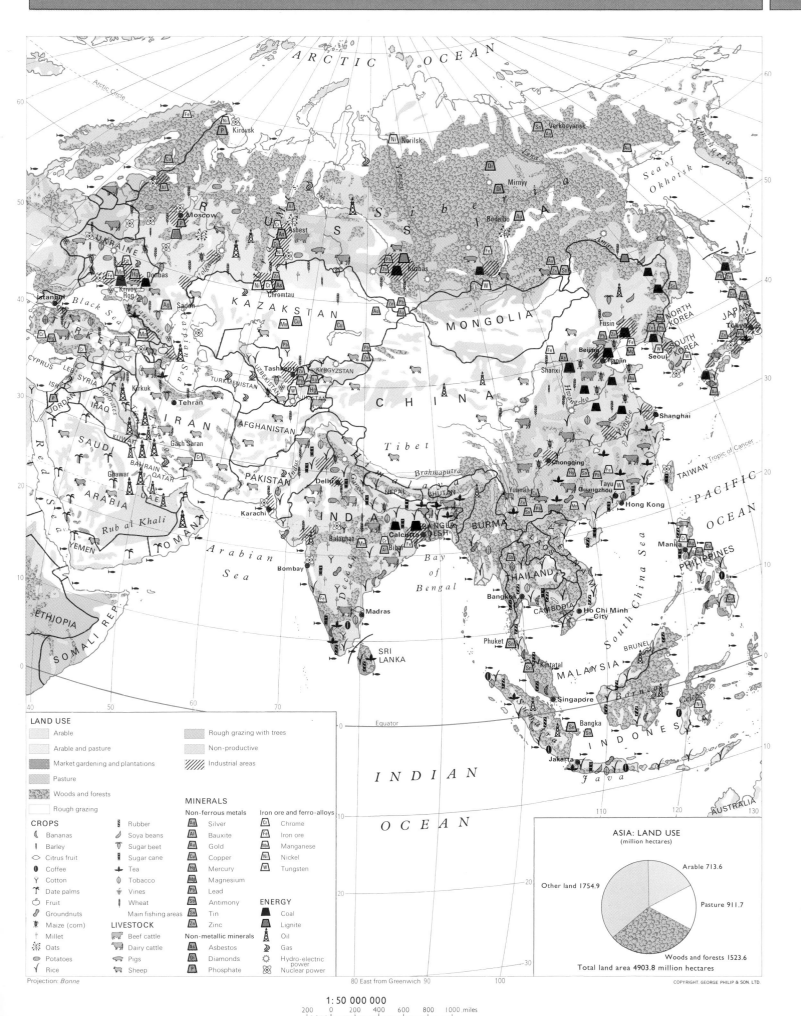

LAND USE

- Arable
- Arable and pasture
- Market gardening and plantations
- Pasture
- Woods and forests
- Rough grazing
- Rough grazing with trees
- Non-productive
- Industrial areas

CROPS

- Bananas
- Barley
- Citrus fruit
- Coffee
- Cotton
- Date palms
- Fruit
- Groundnuts
- Maize (corn)
- Millet
- Oats
- Potatoes
- Rice
- Rubber
- Soya beans
- Sugar beet
- Sugar cane
- Tea
- Tobacco
- Vines
- Wheat
- Main fishing areas

LIVESTOCK

- Beef cattle
- Dairy cattle
- Pigs
- Sheep

MINERALS

Non-ferrous metals

- Ag Silver
- Al Bauxite
- Au Gold
- Cu Copper
- Hg Mercury
- Mg Magnesium
- Pb Lead
- Sb Antimony
- Sn Tin
- Zn Zinc

Non-metallic minerals

- As Asbestos
- Di Diamonds
- P Phosphate

Iron ore and ferro-alloys

- Cr Chrome
- Fe Iron ore
- Mn Manganese
- Ni Nickel
- W Tungsten

ENERGY

- Coal
- Lignite
- Oil
- Gas
- Hydro-electric power
- Nuclear power

ASIA: LAND USE
(million hectares)

- Arable 713.6
- Pasture 911.7
- Woods and forests 1523.6
- Other land 1754.9

Total land area 4903.8 million hectares

Projection: Bonne

80 East from Greenwich 90   100

1:50 000 000

200 0 200 400 600 800 1000 miles

200 0 400 800 1200 1600 km

COPYRIGHT. GEORGE PHILIP & SON, LTD.

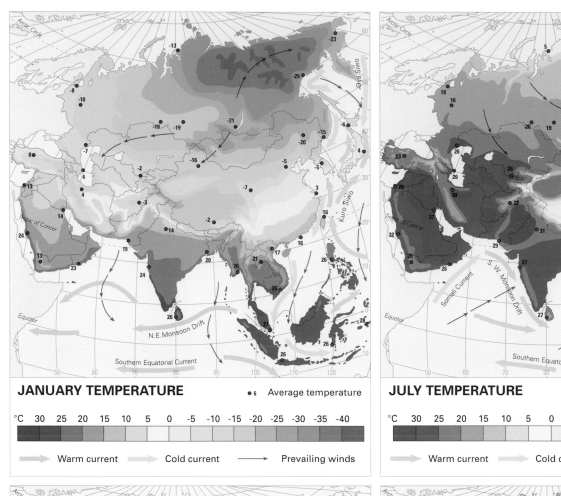

JANUARY TEMPERATURE

● 6 Average temperature

°C 30 25 20 15 10 5 0 -5 -10 -15 -20 -25 -30 -35 -40

Warm current   Cold current   → Prevailing winds

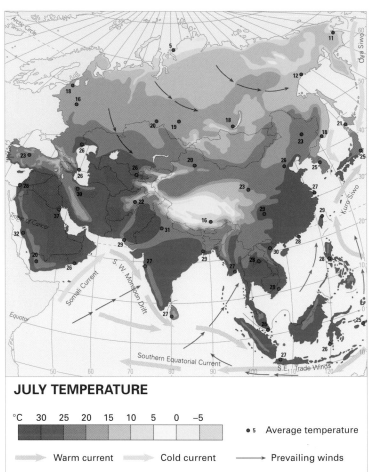

JULY TEMPERATURE

°C 30 25 20 15 10 5 0 -5

● 5 Average temperature

Warm current   Cold current   → Prevailing winds

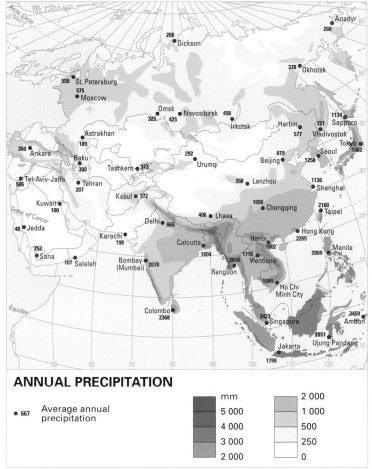

ANNUAL PRECIPITATION

● 667 Average annual precipitation

mm
5 000
4 000
3 000
2 000

2 000
1 000
500
250
0

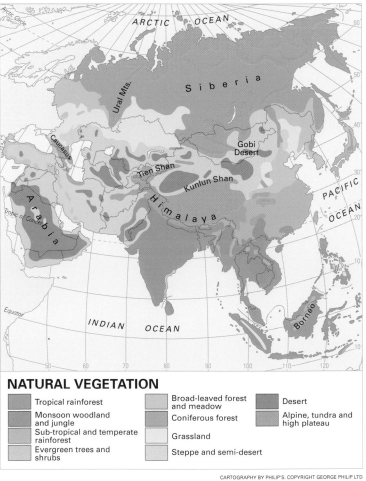

NATURAL VEGETATION

Tropical rainforest

Monsoon woodland and jungle

Sub-tropical and temperate rainforest

Evergreen trees and shrubs

Broad-leaved forest and meadow

Coniferous forest

Grassland

Steppe and semi-desert

Desert

Alpine, tundra and high plateau

Projection: *Modified Hammer Equal Area*   1 : 105 000 000

CARTOGRAPHY BY PHILIP'S. COPYRIGHT GEORGE PHILIP LTD

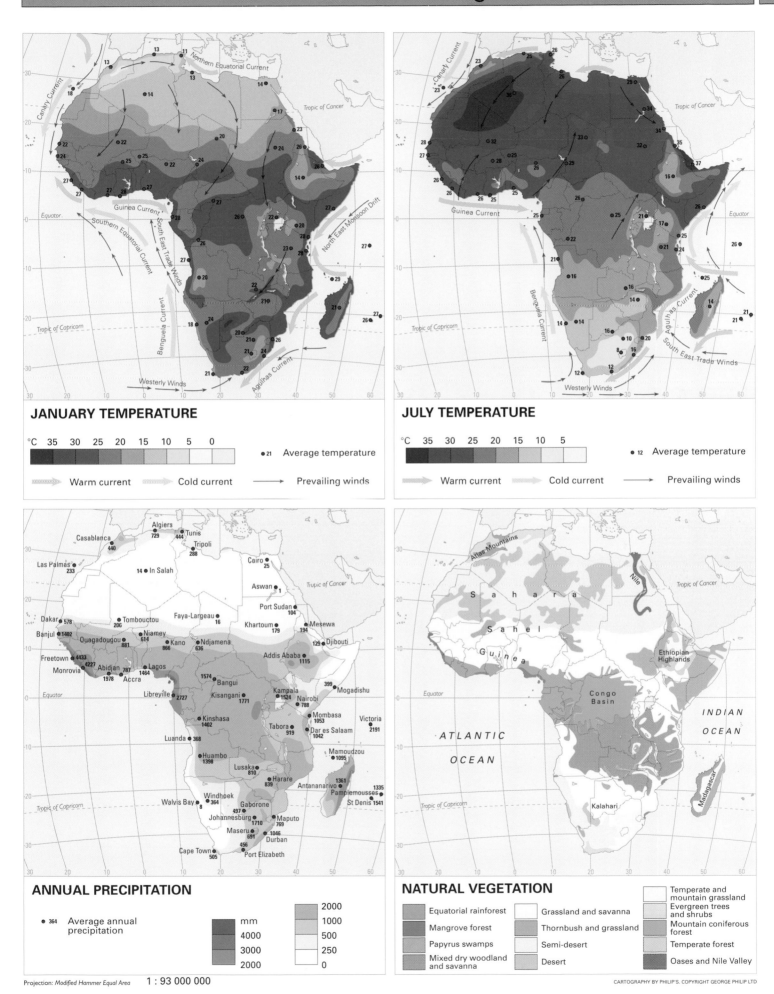

JANUARY TEMPERATURE

°C 35 30 25 20 15 10 5 0

● 21 Average temperature

▷ Warm current ▷ Cold current → Prevailing winds

JULY TEMPERATURE

°C 35 30 25 20 15 10 5

● 12 Average temperature

▷ Warm current ▷ Cold current → Prevailing winds

ANNUAL PRECIPITATION

● 364 Average annual precipitation

mm
2000
4000 1000
3000 500
2000 250
0

NATURAL VEGETATION

Temperate and mountain grassland
Equatorial rainforest   Grassland and savanna   Evergreen trees and shrubs
Mangrove forest   Thornbush and grassland   Mountain coniferous forest
Papyrus swamps   Semi-desert   Temperate forest
Mixed dry woodland and savanna   Desert   Oases and Nile Valley

Projection: *Modified Hammer Equal Area*   1 : 93 000 000

CARTOGRAPHY BY PHILIP'S. COPYRIGHT GEORGE PHILIP LTD

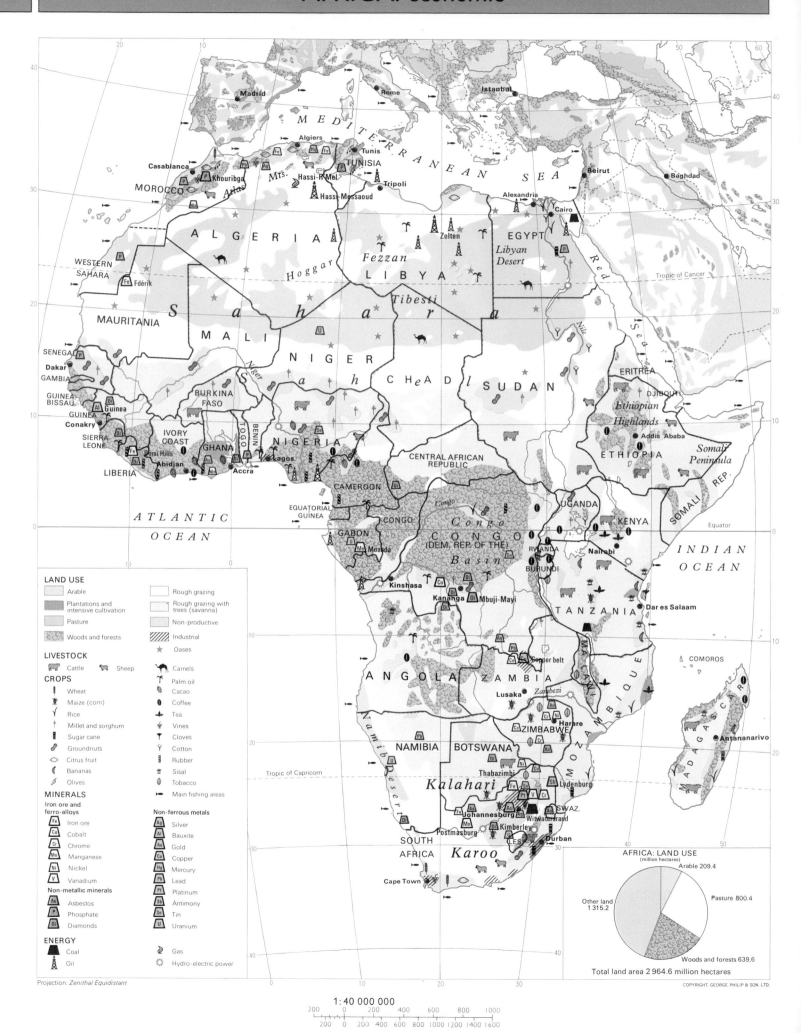

LAND USE
- Arable
- Plantations and intensive cultivation
- Pasture
- Woods and forests
- Rough grazing
- Rough grazing with trees (savanna)
- Non-productive
- Industrial
- ★ Oases

LIVESTOCK
- Cattle
- Sheep
- Camels

CROPS
- Wheat
- Maize (corn)
- Rice
- Millet and sorghum
- Sugar cane
- Groundnuts
- Citrus fruit
- Bananas
- Olives
- Palm oil
- Cacao
- Coffee
- Tea
- Vines
- Cloves
- Cotton
- Rubber
- Sisal
- Tobacco
- Main fishing areas

MINERALS
Iron ore and ferro-alloys
- Fe Iron ore
- Co Cobalt
- Cr Chrome
- Mn Manganese
- Ni Nickel
- V Vanadium

Non-metallic minerals
- As Asbestos
- P Phosphate
- Di Diamonds

Non-ferrous metals
- Ag Silver
- Al Bauxite
- Au Gold
- Cu Copper
- Hg Mercury
- Pb Lead
- Pt Platinum
- Sb Antimony
- Sn Tin
- U Uranium

ENERGY
- Coal
- Oil
- Gas
- Hydro-electric power

AFRICA: LAND USE
(million hectares)
- Arable 209.4
- Pasture 800.4
- Woods and forests 639,6
- Other land 1 315.2
Total land area 2 964.6 million hectares

Projection: Zenithal Equidistant

COPYRIGHT. GEORGE PHILIP & SON. LTD.

1:40 000 000

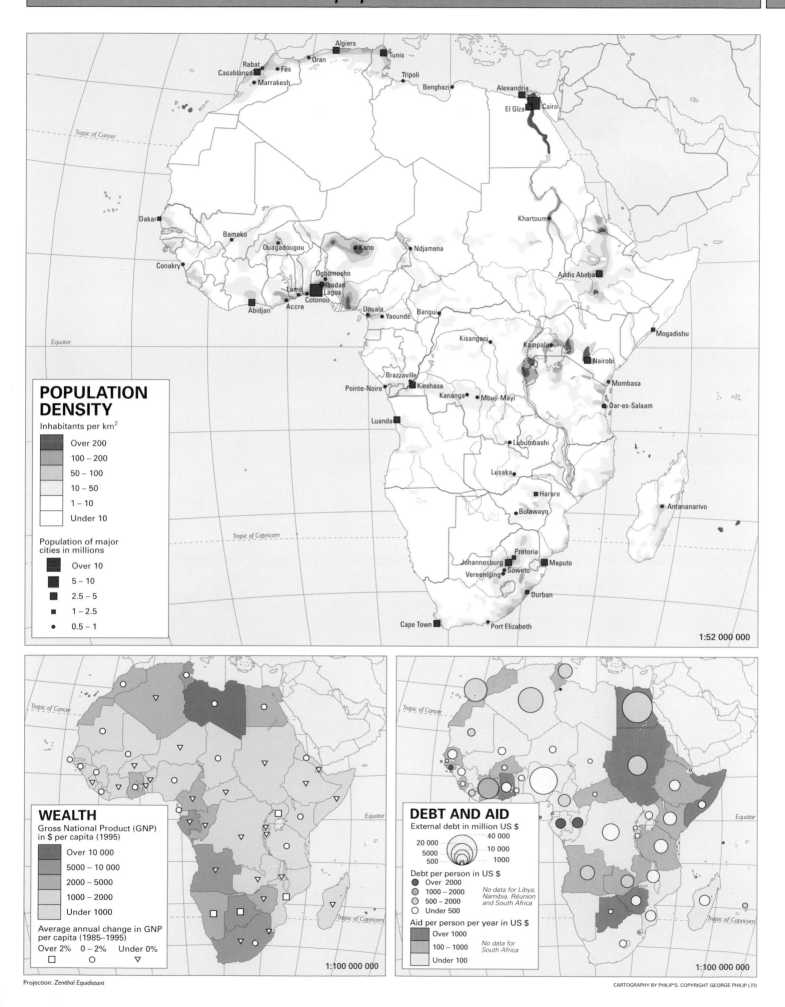

POPULATION DENSITY

Inhabitants per km²

- Over 200
- 100 – 200
- 50 – 100
- 10 – 50
- 1 – 10
- Under 10

Population of major cities in millions

- Over 10
- 5 – 10
- 2.5 – 5
- 1 – 2.5
- 0.5 – 1

1:52 000 000

WEALTH

Gross National Product (GNP) in $ per capita (1995)

- Over 10 000
- 5000 – 10 000
- 2000 – 5000
- 1000 – 2000
- Under 1000

Average annual change in GNP per capita (1985–1995)

Over 2% □   0 – 2% ○   Under 0% ▽

1:100 000 000

DEBT AND AID

External debt in million US $

20 000   40 000
5000   10 000
500   1000

Debt per person in US $

- Over 2000
- 1000 – 2000
- 500 – 2000
- Under 500

No data for Libya, Namibia, Réunion and South Africa

Aid per person per year in US $

- Over 1000
- 100 – 1000
- Under 100

No data for South Africa

1:100 000 000

Projection: *Zenithal Equidistant*

CARTOGRAPHY BY PHILIP'S. COPYRIGHT GEORGE PHILIP LTD

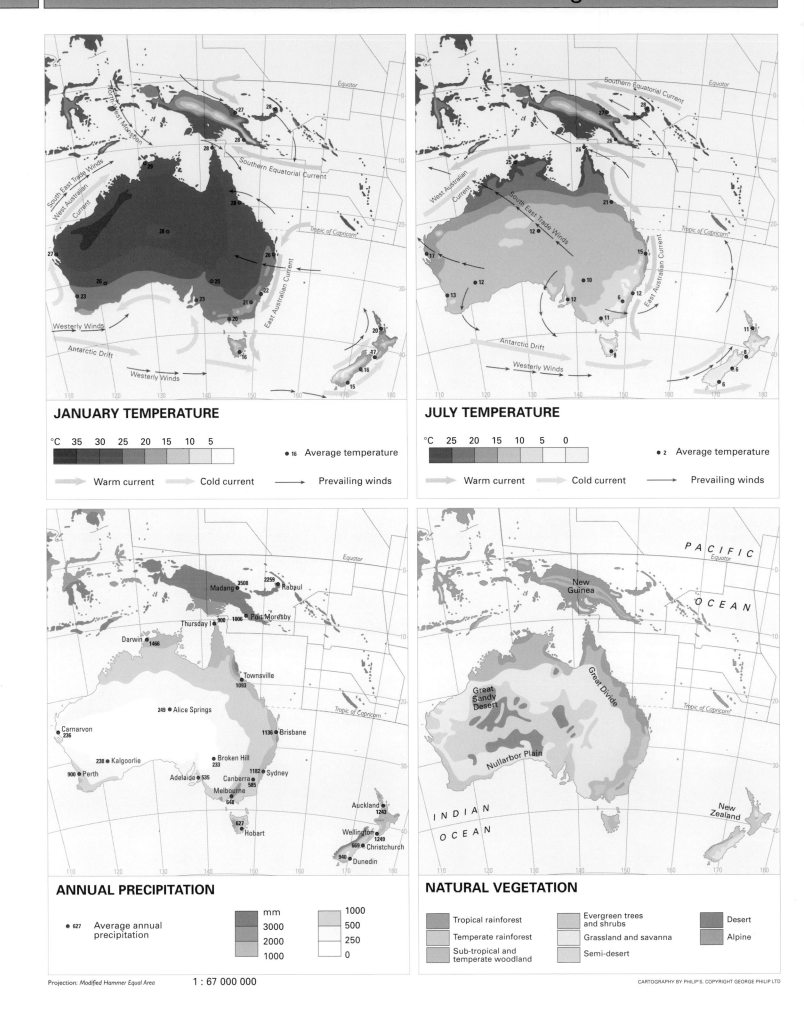

JANUARY TEMPERATURE

°C   35   30   25   20   15   10   5

● 16   Average temperature

Warm current   Cold current   Prevailing winds

JULY TEMPERATURE

°C   25   20   15   10   5   0

● 2   Average temperature

Warm current   Cold current   Prevailing winds

ANNUAL PRECIPITATION

● 627   Average annual precipitation

mm	
3000	1000
2000	500
1000	250
	0

NATURAL VEGETATION

	Tropical rainforest		Evergreen trees and shrubs		Desert
	Temperate rainforest		Grassland and savanna		Alpine
	Sub-tropical and temperate woodland		Semi-desert		

Projection: *Modified Hammer Equal Area*   1 : 67 000 000

CARTOGRAPHY BY PHILIP'S. COPYRIGHT GEORGE PHILIP LTD

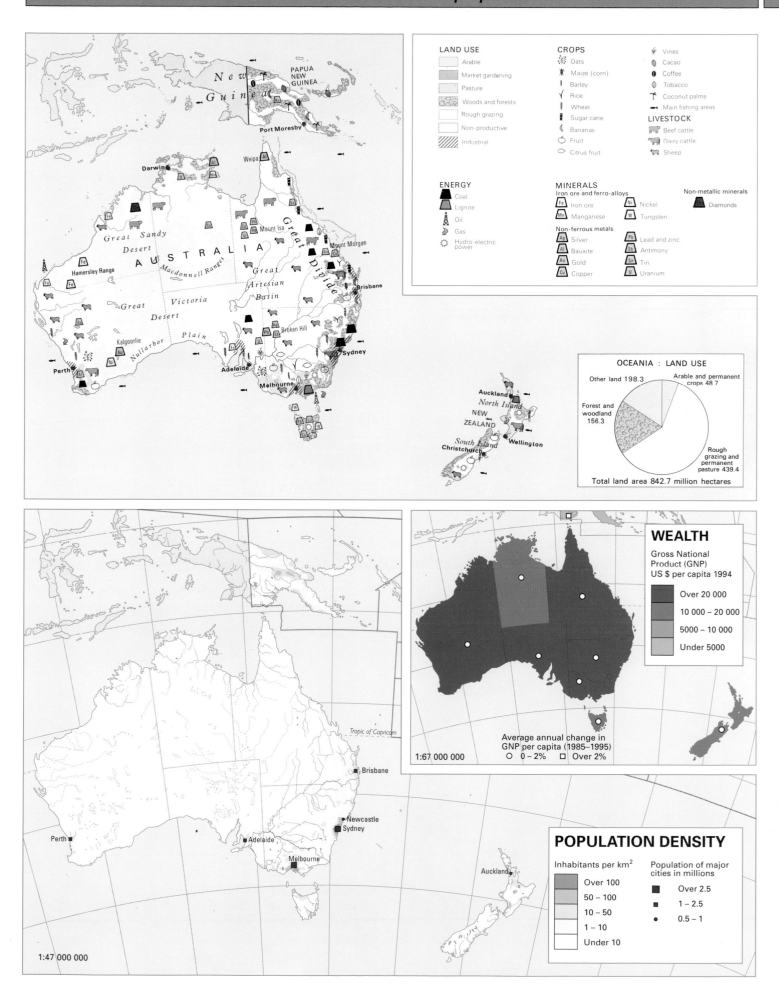

LAND USE
- Arable
- Market gardening
- Pasture
- Woods and forests
- Rough grazing
- Non-productive
- Industrial

CROPS
- Oats
- Maize (corn)
- Barley
- Rice
- Wheat
- Sugar cane
- Bananas
- Fruit
- Citrus fruit

- Vines
- Cacao
- Coffee
- Tobacco
- Coconut palms
- Main fishing areas

LIVESTOCK
- Beef cattle
- Dairy cattle
- Sheep

ENERGY
- Coal
- Lignite
- Oil
- Gas
- Hydro-electric power

MINERALS
Iron ore and ferro-alloys
- Fe Iron ore
- Mn Manganese
- Ni Nickel
- W Tungsten

Non-ferrous metals
- Ag Silver
- Al Bauxite
- Au Gold
- Cu Copper
- Pb Lead and zinc
- Sb Antimony
- Sn Tin
- U Uranium

Non-metallic minerals
- Diamonds

OCEANIA : LAND USE

Other land 198.3

Arable and permanent crops 48.7

Forest and woodland 156.3

Rough grazing and permanent pasture 439.4

Total land area 842.7 million hectares

WEALTH

Gross National Product (GNP) US $ per capita 1994
- Over 20 000
- 10 000 – 20 000
- 5000 – 10 000
- Under 5000

Average annual change in GNP per capita (1985–1995)
- ○ 0 – 2%
- □ Over 2%

1:67 000 000

POPULATION DENSITY

Inhabitants per km²
- Over 100
- 50 – 100
- 10 – 50
- 1 – 10
- Under 10

Population of major cities in millions
- Over 2.5
- 1 – 2.5
- 0.5 – 1

1:47 000 000

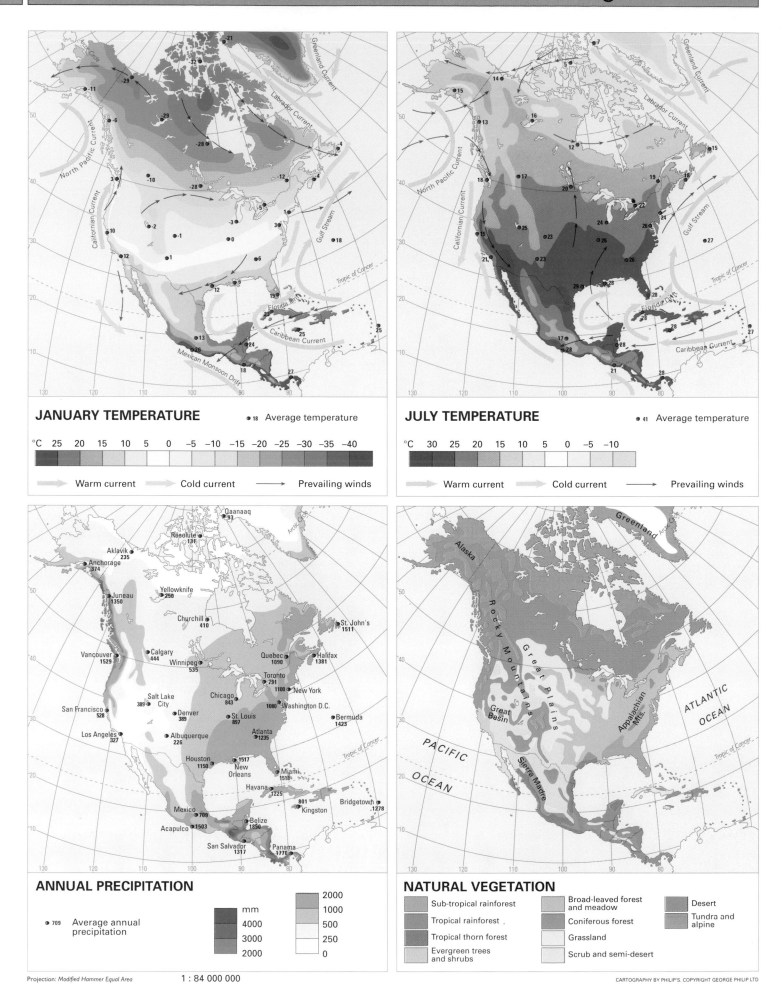

JANUARY TEMPERATURE   ● 18 Average temperature

°C 25 20 15 10 5 0 −5 −10 −15 −20 −25 −30 −35 −40

→ Warm current   → Cold current   → Prevailing winds

JULY TEMPERATURE   ● 41 Average temperature

°C 30 25 20 15 10 5 0 −5 −10

→ Warm current   → Cold current   → Prevailing winds

ANNUAL PRECIPITATION

● 709 Average annual precipitation

mm	
	2000
	1000
4000	500
3000	250
2000	0

NATURAL VEGETATION

Sub-tropical rainforest	Broad-leaved forest and meadow	Desert
Tropical rainforest	Coniferous forest	Tundra and alpine
Tropical thorn forest	Grassland	
Evergreen trees and shrubs	Scrub and semi-desert	

Projection: *Modified Hammer Equal Area*   1 : 84 000 000

CARTOGRAPHY BY PHILIP'S. COPYRIGHT GEORGE PHILIP LTD

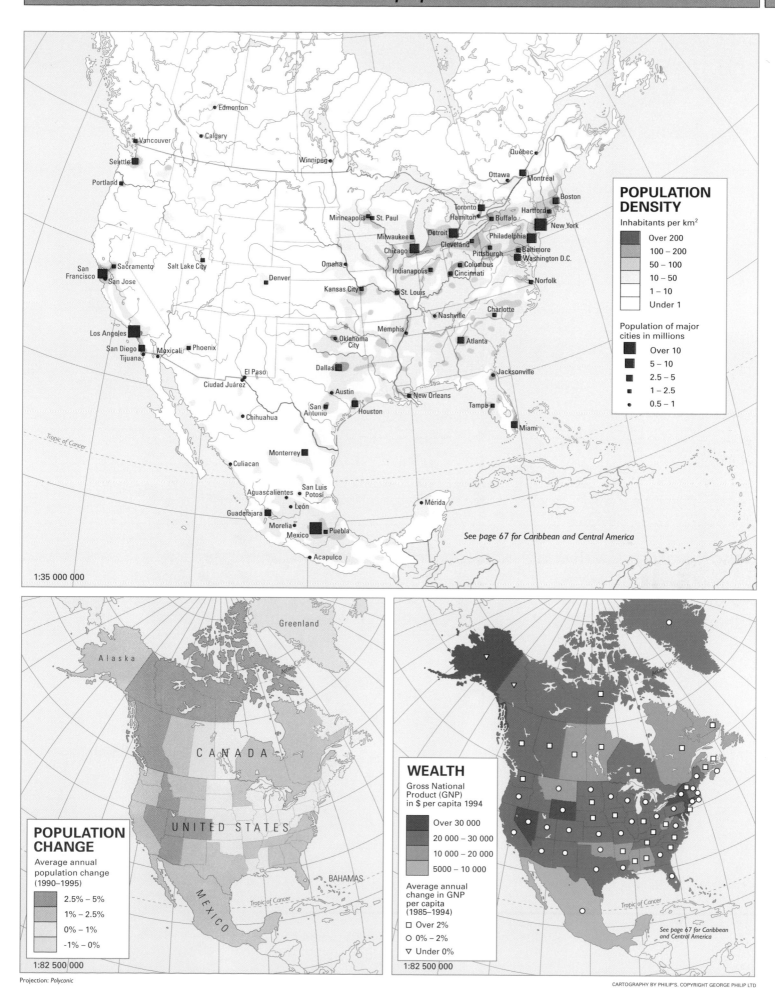

POPULATION DENSITY

Inhabitants per km²

- Over 200
- 100 – 200
- 50 – 100
- 10 – 50
- 1 – 10
- Under 1

Population of major cities in millions

- Over 10
- 5 – 10
- 2.5 – 5
- 1 – 2.5
- 0.5 – 1

See page 67 for Caribbean and Central America

1:35 000 000

POPULATION CHANGE

Average annual population change (1990–1995)

- 2.5% – 5%
- 1% – 2.5%
- 0% – 1%
- -1% – 0%

1:82 500 000

WEALTH

Gross National Product (GNP) in $ per capita 1994

- Over 30 000
- 20 000 – 30 000
- 10 000 – 20 000
- 5000 – 10 000

Average annual change in GNP per capita (1985–1994)

- □ Over 2%
- ○ 0% – 2%
- ▽ Under 0%

See page 67 for Caribbean and Central America

1:82 500 000

Projection: *Polyconic*

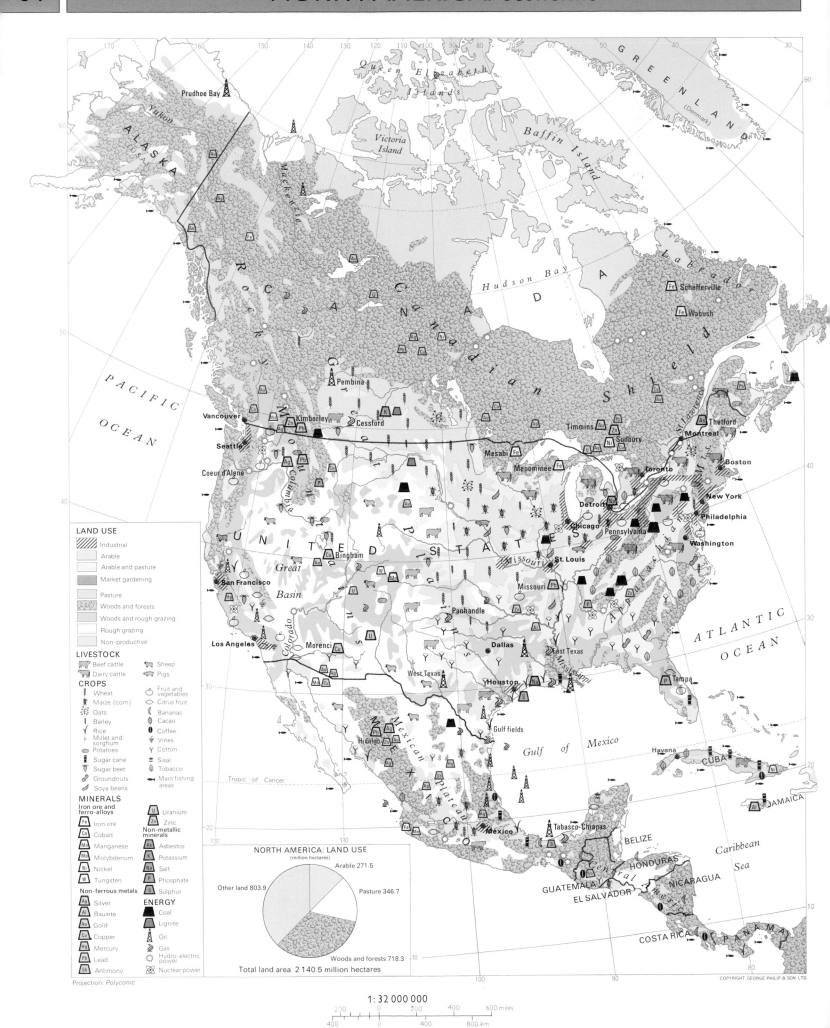

LAND USE
- Industrial
- Arable
- Arable and pasture
- Market gardening
- Pasture
- Woods and forests
- Woods and rough grazing
- Rough grazing
- Non-productive

LIVESTOCK
- Beef cattle
- Dairy cattle
- Sheep
- Pigs

CROPS
- Wheat
- Maize (corn)
- Oats
- Barley
- Rice
- Millet and sorghum
- Potatoes
- Sugar cane
- Sugar beet
- Groundnuts
- Soya beans
- Fruit and vegetables
- Citrus fruit
- Bananas
- Cacao
- Coffee
- Vines
- Cotton
- Sisal
- Tobacco
- Main fishing areas

MINERALS
Iron ore and ferro-alloys
- Fe Iron ore
- Co Cobalt
- Mn Manganese
- Mo Molybdenum
- Ni Nickel
- W Tungsten

Non-ferrous metals
- Ag Silver
- Al Bauxite
- Au Gold
- Cu Copper
- Hg Mercury
- Pb Lead
- Sb Antimony

- U Uranium
- Zn Zinc

Non-metallic minerals
- As Asbestos
- K Potassium
- Na Salt
- P Phosphate
- S Sulphur

ENERGY
- Coal
- Lignite
- Oil
- Gas
- Hydro-electric power
- Nuclear power

NORTH AMERICA: LAND USE
(million hectares)

Arable 271.5
Other land 803.9
Pasture 346.7
Woods and forests 718.3

Total land area 2 140.5 million hectares

Projection: *Polyconic*

1 : 32 000 000

200   0   200   400   600 miles
400   0   400   800 km

COPYRIGHT. GEORGE PHILIP & SON. LTD

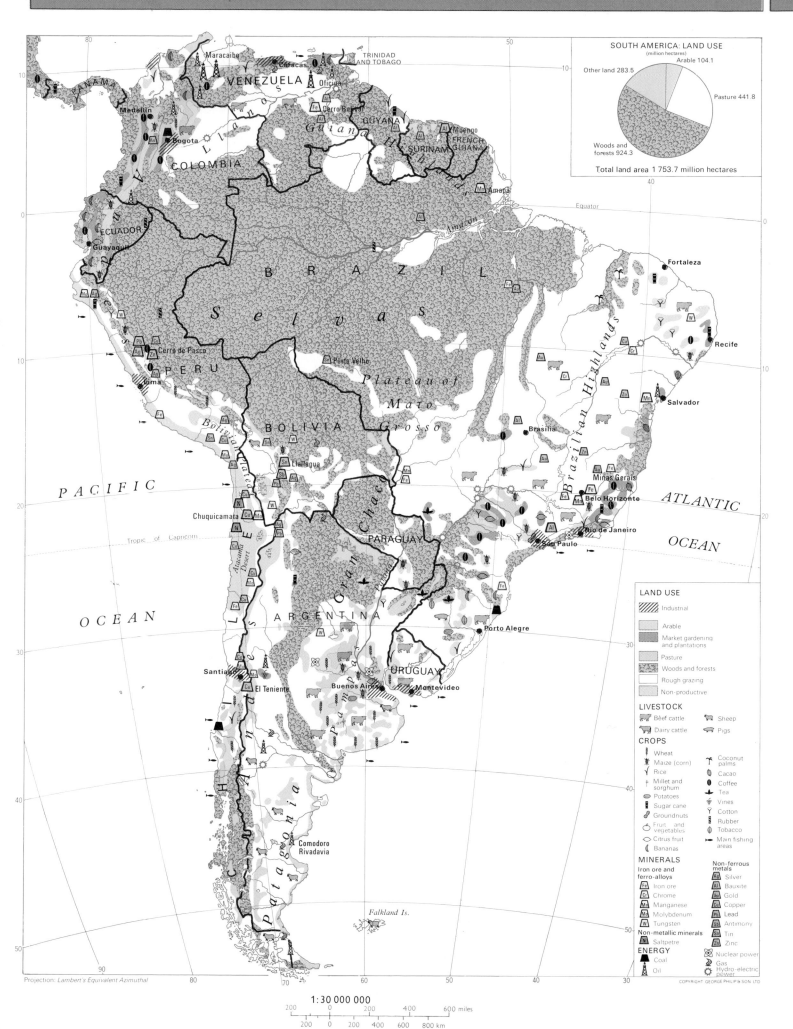

SOUTH AMERICA: LAND USE
(million hectares)

Arable 104.1

Other land 283.5

Pasture 441.8

Woods and forests 924.3

Total land area 1 753.7 million hectares

LAND USE

- Industrial
- Arable
- Market gardening and plantations
- Pasture
- Woods and forests
- Rough grazing
- Non-productive

LIVESTOCK

- Beef cattle
- Sheep
- Dairy cattle
- Pigs

CROPS

- Wheat
- Maize (corn)
- Rice
- Millet and sorghum
- Potatoes
- Sugar cane
- Groundnuts
- Fruit and vegetables
- Citrus fruit
- Bananas
- Coconut palms
- Cacao
- Coffee
- Tea
- Vines
- Cotton
- Rubber
- Tobacco
- Main fishing areas

MINERALS

Iron ore and ferro-alloys

- Fe Iron ore
- Cr Chrome
- Mn Manganese
- Mo Molybdenum
- W Tungsten

Non-metallic minerals

- N Saltpetre

ENERGY

- Coal
- Oil

Non-ferrous metals

- Ag Silver
- Al Bauxite
- Au Gold
- Cu Copper
- Pb Lead
- Sb Antimony
- Sn Tin
- Zn Zinc

- Nuclear power
- Gas
- Hydro-electric power

Projection: Lambert's Equivalent Azimuthal

1:30 000 000

200   0   200   400   600 miles

200   0   200   400   600   800 km

COPYRIGHT. GEORGE PHILIP & SON. LTD

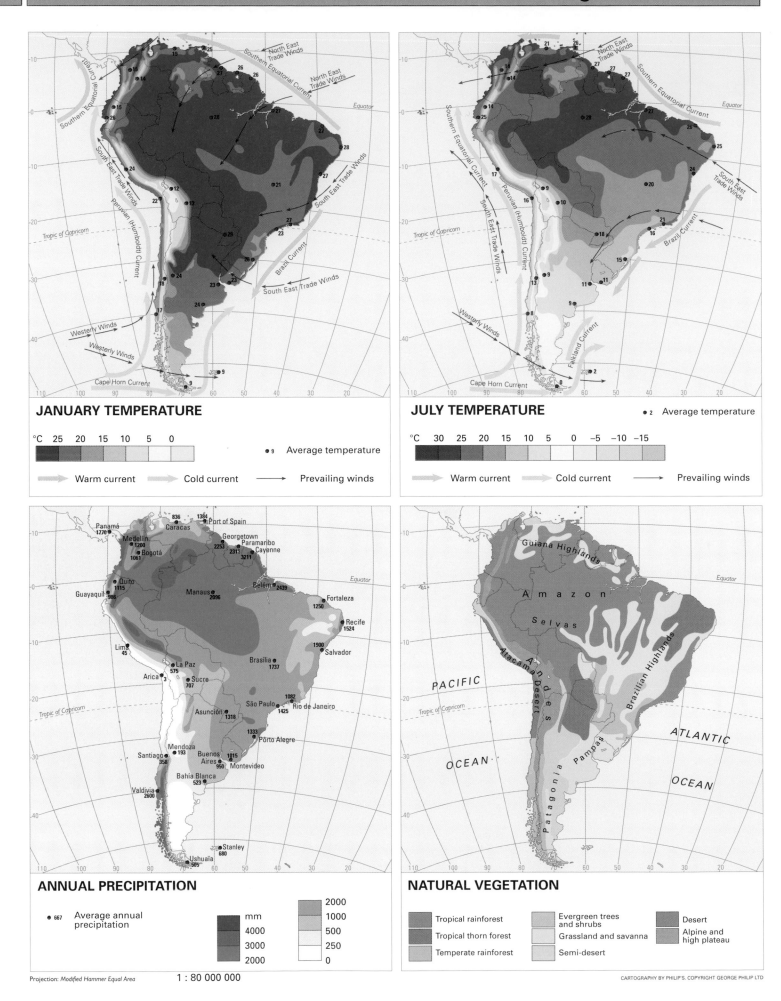

JANUARY TEMPERATURE

°C 25 20 15 10 5 0

● 9 Average temperature

⟹ Warm current   ⟹ Cold current   → Prevailing winds

JULY TEMPERATURE

● 2 Average temperature

°C 30 25 20 15 10 5 0 −5 −10 −15

⟹ Warm current   ⟹ Cold current   → Prevailing winds

ANNUAL PRECIPITATION

● 667 Average annual precipitation

mm
4000
3000
2000

2000
1000
500
250
0

NATURAL VEGETATION

Tropical rainforest

Tropical thorn forest

Temperate rainforest

Evergreen trees and shrubs

Grassland and savanna

Semi-desert

Desert

Alpine and high plateau

Projection: *Modified Hammer Equal Area*   1 : 80 000 000

CARTOGRAPHY BY PHILIP'S. COPYRIGHT GEORGE PHILIP LTD

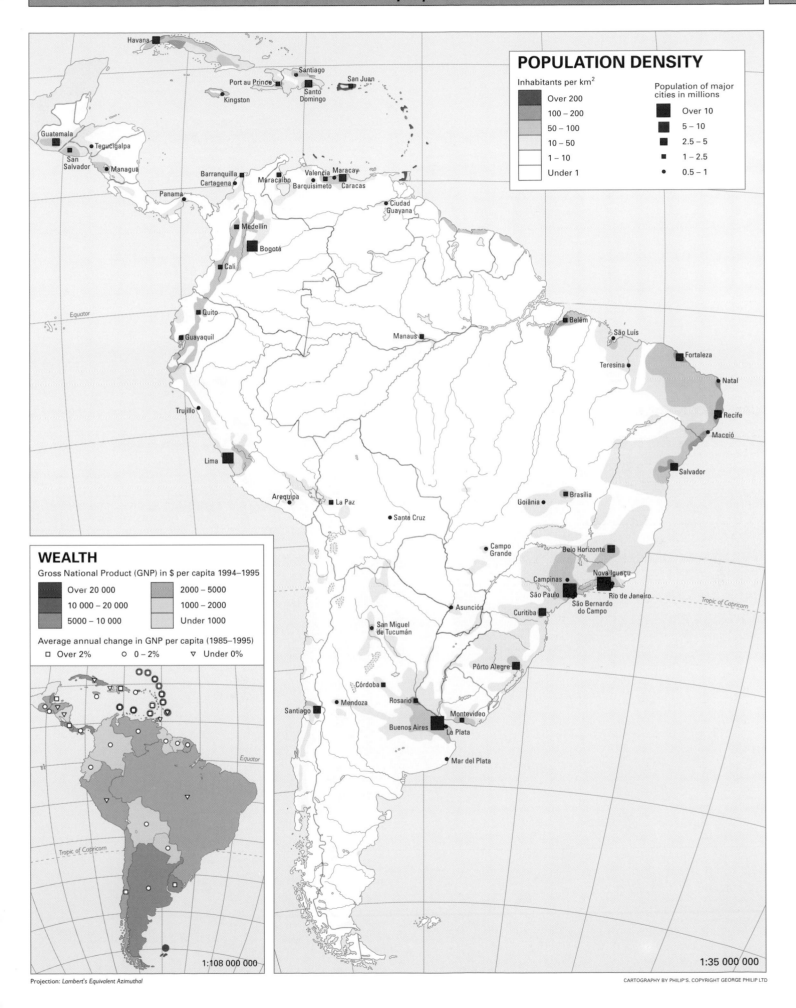

POPULATION DENSITY

Inhabitants per km²

Over 200
100 – 200
50 – 100
10 – 50
1 – 10
Under 1

Population of major cities in millions

Over 10
5 – 10
2.5 – 5
1 – 2.5
0.5 – 1

WEALTH

Gross National Product (GNP) in $ per capita 1994–1995

Over 20 000
10 000 – 20 000
5000 – 10 000
2000 – 5000
1000 – 2000
Under 1000

Average annual change in GNP per capita (1985–1995)

☐ Over 2%   ○ 0 – 2%   ▽ Under 0%

1:108 000 000

1:35 000 000

Projection: *Lambert's Equivalent Azimuthal*

CARTOGRAPHY BY PHILIP'S. COPYRIGHT GEORGE PHILIP LTD

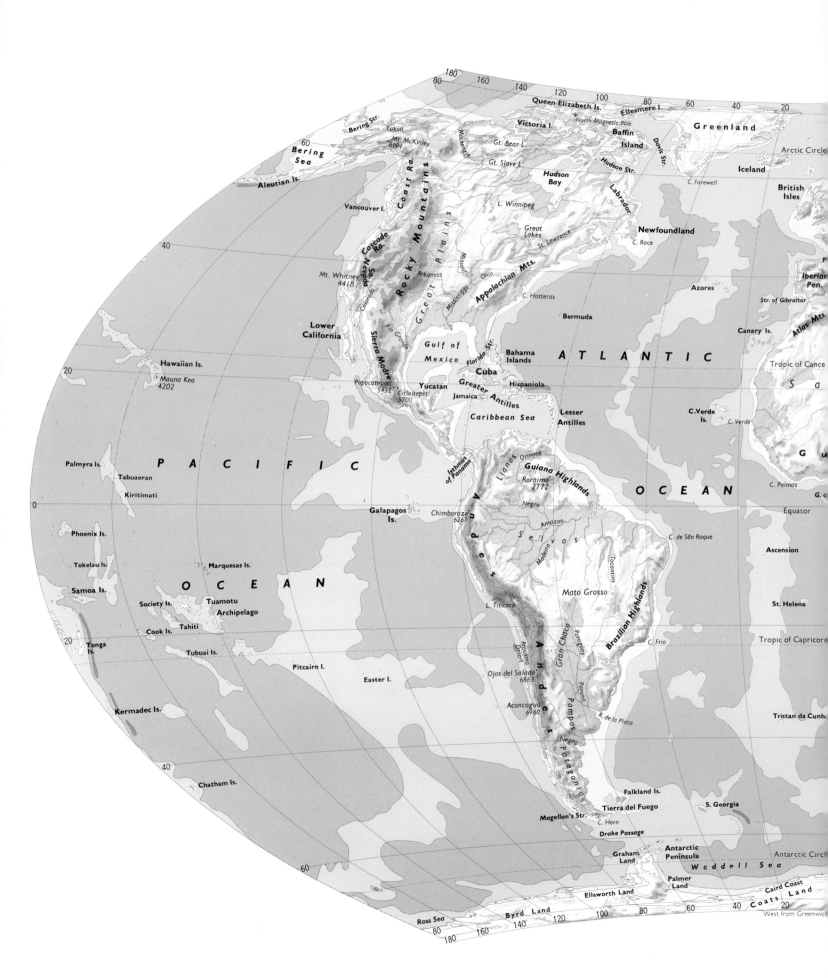

180   160   140   120   100   80   60   40   20
80
60   Bering Str.   Yukon   Mt. McKinley   Victoria I.   North Magnetic Pole   Queen Elizabeth Is.   Ellesmere I.   Greenland
        6194   Baffin   Arctic Circle
Bering   Coast Ra.   Mackenzie   Gt. Bear L.   Island   Davis Str.
Sea   Hudson Str.
Aleutian Is.   Vancouver I.   Rocky Mountains   Gt. Slave L.   Hudson   Labrador   C. Farewell   Iceland   British
40   Bay   Isles
            Cascade Ra.   L. Winnipeg   Great   Newfoundland
            Sierra Nevada   Great Plains   Lakes   St. Lawrence   C. Race
Mt. Whitney   Arkansas   Missouri   Ohio   Appalachian Mts.   Azores   Iberian
        4418   Colorado   Pen.
            Rio Grande   Mississippi   C. Hatteras   Bermuda   Str. of Gibraltar
Lower   Canary Is.   Atlas Mts.
California   Sierra Madre   Gulf of   Florida Str.   Bahama   Tropic of Cancer
20   Mexico   Islands   A T L A N T I C   S a
Hawaiian Is.   Popocatepetl   Cuba
    Mauna Kea   5452   Yucatan   Greater   Hispaniola   C. Verde
    4202   Citlaltepetl   Antilles   Jamaica   Is.   C. Verde   G u
            5700   Lesser
Palmyra Is.   Caribbean Sea   Antilles   O C E A N
Tabuaeran   Isthmus   Llanos   Orinoco   C. Palmas
Kiritimati   P A C I F I C   of Panama   Guiana Highlands   G. o
                    Andes   Roraima
0   2772   Negro
Galapagos   Chimborazo   Equator
Phoenix Is.   Is.   6267   Amazon   C. de São Roque
                Selvas   Madeira   Ascension
Tokelau Is.   Marquesas Is.   Tocantins   St. Helena
Samoa Is.   O C E A N   Mato Grosso
    Society Is.   Tuamotu   L. Titicaca   Brazilian Highlands
Cook Is.   Tahiti   Archipelago   Paraguay   C. Frio
20   Andes   Gran Chaco   Tropic of Capricorn
Tonga   Tubuai Is.   Atacama   Ojos del Salado   Parana
Is.   Pitcairn I.   Desert   6863
            Easter I.   Aconcagua   Pampas
Kermadec Is.   6960   R. de la Plata   Tristan da Cunha
                    Negro   Patagonia
                    Falkland Is.
40   Chatham Is.   S. Georgia
                Tierra del Fuego
            Magellan's Str.   C. Horn
                Drake Passage
                Graham   Antarctic   Antarctic Circle
60   Land   Peninsula   Palmer   Weddell Sea
        Ross Sea   Byrd Land   Ellsworth Land   Land   Caird Coast
                                            Coats Land
    180   160   140   120   100   80   60   40   West from Greenwich

Projection: Hammer Equal Area

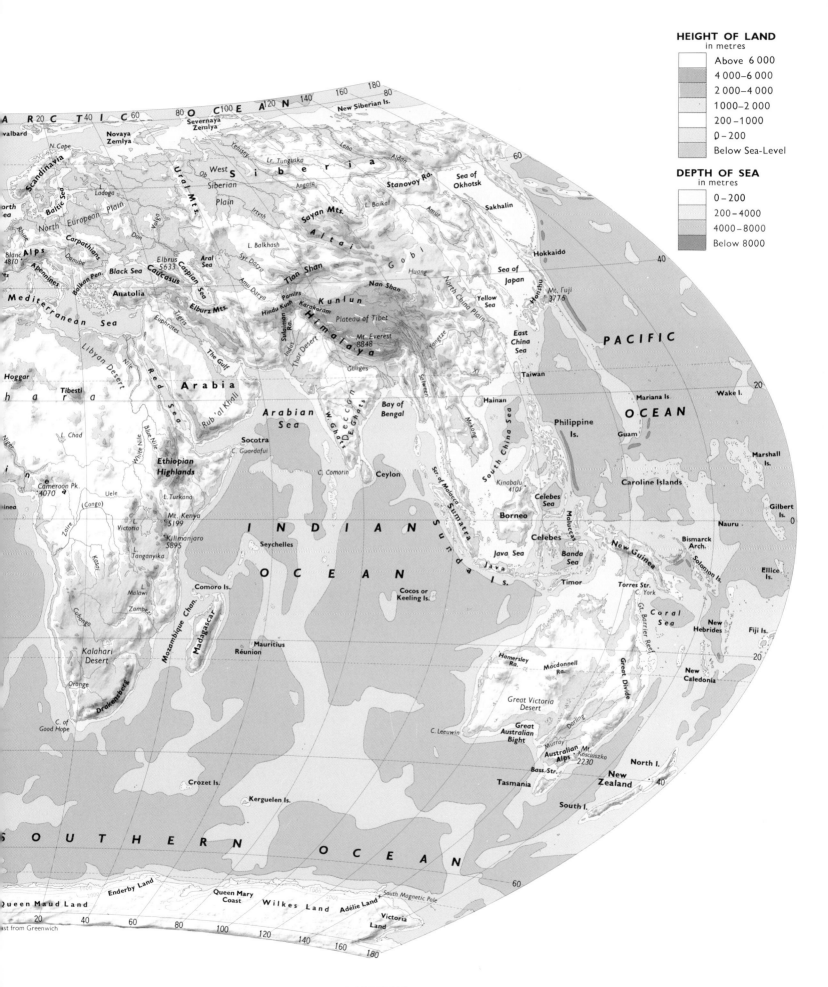

HEIGHT OF LAND
in metres

Above 6 000
4 000–6 000
2 000–4 000
1000–2 000
200–1000
0–200
Below Sea-Level

DEPTH OF SEA
in metres

0–200
200–4000
4000–8000
Below 8000

1:80 000 000

Copyright, George Philip & Son, Ltd.

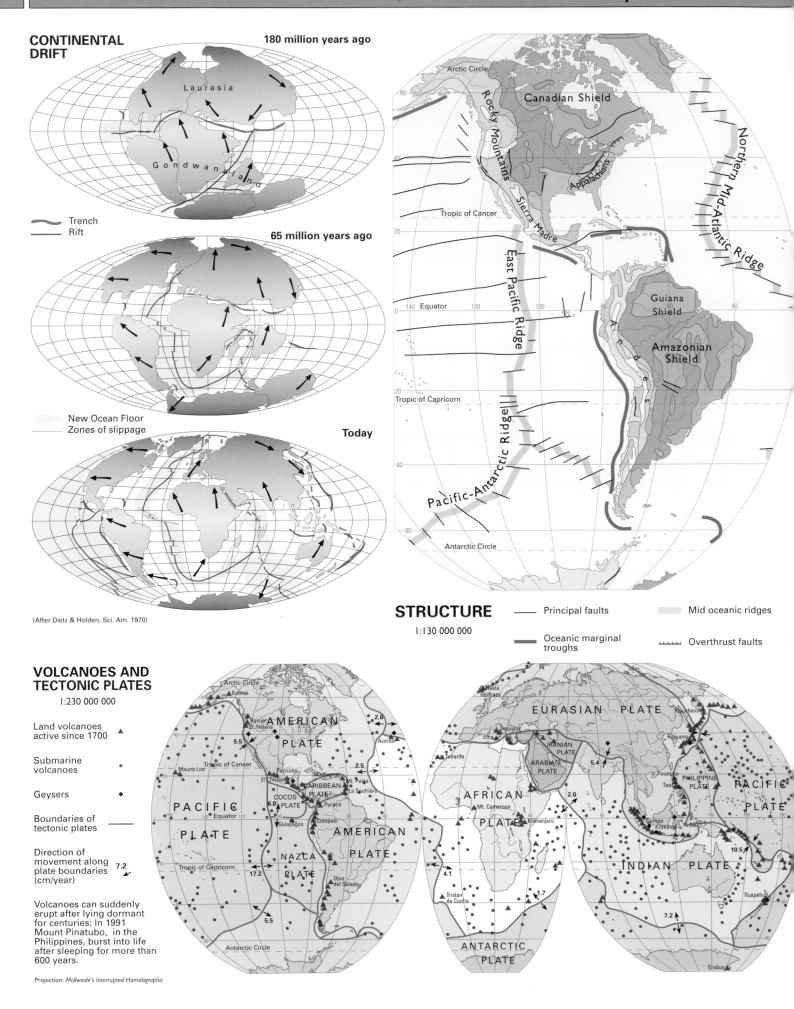

CONTINENTAL DRIFT

180 million years ago

Laurasia

Gondwanaland

∿ Trench
— Rift

65 million years ago

New Ocean Floor
— Zones of slippage

Today

(After Dietz & Holden, Sci. Am. 1970)

Arctic Circle

Canadian Shield

Rocky Mountains

Appalachians

Tropic of Cancer

Sierra Madre

Equator

East Pacific Ridge

Guiana Shield

Amazonian Shield

Andes

Tropic of Capricorn

Pacific-Antarctic Ridge

Northern Mid-Atlantic Ridge

Antarctic Circle

STRUCTURE

1:130 000 000

— Principal faults
━ Oceanic marginal troughs

▒ Mid oceanic ridges
⊥⊥⊥ Overthrust faults

VOLCANOES AND TECTONIC PLATES

1:230 000 000

Land volcanoes active since 1700 ▲

Submarine volcanoes •

Geysers ✛

Boundaries of tectonic plates ——

Direction of movement along plate boundaries (cm/year) 7.2

Volcanoes can suddenly erupt after lying dormant for centuries: In 1991 Mount Pinatubo, in the Philippines, burst into life after sleeping for more than 600 years.

Projection: *Mollweide's Interrupted Homolographic*

Arctic Circle
Katmai
Rainier
St. Helens
AMERICAN PLATE
2.6
Azores
5.5
Mauna Loa
Tropic of Cancer
Paricutin
2.5
Mangaroa
El Chichón
Mt. Pelée
CARIBBEAN PLATE
La Soufrière
COCOS PLATE
6.0
Puracé
PACIFIC PLATE
Equator
Galapagos
Cotopaxi
AMERICAN PLATE
NAZCA PLATE
Tropic of Capricorn
7.2
17.2
Ojos del Salado
5.5
Antarctic Circle

Hekla
Heimaey
EURASIAN PLATE
Khyuchevsk
Vesuvius
Etna
IRANIAN PLATE
ARABIAN PLATE
Fujiyama
Tenerife
5.4
Pinatubo
AFRICAN PLATE
Taal
PHILIPPINE PLATE
PACIFIC PLATE
Mt. Cameroon
2.0
Dempo
Kilimanjaro
Krakatoa
4.1
10.5
INDIAN PLATE
Tristan da Cunha
1.7
Ruapehu
7.2
ANTARCTIC PLATE
Erebus

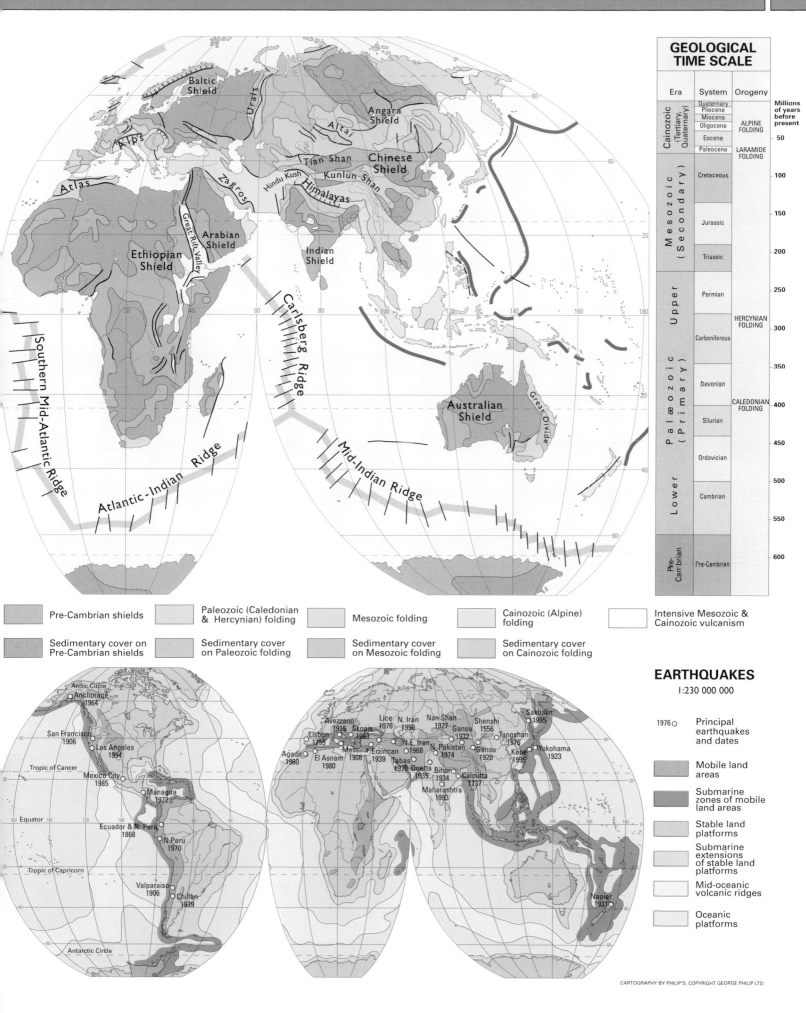

GEOLOGICAL TIME SCALE

Era	System	Orogeny	Millions of years before present
Cainozoic (Tertiary, Quaternary)	Quaternary		
	Pliocene	ALPINE FOLDING	
	Miocene		
	Oligocene		50
	Eocene		
	Paleocene	LARAMIDE FOLDING	
Mesozoic (Secondary)	Cretaceous		100
	Jurassic		150
	Triassic		200
Palaeozoic (Primary) — Upper	Permian		250
	Carboniferous	HERCYNIAN FOLDING	300
	Devonian		350
	Silurian	CALEDONIAN FOLDING	400
Palaeozoic (Primary) — Lower	Ordovician		450
	Cambrian		500
			550
Pre-Cambrian	Pre-Cambrian		600

Pre-Cambrian shields

Paleozoic (Caledonian & Hercynian) folding

Mesozoic folding

Cainozoic (Alpine) folding

Intensive Mesozoic & Cainozoic vulcanism

Sedimentary cover on Pre-Cambrian shields

Sedimentary cover on Paleozoic folding

Sedimentary cover on Mesozoic folding

Sedimentary cover on Cainozoic folding

EARTHQUAKES

1:230 000 000

1976 ○ Principal earthquakes and dates

Mobile land areas

Submarine zones of mobile land areas

Stable land platforms

Submarine extensions of stable land platforms

Mid-oceanic volcanic ridges

Oceanic platforms

CARTOGRAPHY BY PHILIP'S. COPYRIGHT GEORGE PHILIP LTD

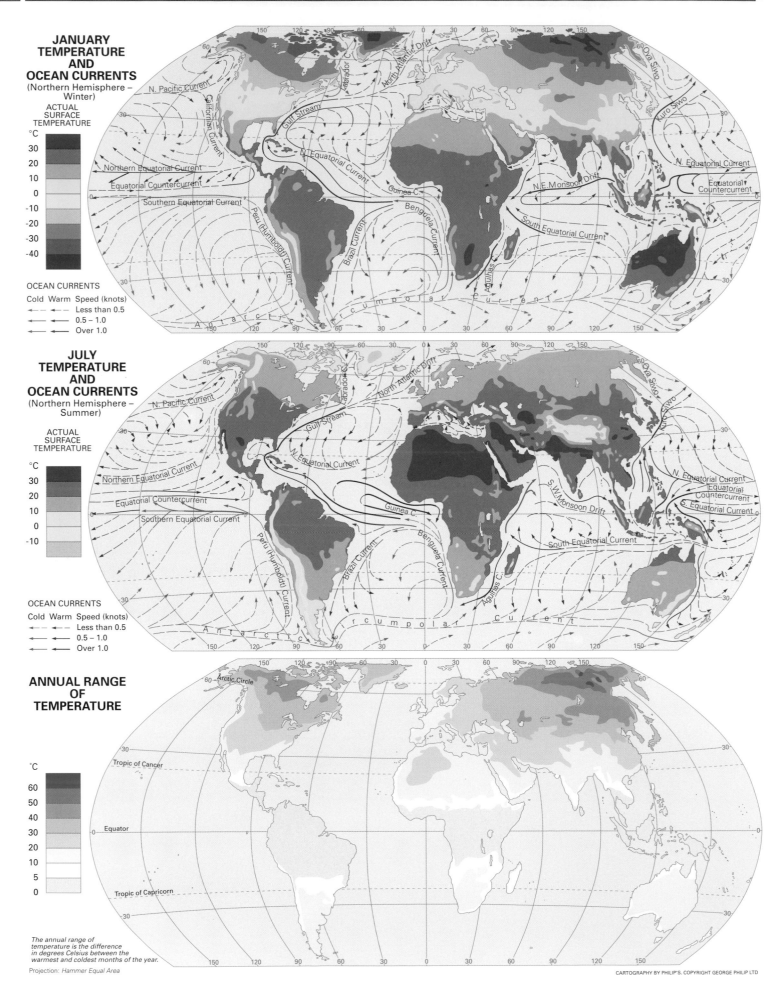

JANUARY TEMPERATURE AND OCEAN CURRENTS
(Northern Hemisphere – Winter)

ACTUAL SURFACE TEMPERATURE

°C
30
20
10
0
-10
-20
-30
-40

OCEAN CURRENTS

Cold Warm Speed (knots)
Less than 0.5
0.5 – 1.0
Over 1.0

JULY TEMPERATURE AND OCEAN CURRENTS
(Northern Hemisphere – Summer)

ACTUAL SURFACE TEMPERATURE

°C
30
20
10
0
-10

OCEAN CURRENTS

Cold Warm Speed (knots)
Less than 0.5
0.5 – 1.0
Over 1.0

ANNUAL RANGE OF TEMPERATURE

°C
60
50
40
30
20
10
5
0

The annual range of temperature is the difference in degrees Celsius between the warmest and coldest months of the year.

Projection: Hammer Equal Area

CARTOGRAPHY BY PHILIP'S. COPYRIGHT GEORGE PHILIP LTD

1 : 190 000 000

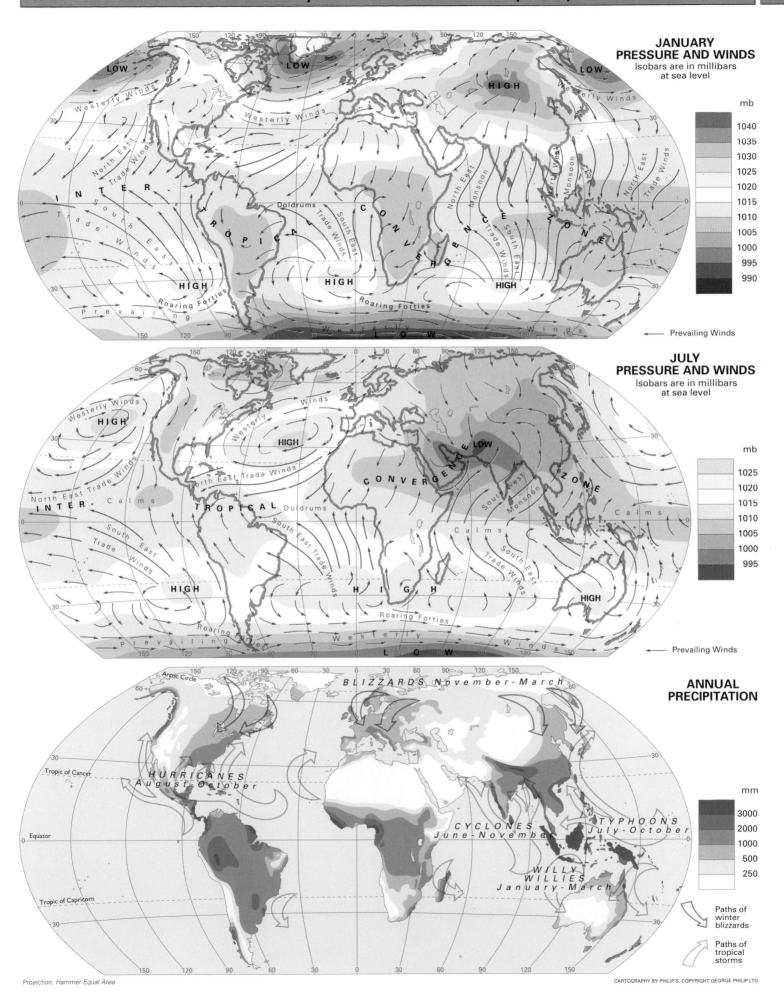

JANUARY PRESSURE AND WINDS
Isobars are in millibars at sea level

mb

1040
1035
1030
1025
1020
1015
1010
1005
1000
995
990

→ Prevailing Winds

JULY PRESSURE AND WINDS
Isobars are in millibars at sea level

mb

1025
1020
1015
1010
1005
1000
995

→ Prevailing Winds

ANNUAL PRECIPITATION

mm

3000
2000
1000
500
250

Paths of winter blizzards

Paths of tropical storms

Projection: Hammer Equal Area

CARTOGRAPHY BY PHILIP'S. COPYRIGHT GEORGE PHILIP LTD

1 : 190 000 000

CLIMATIC REGIONS — after Köppen

Köppen's classification recognises five major climatic regions corresponding broadly to the five principal vegetation types and these are designated by the letters A, B, C, D and E. Each one of these are subdivided on the basis of temperature and rainfall. This map shows a climate graph for a selected place within each of the 12 sub-regions.

TROPICAL RAINY CLIMATES A

Af	Rain Forest Climate	All mean monthly temperatures above 18°C and an annual variation in temperature of less than 6°C
Am	Monsoon Climate	
Aw	Savanna Climate	All monthly temperatures above 18°C but with an annual variation in temperature of less than 12°C

DRY CLIMATES B

BS	Steppe Climate	The principal difference between this grouping and groups A, C, D and E is the combination of a wide range of temperatures with low rainfall
BW	Desert Climate	

WARM TEMPERATE RAINY CLIMATES C

The climatic group is separated from group A by having the mean temperature of the coolest month below 18°C but above -3°C. The mean temperature of the warmest month is over 10°C.

Cw	Dry Winter Climate	The wettest month of summer has at least ten times as much rain as the driest winter month
Cs	Dry Summer Climate (Mediterranean)	The wettest month of winter has at least three times as much rain as the driest month of summer. The driest summer month itself has less than 30mm rainfall.
Cf	Climate with no Dry Season	Even rainfall throughout the year.

COLD TEMPERATE RAINY CLIMATES D

Dw	Dry Winter Climate	The mean temperature of the coldest month is below -3°C but the mean temperature of the warmest month is still over 10°C.
Df	Climate with no Dry Season	

POLAR CLIMATES E

ET	Tundra Climate	The mean temperature of the warmest month is below 10°C giving permanently frozen subsoil.
EF	Polar Climate	The mean temperature of the warmest month is below 0°C giving permanently ice and snow.

The classification is in some cases subdivided by the addition of the following letters after the major types :-

Used with groups C and D	**a**	Hot summer – mean temperature of the hottest month above 22°C and with more than four months of over 10°C.
	b	Warm summer – mean temperature of the hottest month below 22°C but still with more than four months of over 10°C.
	c	Cool short summer – mean temperature of the hottest month below 22°C but with less than four months of over 10°C.
Used with group D	**d**	Cool short summer and cold winter – mean temperature of the hottest month below 22°C and of the coolest month below -38°C
Used with group B	**h**	Hot dry climate – mean annual temperature above 18°C.
	k	Cool dry climate – mean annual temperature below 18°C.
Used with group E	**H**	Polar climate due to elevation being over 1500m.

Climate graphs: QUEBEC Df; EISMITTE EF; EDMONTON BS; LA PAZ ET; BUENOS AIRES Cf

Colour of climate region on map
Average monthly daily maximum temperature
Average monthly temperature
Average monthly daily minimum temperature
Average annual rainfall
Average monthly rainfall
Months of the year

SOIL REGIONS

1:220 000 000
after Glinka, Stremme, Marbut, and others

- Tundra soil
- Podzols
- Brown forest soil
- Lightly leached dry forest soil
- Red and yellow sub-tropical forest soil
- Reddish savanna soil and tropical red earths
- Laterites
- Chernozem
- Degraded chernozem
- Black savanna soil
- Chestnut steppe soil
- Grey and brown desert steppe soils
- Alluvium
- Mountain and high plateau soils
- Oases soil
- Tropical and mangrove swamp

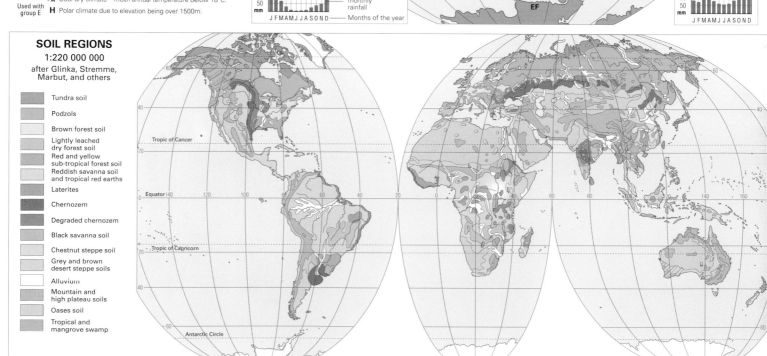

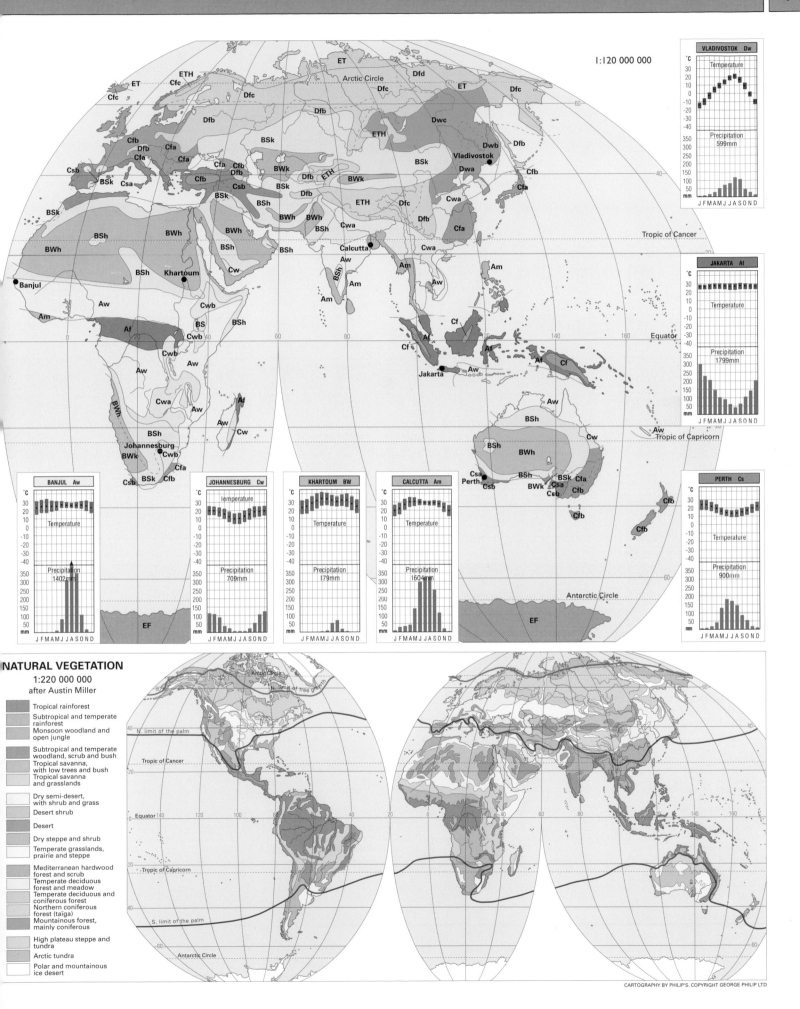

NATURAL VEGETATION
1:220 000 000
after Austin Miller

- Tropical rainforest
- Subtropical and temperate rainforest
- Monsoon woodland and open jungle
- Subtropical and temperate woodland, scrub and bush
- Tropical savanna, with low trees and bush
- Tropical savanna and grasslands
- Dry semi-desert, with shrub and grass
- Desert shrub
- Desert
- Dry steppe and shrub
- Temperate grasslands, prairie and steppe
- Mediterranean hardwood forest and scrub
- Temperate deciduous forest and meadow
- Temperate deciduous and coniferous forest
- Northern coniferous forest (taiga)
- Mountainous forest, mainly coniferous
- High plateau steppe and tundra
- Arctic tundra
- Polar and mountainous ice desert

1:120 000 000

CARTOGRAPHY BY PHILIP'S. COPYRIGHT GEORGE PHILIP LTD

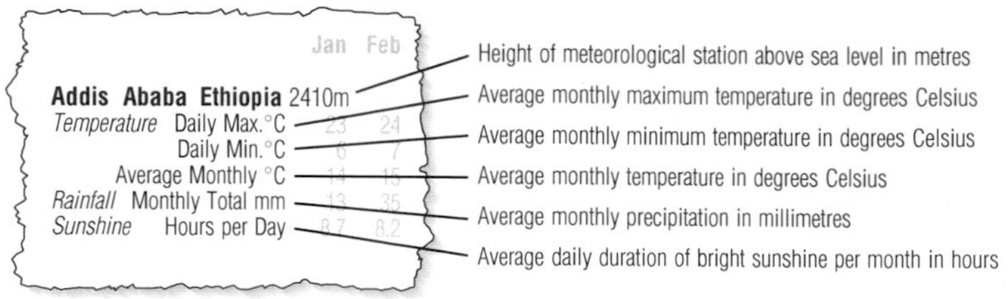
Jan Feb
Addis Ababa Ethiopia 2410m
Temperature Daily Max.°C 23 24
Daily Min.°C 6 7
Average Monthly °C 14 15
Rainfall Monthly Total mm 13 35
Sunshine Hours per Day 8.7 8.2
Height of meteorological station above sea level in metres
Average monthly maximum temperature in degrees Celsius
Average monthly minimum temperature in degrees Celsius
Average monthly temperature in degrees Celsius
Average monthly precipitation in millimetres
Average daily duration of bright sunshine per month in hours

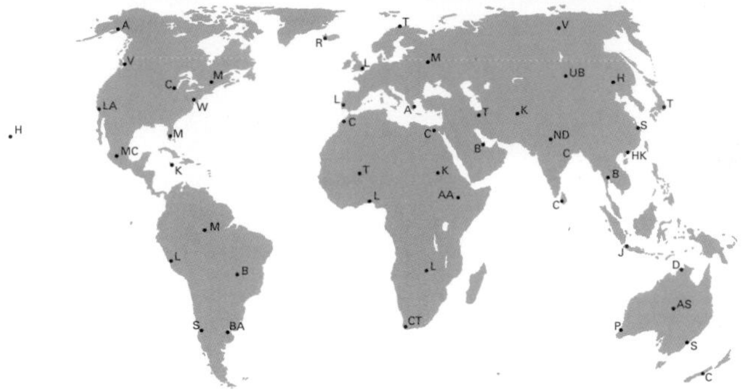

Addis Ababa Ethiopia 2410m	Jan	Feb	Mar	Apr	May	June	July	Aug	Sep	Oct	Nov	Dec	Year
Temperature Daily Max.°C	23	24	25	24	25	23	20	20	21	22	23	22	23
Daily Min.°C	6	7	9	10	9	10	11	11	10	7	5	5	8
Average Monthly °C	14	15	17	17	17	16	16	15	15	15	14	14	15
Rainfall Monthly Total mm	13	35	67	91	81	117	247	255	167	29	8	5	1115
Sunshine Hours per Day	8.7	8.2	7.6	8.1	6.5	4.8	2.8	3.2	5.2	7.6	6.7	7	6.4

Alice Springs Australia 580m	Jan	Feb	Mar	Apr	May	June	July	Aug	Sep	Oct	Nov	Dec	Year
Temperature Daily Max.°C	35	35	32	27	23	19	19	23	27	31	33	35	28
Daily Min.°C	21	20	17	12	8	5	4	6	10	15	18	20	13
Average Monthly °C	28	27	25	20	15	12	12	14	18	23	25	27	21
Rainfall Monthly Total mm	44	33	27	10	15	13	7	8	7	18	29	38	249
Sunshine Hours per Day	10.3	10.4	9.3	9.2	8	8	8.9	9.8	10	9.7	10.1	10	9.5

Anchorage USA 183m	Jan	Feb	Mar	Apr	May	June	July	Aug	Sep	Oct	Nov	Dec	Year
Temperature Daily Max.°C	-7	-3	0	7	13	18	19	17	13	6	-2	-6	-6
Daily Min.°C	-15	-12	-9	-2	4	8	10	9	5	-2	-9	-14	-2
Average Monthly °C	-11	-7	-4	3	9	13	15	13	9	2	-5	-10	-4
Rainfall Monthly Total mm	20	18	13	11	13	25	47	64	64	47	28	24	374
Sunshine Hours per Day	2.4	4.1	6.6	8.3	8.3	9.2	8.5	6	4.4	3.1	2.6	1.6	5.4

Athens Greece 107m	Jan	Feb	Mar	Apr	May	June	July	Aug	Sep	Oct	Nov	Dec	Year
Temperature Daily Max.°C	13	14	16	20	25	30	33	33	29	24	19	15	23
Daily Min.°C	6	7	8	11	16	20	23	23	19	15	12	8	14
Average Monthly °C	10	10	12	16	20	25	28	28	24	20	15	11	18
Rainfall Monthly Total mm	62	37	37	23	23	14	6	7	15	51	56	71	402
Sunshine Hours per Day	3.9	5.2	5.8	7.7	8.9	10.7	11.9	11.5	9.4	6.8	4.8	3.8	7.3

Bahrain City Bahrain 2m	Jan	Feb	Mar	Apr	May	June	July	Aug	Sep	Oct	Nov	Dec	Year
Temperature Daily Max.°C	20	21	25	29	33	36	37	38	36	32	27	22	30
Daily Min.°C	14	15	18	22	25	29	31	32	29	25	22	16	23
Average Monthly °C	17	18	21	25	29	32	34	35	32	29	25	19	26
Rainfall Monthly Total mm	18	12	10	9	2	0	0	0	0	0.4	3	16	70
Sunshine Hours per Day	5.9	6.9	7.9	8.8	10.6	13.2	12.1	12	12	10.3	7.7	6.4	9.5

Bangkok Thailand 10m	Jan	Feb	Mar	Apr	May	June	July	Aug	Sep	Oct	Nov	Dec	Year
Temperature Daily Max.°C	32	33	34	35	34	33	32	32	32	31	31	31	33
Daily Min.°C	20	23	24	26	25	25	25	24	24	24	23	20	24
Average Monthly °C	26	28	29	30	30	29	28	28	28	28	27	26	28
Rainfall Monthly Total mm	9	30	36	82	165	153	168	183	310	239	55	8	1438
Sunshine Hours per Day	8.2	8	8	10	7.5	6.1	4.7	5.2	5.2	6.1	7.3	7.8	7

Brasilia Brazil 910m	Jan	Feb	Mar	Apr	May	June	July	Aug	Sep	Oct	Nov	Dec	Year
Temperature Daily Max.°C	28	28	28	28	27	27	27	29	30	29	28	27	28
Daily Min.°C	18	18	18	17	15	13	13	14	16	18	18	18	16
Average Monthly °C	23	23	23	22	21	20	20	21	23	24	23	22	22
Rainfall Monthly Total mm	252	204	227	93	17	3	6	3	30	127	255	343	1560
Sunshine Av. Monthly Dur.	5.8	5.7	6	7.4	8.7	9.3	9.6	9.8	7.9	6.5	4.8	4.4	7.2

Buenos Aires Argentina 25m	Jan	Feb	Mar	Apr	May	June	July	Aug	Sep	Oct	Nov	Dec	Year
Temperature Daily Max.°C	30	29	26	22	18	14	14	16	18	21	25	28	22
Daily Min.°C	17	17	16	12	9	5	6	6	8	10	14	16	11
Average Monthly °C	23	23	21	17	13	10	10	11	13	15	19	22	16
Rainfall Monthly Total mm	79	71	109	89	76	61	56	61	79	86	84	99	950
Sunshine Hours per Day	9.2	8.5	7.5	6.8	4.9	3.5	3.8	5.2	6	6.8	8.1	8.5	6.6

Cairo Egypt 75m	Jan	Feb	Mar	Apr	May	June	July	Aug	Sep	Oct	Nov	Dec	Year
Temperature Daily Max.°C	19	21	24	28	32	35	35	35	33	30	26	21	28
Daily Min.°C	9	9	12	14	18	20	22	22	20	18	14	10	16
Average Monthly °C	14	15	18	21	25	28	29	28	26	24	20	16	22
Rainfall Monthly Total mm	4	4	3	1	2	1	0	0	1	1	3	7	27
Sunshine Hours per Day	6.9	8.4	8.7	9.7	10.5	11.9	11.7	11.3	10.4	9.4	8.3	6.4	9.5

Calcutta India 5m	Jan	Feb	Mar	Apr	May	June	July	Aug	Sep	Oct	Nov	Dec	Year
Temperature Daily Max.°C	27	29	34	36	35	34	32	32	32	32	29	26	31
Daily Min.°C	13	15	21	24	25	26	26	26	26	23	18	13	21
Average Monthly °C	20	22	27	30	30	30	29	29	29	28	23	20	26
Rainfall Monthly Total mm	10	30	34	44	140	297	325	332	253	114	20	5	1604
Sunshine Hours per Day	8.6	8.7	8.9	9	8.7	5.4	4.1	4.1	5.1	6.5	8.3	8.4	7.1

Cape Town South Africa 44m	Jan	Feb	Mar	Apr	May	June	July	Aug	Sep	Oct	Nov	Dec	Year
Temperature Daily Max.°C	26	26	25	23	20	18	17	18	19	21	24	25	22
Daily Min.°C	15	15	14	11	9	7	7	7	8	10	13	15	11
Average Monthly °C	21	20	20	17	14	13	12	12	14	16	18	20	16
Rainfall Monthly Total mm	12	19	17	42	67	98	68	76	36	45	12	13	505
Sunshine Hours per Day	11.4	10.2	9.4	7.7	6.1	5.7	6.4	6.6	7.6	8.6	10.2	10.9	8.4

Casablanca Morocco 59m	Jan	Feb	Mar	Apr	May	June	July	Aug	Sep	Oct	Nov	Dec	Year
Temperature Daily Max.°C	17	18	20	21	22	24	26	26	26	24	21	18	22
Daily Min.°C	8	9	11	12	15	18	19	20	18	15	12	10	14
Average Monthly °C	13	13	15	16	18	21	23	23	22	20	17	14	18
Rainfall Monthly Total mm	78	61	54	37	20	3	0	1	6	28	58	94	440
Sunshine Hours per Day	5.2	6.3	7.3	9	9.4	9.7	10.2	9.7	9.1	7.4	5.9	5.3	7.9

Chicago USA 186m	Jan	Feb	Mar	Apr	May	June	July	Aug	Sep	Oct	Nov	Dec	Year
Temperature Daily Max.°C	0.6	1.5	6.4	14.1	20.6	26.4	28.9	28	23.8	17.4	8.4	2.1	14.9
Daily Min.°C	-7	-6	-2	5	11	16	20	19	14	8	0	-5	-6
Average Monthly °C	-3	-2	2	9	16	21	24	23	19	13	4	-2	4
Rainfall Monthly Total mm	47	41	70	77	96	103	86	80	69	71	56	48	844
Sunshine Hours per Day	4	5	6.6	6.9	8.9	10.2	10	9.2	8.2	6.9	4.5	3.7	7

Christchurch New Zealand 5m	Jan	Feb	Mar	Apr	May	June	July	Aug	Sep	Oct	Nov	Dec	Year
Temperature Daily Max.°C	21	21	19	17	13	11	10	11	14	17	19	21	16
Daily Min.°C	12	12	10	7	4	2	1	3	5	7	8	11	7
Average Monthly °C	16	16	15	12	9	6	6	7	9	12	13	16	11
Rainfall Monthly Total mm	56	46	43	46	76	69	61	58	51	51	51	61	669
Sunshine Hours per Day	7	6.5	5.6	4.7	4.3	3.9	4.1	4.7	5.6	6.1	6.9	6.3	5.5

Colombo Sri Lanka 10m	Jan	Feb	Mar	Apr	May	June	July	Aug	Sep	Oct	Nov	Dec	Year
Temperature Daily Max.°C	30	31	31	31	30	30	29	29	30	29	29	30	30
Daily Min.°C	22	22	23	24	25	25	25	25	25	24	23	22	24
Average Monthly °C	26	26	27	28	28	27	27	27	27	27	26	26	27
Rainfall Monthly Total mm	101	66	118	230	394	220	140	102	174	348	333	142	2368
Sunshine Hours per Day	7.9	9	8.1	7.2	6.4	5.4	6.1	6.3	6.2	6.5	6.4	7.8	6.9

Darwin Australia 30m	Jan	Feb	Mar	Apr	May	June	July	Aug	Sep	Oct	Nov	Dec	Year
Temperature Daily Max.°C	32	32	33	33	33	31	31	32	33	34	34	33	33
Daily Min.°C	25	25	25	24	23	21	19	21	23	25	26	26	24
Average Monthly °C	29	29	29	29	28	26	25	26	28	29	30	29	28
Rainfall Monthly Total mm	405	309	279	77	8	2	0	1	15	48	108	214	1466
Sunshine Hours per Day	5.8	5.8	6.6	9.8	9.3	10	9.9	10.4	10.1	9.4	9.6	6.8	8.6

Harbin China 175m	Jan	Feb	Mar	Apr	May	June	July	Aug	Sep	Oct	Nov	Dec	Year
Temperature Daily Max.°C	-14	-9	0	12	21	26	29	27	20	12	-1	-11	9
Daily Min.°C	-26	-23	-12	-1	7	14	18	16	8	0	-12	-22	-3
Average Monthly °C	-20	-16	-6	6	14	20	23	22	14	6	-7	-17	3
Rainfall Monthly Total mm	4	6	17	23	44	92	167	119	52	36	12	5	577
Sunshine Hours per Day	6.4	7.8	8	7.8	8.3	8.6	8.6	8.2	7.2	6.9	6.1	5.7	7.5

Hong Kong China 35m	Jan	Feb	Mar	Apr	May	June	July	Aug	Sep	Oct	Nov	Dec	Year
Temperature Daily Max.°C	18	18	20	24	28	30	31	31	30	27	24	20	25
Daily Min.°C	13	13	16	19	23	26	26	26	25	23	19	15	20
Average Monthly °C	16	15	18	22	25	28	28	28	27	25	21	17	23
Rainfall Monthly Total mm	30	60	70	133	332	479	286	415	364	33	46	17	2265
Sunshine Hours per Day	4.7	3.5	3.1	3.8	5	5.4	6.8	6.5	6.6	7	6.2	5.5	5.3

Honolulu Hawaii 5m	Jan	Feb	Mar	Apr	May	June	July	Aug	Sep	Oct	Nov	Dec	Year
Temperature Daily Max.°C	26	26	26	27	28	29	29	29	30	29	28	26	28
Daily Min.°C	19	19	19	20	21	22	23	23	23	22	21	20	21
Average Monthly °C	23	22	23	23	24	26	26	26	26	26	24	23	24
Rainfall Monthly Total mm	96	84	73	33	25	8	11	23	25	47	55	76	556
Sunshine Hours per Day	7.3	7.7	8.3	8.6	8.8	9.1	9.4	9.3	9.2	8.3	7.5	6.2	8.3

Jakarta Indonesia 10m	Jan	Feb	Mar	Apr	May	June	July	Aug	Sep	Oct	Nov	Dec	Year
Temperature Daily Max.°C	29	29	30	31	31	31	31	31	31	31	30	29	30
Daily Min.°C	23	23	23	24	24	23	23	23	23	23	23	23	23
Average Monthly °C	26	26	27	27	27	27	27	27	27	27	27	26	27
Rainfall Monthly Total mm	300	300	211	147	114	97	64	43	66	112	142	203	1799
Sunshine Av. Monthly Dur.	6.1	6.5	7.7	8.5	8.4	8.5	9.1	9.5	9.6	9	7.7	7.1	8.1

Kabul Afghanistan 1791 m	Jan	Feb	Mar	Apr	May	June	July	Aug	Sep	Oct	Nov	Dec	Year
Temperature Daily Max.°C	2	4	12	19	26	31	33	33	30	22	17	8	20
Daily Min.°C	-8	-6	1	6	11	13	16	15	11	6	1	-3	5
Average Monthly °C	-3	-1	6	13	18	22	25	24	20	14	9	3	12
Rainfall Monthly Total mm	28	61	72	117	33	1	7	1	0	1	37	14	372
Sunshine Av. Monthly Dur.	5.9	6	5.7	6.8	10.1	11.5	11.4	11.2	9.8	9.4	7.8	6.1	8.5

Khartoum Sudan 380m	Jan	Feb	Mar	Apr	May	June	July	Aug	Sep	Oct	Nov	Dec	Year
Temperature Daily Max.°C	32	33	37	40	42	41	38	36	38	39	35	32	37
Daily Min.°C	16	17	20	23	26	27	26	25	25	25	21	17	22
Average Monthly °C	24	25	28	32	34	34	32	30	32	32	28	25	30
Rainfall Monthly Total mm	0	0	0	1	7	5	56	80	28	2	0	0	179
Sunshine Av. Monthly Dur.	10.6	11.2	10.4	10.8	10.4	10.1	8.6	8.6	9.6	10.3	10.8	10.6	10.2

ngston Jamaica 35m

	Jan	Feb	Mar	Apr	May	June	July	Aug	Sep	Oct	Nov	Dec	Year
mperature Daily Max.°C	30	30	30	31	31	32	32	32	32	31	31	31	31
Daily Min.°C	20	20	20	21	22	24	23	23	23	23	22	21	22
Average Monthly °C	25	25	25	26	26	28	28	28	27	27	26	26	26
infall Monthly Total mm	23	15	23	31	102	89	38	91	99	180	74	36	801
nshine Av. Monthly Dur.	8.3	8.8	8.7	8.7	8.3	7.8	8.5	8.5	7.6	7.3	8.3	7.7	8.2

gos Nigeria 40m

	Jan	Feb	Mar	Apr	May	June	July	Aug	Sep	Oct	Nov	Dec	Year
mperature Daily Max.°C	32	33	33	32	31	29	28	28	29	30	31	32	31
Daily Min.°C	22	23	23	23	23	22	22	21	22	22	23	22	22
Average Monthly °C	27	28	28	28	27	26	25	24	25	26	27	27	26
infall Monthly Total mm	28	41	99	99	203	300	180	56	180	190	63	25	1464
nshine Av. Monthly Dur.	5.9	6.8	6.3	6.1	5.6	3.8	2.8	3.3	3	5.1	6.6	6.5	5.2

ma Peru 120m

	Jan	Feb	Mar	Apr	May	June	July	Aug	Sep	Oct	Nov	Dec	Year
mperature Daily Max.°C	28	29	29	27	24	20	20	19	20	22	24	26	24
Daily Min.°C	19	20	19	17	16	15	14	14	14	15	16	17	16
Average Monthly °C	24	24	24	22	20	17	17	16	17	18	20	21	20
infall Monthly Total mm	1	1	1	1	5	5	8	8	8	3	3	1	45
nshine Av. Monthly Dur.	6.3	6.8	6.9	6.7	4	1.4	1.1	1	1.1	2.5	4.1	5	3.9

sbon Portugal 77m

	Jan	Feb	Mar	Apr	May	June	July	Aug	Sep	Oct	Nov	Dec	Year
mperature Daily Max.°C	14	15	17	20	21	25	27	28	26	22	17	15	21
Daily Min.°C	8	8	10	12	13	15	17	17	17	14	11	9	13
Average Monthly °C	11	12	14	16	17	20	22	23	21	18	14	12	17
infall Monthly Total mm	111	76	109	54	44	16	3	4	33	62	93	103	708
nshine Av. Monthly Dur.	4.7	5.9	6	8.3	9.1	10.6	11.4	10.7	8.4	6.7	5.2	4.6	7.7

ndon (Kew) United Kingdom 5m

	Jan	Feb	Mar	Apr	May	June	July	Aug	Sep	Oct	Nov	Dec	Year
mperature Daily Max.°C	6	7	10	13	17	20	22	21	19	14	10	7	14
Daily Min.°C	2	2	3	6	8	12	14	13	11	8	5	4	7
Average Monthly °C	4	5	7	9	12	16	18	17	15	11	8	5	11
infall Monthly Total mm	54	40	37	37	46	45	57	59	49	57	64	48	593
nshine Av. Monthly Dur.	1.7	2.3	3.5	5.7	6.7	7	6.6	6	5	3.3	1.9	1.4	4.3

s Angeles USA 30m

	Jan	Feb	Mar	Apr	May	June	July	Aug	Sep	Oct	Nov	Dec	Year
mperature Daily Max.°C	18	18	18	19	20	22	24	24	24	23	22	19	21
Daily Min.°C	7	8	9	11	13	15	17	17	16	14	11	9	12
Average Monthly °C	12	13	14	15	17	18	21	21	20	18	16	14	17
infall Monthly Total mm	69	74	46	28	3	3	0	0	5	10	28	61	327
nshine Av. Monthly Dur.	6.9	8.2	8.9	8.8	9.5	10.3	11.7	11	10.1	8.6	8.2	7.6	9.2

saka Zambia 1154m

	Jan	Feb	Mar	Apr	May	June	July	Aug	Sep	Oct	Nov	Dec	Year
mperature Daily Max.°C	26	26	26	27	25	23	23	26	29	31	29	27	27
Daily Min.°C	17	17	16	15	12	10	9	11	15	18	18	17	15
Average Monthly °C	22	22	21	21	18	17	16	19	22	25	23	22	21
infall Monthly Total mm	224	173	90	19	3	1	0	1	1	17	85	196	810
nshine Av. Monthly Dur.	5.1	5.4	6.9	8.9	9	9	9.1	9.6	9.5	9	7	5.5	7.8

anaus Brazil 45m

	Jan	Feb	Mar	Apr	May	June	July	Aug	Sep	Oct	Nov	Dec	Year
mperature Daily Max.°C	31	31	31	31	31	31	32	33	34	34	33	32	32
Daily Min.°C	24	24	24	24	24	24	24	24	24	25	25	24	24
Average Monthly °C	28	28	28	27	28	28	28	29	29	29	29	28	28
infall Monthly Total mm	278	278	300	287	193	99	61	41	62	112	165	220	2096
nshine Av. Monthly Dur.	3.9	4	3.6	3.9	5.4	6.9	7.9	8.2	7.5	6.6	5.9	4.9	5.7

exico City Mexico 2309m

	Jan	Feb	Mar	Apr	May	June	July	Aug	Sep	Oct	Nov	Dec	Year
mperature Daily Max.°C	21	23	26	27	26	25	23	24	23	22	21	21	24
Daily Min.°C	5	6	7	9	10	11	11	11	11	9	6	5	8
Average Monthly °C	13	15	16	18	18	18	17	17	17	16	14	13	16
infall Monthly Total mm	8	4	9	23	57	111	160	149	119	46	16	7	709
nshine Av. Monthly Dur.	7.3	8.1	8.5	8.1	7.8	7	6.2	6.4	5.6	6.3	7	7.3	7.1

ami USA 2m

	Jan	Feb	Mar	Apr	May	June	July	Aug	Sep	Oct	Nov	Dec	Year
mperature Daily Max.°C	24	25	27	28	30	31	32	32	31	29	27	25	28
Daily Min.°C	14	15	16	19	21	23	24	24	24	22	18	15	20
Average Monthly °C	19	20	21	23	25	27	28	28	27	25	22	20	24
infall Monthly Total mm	51	48	58	99	163	188	170	178	241	208	71	43	1518
nshine Av. Monthly Dur.	7.7	8.3	8.7	9.4	8.9	8.5	8.7	8.4	7.1	6.5	7.5	7.1	8.1

ontreal Canada 57m

	Jan	Feb	Mar	Apr	May	June	July	Aug	Sep	Oct	Nov	Dec	Year
mperature Daily Max.°C	-6	-4	2	11	18	23	26	25	20	14	5	-3	11
Daily Min.°C	-13	-11	-5	2	9	14	17	16	11	6	0	-9	3
Average Monthly °C	-9	-8	-2	6	13	19	22	20	16	10	3	-6	7
infall Monthly Total mm	87	76	86	83	81	91	98	87	96	84	89	89	1047
nshine Av. Monthly Dur.	2.8	3.4	4.5	5.2	6.7	7.7	8.2	7.7	5.6	4.3	2.4	2.2	5.1

oscow Russia 156m

	Jan	Feb	Mar	Apr	May	June	July	Aug	Sep	Oct	Nov	Dec	Year
mperature Daily Max.°C	-6	-4	1	9	18	22	24	22	17	10	1	-5	9
Daily Min.°C	-14	-16	-11	-1	5	9	12	9	4	-2	-6	-12	-2
Average Monthly °C	-10	-10	-5	4	12	15	18	16	10	4	-2	-8	4
infall Monthly Total mm	31	28	33	35	52	67	74	74	58	51	36	36	575
nshine Av. Monthly Dur.	1	1.9	3.7	5.2	7.8	8.3	8.4	7.1	4.4	2.4	1	0.6	4.4

w Delhi India 220m

	Jan	Feb	Mar	Apr	May	June	July	Aug	Sep	Oct	Nov	Dec	Year
mperature Daily Max.°C	21	24	29	36	41	39	35	34	34	34	28	23	32
Daily Min.°C	6	10	14	20	26	28	27	26	24	17	11	7	18
Average Monthly °C	14	17	22	28	33	34	31	30	29	26	20	15	25
infall Monthly Total mm	25	21	13	8	13	77	178	184	123	10	2	11	665
nshine Av. Monthly Dur.	7.7	8.2	8.2	8.7	9.2	7.9	6	6.3	6.9	9.4	8.7	8.3	8

Perth Australia 60m

	Jan	Feb	Mar	Apr	May	June	July	Aug	Sep	Oct	Nov	Dec	Year
Temperature Daily Max.°C	29	30	27	25	21	18	17	18	19	21	25	27	23
Daily Min.°C	17	18	16	14	12	10	9	9	10	11	14	16	13
Average Monthly °C	23	24	22	19	16	14	13	13	15	16	19	22	18
Rainfall Monthly Total mm	8	13	22	44	128	189	177	145	84	58	19	13	900
Sunshine Av. Monthly Dur.	10.4	9.8	8.8	7.5	5.7	4.8	5.4	6	7.2	8.1	9.6	10.4	7.8

Reykjavik Iceland 18m

	Jan	Feb	Mar	Apr	May	June	July	Aug	Sep	Oct	Nov	Dec	Year
Temperature Daily Max.°C	2	3	5	6	10	13	15	14	12	8	5	4	8
Daily Min.°C	-3	-3	-1	1	4	7	9	8	6	3	0	-2	3
Average Monthly °C	0	0	2	4	7	10	12	11	9	5	3	1	5
Rainfall Monthly Total mm	89	64	62	56	42	42	50	56	67	94	78	79	779
Sunshine Av. Monthly Dur.	0.8	2	3.6	4.5	5.9	6.1	5.8	5.4	3.5	2.3	1.1	0.3	3.7

Santiago Chile 520m

	Jan	Feb	Mar	Apr	May	June	July	Aug	Sep	Oct	Nov	Dec	Year
Temperature Daily Max.°C	30	29	27	24	19	15	15	17	19	22	26	29	23
Daily Min.°C	12	11	10	7	5	3	3	4	6	7	9	11	7
Average Monthly °C	21	20	18	15	12	9	9	10	12	15	17	20	15
Rainfall Monthly Total mm	3	3	5	13	64	84	76	56	31	15	8	5	363
Sunshine Av. Monthly Dur.	10.8	8.9	8.5	5.5	3.6	3.3	3.3	3.6	4.8	6.1	8.7	10.1	6.4

Shanghai China 5m

	Jan	Feb	Mar	Apr	May	June	July	Aug	Sep	Oct	Nov	Dec	Year
Temperature Daily Max.°C	8	8	13	19	24	28	32	32	27	23	17	10	20
Daily Min.°C	-1	0	4	9	14	19	23	23	19	13	7	2	11
Average Monthly °C	3	4	8	14	19	23	27	27	23	18	12	6	15
Rainfall Monthly Total mm	48	59	84	94	94	180	147	142	130	71	51	36	1136
Sunshine Av. Monthly Dur.	4	3.7	4.4	4.8	5.4	4.7	6.9	7.5	5.3	5.6	4.7	4.5	5.1

Sydney Australia 40m

	Jan	Feb	Mar	Apr	May	June	July	Aug	Sep	Oct	Nov	Dec	Year
Temperature Daily Max.°C	26	26	25	22	19	17	17	18	20	22	24	25	22
Daily Min.°C	18	19	17	14	11	9	8	9	11	13	16	17	14
Average Monthly °C	22	22	21	18	15	13	12	13	16	18	20	21	18
Rainfall Monthly Total mm	89	101	127	135	127	117	117	76	74	71	74	74	1182
Sunshine Av. Monthly Dur.	7.5	7	6.4	6.1	5.7	5.3	6.1	7	7.3	7.5	7.5	7.5	6.8

Tehran Iran 1191m

	Jan	Feb	Mar	Apr	May	June	July	Aug	Sep	Oct	Nov	Dec	Year
Temperature Daily Max.°C	9	11	16	21	29	30	37	36	29	24	16	11	22
Daily Min.°C	-1	1	4	10	16	20	23	23	18	12	6	1	11
Average Monthly °C	4	6	10	15	22	25	30	29	23	18	11	6	17
Rainfall Monthly Total mm	37	23	36	31	14	2	1	1	1	5	29	27	207
Sunshine Av. Monthly Dur.	5.9	6.7	7.5	7.4	8.6	11.6	11.2	11	10.1	7.6	6.9	6.3	8.4

Timbuktu Mali 269m

	Jan	Feb	Mar	Apr	May	June	July	Aug	Sep	Oct	Nov	Dec	Year
Temperature Daily Max.°C	31	35	38	41	43	42	38	35	38	40	37	31	37
Daily Min.°C	13	16	18	22	26	27	25	24	24	23	18	14	21
Average Monthly °C	22	25	28	31	34	34	32	30	31	31	28	23	29
Rainfall Monthly Total mm	0	0	0	1	4	20	54	93	31	3	0	0	206
Sunshine Av. Monthly Dur.	9.1	9.6	9.6	9.7	9.8	9.4	9.6	9	9.3	9.5	9.5	8.9	9.4

Tokyo Japan 5m

	Jan	Feb	Mar	Apr	May	June	July	Aug	Sep	Oct	Nov	Dec	Year
Temperature Daily Max.°C	9	9	12	18	22	25	29	30	27	20	16	11	19
Daily Min.°C	-1	-1	3	4	13	17	22	23	19	13	7	1	10
Average Monthly °C	4	4	8	11	18	21	25	26	23	17	11	6	14
Rainfall Monthly Total mm	48	73	101	135	131	182	146	147	217	220	101	61	1562
Sunshine Av. Monthly Dur.	6	5.9	5.7	6	6.2	5	5.8	6.6	4.5	4.4	4.8	5.4	5.5

Tromsø Norway 100m

	Jan	Feb	Mar	Apr	May	June	July	Aug	Sep	Oct	Nov	Dec	Year
Temperature Daily Max.°C	-2	-2	0	3	7	12	16	14	10	5	2	0	5
Daily Min.°C	-6	-6	-5	-2	1	6	9	8	5	1	-2	-4	0
Average Monthly °C	-4	-4	-3	0	4	9	13	11	7	3	0	-2	3
Rainfall Monthly Total mm	96	79	91	65	61	59	56	80	109	115	88	95	994
Sunshine Av. Monthly Dur.	0.1	1.6	2.9	6.1	5.7	6.9	7.9	4.8	3.5	1.7	0.3	0	3.52

Ulan Bator Mongolia 1305m

	Jan	Feb	Mar	Apr	May	June	July	Aug	Sep	Oct	Nov	Dec	Year
Temperature Daily Max.°C	-19	-13	-4	7	13	21	22	21	14	6	-6	-16	4
Daily Min.°C	-32	-29	-22	-8	-2	7	11	8	2	-8	-20	-28	-11
Average Monthly °C	-26	-21	-13	-1	6	14	16	14	8	-1	-13	-22	-4
Rainfall Monthly Total mm	1	1	2	5	10	28	76	51	23	5	5	2	209
Sunshine Av. Monthly Dur.	6.4	7.8	8	7.8	8.3	8.6	8.6	8.2	7.2	6.9	6.1	5.7	7.5

Vancouver Canada 5m

	Jan	Feb	Mar	Apr	May	June	July	Aug	Sep	Oct	Nov	Dec	Year
Temperature Daily Max.°C	6	7	10	14	17	20	23	22	19	14	9	7	14
Daily Min.°C	0	1	3	5	8	11	13	12	10	7	3	2	6
Average Monthly °C	3	4	6	9	13	16	18	17	14	10	6	4	10
Rainfall Monthly Total mm	214	161	151	90	69	65	39	44	83	172	198	243	1529
Sunshine Av. Monthly Dur.	1.6	3	3.8	5.9	7.5	7.4	9.5	8.2	6	3.7	2	1.4	5

Verkhoyansk Russia 137m

	Jan	Feb	Mar	Apr	May	June	July	Aug	Sep	Oct	Nov	Dec	Year
Temperature Daily Max.°C	-47	-40	-20	-1	11	21	24	21	12	-8	-33	-42	-8
Daily Min.°C	-51	-48	-40	-25	-7	4	6	1	-6	-20	-39	-50	-23
Average Monthly °C	-49	-44	-30	-13	2	12	15	11	3	-14	-36	-46	-16
Rainfall Monthly Total mm	7	5	5	4	5	25	33	30	13	11	10	7	155
Sunshine Av. Monthly Dur.	0	2.6	6.9	9.6	9.7	10	9.7	7.5	4.1	2.4	0.6	0	5.4

Washington USA 22m

	Jan	Feb	Mar	Apr	May	June	July	Aug	Sep	Oct	Nov	Dec	Year
Temperature Daily Max.°C	7	8	12	19	25	29	31	30	26	20	14	8	19
Daily Min.°C	-1	-1	2	8	13	18	21	20	16	10	4	-1	9
Average Monthly °C	3	3	7	13	19	24	26	25	21	15	9	4	14
Rainfall Monthly Total mm	84	68	96	85	103	88	108	120	100	78	75	75	1080
Sunshine Av. Monthly Dur.	4.4	5.7	6.7	7.4	8.2	8.8	8.6	8.2	7.5	6.5	5.3	4.5	6.8

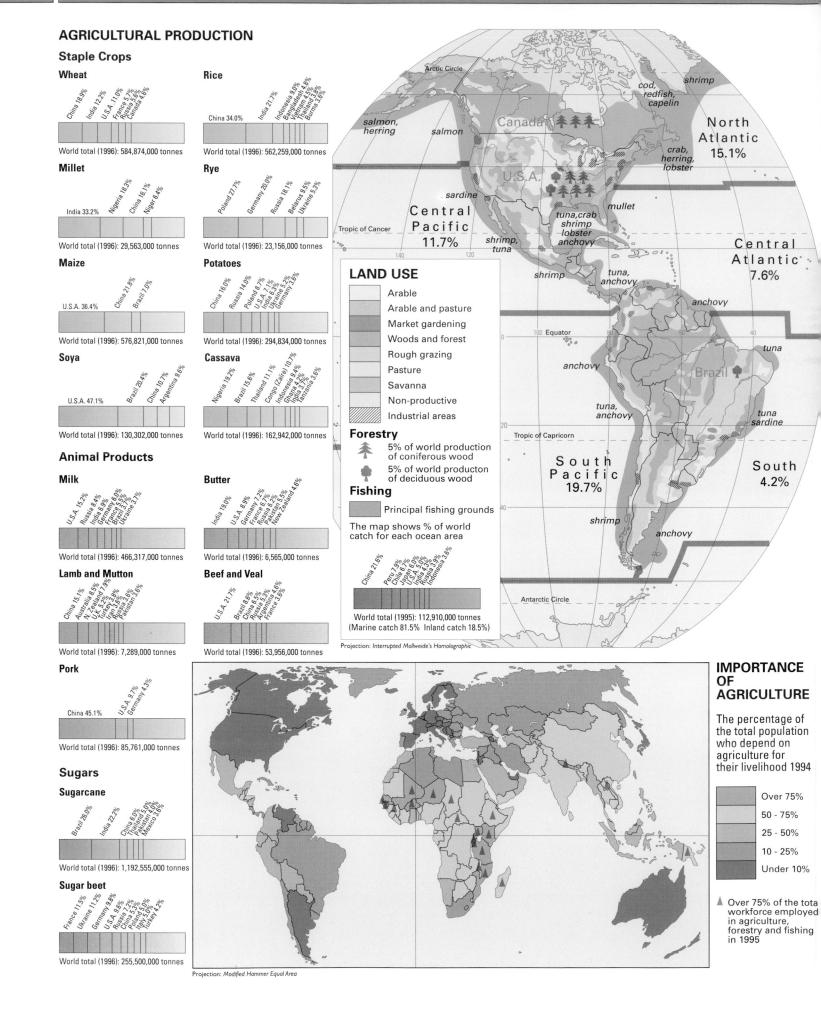

AGRICULTURAL PRODUCTION

Staple Crops

Wheat

China 18.9% · India 12.2% · U.S.A. 11.0% · France 5.7% · Russia 5.6% · Canada 4.6%

World total (1996): 584,874,000 tonnes

Rice

China 34.0% · India 21.7% · Indonesia 9.0% · Bangladesh 4.8% · Vietnam 4.5% · Thailand 3.6% · Burma 3.6%

World total (1996): 562,259,000 tonnes

Millet

India 33.2% · Nigeria 18.3% · China 16.1% · Niger 6.4%

World total (1996): 29,563,000 tonnes

Rye

Poland 27.7% · Germany 20.0% · Russia 18.1% · Belarus 9.5% · Ukraine 5.3%

World total (1996): 23,156,000 tonnes

Maize

U.S.A. 36.4% · China 21.8% · Brazil 7.0%

World total (1996): 576,821,000 tonnes

Potatoes

China 16.0% · Russia 14.0% · Poland 8.7% · U.S.A. 7.1% · Ukraine 5.2% · India 6.3% · Germany 3.6%

World total (1996): 294,834,000 tonnes

Soya

U.S.A. 47.1% · Brazil 20.4% · China 10.7% · Argentina 9.6%

World total (1996): 130,302,000 tonnes

Cassava

Nigeria 19.2% · Brazil 15.6% · Thailand 11.1% · Congo (Zaire) 10.7% · Indonesia 9.4% · Ghana 4.2% · India 3.7% · Tanzania 3.6%

World total (1996): 162,942,000 tonnes

Animal Products

Milk

U.S.A. 15.2% · Russia 8.4% · India 6.9% · Germany 6.0% · France 5.5% · Brazil 3.5% · Ukraine 3.7%

World total (1996): 466,317,000 tonnes

Butter

India 19.0% · U.S.A. 8.9% · Germany 7.2% · France 6.7% · Russia 6.6% · Pakistan 6.2% · New Zealand 4.6%

World total (1996): 6,565,000 tonnes

Lamb and Mutton

China 15.1% · Australia 8.5% · N. Zealand 7.9% · Turkey 3.9% · U.K. 5.5% · Iran 3.6% · Pakistan 3.6%

World total (1996): 7,289,000 tonnes

Beef and Veal

U.S.A. 21.7% · Brazil 8.6% · China 6.5% · Russia 5.3% · Argentina 4.6% · France 3.6%

World total (1996): 53,956,000 tonnes

Pork

China 45.1% · U.S.A. 9.7% · Germany 4.3%

World total (1996): 85,761,000 tonnes

Sugars

Sugarcane

Brazil 26.0% · India 22.2% · China 6.0% · Thailand 5.0% · Pakistan 4.0% · Mexico 3.6%

World total (1996): 1,192,555,000 tonnes

Sugar beet

France 11.5% · Ukraine 11.2% · Germany 9.8% · U.S.A. 9.6% · Russia 7.2% · China 5.3% · Poland 5.0% · Italy 5.0% · Turkey 4.2%

World total (1996): 255,500,000 tonnes

Projection: *Modified Hammer Equal Area*

LAND USE

- Arable
- Arable and pasture
- Market gardening
- Woods and forest
- Rough grazing
- Pasture
- Savanna
- Non-productive
- Industrial areas

Forestry

🌲 5% of world production of coniferous wood

🌳 5% of world producton of deciduous wood

Fishing

Principal fishing grounds

The map shows % of world catch for each ocean area

China 21.6% · Peru 7.9% · Chile 6.7% · Japan 5.0% · U.S.A. 5.0% · India 4.3% · Russia 4.3% · Indonesia 3.6%

World total (1995): 112,910,000 tonnes
(Marine catch 81.5% Inland catch 18.5%)

Projection: *Interrupted Mollweide's Homolographic*

Map labels

Arctic Circle

cod, redfish, capelin · shrimp

salmon, herring · salmon · Canada

North Atlantic 15.1%

crab, herring, lobster

U.S.A.

sardine · mullet · tuna,crab shrimp lobster anchovy

Central Pacific 11.7%

Tropic of Cancer

shrimp, tuna

Central Atlantic 7.6%

shrimp · tuna, anchovy · anchovy

Equator

anchovy · Brazil · tuna

tuna, anchovy · tuna sardine

Tropic of Capricorn

South Pacific 19.7%

South 4.2%

shrimp · anchovy

Antarctic Circle

IMPORTANCE OF AGRICULTURE

The percentage of the total population who depend on agriculture for their livelihood 1994

- Over 75%
- 50 – 75%
- 25 – 50%
- 10 – 25%
- Under 10%

▲ Over 75% of the total workforce employed in agriculture, forestry and fishing in 1995

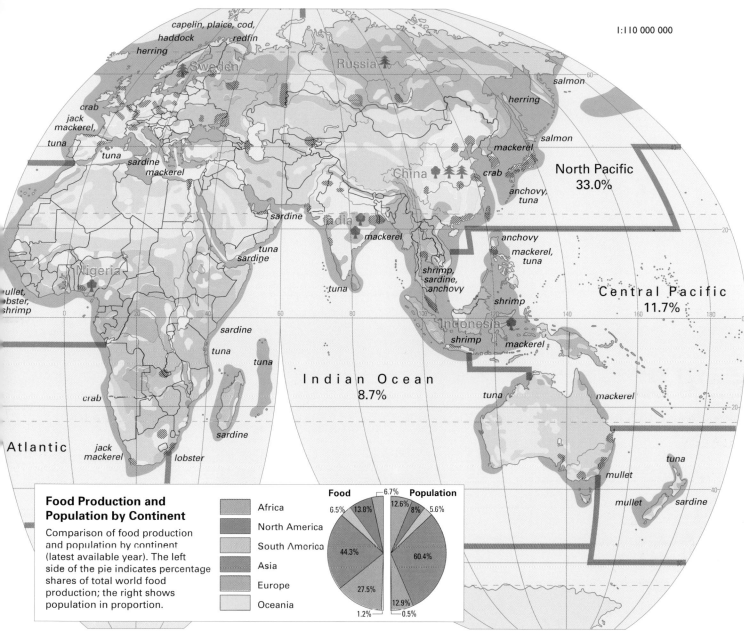

1:110 000 000

capelin, plaice, cod,
haddock   redfin
herring

Sweden

Russia

crab
jack
mackerel,
tuna

tuna

tuna

sardine
mackerel

salmon

herring

salmon

China

mackerel

crab

North Pacific
33.0%

anchovy,
tuna

sardine

India

mackerel

anchovy

mackerel,
tuna

Central Pacific
11.7%

Nigeria

tuna
sardine

tuna

shrimp,
sardine,
anchovy

shrimp

mullet,
lobster,
shrimp

sardine

tuna

tuna

Indonesia

shrimp

mackerel

Indian Ocean
8.7%

tuna

mackerel

crab

sardine

Atlantic

jack
mackerel

lobster

tuna

mullet

mullet

sardine

Food Production and Population by Continent

Comparison of food production and population by continent (latest available year). The left side of the pie indicates percentage shares of total world food production; the right shows population in proportion.

Africa
North America
South America
Asia
Europe
Oceania

Food   6.7%   **Population**
6.5% 13.8%   12.6% 8% 5.6%

44.3%   60.4%

27.5%   12.9%
1.2%   0.5%

TRADE IN AGRICULTURAL PRODUCTS

Balance of trade in agricultural products (food and live animals) by value (latest available year)

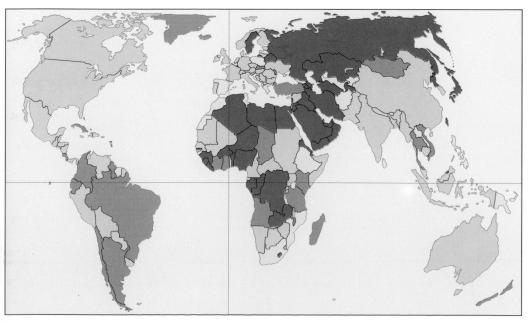

50% more exports than imports
10% more exports than imports
10% either side
10% more imports than exports
50% more imports than exports

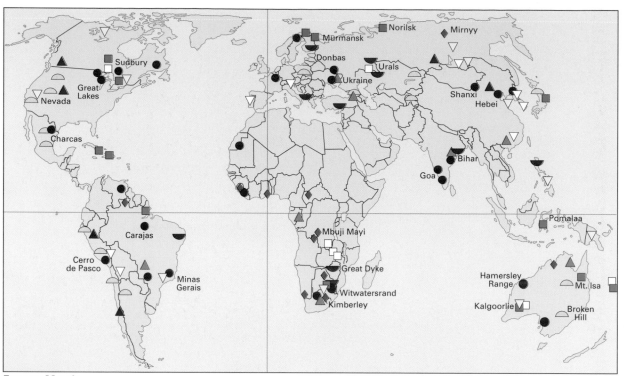

Precious Metals

▽ Gold
World total (1994)
2 290 tonnes

South Africa	25.3%
U.S.A.	14.2%
Australia	11.2%
Russia	6.4%
Canada	6.4%

◠ Silver
World total (1994)
13 900 tonnes

Mexico	16.8%
Peru	12.2%
U.S.A.	10.6%
Australia	7.6%
Chile	7.1%

◆ Diamonds
World total (1994)
106 000 000 carats

Australia	34.0%
Russia	18.9%
Congo (Zaïre)	16.8%
Botswana	15.6%
South Africa	8.0%

Ferrous Metals

● Iron Ore		■ Nickel		◗ Chrome		▲ Manganese		☐ Cobalt		▲ Molybdenum		▽ Tungsten	
World total (1994)		World total (1994)		World total (1994)		World total (1994)		World total (1994)		World total (1994)		World total (1994)	
995 000 000 tonnes		810 000 tonnes		9 600 000 tonnes		22 180 000 tonnes		18 500 tonnes		104 000 tonnes		25 500 tonnes	
China	24.1%	Russia	22.2%	South Africa	37.4%	Ukraine	32.1%	Canada	23.4%	U.S.A.	45.0%	China	64.7%
Brazil	16.7%	Japan	13.7%	Kazakstan	21.0%	China	18.8%	Zambia	18.9%	China	16.8%	Russia	15.7%
Australia	12.9%	Canada	13.0%	India	9.5%	South Africa	14.4%	Russia	17.8%	Chile	15.4%	Portugal	3.9%
Russia	7.4%	Norway	8.4%	Turkey	8.2%	Gabon	10.9%	Australia	11.4%	Canada	9.2%	North Korea	3.5%
U.S.A.	5.9%	Australia	5.7%	Finland	6.0%	Brazil	7.7%	Congo (Zaïre)	10.8%	Russia	4.3%	Peru	3.1%

Fertilizers

▪ Nitrates
World total (1993)
79 932 000 tonnes

China	20.0%
U.S.A.	17.2%
India	9.3%
Russia	7.1%
Canada	3.7%

△ Phosphates
World total (1994)
37 900 000 tonnes

U.S.A.	31.9%
China	18.5%
Morocco	15.6%
Russia	7.4%
Tunisia	4.3%

▽ Potash
World total (1994)
22 500 000 tonnes

Canada	35.7%
Germany	14.6%
Belarus	11.4%
Russia	11.0%
U.S.A.	6.2%

Non-Ferrous Metals

▪ Copper		▲ Lead		● Bauxite		▽ Tin		◆ Zinc		◡ Mercury	
World total (1994)		World total (1994)		World total (1994)		World total (1994)		World total (1994)		World total (1994)	
9 750 000 tonnes		5 380 000 tonnes		107 000 000 tonnes		199 000 tonnes		7 360 000 tonnes		1 760 tonnes	
U.S.A.	17.5%	U.S.A.	23.4%	Australia	39.0%	China	26.6%	China	13.2%	China	28.4%
Chile	13.1%	France	8.3%	Guinea	13.5%	Malaysia	21.1%	Japan	9.7%	Algeria	27.0%
Japan	11.5%	China	7.6%	Brazil	7.6%	Indonesia	15.6%	Canada	9.4%	Spain	17.0%
Russia	6.0%	U.K.	6.4%	India	5.0%	Brazil	15.2%	Germany	4.9%	Kyrgyzstan	11.4%
Canada	5.7%	Germany	6.2%	China	3.5%	Bolivia	7.7%	U.S.A.	4.8%	Finland	5.7%

Projection: *Modified Hammer Equal Area*

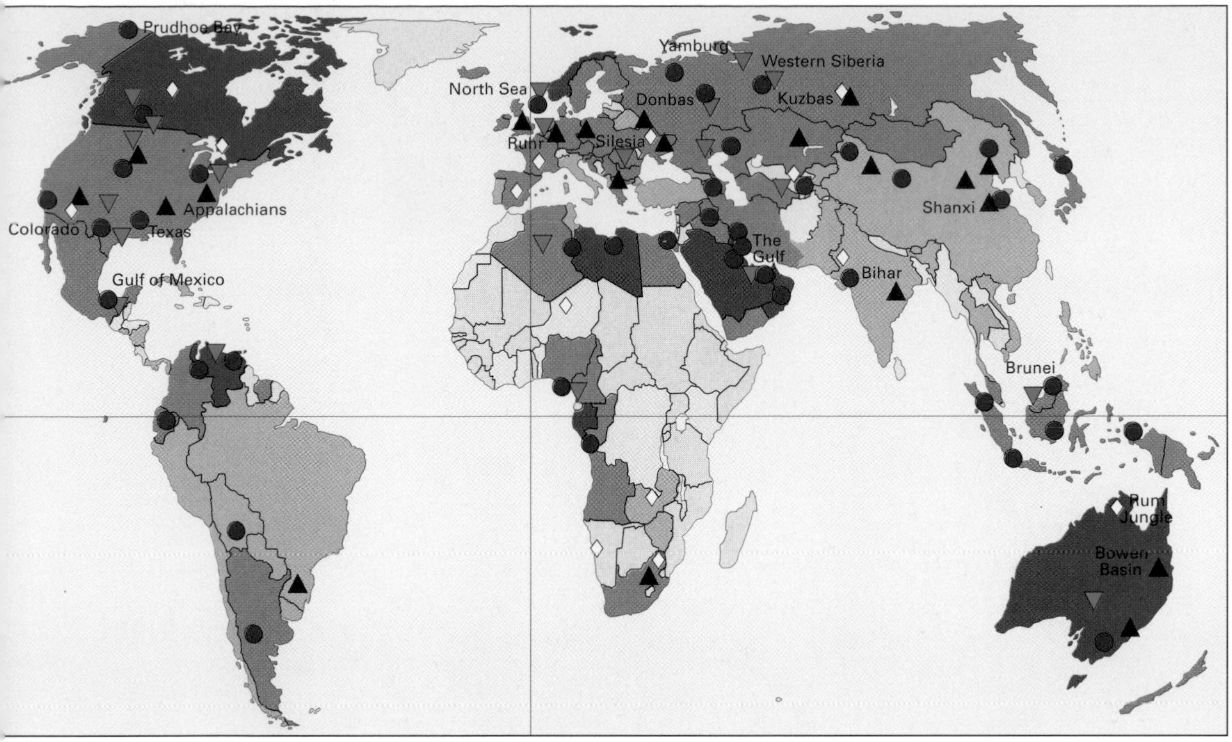

ENERGY PRODUCTION

Primary energy production expressed in kilograms of coal equivalent per person 1994

- Over 10 000 kg per person
- 1 000 – 10 000 kg per person
- 100 – 1 000 kg per person
- 10 – 100 kg per person
- Under 10 kg per person

- ● Oil
- ▼ Natural gas
- ▲ Coal and lignite
- ◇ Uranium *(the fuel used to generate nuclear power)*

In developing countries traditional fuels are still very important. Sometimes called biomass fuels, they include wood, charcoal and dried dung. The pie graph for Nigeria at the foot of the page shows their importance.

Map labels: Prudhoe Bay, North Sea, Yamburg, Western Siberia, Donbas, Kuzbas, Ruhr, Silesia, Colorado, Texas, Appalachians, Gulf of Mexico, The Gulf, Shanxi, Bihar, Brunei, Rum Jungle, Bowen Basin

Oil		Natural Gas		Coal (bituminous)		Coal (lignite)		Uranium		Nuclear Power		Hydro-Electric Power	
World total (1994) 3 183 500 000 tonnes		World total (1993) 2 658 000 000 tonnes of coal equivalent		World total (1993) 3 160 000 000 tonnes		World total (1993) 1 265 000 000 tonnes		World total (1993) 32 532 tonnes (metal content)		World total (1994) 820 000 000 tonnes of coal equivalent		World total (1994) 922 000 000 tonnes of coal equivalent	
Saudi Arabia	13.2%	Canada	28.2%	China	36.0%	U.S.A.	23.7%	Canada	28.2%	U.S.A.	31.0%	Canada	12.8%
U.S.A.	12.6%	Nigeria	9.0%	U.S.A.	17.6%	Germany	17.5%	Niger	9.0%	France	16.3%	U.S.A.	12.2%
Russia	9.9%	Kazakstan	8.3%	India	7.9%	Russia	9.1%	Kazakstan	8.3%	Japan	11.8%	Former U.S.S.R.	10.4%
Iran	5.7%	Uzbekistan	8.0%	Russia	6.3%	China	7.4%	Uzbekistan	8.0%	Former U.S.S.R.	7.9%	Brazil	10.3%
Mexico	4.9%	Russia	7.4%	Australia South Africa }	5.8%	Poland	5.4%	Russia	7.4%	Germany	6.9%	China	6.9%

ENERGY CONSUMPTION

Primary energy consumption expressed in kilograms of coal equivalent per person 1994

- Over 10 000 kg per person
- 5 000 – 10 000 kg per person
- 1 000 – 5 000 kg per person
- 100 – 1 000 kg per person
- Under 100 kg per person

Energy consumption by Continent 1991

		Change 1990-91
Europe*	38.3%	(-0.2%)
North America	30.0%	(+2.4%)
Asia	25.0%	(+1.9%)
South America	3.0%	(-2.9%)
Africa	2.4%	(-0.4%)
Australasia	1.3%	(no change)
*includes former U.S.S.R.		

Projection: Modified Hammer Equal Area

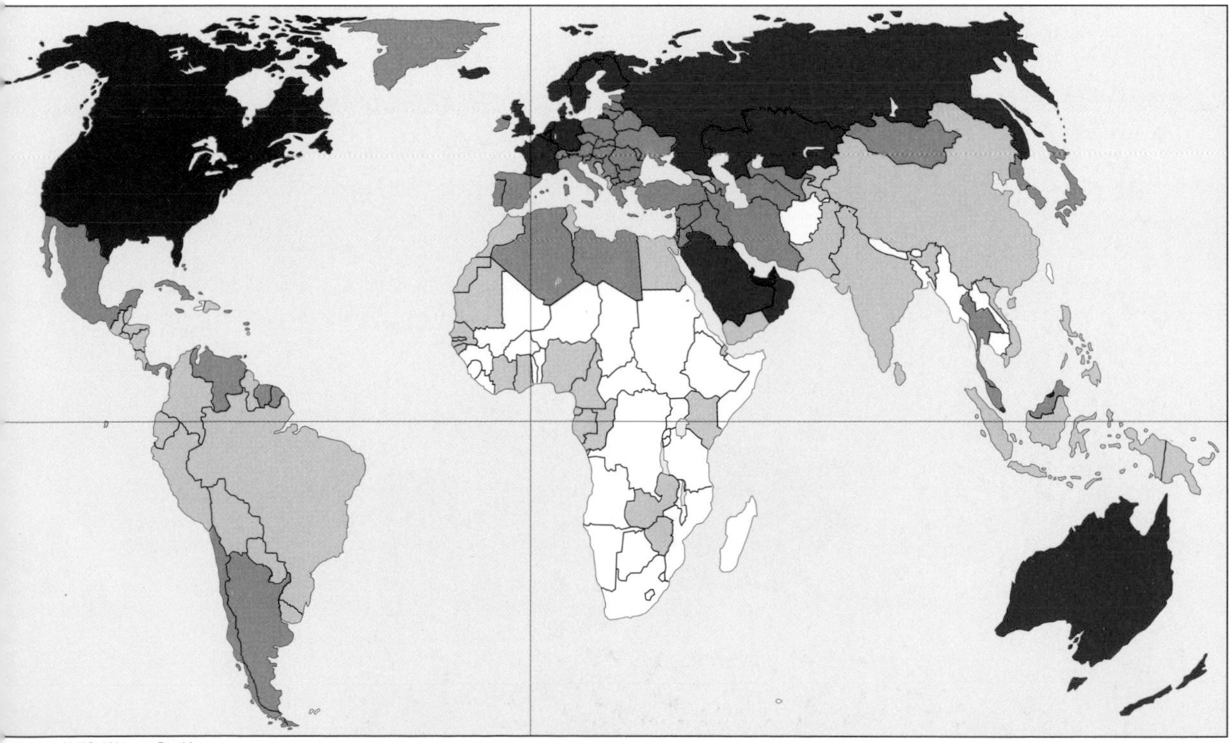

TYPE OF ENERGY CONSUMED BY SELECTED COUNTRIES 1993

- Coal & Lignite
- Oil
- Natural gas
- Hydro-electricity
- Nuclear electricity
- Traditional Fuels

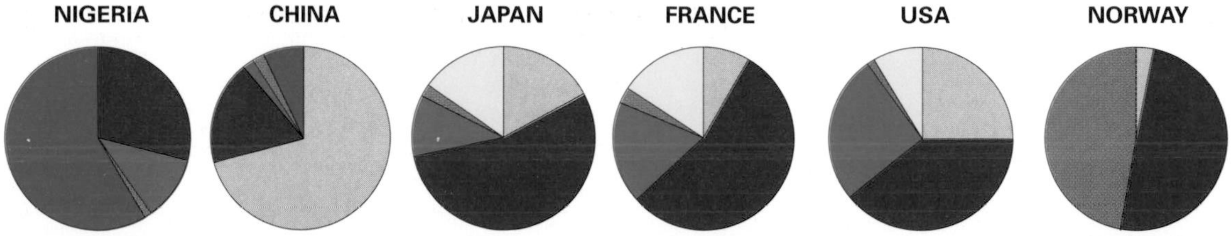

NIGERIA 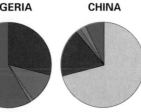 **CHINA** 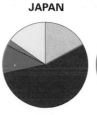 **JAPAN** **FRANCE** **USA** 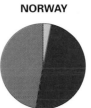 **NORWAY**

CARTOGRAPHY BY PHILIP'S. COPYRIGHT GEORGE PHILIP LTD.

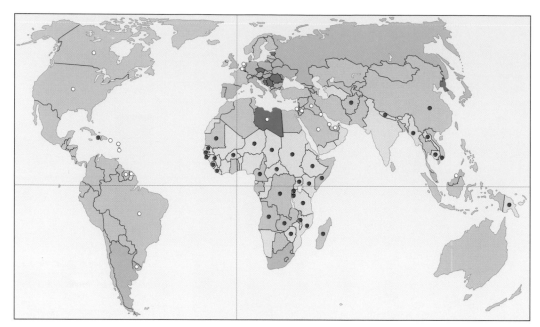

EMPLOYMENT IN INDUSTRY

Percentage of total workforce employed in manufacturing and mining 1995

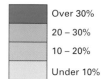

- Over 30%
- 20 – 30%
- 10 – 20%
- Under 10%

●   Over two thirds of total workforce employed in agriculture

○   Over a third of total workforce employed in service industries (work in offices, shops, tourism, transport, construction and government)

INDUSTRIAL PRODUCTION

Industrial output (mining, manufacturing, construction, energy and water production), top 40 nations, US $ billion (1991)

1.	U.S.A.	1,627	21. Saudi Arabia	56
2.	Japan	1,412	22. Indonesia	48
3.	Germany	614	23. Spain	47
4.	Italy	380	24. Argentina	46
5.	France	348	25. Poland	39
6.	U.K.	324	26. Norway	38
7.	Former U.S.S.R.	250	27. Finland	37
8.	Brazil	161	28. Thailand	36
9.	China	155	29. Turkey	33
10.	South Korea	127	30. Denmark	31
11.	Canada	117	31. Israel	23
12.	Australia	93	32. Iran	20
	Netherlands	93	33. Ex- Czechoslovakia	19
14.	Taiwan	86	34. Hong Kong	17
15.	Mexico	85	Portugal (1989)	17
16.	Sweden	70	36. Algeria	16
17.	Switzerland (1989)	61	Greece	16
18.	India	60	38. Iraq	15
19.	Austria	59	Philippines	15
	Belgium	59	Singapore	15

Graphs show the top ten producing countries for selected industrial goods.

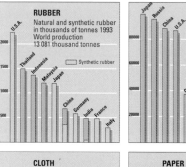

RUBBER
Natural and synthetic rubber in thousands of tonnes 1993
World production 13 081 thousand tonnes

☐ Synthetic rubber

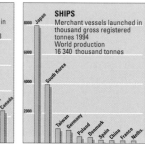

STEEL
Production in thousand tonnes 1993

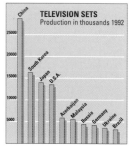

SHIPS
Merchant vessels launched in thousand gross registered tonnes 1994
World production 16 340 thousand tonnes

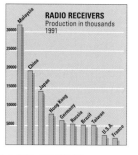

TELEVISION SETS
Production in thousands 1992

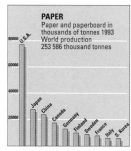

CLOTH
Includes woven cotton and wool, silk, linen, jute, and man-made fabrics in thousands of tonnes 1991

☐ Synthetic fabrics

PAPER
Paper and paperboard in thousands of tonnes 1993
World production 253 586 thousand tonnes

CARS
Passenger cars in thousands 1993

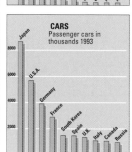

RADIO RECEIVERS
Production in thousands 1991

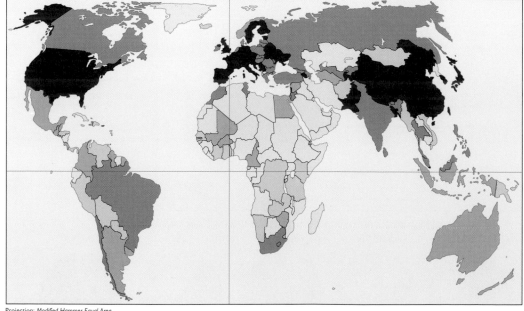

INDUSTRY AND TRADE

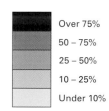

Manufactured goods (inc. machinery & transport) as a percentage of total exports (latest available year)

- Over 75%
- 50 – 75%
- 25 – 50%
- 10 – 25%
- Under 10%

The Far East and South-East Asia (Japan 98.3%, Macau 97.8%, Taiwan 92.7%, Hong Kong 93.0%, South Korea 93.4%) are most dominant, but many countries in Europe (e.g. Slovenia 92.4%) are also heavily dependent on manufactured goods.

DEPENDENCE ON TRADE

Value of exports as a percentage
of G.N.P. (Gross National Product)
1995

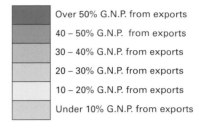

Over 50% G.N.P. from exports

40 – 50% G.N.P. from exports

30 – 40% G.N.P. from exports

20 – 30% G.N.P. from exports

10 – 20% G.N.P. from exports

Under 10% G.N.P. from exports

● Most dependent on industrial
exports (over 75% of total exports)

○ Most dependent on fuel exports
(over 75% of total exports)

● Most dependent on metal and
mineral exports (over 75% of total
exports)

BALANCE OF TRADE

Value of exports in proportion to
the value of imports 1995

Exports exceed
imports by:

More than 40%

10 – 40%

10% either side

10 – 40%

Imports exceed
exports by:

More than 40%

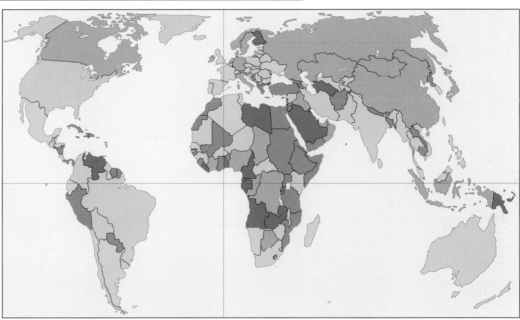

SHARE OF WORLD TRADE

Percentage share of total world
exports by value 1995

Over 10% of world trade

5 – 10% of world trade

1 – 5% of world trade

0.5 – 1% of world trade

0.1 – 0.5% of world trade

Under 0.1% of world trade

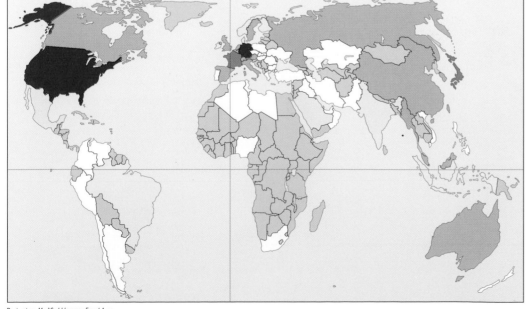

Projection: *Modified Hammer Equal Area*

CARTOGRAPHY BY PHILIP'S. COPYRIGHT GEORGE PHILIP LTD

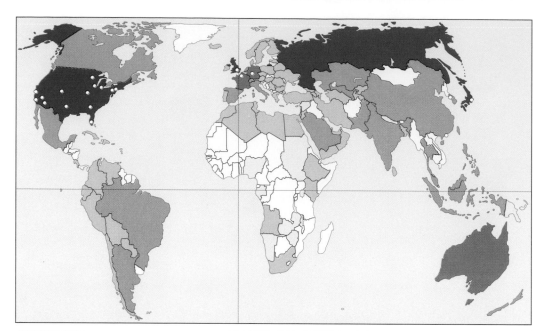

AIR TRAVEL

Passenger kilometres flown 1994

Passenger kilometres are the number of passengers (international and domestic) multiplied by the distance flown by each passenger from airport of origin.

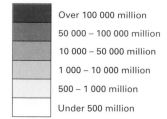

- Over 100 000 million
- 50 000 – 100 000 million
- 10 000 – 50 000 million
- 1 000 – 10 000 million
- 500 – 1 000 million
- Under 500 million

○   Major airports (handling over 25 million passengers in 1995)

World's busiest airports (total passengers)		World's busiest airports (international passengers)	
1. Chicago	(O'Hare)	1. London	(Heathrow)
2. Atlanta	(Hartsfield)	2. London	(Gatwick)
3. Dallas	(Dallas/Ft Worth)	3. Frankfurt	(International)
4. London	(Heathrow)	4. New York	(Kennedy)
5. Los Angeles	(Intern'l)	5. Paris	(De Gaulle)

TOURISM

Tourism receipts as a percentage of G.N.P. (Gross National Product) 1994

- Over 10% of G.N.P from tourism
- 5 – 10% of G.N.P. from tourism
- 2.5 – 5% of G.N.P. from tourism
- 1 – 2.5% of G.N.P. from tourism
- 0.5 – 1% of G.N.P. from tourism
- Under 0.5% of G.N.P. from tourism

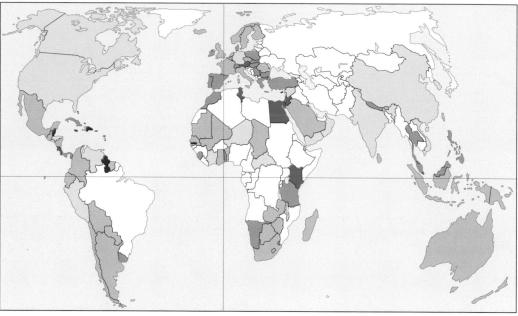

Countries spending the most on promoting tourism, millions of US $ (1996)		Fastest growing tourist destinations, % change in receipts (1994–5)	
Australia	88	South Korea	49%
Spain	79	Czech Republic	27%
U.K.	79	India	21%
France	73	Russia	19%
Singapore	54	Philippines	18%

TOURIST DESTINATIONS

- ■ Cultural & historical centres
- □ Coastal resorts
- □ Ski resorts
- ■ Centres of entertainment
- ■ Places of pilgrimage
- ■ Places of great natural beauty

— Popular holiday cruise routes

Projection: *Modified Hammer Equal Area*

TIME ZONES

Note: Certain of the time zones are affected by the incidence of "Summer Time" in countries where it is adopted.

Legend:
- Zones using Greenwich Mean Time
- Zones slow of Greenwich Mean Time
- Half hour zones
- Zones fast of Greenwich Mean Time
- - - - - International boundaries
- —— Time zone boundaries
- —— International date line
- —— Selected air routes
- 10PM — Actual Solar Time when noon at Greenwich is shown along the top of the map
- 10 — Hours slow or fast of Greenwich Mean Time
- Equatorial scale: 1:220 000 000

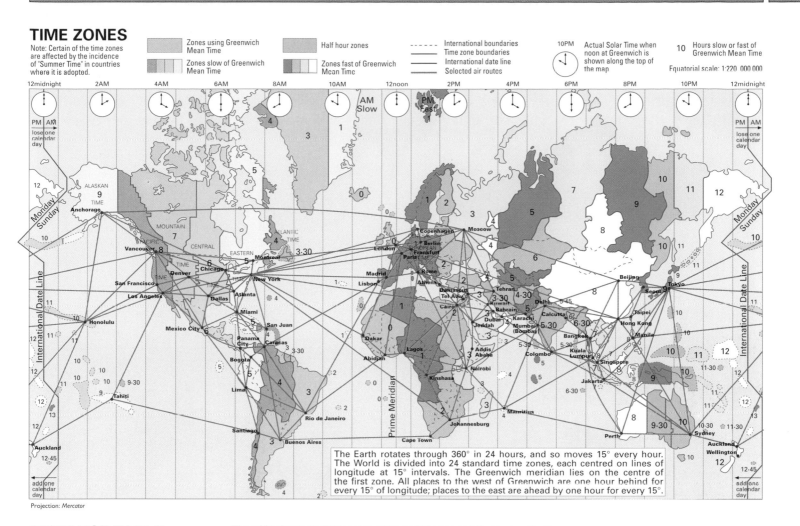

> The Earth rotates through 360° in 24 hours, and so moves 15° every hour. The World is divided into 24 standard time zones, each centred on lines of longitude at 15° intervals. The Greenwich meridian lies on the centre of the first zone. All places to the west of Greenwich are one hour behind for every 15° of longitude; places to the east are ahead by one hour for every 15°.

Projection: *Mercator*

DISTANCE TABLE

The table shows air distances in miles and kilometres between twenty-four major cities. Known as 'Great Circle' distances, these measure the shortest routes between cities, which aircraft use where possible.

Miles (upper-right triangle)

	Beijing	Bogotá	Buenos Aires	Cairo	Calcutta	Caracas	Chicago	Hong Kong	Honolulu	Johannesburg	Lagos	London	Los Angeles	Mexico City	Moscow	Nairobi	New York	Paris	Rio de Janeiro	Rome	Singapore	Sydney	Tokyo	Wellington	City
		9263	11972	4688	2031	8947	6588	1220	6070	7276	7119	5057	6251	7742	3600	5727	6020	5110	10773	5049	2783	5561	1304	6700	Beijing
			2911	6971	10223	637	2710	10480	5697	7125	5319	5262	3478	1961	6758	7672	2481	5358	2820	5831	11990	8903	8851	7527	Bogota
				7341	10268	3167	5599	11481	7558	5025	4919	6917	6122	4591	8374	6463	5298	6867	1214	6929	9867	7332	11410	6202	Buenos Aires
					3541	6340	6127	5064	8838	3894	2432	2180	7580	7687	1803	2197	5605	1994	6149	1325	5137	8959	5947	10268	Cairo
						9609	7978	1653	7048	5256	5727	4946	8152	9494	3438	3839	7921	4883	9366	4486	1800	5678	3195	7055	Calcutta
							2502	10166	6009	6847	4810	4664	3612	2228	6175	7173	2131	4738	2825	5196	11407	9534	8801	8154	Caracas
								7783	4247	8689	5973	3949	1742	1694	4971	8005	711	4132	5311	4809	9369	9243	6299	8358	Chicago
									5543	6669	7360	5980	7232	8775	4439	5453	8047	5984	11001	5769	1615	4582	1786	5857	Hong Kong
										11934	10133	7228	2558	3781	7036	10739	4958	7437	8290	8026	6721	5075	3854	4669	Honolulu
											2799	5637	10362	9063	5692	1818	7979	5426	4420	4811	5381	6860	8418	7308	Johannesburg
												3118	7713	6879	3886	2366	5268	2929	3750	2510	6925	9643	8376	9973	Lagos
													5442	5552	1552	4237	3463	212	5778	889	6743	10558	5942	11691	London
														1549	6070	9659	2446	5645	6310	6331	8776	7502	5475	6719	Los Angeles
															6664	9207	2090	5717	4780	6365	10321	8058	7024	6897	Mexico City
																3942	4666	1545	7184	1477	5237	9008	4651	10283	Moscow
																	7358	4029	5548	3350	4635	7552	6996	8490	Nairobi
																		3626	4832	4280	9531	9935	6741	8951	New York
																			5708	687	6671	10539	6038	11798	Paris
																				5725	9763	8389	11551	7367	Rio de Janeiro
																					6229	10143	6127	11523	Rome
																						3915	3306	5298	Singapore
																							4861	1383	Sydney
																								5762	Tokyo
																									Wellington

Kms (lower-left triangle)

Kms	Beijing	Bogotá	Buenos Aires	Cairo	Calcutta	Caracas	Chicago	Hong Kong	Honolulu	Johannesburg	Lagos	London	Los Angeles	Mexico City	Moscow	Nairobi	New York	Paris	Rio de Janeiro	Rome	Singapore	Sydney	Tokyo
Beijing																							
Bogota	14908																						
Buenos Aires	19268	4685																					
Cairo	7544	11218	11814																				
Calcutta	3269	16453	16524	5699																			
Caracas	14399	1026	5096	10203	15464																		
Chicago	10603	4361	9011	9860	12839	4027																	
Hong Kong	1963	16865	18478	8150	2659	16360	12526																
Honolulu	8160	9169	12164	14223	11343	9670	6836	8921															
Johannesburg	11710	11467	8088	6267	8459	11019	13984	10732	19206														
Lagos	11457	8561	7916	3915	9216	7741	9612	11845	16308	4505													
London	8138	8468	11131	3508	7961	7507	6356	9623	11632	9071	5017												
Los Angeles	10060	5596	9852	12200	13120	5812	2804	11639	4117	16676	12414	8758											
Mexico City	12460	3156	7389	12372	15280	3586	2726	14122	6085	14585	11071	8936	2493										
Moscow	5794	10877	13477	2902	5534	9938	8000	7144	11323	9161	6254	2498	9769	10724									
Nairobi	9216	12347	10402	3536	6179	11544	12883	8776	17282	2927	3807	6819	15544	14818	6344								
New York	10988	3993	8526	9020	12747	3430	1145	12950	7980	12841	8477	5572	3936	3264	7510	11842							
Paris	8217	8622	11051	3210	7858	7625	6650	9630	11968	8732	4714	342	9085	9200	2486	6485	5836						
Rio de Janeiro	17338	4539	1953	9896	15073	4546	8547	17704	13342	7113	6035	9299	10155	7693	11562	8928	7777	9187					
Rome	8126	9383	11151	2133	7219	8363	7739	9284	12916	7743	4039	1431	10243	2376	5391	6888	1105	9214					
Singapore	4478	19296	15879	8267	2897	18359	15078	2599	10816	8660	11145	10852	14123	16610	8428	7460	15339	10737	15712	10025			
Sydney	8949	14327	11800	14418	9138	15343	14875	7374	8168	11040	15519	16992	12073	12969	14497	12153	15989	16962	13501	16324	6300		
Tokyo	2099	14245	18362	9571	5141	14164	10137	2874	6202	13547	13480	9562	8811	11304	7485	11260	10849	9718	18589	9861	5321	7823	
Wellington	10782	12113	9981	16524	11354	13122	13451	9427	7513	11761	16050	18814	10814	11100	16549	13664	14405	18987	11855	18545	8526	2226	9273

CARTOGRAPHY BY PHILIP'S.

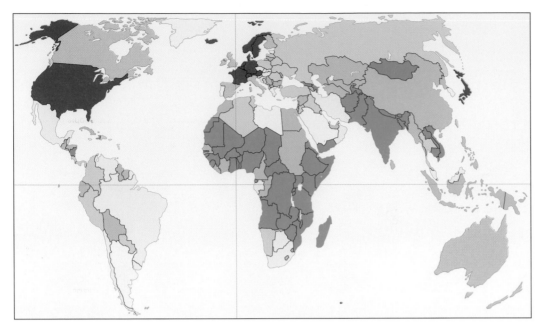

WEALTH

The value of total production in 1995 divided by the population.
(The Gross National Product per capita)

	Over 400% of world average
	200 – 400% of world average
	100 – 200% of world average

World average wealth per person $5 714

	50 – 100% of world average
	25 – 50% of world average
	10 – 25% of world average
	Under 10% of world average

Top 5 countries		Bottom 5 countries	
Luxembourg	$41 210	Mozambique	$80
Switzerland	$40 630	Ethiopia	$100
Japan	$39 640	Congo (Zaïre)	$120
Norway	$31 250	Tanzania	$120
Denmark	$29 890	Burundi	$160
		U.K.	$18 700

CAR OWNERSHIP

Number of people per car
(latest available year)

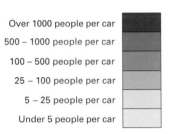

	Over 1000 people per car
	500 – 1000 people per car
	100 – 500 people per car
	25 – 100 people per car
	5 – 25 people per car
	Under 5 people per car

Most people per car		Most cars (millions)	
Nepal	4247	U.S.A.	143.8
Bangladesh	2618	Germany	39.1
Cambodia	2328	Japan	39.0
Somalia	1790	Italy	29.6
Ethiopia	1423	France	24.0

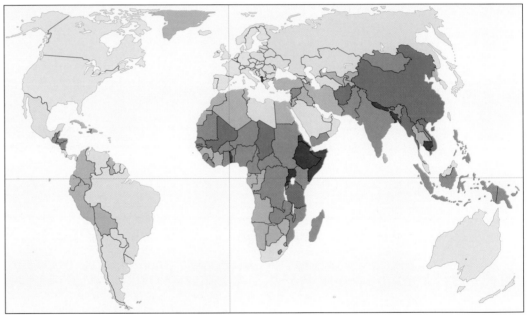

HUMAN DEVELOPMENT INDEX

The Human Development Index (H.D.I.) 1994 includes social and economic indicators and is calculated by the U.N. Development Programme as a measure of national human progress. Wealthy developed countries measure highest on the index.

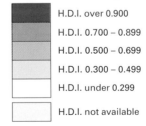

	H.D.I. over 0.900
	H.D.I. 0.700 – 0.899
	H.D.I. 0.500 – 0.699
	H.D.I. 0.300 – 0.499
	H.D.I. under 0.299
	H.D.I. not available

Top 5 countries		Bottom 5 countries	
Canada	0.960	Mali	0.229
France	0.946	Burkina Faso	0.221
Norway	0.943	Niger	0.206
U.S.A.	0.942	Rwanda	0.187
Iceland	0.942	Sierra Leone	0.176
		U.K.	0.931

Projection: *Modified Hammer Equal Area*

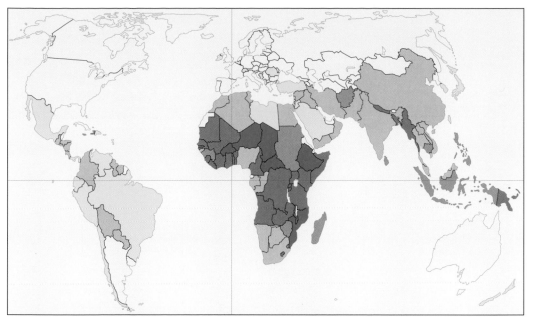

HEALTH CARE

Number of people per doctor 1993

- Over 25 000 people per doctor
- 10 000 – 25 000 people per doctor
- 5 000 – 10 000 people per doctor
- 1 000 – 5 000 people per doctor
- 500 – 1 000 people per doctor
- Under 500 people per doctor

Most people per doctor 1993		Least people per doctor 1993	
Niger	53 986	Georgia	182
Malawi	44 205	Italy	207
Mozambique	36 225	Israel	220
Burkina Faso	34 804	Russia	222
Ethiopia	32 499	Ukraine	227
		U.K.	300

ILLITERACY & EDUCATION

Percentage of total population unable to read or write 1995

- Over 75% of population illiterate
- 50 – 75% of population illiterate
- 25 – 50% of population illiterate
- 10 – 25% of population illiterate
- Under 10% of population illiterate

• Less than 6 years compulsory education per child

Educational expenditure per person (latest available year)

Top five countries		Bottom five countries	
Norway	$2,820	Congo (Zaïre)	$1
Denmark	$2,450	Somalia	$2
Switzerland	$2,256	Sierra Leone	$2
Japan	$1,853	Nigeria	$3
Finland	$1,706	Haiti	$3
U.K.	$1,009		

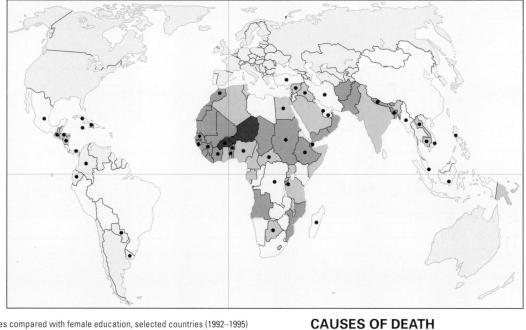

FERTILITY & EDUCATION
Fertility rates compared with female education, selected countries (1992–1995)

- Fertility rate: average number of children borne per woman
- Percentage of females aged 12 – 17 in secondary education

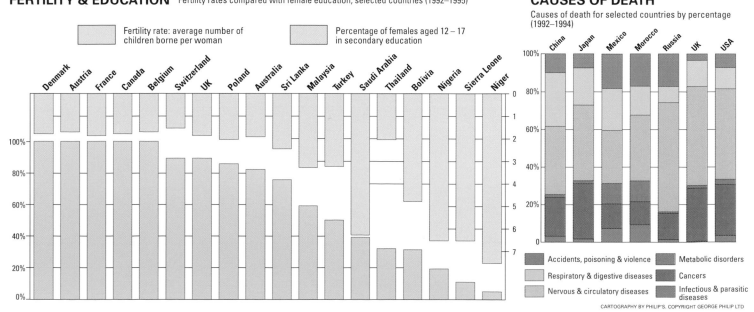

CAUSES OF DEATH
Causes of death for selected countries by percentage (1992–1994)

- Accidents, poisoning & violence
- Respiratory & digestive diseases
- Nervous & circulatory diseases
- Metabolic disorders
- Cancers
- Infectious & parasitic diseases

CARTOGRAPHY BY PHILIP'S. COPYRIGHT GEORGE PHILIP LTD

AGE DISTRIBUTION PYRAMIDS

The bars represent the percentage of the total population (males plus females) in the age group shown.

Developed countries such as the U.K. have populations evenly spread across age groups and usually a growing percentage of elderly people. Developing countries such as Kenya have the great majority of their people in the younger age groups, about to enter their most fertile years.

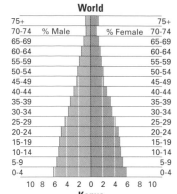

World

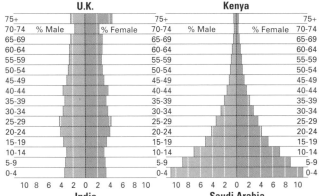

U.K.   Kenya

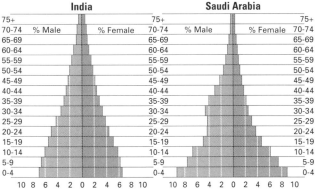

India   Saudi Arabia

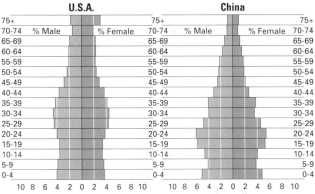

U.S.A.   China

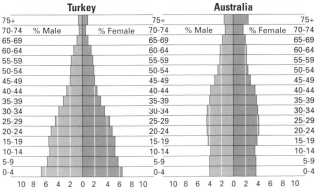

Turkey   Australia

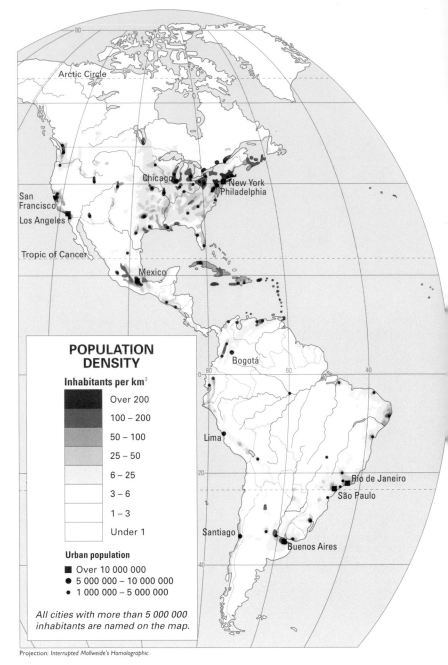

POPULATION DENSITY

Inhabitants per km²

- Over 200
- 100 – 200
- 50 – 100
- 25 – 50
- 6 – 25
- 3 – 6
- 1 – 3
- Under 1

Urban population

- ■ Over 10 000 000
- ● 5 000 000 – 10 000 000
- • 1 000 000 – 5 000 000

All cities with more than 5 000 000 inhabitants are named on the map.

Projection: Interrupted Mollweide's Homolographic

POPULATION CHANGE 1930-2020

Population totals are in millions

Figures in italics represent the percentage average annual increase for the period shown

	1930	1930-1960	1960	1960-1990	1990	1990-2020	2020
World	2013	*1.4%*	3019	*1.9%*	5292	*1.4%*	8062
Africa	155	*2.0%*	281	*2.85*	648	*2.7%*	1441
North America	135	*1.3%*	199	*1.1%*	276	*0.6%*	327
Latin America*	129	*1.8%*	218	*2.4%*	448	*1.6%*	719
Asia	1073	*1.5%*	1669	*2.1%*	3108	*1.4%*	4680
Europe	355	*0.6%*	425	*0.55*	498	*0.1%*	514
Oceania	10	*1.4%*	16	*1.75*	27	*1.1%*	37
C.I.S.†	176	*0.7%*	214	*1.0%*	288	*0.6%*	343

* South America plus Central America, Mexico, and the West Indies
† Commonwealth of Independent States, formerly the U.S.S.R.

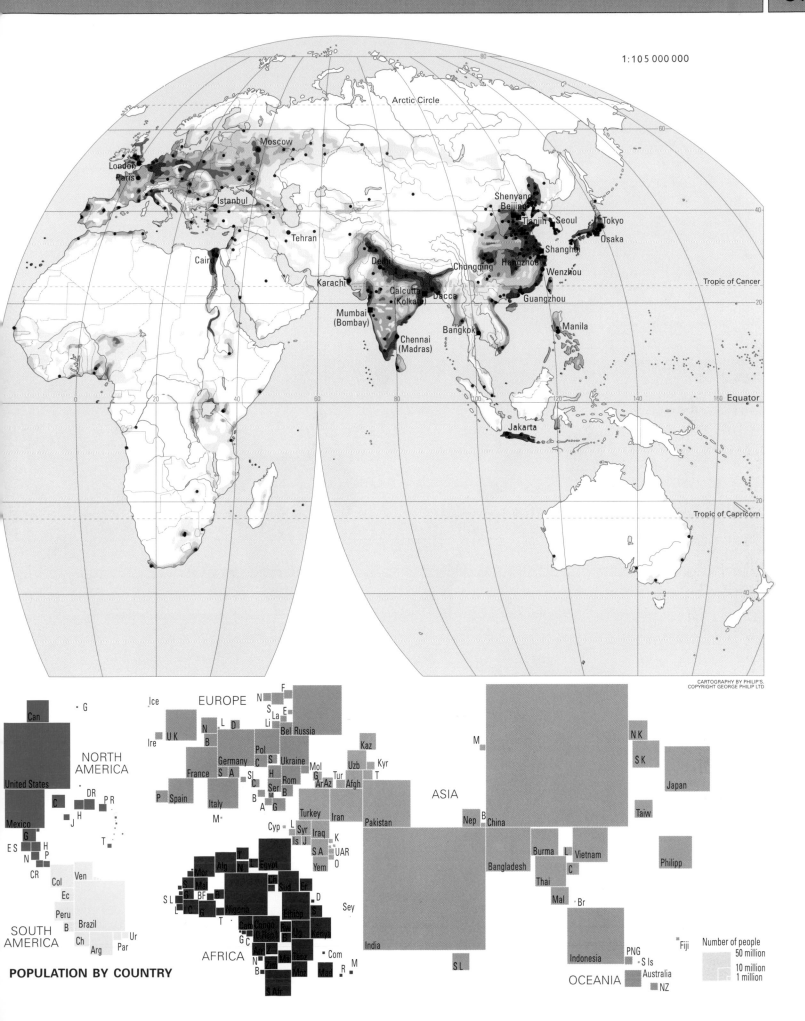

1:105 000 000

Arctic Circle

Moscow

London
Paris

Istanbul

Tehran

Cairo

Shenyang
Beijing
Tianjin   Seoul   Tokyo
Osaka
Delhi   Shanghai
Karachi   Chongqing   Hangzhou
Calcutta   Wenzhou
(Kolkata) Dacca
Mumbai   Guangzhou
(Bombay)
Chennai   Bangkok   Manila
(Madras)

Tropic of Cancer

Equator

Jakarta

Tropic of Capricorn

CARTOGRAPHY BY PHILIP'S.
COPYRIGHT GEORGE PHILIP LTD

POPULATION BY COUNTRY

EUROPE

ASIA

NORTH
AMERICA

SOUTH
AMERICA

AFRICA

OCEANIA

Number of people
50 million
10 million
1 million

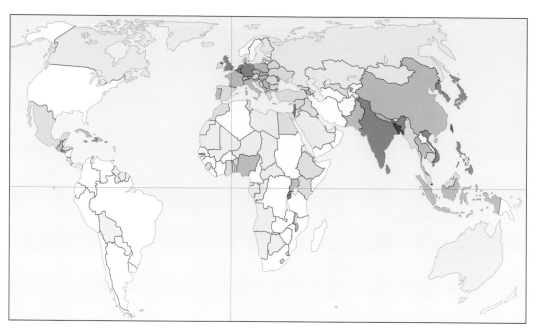

POPULATION DENSITY BY COUNTRY

Density of people per square kilometre 1997

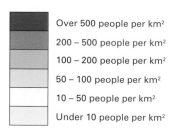

Over 500 people per km²

200 – 500 people per km²

100 – 200 people per km²

50 – 100 people per km²

10 – 50 people per km²

Under 10 people per km²

Top 5 countries		Bottom 5 countries	
Macau	22 111 per km²	Namibia	1.9 per km²
Monaco	20 805 per km²	French Guiana	1.5 per km²
Singapore	5 246 per km²	Mongolia	1.4 per km²
Malta	1 172 per km²	W. Sahara	0.8 per km²
Bangladesh	953 per km²	Greenland	0.2 per km²

U.K. 243 per km²

POPULATION CHANGE 1990-2000

The predicted population change for the years 1990-2000

Over 40% population gain

30 – 40% population gain

20 – 30% population gain

10 – 20% population gain

0 – 10% population gain

No change or population loss

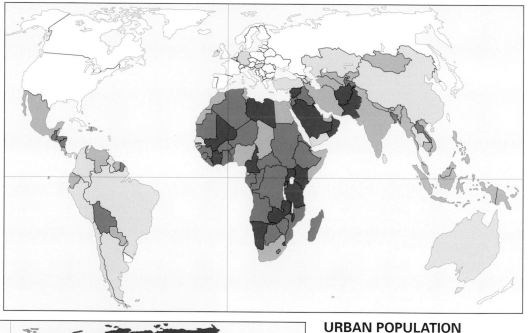

Top 5 countries		Bottom 5 countries	
Kuwait	+75.9%	Belgium	-0.1%
Namibia	+62.5%	Hungary	-0.2%
Afghanistan	+60.1%	Grenada	-2.4%
Mali	+55.5%	Germany	-3.2%
Tanzania	+54.6%	Tonga	-3.2%

U.K. +2.0%

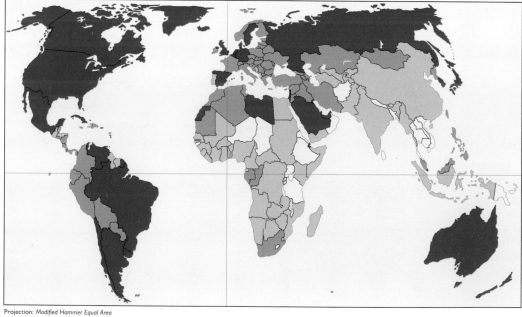

URBAN POPULATION

Percentage of total population living in towns and cities 1995

Over 75%

50 – 75%

25 – 50%

10 – 25%

Under 10%

Most urbanized		Least urbanized	
Singapore	100%	Bhutan	6%
Belgium	97%	Rwanda	6%
Kuwait	97%	Burundi	7%
Iceland	92%	Uganda	12%
Venezuela	92%	Malawi	13%

U.K. 89%

Projection: *Modified Hammer Equal Area*

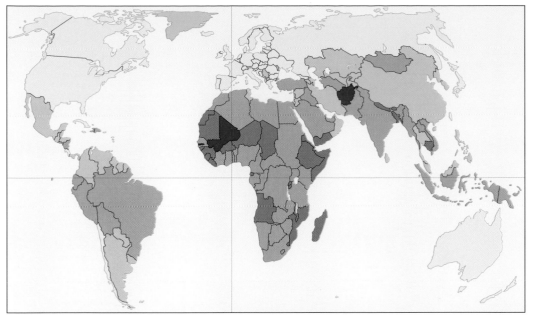

CHILD MORTALITY

The number of babies who died
under the age of one
(average 1990–95)

Over 150 deaths per 1 000 births	
100 – 150 deaths per 1 000 births	
50 – 100 deaths per 1 000 births	
20 – 50 deaths per 1 000 births	
10 – 20 deaths per 1 000 births	
Under 10 deaths per 1 000 births	

Highest child mortality		Lowest child mortality	
Afghanistan	162 deaths	Hong Kong	6 deaths
Mali	159 deaths	Denmark	6 deaths
Sierra Leone	143 deaths	Japan	5 deaths
Guinea-Bissau	140 deaths	Iceland	5 deaths
Malawi	138 deaths	Finland	5 deaths
		U.K.	8 deaths

LIFE EXPECTANCY

Average expected lifespan
of babies born in 1997

Over 75 years	
70 – 75 years	
65 – 70 years	
60 – 65 years	
55 – 60 years	
50 – 55 years	
Under 50 years	

Highest life expectancy		Lowest life expectancy	
Iceland	81 years	Tanzania	42 years
Japan	80 years	Niger	41 years
Australia	80 years	Uganda	40 years
Canada	79 years	Rwanda	39 years
Luxembourg	79 years	Malawi	35 years
		U.K.	77 years

FAMILY SIZE

The average number of children a woman
can expect to bear during her lifetime 1995

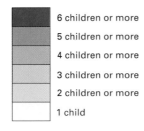

6 children or more	
5 children or more	
4 children or more	
3 children or more	
2 children or more	
1 child	

Most children per family

Yemen	7.4
Niger	7.4
Somalia	7.0
Oman	7.0
Ethiopia	7.0
U.K.	1.7

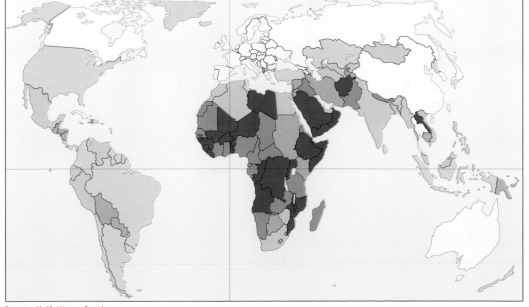

Projection: *Modified Hammer Equal Area*

CARTOGRAPHY BY PHILIP'S. COPYRIGHT GEORGE PHILIP LTD

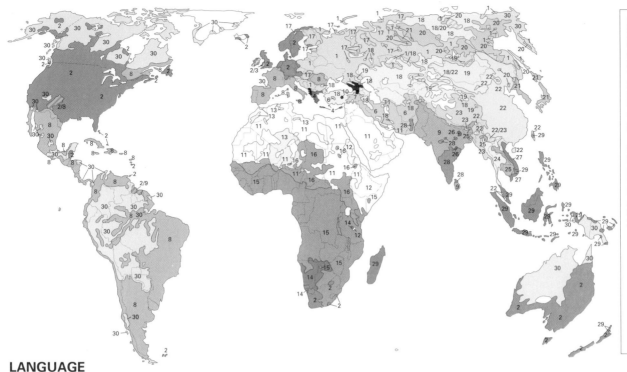

MOTHER TONGUES
Chinese 1069 million (Mandarin 864), English 443, Hindi 352, Spanish 341, Russian 293, Arabic 197, Bengali 184, Portuguese 173, Malay-Indonesian 142, Japanese 125, French 121, German 118, Urdu 92, Punjabi 84, Korean 71.

OFFICIAL LANGUAGES
English 27% of world population, Chinese 19%, Hindi 13.5%, Spanish 5.4%, Russian 5.2%, French 4.2%, Arabic 3.3%, Portuguese 3%, Malay 3%, Bengali 2.9%, Japanese 2.3%

Language can be classified by ancestry and structure . For example the Romance and Germanic groups are both derived from an Indo-European language believed to have been spoken 5000 years ago.

LANGUAGE

INDO-EUROPEAN FAMILY
- 1 Balto-Slavic group (incl. Russian, Ukrainian)
- 2 Germanic group (incl. English, German)
- 3 Celtic group
- 4 Greek
- 5 Albanian
- 6 Iranian group
- 7 Armenian
- 8 Romance group (incl. Spanish, Portuguese, French, Italian)
- 9 Indo-Aryan group (incl. Hindi, Bengali, Urdu, Punjabi, Marathi)
- 10 CAUCASIAN FAMILY

AFRO-ASIATIC FAMILY
- 11 Semitic group (incl. Arabic)
- 12 Kushitic group
- 13 Berber group
- 14 KHOISAN FAMILY
- 15 NIGER-CONGO FAMILY
- 16 NILO-SAHARAN FAMILY
- 17 URALIC FAMILY

ALTAIC FAMILY
- 18 Turkic group
- 19 Mongolian group
- 20 Tungus-Manchu group
- 21 Japanese and Korean

SINO-TIBETAN FAMILY
- 22 Sinitic (Chinese) languages
- 23 Tibetic-Burmic languages
- 24 TAI FAMILY

AUSTRO-ASIATIC FAMILY
- 25 Mon-Khmer group
- 26 Munda group
- 27 Vietnamese
- 28 DRAVIDIAN FAMILY (incl. Telugu, Tamil)
- 29 AUSTRONESIAN FAMILY (incl. Malay-Indonesian)
- 30 OTHER LANGUAGES

RELIGION

- Roman Catholicism
- Orthodox and other Eastern Churches
- Protestantism
- Sunni Islam
- Shia Islam
- Buddhism
- Hinduism
- Confucianism
- Judaism
- Shintoism
- Primitive Religions

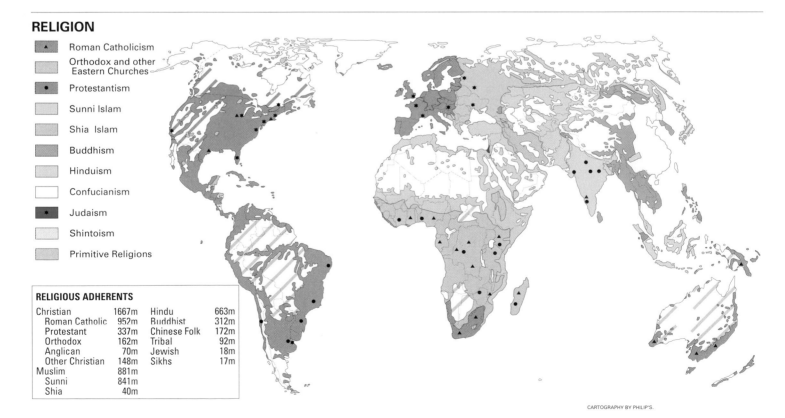

RELIGIOUS ADHERENTS

Christian	1667m	Hindu	663m
Roman Catholic	952m	Buddhist	312m
Protestant	337m	Chinese Folk	172m
Orthodox	162m	Tribal	92m
Anglican	70m	Jewish	18m
Other Christian	148m	Sikhs	17m
Muslim	881m		
Sunni	841m		
Shia	40m		

CARTOGRAPHY BY PHILIP'S.

UNITED NATIONS

Created in 1945 to promote peace and co-operation and based in New York, the United Nations is the world's largest international organization, with 185 members and an annual budget of US $2.6 billion (1996–97). Each member of the General Assembly has one vote, while the permanent members of the 15-nation Security Council – USA, Russia, China, UK and France – hold a veto. The Secretariat is the UN's principal administrative arm. The 54 members of the Economic and Social Council are responsible for economic, social, cultural, educational, health and related matters. The UN has 16 specialized agencies – based in Canada, France, Switzerland and Italy – as well as the USA – which help members in fields such as education (UNESCO), agriculture (FAO), medicine (WHO) and finance (IFC). By the end of 1994, all the original 11 trust territories of The Trusteeship Council had become independent.

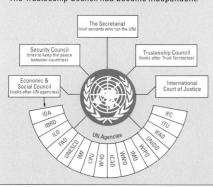

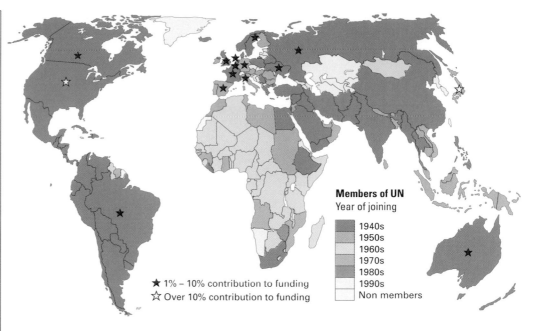

Members of UN
Year of joining

- 1940s
- 1950s
- 1960s
- 1970s
- 1980s
- 1990s
- Non members

★ 1% – 10% contribution to funding
☆ Over 10% contribution to funding

MEMBERSHIP OF THE UN In 1945 there were 51 members; by December 1994 membership had increased to 185 following the admission of Palau. There are 7 independent states which are not members of the UN – Kiribati, Nauru, Switzerland, Taiwan, Tonga, Tuvalu and the Vatican City. All the successor states of the former USSR had joined by the end of 1992. The official languages of the UN are Chinese, English, French, Russian, Spanish and Arabic.
FUNDING The UN budget for 1996–97 was US $2.6 billion. Contributions are assessed by the members' ability to pay, with the maximum 25% of the total, the minimum 0.01%. Contributions for 1996 were: USA 25.0%, Japan 15.4%, Germany 9.0%, France 6.4%, UK 5.3%, Italy 5.2%, Russia 4.5%, Canada 3.1%, Spain 2.4%, Brazil 1.6%, Netherlands 1.6%, Australia 1.5%, Sweden 1.2%, Ukraine 1.1%, Belgium 1.0%.

INTERNATIONAL ORGANIZATIONS

EU European Union (evolved from the European Community in 1993). The 15 members - Austria, Belgium, Denmark, Finland, France, Germany, Greece, Ireland, Italy, Luxembourg, Netherlands, Portugal, Spain, Sweden and the UK - aim to integrate economies, co-ordinate social developments and bring about political union. These members of what is now the world's biggest market share agricultural and industrial policies and tariffs on trade. The original body, the European Coal and Steel Community (ECSC), was created in 1951 following the signing of the Treaty of Paris.
EFTA European Free Trade Association (formed in 1960). Portugal left the original 'Seven' in 1989 to join what was then the EC, followed by Austria, Finland and Sweden in 1995. Only 4 members remain: Norway, Iceland, Switzerland and Liechtenstein.
ACP African-Caribbean-Pacific (formed in 1963). Members have economic ties with the EU.
NATO North Atlantic Treaty Organization (formed in 1949). It continues after 1991 despite the winding up of the Warsaw Pact. There are 19 member nations.
OAS Organization of American States (formed in 1948). It aims to promote social and economic co-operation between developed countries of North America and developing nations of Latin America.
ASEAN Association of South-east Asian Nations (formed in 1967). Burma and Laos joined in July 1997.
OAU Organization of African Unity (formed in 1963). Its 53 members represent over 94% of Africa's population. Arabic, French, Portuguese and English are recognized as working languages.
LAIA Latin American Integration Association (1980). Its aim is to promote freer regional trade.
OECD Organization for Economic Co-operation and Development (formed in 1961). It comprises the 29 major Western free-market economies. 'G7' is its' inner group' comprising the USA, Canada, Japan, UK, Germany, Italy and France. Russia attended the G7 summit in June 1997 ('Summit of the Eight').
COMMONWEALTH The Commonwealth of Nations evolved from the British Empire; it comprises 16 Queen's realms, 32 republics and 5 indigenous monarchies, giving a total of 53.
OPEC Organization of Petroleum Exporting Countries (formed in 1960). It controls about three-quarters of the world's oil supply. Gabon left the organization in 1996.

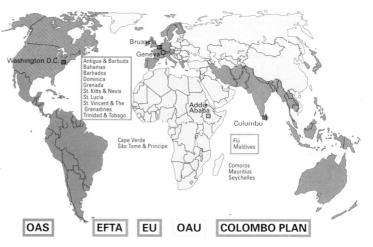

OAS   EFTA   EU   OAU   COLOMBO PLAN

ARAB LEAGUE (formed in 1945). The League's aim is to promote economic, social, political and military co-operation. There are 21 member nations.
COLOMBO PLAN (formed in 1951). Its 26 members aim to promote economic and social development in Asia and the Pacific.

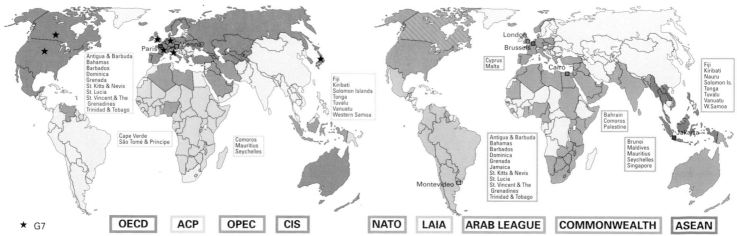

★ G7   OECD   ACP   OPEC   CIS   NATO   LAIA   ARAB LEAGUE   COMMONWEALTH   ASEAN

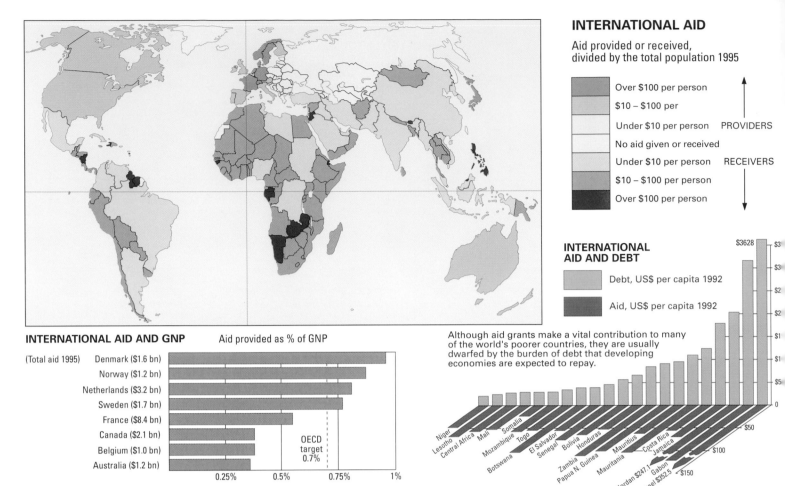

INTERNATIONAL AID

Aid provided or received,
divided by the total population 1995

- Over $100 per person
- $10 – $100 per
- Under $10 per person — PROVIDERS
- No aid given or received
- Under $10 per person — RECEIVERS
- $10 – $100 per person
- Over $100 per person

INTERNATIONAL AID AND DEBT

- Debt, US$ per capita 1992
- Aid, US$ per capita 1992

Although aid grants make a vital contribution to many of the world's poorer countries, they are usually dwarfed by the burden of debt that developing economies are expected to repay.

$3628

Niger, Lesotho, Central Africa, Mali, Somalia, Mozambique, Togo, Botswana, El Salvador, Senegal, Bolivia, Honduras, Zambia, Papua N. Guinea, Mauritania, Mauritius, Costa Rica, Jamaica, Jordan $247.1, Gabon, Israel $352.5

$50 $100 $150

INTERNATIONAL AID AND GNP

Aid provided as % of GNP

(Total aid 1995)
- Denmark ($1.6 bn)
- Norway ($1.2 bn)
- Netherlands ($3.2 bn)
- Sweden ($1.7 bn)
- France ($8.4 bn)
- Canada ($2.1 bn)
- Belgium ($1.0 bn)
- Australia ($1.2 bn)

OECD target 0.7%

0.25%   0.5%   0.75%   1%

INTERNATIONAL MIGRATION

Foreign born as a %
of total population
(latest year)

- Over 7.5%
- 3 – 7.5%
- 1.5 – 3%
- Under 1.5%
- No available data

Major migrations since 1945
1. 18m E. Europeans to Germany 1945 –
2. 4m Europeans to N. America 1945 –
3. 2.4m Jews to Israel 1945 –
4. 2m Irish & Commonwealth to U.K. 1945 –
5. 2m Europeans to Australia 1945
6. 2m N. Africans & S. Europeans to France 1946 –
7. 5m Chinese to Japan & Korea 1947 –
8. 2.9m Palestinian refugees 1947
9. 25m Indian & Pakistani refugees 1947–
10. 9m Mexicans to N. America 1950 –
11. 5m Korean refugees 1950 – 54
12. 4.7m C. Americans & W. Indians to N. America 1960–
13. 1.5m workers to S. Africa 1960 –
14. 2.4m S. Asian workers to the Gulf 1970 –
15. 3m workers to Nigeria & Ivory Coast 1970 –
16. 2m Bangladeshi & Pakistani refugees 1972 –
17. 1.5m Vietnamese & Cambodian refugees 1975 –
18. 6.1m Afghan refugees 1979 –
19. 2.9m Egyptian workers to Libya & the Gulf 1980 –
20. 2m workers to Argentina 1980 –
21. 1.7m Mozambique refugees 1985 –
22. 1.7m Yugoslav refugees 1992 –
23. 2.6m Rwanda - Burundi refugees 1994–

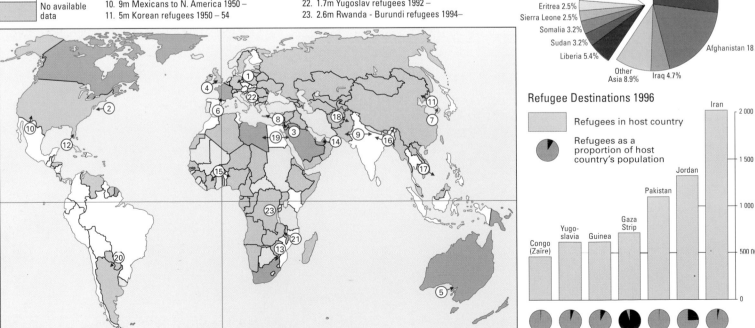

INTERNATIONAL REFUGEES

Origins of Refugees   World Total 1996: 13.6 millic

- Other Europe 7.0%
- North & South America 0.7%
- Bosnia-Herz. 6.9%
- Palestine 27.1%
- Other Africa 9.1%
- Other Africa 9.1%
- Eritrea 2.5%
- Sierra Leone 2.5%
- Somalia 3.2%
- Sudan 3.2%
- Liberia 5.4%
- Afghanistan 18
- Other Asia 8.9%
- Iraq 4.7%

Refugee Destinations 1996

- Refugees in host country
- Refugees as a proportion of host country's population

Iran — 2 000

Congo (Zaïre), Yugo-slavia, Guinea, Gaza Strip, Pakistan, Jordan, Iran

1 500   1 000   500

HOUSING

Number of people per household
(latest available year)

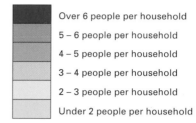

- Over 6 people per household
- 5 – 6 people per household
- 4 – 5 people per household
- 3 – 4 people per household
- 2 – 3 people per household
- Under 2 people per household

Expenditure on housing and energy as a
percentage of total consumer spending

- ♠ Over 20% spent
- △ Under 5% spent

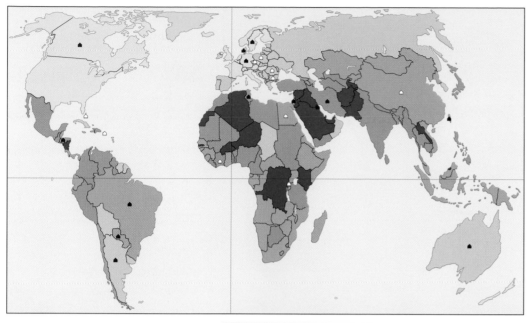

WATER SUPPLY

Percentage of total population with
access to safe drinking water
(average 1990 – 1996)

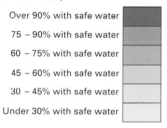

- Over 90% with safe water
- 75 – 90% with safe water
- 60 – 75% with safe water
- 45 – 60% with safe water
- 30 – 45% with safe water
- Under 30% with safe water

Least well provided countries

Afghanistan	23%	Papua New Guinea	28%
Chad	24%	Haiti	28%
Ethiopia	25%	Madagascar	29%

Average daily domestic water
consumption per person

△ Under 80 litres   ♦ Over 320 litres

*80 litres of water a day is considered
necessary for a reasonable quality of life*

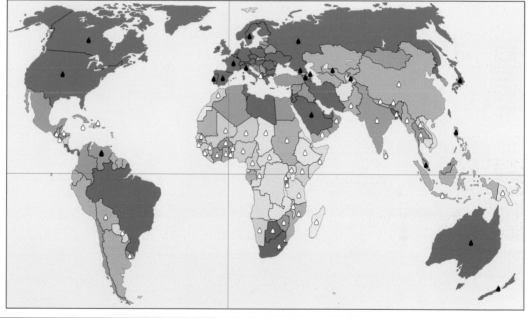

DAILY FOOD CONSUMPTION

Average daily food intake
in calories per person 1992

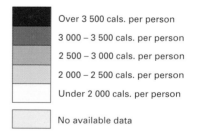

- Over 3 500 cals. per person
- 3 000 – 3 500 cals. per person
- 2 500 – 3 000 cals. per person
- 2 000 – 2 500 cals. per person
- Under 2 000 cals. per person
- No available data

Top 5 countries		Bottom 5 countries	
Ireland	3 847	Mozambique	1 680
Greece	3 815	Liberia	1 640
Cyprus	3 779	Ethiopia	1 610
U.S.A.	3 732	Afghanistan	1 523
Spain	3 708	Somalia	1 499
	U.K.	3 317	

Malnutrition in children under 5 years

- ■ Over 50% of children
- ■ 25 – 50% of children

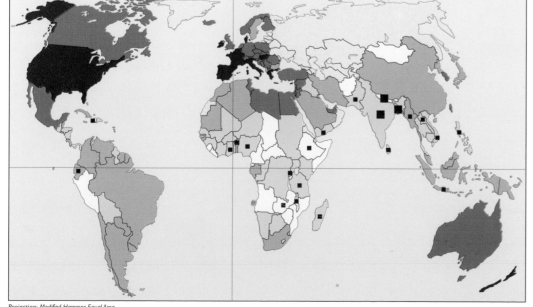

Projection: *Modified Hammer Equal Area*

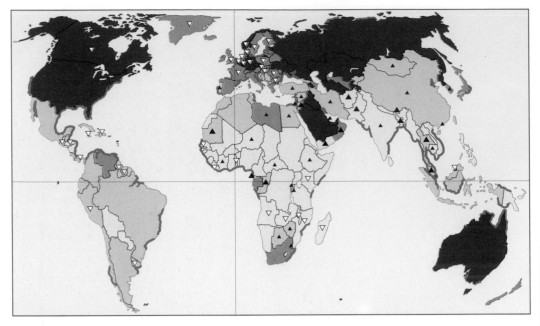

GLOBAL WARMING

Carbon dioxide emissions in tonnes per person per year (1992)

■	Over 10 tonnes of CO_2
■	5 – 10 tonnes of CO_2
■	1 – 5 tonnes of CO_2
■	Under 1 tonne of CO_2

Changes in CO_2 emissions 1980 – 1990

▲	Over 100% increase in emissions
▲	50 – 100% increase in emissions
▽	Reduction in emissions
▬	Coasts in danger of flooding from rising sea levels caused by global warming

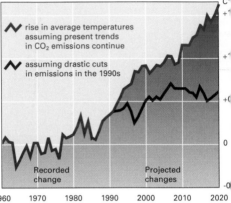

rise in average temperatures assuming present trends in CO_2 emissions continue

assuming drastic cuts in emissions in the 1990s

Recorded change

Projected changes

1960 1970 1980 1990 2000 2010 2020

Largest percentage share of total world greenhouse gas emissions 1992

5%	10%	15%	20%

U.S.A.
Former U.S.S.R.
China
Japan
Brazil
Germany
India
U.K.

Contribution to the greenhouse effect by the major heat-absorbing gases in the atmosphere

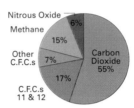

Nitrous Oxide 6%
Methane 15%
Other C.F.C.s 7%
Carbon Dioxide 55%
C.F.C.s 11 & 12 17%

THE GREENHOUSE EFFECT

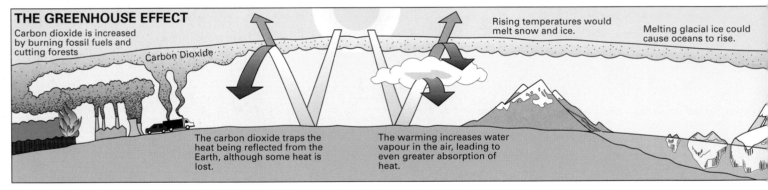

Carbon dioxide is increased by burning fossil fuels and cutting forests

Carbon Dioxide

Rising temperatures would melt snow and ice.

Melting glacial ice could cause oceans to rise.

The carbon dioxide traps the heat being reflected from the Earth, although some heat is lost.

The warming increases water vapour in the air, leading to even greater absorption of heat.

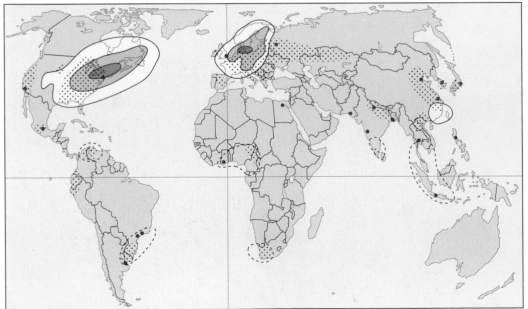

ACID RAIN

Acid rain is caused by high levels of sulphur and nitrogen in the atmosphere. They combine with water vapour and oxygen to form acids (H_2SO_4 and HNO_3) which fall as precipitation.

⋮⋮	Main areas of sulphur and nitrogen emissions (from the burning of fossil fuels)
●	Major cities with levels of air pollution exceeding World Health Organisation guidelines

Areas of acid deposition

(pH numbers measure acidity: normal rain is pH 5.

■	pH less than 4.0 (most acidic)
■	pH 4.0 – 4.5
□	pH 4.5 – 5.0
⬚	Potential problem areas

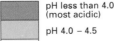

Projection: *Modified Hammer Equal Area*

WATER POLLUTION

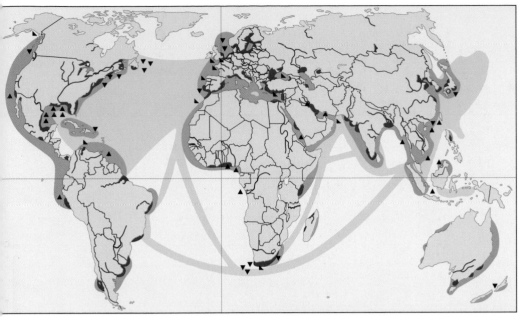

	Severely polluted sea areas and lakes
	Less polluted sea areas and lakes
	Areas of frequent oil pollution by shipping

- ◣ Major oil tanker spills
- ▲ Major oil rig blow-outs
- ▼ Offshore dumpsites for industrial and municipal waste
- ——— Severely polluted rivers and estuaries

Sources of marine oil pollution		Sources of river pollution	
Tanker operations	22%	Agriculture	64%
Municipal waste	22%	Mining	9%
Tanker accidents	13%	Land disposal	9%
River runoff	12%	Forestry	6%
Others	31%	Others	11%

DESERTIFICATION

Existing deserts	
Areas with a high risk of desertification	
Areas with a moderate risk of desertification	

DEFORESTATION IN THE TROPICS

Former areas of rainforest	
Existing rainforest	

Deforestation 1990-1995

	Extent of forest cleared annually (thousand ha)	Annual deforestation rate (%)
Brazil	2554	0.5
Indonesia	1084	1.0
Congo (Zaire)	740	0.7
Bolivia	581	1.2
Mexico	508	0.9
Venezuela	503	1.1
Malaysia	400	2.4

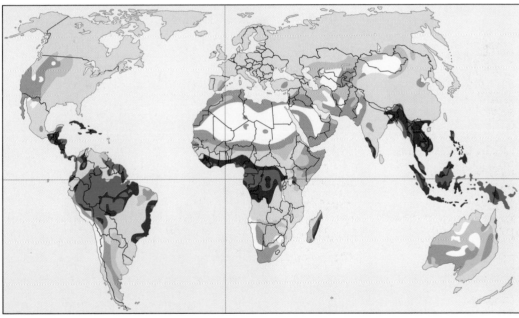

NATURAL DISASTERS

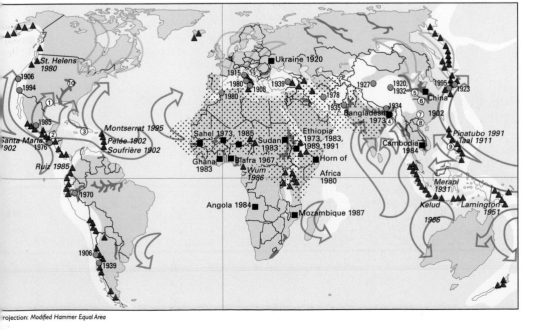

- ▢ Earthquake zones
- ● Major earthquakes since 1900 (with dates)
- ▲ Major volcanoes (notable eruptions since 1900 with dates)
- Areas liable to flood
- ⇨ Paths of tropical storms
- ⇨ Paths of winter blizzards
- Areas liable to invasion by locusts
- ■ Major famines since 1900 (with dates)
- ⑨ Major storms and floods

1	Texas 1900
2	Central America 1966, 1974
3	West Indies 1928, 1963, 1979, 1988
4	Bangladesh 1960, 1963, 1965, 1970, 1985, 1988, 1989, 1991
5	Huang He 1887, 1931
6	Yangtze 1911, 1989, 1995
7	Hunan 1991
8	Haiphong 1881
9	Philippines 1970, 1991
10	Mississippi 1993

Projection: Modified Hammer Equal Area

CARTOGRAPHY BY PHILIP'S. COPYRIGHT GEORGE PHILIP LTD

	Population									Land and Agriculture					Energy	Trade	
	Population Total 1997	Population Density 1997	Average Annual Change 1970-80	Average Annual Change 1990-97	Birth Rate 1997	Death Rate 1997	Fertility Rate 1995	Life Expectancy Average 1997	Urban Population 1995	Land Area	Arable and Permanent Crops	Permanent grassland	Forest	Agriculture Population 1995	Consumption per capita 1994	Imports per capita 1995	Exports per capita 1995
	millions	persons per km²	%	%	births per thousand population	deaths per thousand population	children	years	%	thousand km²	% of land area	% of land area	% of land area	% of economically active pop.	tonnes of coal	US $	US $
Afghanistan	23	35	1.7	4.8	43	18	6.9	46	20	652	12	46	3	69	0.04	19	6
Albania	3.6	131	2.3	1.5	22	8	2.6	68	37	27.4	26	15	38	54	0.3	178	42
Algeria	29.3	12	3.1	2.3	28	6	3.5	69	56	2382	3	13	2	24	1.58	375	375
Angola	11.2	9	3.3	1.6	44	17	6.9	47	32	1247	3	43	18	74	0.08	198	309
Argentina	35.4	13	1.7	1.3	20	8	2.7	74	88	2737	10	52	19	11	2.15	579	603
Armenia	3.8	134	2	1.9	17	8	1.8	69	69	28.4	20	54	15	15	0.61	105	603
Australia	18.4	2	1.6	1.2	14	7	1.9	80	86	7644	6	54	19	5	7.61	3342	2942
Austria	8.2	99	0.1	1.1	11	10	1.5	77	65	82.7	18	24	39	7	4.16	8253	7166
Azerbaijan	7.7	89	1.8	1	22	9	2.3	65	56	86.1	23	52	11	30	2.6	105	86
Bahamas	0.3	28	2.1	1.5	18	6	2	73	85	10	1	0	32	5	2.97	4439	5418
Bangladesh	124	953	2.8	1	30	11	3.5	56	18	130	74	5	15	62	0.09	55	27
Barbados	0.3	616	0.4	0.6	15	8	1.8	75	46	0.43	37	5	12	6	1.58	2946	915
Belarus	10.5	51	0.7	0.3	11	13	1.4	69	69	208	31	14	34	18	3.38	297	243
Belgium	10.2	335	0.2	0.5	12	10	1.6	77	97	30.5	24	21	21	3	6.86	14702	16078
Benin	5.8	52	2.5	2.9	46	13	6	53	36	111	17	4	31	60	0.05	125	34
Bolivia	7.7	7	2.6	2.4	32	10	4.5	60	62	1084	2	24	53	45	0.49	192	149
Bosnia-Herzegovina	3.6	70	1	-2.7	6	7	1	60	41	51.2	16	24	39	10	0.36	204	12
Botswana	1.5	3	3.8	2.2	33	7	4.4	62	31	567	1	45	47	39	...	1153	1302
Brazil	159.5	19	2.4	1.4	20	9	2.4	62	78	8457	6	22	58	19	0.85	345	298
Bulgaria	8.6	77	0.4	-0.7	8	14	1.2	71	71	111	38	16	35	11	3.26	598	606
Burkina Faso	10.9	40	2.3	2.8	46	20	6.7	42	27	274	13	22	50	92	0.05	54	53
Burma	47.5	72	2.4	1.9	30	11	3.4	57	27	658	15	1	49	72	0.08	30	19
Burundi	6.3	243	1.6	0.5	42	15	6.5	49	7	25.7	46	39	13	91	0.02	39	18
Cambodia	10.5	59	-0.8	3.5	43	15	4.7	50	21	177	22	8	69	73	0.02	43	24
Cameroon	13.8	30	2.7	2.6	42	14	5.7	52	45	465	15	4	77	68	0.14	94	154
Canada	30.2	3	1.2	1.9	13	7	1.7	79	77	9221	5	3	54	3	11.21	5676	6491
Central African Rep.	3.4	5	2.3	1.8	40	18	5.1	45	39	623	3	5	75	79	0.04	54	52
Chad	6.8	5	2.1	2.5	44	17	5.9	48	22	1259	3	36	26	81	0.01	67	77
Chile	14.7	20	1.6	1.6	18	6	2.3	75	85	749	6	18	22	17	1.45	1121	1130
China	1210	130	1.8	1.2	17	7	1.9	70	29	9326	10	43	14	71	0.92	106	122
Colombia	35.9	35	2.3	1.2	21	5	2.8	73	73	1039	5	39	48	24	1	395	288
Congo	2.7	8	2.8	2.9	39	17	6	46	59	342	0	29	58	45	0.34	259	325
Congo (Zaïre)	47.2	21	2.9	4.1	48	17	6	47	29	2267	3	7	77	66	0.06	8	9
Costa Rica	3.5	69	2.8	2.2	23	4	2.8	76	50	51.1	10	46	31	22	0.87	977	811
Croatia	4.9	86	0.4	0.2	10	11	1.5	73	55	56.4	22	20	38	15	1.59	1586	969
Cuba	11.3	102	1.3	0.8	13	7	1.7	75	75	110	31	27	24	16	1.14	258	146
Cyprus	0.8	83	0.2	1.4	15	8	2.2	77	68	9.24	15	0	13	10	3.03	4986	1661
Czech Rep.	10.5	136	0.5	0.3	11	11	1.3	74	65	77	44	12	34	11	4.97	2450	2099
Denmark	5.4	126	0.4	0.3	12	10	1.8	78	86	42.4	56	7	10	4	5.15	8266	9378
Dominican Rep.	8.2	168	2.6	1.8	23	6	2.9	69	62	48.4	31	43	12	21	0.65	376	97
Ecuador	11.8	43	3	1.6	25	5	3.2	72	59	277	11	18	56	29	0.77	366	376
Egypt	63	63	2.1	2.6	28	9	3.4	62	45	995	4	0	0	33	0.66	199	58
El Salvador	6	287	2.3	1.8	27	6	3.7	69	52	20.7	35	29	5	32	0.5	504	176
Estonia	1.5	34	0.8	-1.1	12	14	1.3	68	73	43.2	27	7	48	14	4.9	1714	1240
Ethiopia	58.5	53	2.4	3.5	46	18	7	47	13	1101	11	20	13	86	0.03	19	7
Finland	5.2	17	0.4	0.6	11	11	1.8	76	63	305	9	0	76	7	7.4	5502	7744
France	58.8	107	0.6	0.7	13	9	1.7	79	74	550	35	19	27	4	5.15	4763	4941
Gabon	1.2	5	4.8	1.5	28	13	5.2	56	73	258	2	18	77	45	0.87	667	2055
Gambia, The	1.2	120	3.3	4.9	44	19	5.3	53	26	10	17	19	10	80	0.1	192	32
Georgia	5.5	78	0.8	0	14	9	1.9	68	58	69.7	16	24	33	25	0.85	39	22
Germany	82.3	236	0.1	0.5	9	11	1.2	76	87	349	34	15	31	3	5.48	5445	6227
Ghana	18.1	80	2.2	2.7	34	11	5.1	57	36	228	19	37	42	56	0.14	129	74
Greece	10.6	82	0.9	0.8	10	10	1.4	78	65	129	27	41	20	20	3.22	2056	899
Guatemala	11.3	104	2.8	2.9	33	7	4.7	66	42	108	18	24	54	51	0.29	310	203
Guinea	7.5	30	1.4	3.8	42	18	6.5	46	30	246	3	44	27	85	0.08	116	97
Guinea-Bissau	1.2	41	4.2	2.6	39	16	6	49	22	28.1	12	38	38	84	0.1	66	22
Guyana	0.8	4	0.7	-0.8	19	10	2.4	59	35	197	3	6	84	20	0.6	594	558
Haiti	7.4	269	1.7	1.8	33	15	4.4	50	32	27.6	33	18	5	66	0.04	91	16
Honduras	6.3	56	3.4	3	33	6	4.6	69	48	112	18	14	54	33	0.31	205	178
Hungary	10.2	110	0.4	-0.6	11	15	1.6	69	64	92.3	54	12	19	14	3.27	1472	1217
Iceland	0.3	3	1.1	1.2	17	6	2.1	81	92	100	0	23	1	10	6.7	6500	6678
India	980	330	2.2	2.5	25	9	3.2	60	27	2973	57	4	23	62	0.37	37	33
Indonesia	203.5	112	2.3	1.8	23	8	2.7	62	33	1812	17	7	62	53	0.47	211	234
Iran	69.5	42	3.2	3.5	33	6	4.5	68	58	1636	11	27	7	36	1.88	537	348
Iraq	22.5	51	3.6	2.5	43	6	5.4	67	73	437	12	9	4	12	1.76	278	383

Wealth							Social Indicators								Aid	
GNP 1995	GNP per capita 1995	Real GDP per capita 1995	Average Annual growth of Real GNP per capita 1985-95	GDP share Agriculture 1995	GDP share Industry 1995	GDP share services 1995	HDI Human Development Index 1994	Food Intake	Population per doctor 1993	% of GNP spent on health 1990-95	% of GNP spent on education 1993-94	%o GNP spent on military 1995	Adult Illiteracy Female	Adult Illiteracy Male	given (*) and received per capita 1994	
million US $	US $	US $	%	%	%	%		calories per day	persons	%	%	%	Female %	Male %	US $	
5000	300	800	-6	52	32	16	...	1523	7000	...	...	9.1	85	53	10	Afghanistan
2199	670	2750	-7	56	21	23	0.655	2605	735	2.7	3	2.8	0	0	21	Albania
44609	1600	5300	-2.6	13	47	40	0.737	2897	1062	4.6	5.6	2.5	51	26	11	Algeria
4422	410	1310	-6.1	12	59	29	0.335	1839	23725	4	...	4.8	71	44	40	Angola
278431	8030	8310	1.9	6	31	63	0.884	2880	330	10.6	3.8	1.7	4	4	7	Argentina
2752	730	2260	-15.1	44	35	21	0.651	...	261	7.8	7.3	4.4	2	1	27	Armenia
337909	18720	18940	1.4	3	28	69	0.931	3179	500	8.4	6	2.5	...	...	*62	Australia
216547	26890	21250	1.9	2	34	64	0.932	3497	231	9.7	5.5	1	0	0	*82	Austria
3601	480	1460	-16.3	27	32	41	0.636	...	257	7.5	5.5	5	4	1	3	Azerbaijan
3297	11940	14710	-1	3	9	88	0.894	2624	700	...	3.9	0.6	2	1	15	Bahamas
28599	240	1380	2.1	31	18	51	0.368	2019	12884	2.4	2.3	1.8	74	51	11	Bangladesh
1745	6560	10620	-0.2	5	17	78	0.907	3207	1000	5	7.5	0.7	3	2	...	Barbados
21356	2070	4220	-5.2	13	35	52	0.806	...	236	6.4	6.1	3.3	3	1	11	Belarus
250710	24710	21660	2.2	2	31	67	0.932	3681	274	8.2	5.6	1.7	0	0	*81	Belgium
2034	370	1760	-0.4	34	12	54	0.368	2532	14216	1.7	...	1.3	74	51	53	Benin
5905	800	2540	1.7	17	30	53	0.589	2094	2348	5	5.4	2.6	24	10	96	Bolivia
11650	2600	...	1.8	...	...	...	...	...	600	...	...	...	23	3	...	Bosnia-Herzegovina
4381	3020	5580	6	5	46	49	0.673	2266	5151	1.9	8.5	7.1	40	20	64	Botswana
579787	3640	5400	-0.7	14	37	49	0.783	2824	844	7.4	1.6	1.5	17	17	2	Brazil
11225	1330	4480	-2.2	13	34	53	0.78	2831	306	4	4.5	3.3	3	1	6	Bulgaria
2417	230	780	-0.1	34	27	39	0.221	2387	34804	5.5	3.6	2.4	91	71	48	Burkina Faso
45100	1000	1050	0.4	63	9	28	0.475	2598	12528	0.9	2.4	6.2	22	11	3	Burma
984	160	630	-1.3	56	18	26	0.247	1941	17153	0.9	3.8	5.3	78	51	46	Burundi
2718	270	1084	2	51	14	35	0.348	2021	9374	7.2	...	4.7	47	20	57	Cambodia
8615	650	2110	-7	39	23	38	0.468	1981	11996	1.4	3.1	1.8	48	25	35	Cameroon
573695	19380	21130	0.4	3	30	67	0.96	3094	464	9.8	7.6	1.6	2	2	*73	Canada
1123	340	1070	-2	44	13	43	0.355	1690	25920	1.7	2.8	1.8	48	32	50	Central African Rep.
1144	180	700	0.5	44	22	34	0.288	1989	30030	1.8	2.2	2.6	65	38	38	Chad
59151	4160	9520	6.1	8	34	58	0.891	2582	942	6.5	2.9	3.8	5	5	11	Chile
744890	620	2920	8	21	48	31	0.626	2727	1063	3.8	2.6	5.7	27	10	3	China
70263	1910	6130	2.8	14	32	54	0.848	2677	1105	7.4	3.7	2	9	9	6	Colombia
1784	680	2050	-3.2	10	38	52	0.5	2296	3713	6.8	8.3	1.7	33	17	50	Congo
5313	120	490	-8.5	51	16	33	0.381	2060	15150	2.4	1	2	32	13	4	Congo (Zaïre)
8884	2610	5850	2.9	17	24	59	0.889	2883	1133	8.5	4.7	0.3	5	5	8	Costa Rica
15508	3250	3960	-20	12	25	63	0.76	...	500	10.1	...	12.6	5	1	...	Croatia
13700	1250	3000	-10	...	...	...	0.723	2833	275	7.9	6.6	2.8	5	4	6	Cuba
8510	11500	13000	4.6	6	43	51	0.907	3779	450	3.9	4.3	4.5	7	2	30	Cyprus
39990	3870	9770	-1.8	6	39	55	0.882	...	273	9.9	5.9	2.8	0	0	5	Czech Rep.
156027	29890	21230	1.5	4	29	67	0.927	3664	360	6.6	8.5	1.8	0	0	*273	Denmark
11390	1460	3870	2.1	15	22	63	0.718	2286	949	5.3	1.9	1.3	18	18	16	Dominican Rep.
15997	1390	4220	0.8	12	36	52	0.775	2583	652	5.3	3	3.4	12	8	21	Ecuador
45507	790	3820	1.1	20	21	59	0.614	3335	1316	4.9	5	4.3	61	36	35	Egypt
9057	1610	2610	2.9	14	22	64	0.592	2663	1515	5	1.6	1.8	30	27	54	El Salvador
4252	2860	4220	-4.3	8	28	64	0.776	...	253	5.9	5.8	5.3	0	0	22	Estonia
5722	100	450	-0.5	57	10	33	0.244	1610	32499	1.1	6.4	2.1	75	55	16	Ethiopia
105174	20580	17760	-0.2	6	37	57	0.94	3018	406	8.3	8.4	2	0	0	*59	Finland
451051	24990	21030	1.5	2	27	71	0.946	3633	334	9.7	5.8	3.1	1	1	*137	France
3759	3490	3650	-1.6	9	59	32	0.562	2500	1987	0.5	3.2	1.7	47	26	138	Gabon
354	320	930	0.3	28	15	57	0.281	2360	14000	1.8	2.7	3.8	75	47	43	Gambia, The
2358	440	1470	-17	67	22	11	0.637	...	182	0.3	1.9	3.4	1	0	106	Georgia
2252343	27510	20070	1.9	1	30	69	0.924	3344	367	9.5	4.8	2	0	0	*81	Germany
6719	390	1990	1.5	46	16	38	0.468	2199	22970	3.5	3.1	1.2	47	24	38	Ghana
85885	8210	11710	1.2	21	36	43	0.923	3815	312	6.4	3	4.6	7	2	...	Greece
14255	1340	3340	0.3	25	19	56	0.572	2255	3999	2.7	1.6	1.4	51	38	21	Guatemala
3593	550	1100	1.4	24	31	45	0.271	2389	7445	0.9	2.2	1.4	78	50	62	Guinea
265	250	790	1.8	46	24	30	0.291	2556	3500	1.1	2.8	3	58	32	113	Guinea-Bissau
493	590	2420	0.8	50	35	15	0.649	2384	3000	10.4	5	1.1	2	1	...	Guyana
1777	250	910	-5.2	44	12	44	0.338	1706	10855	3.6	1.4	2.1	58	52	104	Haiti
3566	600	1900	0.2	21	33	46	0.575	2305	1266	5.6	4	1.3	27	27	75	Honduras
42129	4120	6410	-1	8	33	59	0.857	3503	306	7.3	6.7	1.4	1	1	7	Hungary
6686	24950	20460	0.3	13	29	58	0.942	3058	360	6.9	5.4	...	0	0	...	Iceland
319660	340	1400	3.1	29	29	42	0.446	2395	2459	3.5	3.8	2.5	62	35	2	India
190105	980	3800	6	17	42	41	0.668	2752	7028	1.5	1.3	1.6	22	10	7	Indonesia
328000	4800	5470	0.5	25	34	41	0.78	2860	3142	4.5	5.9	3.9	24	22	3	Iran
36200	1800	3150	...	28	20	52	0.531	2121	1659	...	5.1	14.8	55	29	16	Iraq

	Population									Land and Agriculture					Energy	Trade	
	Population Total 1997	Population Density 1997	Average Annual Change 1970-80	Average Annual Change 1990-97	Birth Rate 1997	Death Rate 1997	Fertility Rate 1995	Life Expectancy Average 1997	Urban Population 1995	Land Area	Arable and Permanent Crops	Permanent grassland	Forest	Agriculture Population 1995	Consumption per capita 1994	Imports per capita 1995	Exports per capita 1995
	millions	persons per km²	%	%	births per thousand population	deaths per thousand population	children	years	%	thousand km²	% of land area	% of land area	% of land area	% of economically active pop.	tonnes of coal	US $	US $
Ireland	3.6	53	1.4	0.5	13	9	1.9	76	58	68.9	19	45	5	13	4.31	9237	12469
Israel	5.9	286	2.7	3.6	20	6	2.4	78	91	20.6	21	7	6	3	3.26	5337	3436
Italy	57.8	196	0.5	0.2	10	10	1.2	78	67	294	38	15	23	7	3.95	3562	4038
Ivory Coast	15.1	47	4	3.4	42	17	5.3	45	46	318	12	41	34	57	0.26	231	301
Jamaica	2.6	240	1.3	0.8	22	6	2.4	75	53	10.8	20	24	17	24	1.66	1089	545
Japan	125.9	334	1.1	0.3	10	8	1.5	80	78	377	12	2	66	6	4.98	2684	3540
Jordan	5.6	63	2.4	4.9	36	4	4.8	73	72	88.9	5	9	1	15	1.01	680	325
Kazakstan	17	6	1.3	0.2	19	10	2.3	64	58	2670	13	70	4	21	5.93	40	70
Kenya	31.9	56	3.8	4.1	32	11	4.7	54	25	570	8	37	30	78	0.12	98	62
Korea, North	24.5	203	2.2	1.7	22	5	2.2	71	61	120	17	0	61	34	4.21	75	41
Korea, South	46.1	466	1.8	1.1	16	6	1.8	74	75	98.7	21	1	65	14	3.77	3013	2788
Kyrgyzstan	4.7	24	2	0.8	26	9	3.3	64	40	191	7	44	4	31	0.76	71	76
Laos	5.2	23	1.7	3.3	41	13	6.5	53	22	231	4	3	54	77	0.04	40	20
Latvia	2.5	38	0.7	-1.3	12	15	1.3	67	72	64.1	28	13	46	14	2.3	697	520
Lebanon	3.2	313	0.8	2.5	28	6	2.8	70	87	10.2	30	1	8	4	1.83	2058	197
Lesotho	2.1	69	2.3	2.7	32	14	4.6	52	23	30.4	11	66	0	39	...	520	58
Liberia	3	30	3.1	2.9	42	12	6.5	59	45	96.8	4	21	48	70	0.06	116	197
Libya	5.5	3	4.4	2.8	44	7	6.1	65	86	1760	1	8	0	6	3.34	1240	2596
Lithuania	3.7	57	0.9	-0.1	14	13	1.5	68	71	65.2	47	7	31	18	3.04	696	545
Luxembourg	0.4	163.5	0.7	1.9	13	8	1.7	79	88	2.6	...	...	...	...	12.82	20295	16090
Macedonia	2.2	86	1.6	0.9	13	9	2.2	72	60	24.9	26	25	39	17	1.9	600	500
Madagascar	15.5	27	2.7	4.8	42	14	5.8	53	27	582	5	41	40	76	0.04	36	25
Malawi	10.3	109	3.2	3.1	41	25	6.6	35	13	94.1	18	20	39	86	0.04	49	41
Malaysia	20.9	64	2.4	2.2	26	5	3.4	70	52	329	23	1	68	23	2.29	3751	3563
Mali	11	9	2.3	4.4	51	19	6.8	47	27	1220	2	25	10	84	0.02	70	42
Malta	0.4	1172	1.1	0.9	15	7	1.9	79	88	0.32	41	0	0	2	1.97	7951	5170
Mauritania	2.4	2	2.4	2.5	47	15	5.2	50	54	1025	0	38	4	49	0.61	284	223
Mauritius	1.2	569	1.6	1.1	19	7	2.2	71	44	2.03	52	3	22	12	0.7	1797	1410
Mexico	97.4	51	2.9	1.8	26	5	3	74	75	1909	13	39	26	24	2.03	508	520
Moldova	4.5	132	1.1	0.3	17	12	2	65	50	33.7	66	13	13	31	1.55	185	162
Mongolia	2.5	2	2.8	1.9	25	8	3.4	61	60	1567	1	75	9	29	1.55	158	208
Morocco	28.1	63	2.4	1.6	27	6	3.4	70	52	446	21	47	20	41	0.47	315	172
Mozambique	19.1	24	2.6	4.3	44	18	6.2	45	32	784	4	56	22	81	0.03	45	10
Namibia	1.7	2	2.5	2	37	8	5	65	34	823	1	46	15	45	...	916	881
Nepal	22.1	162	2.6	2.1	37	12	5.3	54	13	137	17	15	42	93	0.03	64	16
Netherlands	15.9	469	0.8	0.9	12	9	1.6	78	89	33.9	28	31	10	4	7.22	11419	12680
New Zealand	3.7	14	1	1.1	15	8	2.1	77	86	268	14	50	28	10	5.47	3951	3882
Nicaragua	4.6	39	3	2.5	33	6	4.1	66	63	119	10	45	26	23	0.36	212	115
Niger	9.7	8	3	3.3	54	24	7.4	41	16	1267	3	8	2	89	0.06	37	27
Nigeria	118	130	2.2	3.1	43	12	5.5	55	38	911	36	44	12	38	0.21	71	94
Norway	4.4	14	0.5	0.8	11	11	1.9	78	73	307	3	0	27	5	7.44	7563	9632
Oman	2.4	11	4.2	6.9	38	4	7	71	13	212	0	5	0	42	5.41	1994	2682
Pakistan	136	176	2.6	2.8	35	11	5.2	59	34	771	28	6	5	48	0.33	88	62
Panama	2.7	37	2.5	1.7	22	5	2.7	74	55	74.4	9	20	44	22	1.2	955	238
Papua New Guinea	4.4	10	2.5	1.8	33	10	4.8	58	16	453	1	0	93	78	0.29	357	651
Paraguay	5.2	13	3	2.8	30	4	4	74	52	397	6	55	32	35	0.38	669	196
Peru	24.5	19	2.7	1.3	24	6	3.1	70	72	1280	3	21	66	33	0.46	392	237
Philippines	73.5	247	2.6	2.4	29	7	3.7	66	52	298	31	4	46	42	0.43	403	249
Poland	38.8	127	0.9	0.1	12	10	1.6	72	64	304	48	13	29	26	3.51	753	593
Portugal	10.1	110	0.8	-0.3	11	10	1.4	76	36	92	32	11	36	14	2.13	3261	2280
Puerto Rico	3.8	432	1.7	1.4	18	8	2.1	75	77	8.86	9	26	16	3	3.07	4300	5900
Romania	22.6	98	0.9	-0.3	10	12	1.4	70	55	230	43	21	29	19	2.54	453	349
Russia	147.8	9	0.6	0	11	16	1.4	64	75	16996	8	5	45	12	6	261	427
Rwanda	7	284	3.3	-0.4	39	21	6.2	39	6	24.7	47	28	10	91	0.03	46	10
Saudi Arabia	19.1	9	5	4.4	38	5	6.2	70	79	2150	2	56	1	14	5.77	1539	2335
Senegal	8.9	46	2.9	2.8	45	11	5.7	57	42	193	12	30	39	74	0.16	156	103
Sierra Leone	4.6	64	2.1	1.5	47	18	6.5	48	35	71.6	8	31	28	67	0.05	30	6
Singapore	3.2	5246	1	2.5	16	5	1.7	79	100	0.61	2	0	5	1	9.67	41639	39553
Slovak Rep.	5.4	112	1.7	0.3	13	9	1.5	73	58	48.1	34	17	41	12	4.07	1250	1025
Slovenia	2	99	0.9	0.2	9	10	1.3	75	50	20.3	14	25	54	5	3.11	4793	4199
Somalia	9.9	16	3.8	1.9	44	13	7	56	27	627	2	69	26	74	0.05	26	5
South Africa	42.3	35	2.3	1.6	27	12	3.9	56	57	1221	11	67	7	11	2.73	718	653
Spain	39.3	79	1.1	0	10	9	1.2	79	77	499	40	21	32	9	3.01	2890	2334
Sri Lanka	18.7	289	1.7	1.2	18	6	2.3	73	22	64.6	29	7	32	47	0.16	290	212
Sudan	31	13	3	3	41	11	4.8	56	35	2376	5	46	18	68	0.06	44	21

GNP 1995 million US $	GNP per capita 1995 US $	Real GDP per capita 1995 US $	Average Annual growth of Real GNP per capita 1985-95 %	GDP share Agriculture 1995 %	GDP share Industry 1995 %	GDP share services 1995 %	HDI Human Development Index 1994	Food Intake calories per day	Population per doctor 1993 persons	% of GNP spent on health 1990-95 %	% of GNP spent on education 1993-94 %	%o GNP spent on military 1995 %	Adult Illiteracy Female %	Adult Illiteracy Male %	Aid given (*) and received per capita 1994 US $	
52765	14710	15680	5.2	9	37	54	0.929	3847	632	7.9	6.4	1.2	0	0	*35	Ireland
87875	15920	16490	2.5	3	32	65	0.913	3050	220	4.1	6	9.2	7	3	226	Israel
088085	19020	19870	1.7	3	31	66	0.921	3561	207	8.3	5.2	1.8	4	2	*37	Italy
9548	660	1580	-4.3	31	20	49	0.368	2491	11739	3.4	...	1	70	50	87	Ivory Coast
3803	1510	3540	3.7	9	38	53	0.736	2607	6420	5.4	4.7	0.6	11	19	43	Jamaica
963587	39640	22110	2.9	2	38	60	0.94	2903	608	7	4.7	1.1	0	0	*106	Japan
6354	1510	4060	-2.8	8	27	65	0.73	3022	554	7.9	3.8	6.7	21	7	127	Jordan
22143	1330	3010	-8.6	12	30	58	0.709	...	254	2.2	5.4	3	4	1	2	Kazakstan
7583	280	1380	0.1	29	17	54	0.463	2075	21970	1.9	6.8	2.3	30	14	42	Kenya
24000	1000	4000	-8	...	...	...	0.765	2833	370	...	...	25.2	5	5	1	Korea, North
435137	9700	11450	7.6	7	43	50	0.89	3285	951	5.4	4.5	3.4	2	2	1	Korea, South
3158	700	1800	-6.9	44	24	32	0.635	...	303	3.5	6.8	3.5	4	1	19	Kyrgyzstan
1694	350	2500	2.7	52	18	30	0.459	2259	4446	2.6	2.3	4.2	56	31	66	Laos
5708	2270	3370	-6.6	9	31	60	0.711	...	278	3.7	6.5	3.2	0	0	14	Latvia
10673	2660	4800	2.7	7	24	69	0.794	3317	537	5.3	2	5.3	10	5	48	Lebanon
1519	770	1780	1.5	10	56	34	0.457	2201	24095	3.5	4.8	5.5	38	19	57	Lesotho
2300	850	1000	1.5	...	...	...	...	1640	25000	8.2	...	4.8	78	46	23	Liberia
38000	7000	6000	1	8	48	44	0.801	3308	957	...	9.6	5.5	37	12	1	Libya
7070	1900	4120	-11.7	11	36	53	0.762	...	235	4.8	4.5	2.4	2	1	14	Lithuania
16876	41210	37930	1	1	33	66	0.899	...	460	6.3	3.1	0.9	0	0	*148	Luxembourg
1813	860	4000	-15	19	44	37	0.748	...	427	7.7	5.6	...	16	6	...	Macedonia
3178	230	640	-2	34	13	53	0.35	2135	8385	1	1.9	1.1	27	12	23	Madagascar
1623	170	750	-0.7	42	27	31	0.32	1825	44205	2.3	3.4	1.2	58	28	40	Malawi
78321	3890	9020	5.7	13	43	44	0.832	2888	2441	1.4	5.3	4.5	22	11	6	Malaysia
2410	250	550	0.6	46	17	37	0.229	2278	18376	1.3	2.1	2.4	77	61	57	Mali
4070	11000	13000	5.1	3	28	69	0.887	3486	410	12.1	5.1	1.1	4	4	...	Malta
1049	460	1540	0.5	27	30	43	0.355	2685	15772	1.5	...	1.9	74	50	99	Mauritania
3815	3380	13210	5.7	9	33	58	0.831	...	1165	2.2	3.7	0.5	21	13	21	Mauritius
304596	3320	6400	0.1	8	26	66	0.853	3146	615	5.3	5.8	0.9	13	8	4	Mexico
3996	920	1600	-8.2	50	28	22	0.612	...	250	5.1	5.5	3.7	6	1	5	Moldova
767	310	1950	-3.8	21	46	33	0.661	1899	371	4.7	5.2	2.4	23	11	88	Mongolia
29545	1110	3340	0.8	14	33	53	0.566	2984	4665	3.4	5.4	4.3	69	43	19	Morocco
1353	80	810	3.6	33	21	46	0.281	1680	36225	4.6	6.2	3.7	77	42	66	Mozambique
3098	2000	4150	2.8	14	29	57	0.57	2134	4328	7.6	8.7	2.7	26	22	125	Namibia
4391	200	1170	2.4	42	22	36	0.347	1957	13634	5	2.9	1	86	59	21	Nepal
371039	24000	19950	1.8	3	27	70	0.94	3222	399	8.8	5.5	2.2	0	0	*172	Netherlands
51655	14340	16360	0.6	7	25	68	0.937	3669	518	7.5	7.3	1.7	1	1	*31	New Zealand
1659	380	2000	-5.8	33	20	47	0.53	2293	2039	7.8	3.8	1.8	33	35	155	Nicaragua
1961	220	750	-2.1	39	18	43	0.206	2257	53986	2.2	3.1	0.9	93	79	30	Niger
28411	260	1220	1.2	43	27	30	0.393	2124	5208	2.7	1.3	2.9	53	33	2	Nigeria
136077	31250	21940	1.6	3	36	61	0.943	3244	308	7.3	9.2	2.6	0	0	*255	Norway
10578	4820	8140	0.3	3	48	49	0.718	...	1131	2.5	4.5	15.1	76	42	29	Oman
59991	460	2230	1.2	26	24	50	0.445	2315	1923	0.8	2.7	6.5	76	50	6	Pakistan
7235	2750	5980	-0.4	11	18	71	0.864	2242	562	7.5	5.2	1.3	10	9	19	Panama
4976	1160	2420	2.1	26	38	36	0.525	2613	12754	2.8	...	1.3	37	19	88	Papua New Guinea
8158	1690	3650	1.1	24	22	54	0.706	2670	1231	4.3	2.9	1.4	9	7	30	Paraguay
55019	2310	3770	-1.6	7	38	55	0.717	1882	939	4.9	1.5	1.6	17	6	18	Peru
71865	1050	2850	1.5	22	32	46	0.672	2257	8273	2.4	2.4	1.6	6	5	109	Philippines
107829	2790	5400	-0.4	6	39	55	0.834	3301	451	4.6	5.5	2.5	2	1	40	Poland
96689	9740	12670	3.7	6	40	54	0.89	3634	353	7.6	5.4	2.9	13	13	*27	Portugal
27750	7500	7000	2.1	1	42	57	...	...	350	...	...	...	10	10	...	Puerto Rico
33488	1480	4360	-4	21	49	30	0.748	3051	538	3.3	3.1	3.1	5	1	3	Romania
331948	2240	4480	-5.1	7	38	55	0.792	...	222	4.8	4.4	7.4	3	0	12	Russia
1128	180	540	-5	37	17	46	0.187	1821	24967	1.9	3.8	4.4	48	30	92	Rwanda
133540	7040	9500	-1.9	6	51	43	0.774	2735	749	2.2	6.4	10.6	50	29	1	Saudi Arabia
5070	600	1780	-1.2	20	18	62	0.326	2262	18192	1.6	4.2	1.9	77	57	82	Senegal
762	180	580	-3.4	42	27	31	0.176	1694	11000	1.6	1.4	5.7	82	55	45	Sierra Leone
79831	26730	22770	6.2	0	36	64	0.9	...	714	3.5	3.3	5.9	14	4	6	Singapore
15848	2950	3610	-2.6	6	33	61	0.873	...	287	6.3	4.9	2.8	0	0	6	Slovak Rep.
16328	8200	10400	-1	5	39	56	0.886	...	500	7.9	6.2	1.5	0	0	...	Slovenia
4625	500	1000	-2.3	65	9	26	...	1499	13300	1.5	0.4	0.9	52	39	61	Somalia
130918	3160	5030	-1	5	31	64	0.716	2695	1500	7.9	7.1	2.9	18	18	10	South Africa
532347	13580	14520	2.6	3	31	66	0.934	3708	261	7.4	4.7	1.5	6	2	*31	Spain
12616	700	3250	2.7	23	25	52	0.711	2273	6843	1.9	3.2	4.9	13	7	31	Sri Lanka
20000	750	1050	0.6	36	18	46	0.333	2202	10000	0.3	...	4.3	65	42	8	Sudan

Wealth — **Social Indicators** — **Aid**

	Population									Land and Agriculture					Energy	Trade	
	Population Total 1997	Population Density 1997	Average Annual Change 1970-80	Average Annual Change 1990-97	Birth Rate 1997	Death Rate 1997	Fertility Rate 1995	Life Expectancy Average 1997	Urban Population 1995	Land Area	Arable and Permanent Crops	Permanent grassland	Forest	Agriculture Population 1995	Consumption per capita 1994	Imports per capita 1995	Exports per capita 1995
	millions	persons per km²	%	%	births per thousand population	deaths per thousand population	children	years	%	thousand km²	% of land area	% of land area	% of land area	% of economically active pop.	tonnes of coal	US $	US $
Surinam	0.5	3	-0.6	1.5	24	6	2.6	70	52	156	0	0	96	20	2.01	1565	873
Swaziland	1	55	3	3.1	43	10	4.6	58	29	17.2	11	62	7	34	...	1090	855
Sweden	8.9	22	0.3	0.7	11	11	1.7	78	84	412	7	1	68	4	6.79	7299	9051
Switzerland	7.1	180	0.2	1	11	10	1.5	78	61	39.6	11	29	32	5	4.5	10938	11088
Syria	15.3	83	3.5	2.9	39	6	4.8	67	52	184	30	45	3	33	1.28	325	280
Taiwan	21.7	603	2	0.9	15	6	1.8	76	76	36	26	11	52	19	2.5	4868	5238
Tajikistan	6	42	3	1.8	34	8	4.2	65	32	143	6	25	4	38	0.58	93	84
Tanzania	31.2	35	3.4	2.8	41	20	5.8	42	24	884	4	40	38	83	0.04	55	23
Thailand	60.8	119	2.7	0.9	17	7	1.8	69	19	511	41	2	26	60	1.07	1236	946
Togo	4.5	82	2.6	3.4	46	10	6.4	58	31	54.4	45	4	17	62	0.08	94	51
Trinidad & Tobago	1.3	253	1.1	0.2	16	7	2.1	70	70	5.13	24	2	46	9	7.53	1329	1904
Tunisia	9.2	59	2.2	1.9	24	5	2.9	73	57	155	32	20	4	24	0.75	886	614
Turkey	63.5	83	2.3	1.1	22	5	2.7	72	65	770	36	16	26	51	1.16	579	350
Turkmenistan	4.8	10	2.7	3.9	29	9	3.8	62	47	488	3	64	9	36	3.68	250	533
Uganda	20.8	104	3	2.4	45	21	6.7	40	12	200	34	9	32	83	0.03	50	22
Ukraine	51.5	85	0.6	-0.1	12	15	1.5	67	69	604	59	13	18	18	4.39	192	187
United Kingdom	58.6	243	0.1	0.3	13	11	1.7	77	90	242	25	46	10	2	5.33	4527	4130
United States	268	28	1.1	1	15	9	2.1	76	77	9573	20	25	30	3	11.39	2929	2222
Uruguay	3.3	19	0.4	0.7	17	9	2.2	75	90	175	7	77	5	14	0.78	899	660
Uzbekistan	23.8	56	2.9	2.1	29	8	3.7	65	42	425	11	50	3	34	2.94	111	138
Venezuela	22.5	26	3.5	1.9	24	5	3.1	72	92	882	4	20	34	11	3.75	553	854
Vietnam	77.1	237	2.3	2.1	22	7	3.1	67	20	325	21	1	30	69	0.16	30	30
Yemen	16.5	31	1.9	5.6	45	9	7.4	60	34	528	3	30	4	57	0.33	165	74
Yugoslavia	10.5	103	1	0.3	14	10	1.9	72	54	102	40	21	26	20	1.22	533	452
Zambia	9.5	13	3.2	2.4	44	24	5.7	45	45	743	7	40	43	74	0.19	12	94
Zimbabwe	12.1	31	3.1	3.7	32	19	3.8	60	32	387	7	44	23	67	0.7	231	183

	Land area thousand sq km	Population 1997 thousands		Land area thousand sq km	Population 1997 thousands		Land area thousand sq km	Population 1997 thousands
American Samoa	0.2	62	French Polynesia	3.66	226	Pitcairn I.	0.05	0.05
Andorra	0.45	75	Gaza Strip	0.36	900	Qatar	11	62
Anguilla	0.1	10	Gibraltar	0.01	28	Réunion	2.5	68
Antigua & Barbuda	0.44	66	Greenland	342	57	St Kitts-Nevis	0.36	4
Aruba	0.19	70	Grenada	0.34	99	St Helena	0.3	
Ascension I.	0.09	1.1	Guadeloupe	1.69	440	St Lucia	0.61	15
Bahrain	0.68	605	Guam	0.55	161	St Pierre & Miquelon	0.23	
Belize	22.8	228	Kiribati	0.73	85	St Vincent & the Grenadines	0.39	11
Bermuda	0.05	65	Kuwait	17.8	2050	San Marino	0.06	2
Bhutan	47	1790	Liechtenstein	0.16	32	Sâo Tomé & Principe	0.96	13
British Virgin Is.	0.15	13	Macau	0.02	450	Seychelles	0.45	7
Brunei	5.27	300	Maldives	0.3	275	Solomon Is.	28	41
Cape Verde Is.	4.03	410	Marshall Is.	0.18	60	Svalbard	63	2
Cayman Is.	0.26	35	Martinique	1.06	405	Tokelau	0.01	
Cocos Is.	0.01	1	Mayotte	0.37	105	Tonga	0.72	10
Comoros	2.23	630	Micronesia	0.7	127	Turks & Caicos Is.	0.43	1
Cook Is.	0.23	20	Monaco	0.002	33	Tuvalu	0.03	1
Djibouti	23.2	650	Montserrat	0.1	12	United Arab Emirates	83.6	2400
Dominica	0.75	78	Nauru	0.02	53	US Virgin Is.	0.34	11
Equatorial Guinea	28.1	420	Netherlands Antilles	0.8	12	Vanuatu	12.2	17
Eritrea	101	3500	New Caledonia	18.3	210	Vatican City	0.0004	
Falkland Is.	12.2	2	Niue	0.26	192	Wallis & Futuna Is.	0.2	1
Faroe Is.	1.4	45	Norfolk I.	0.04	2	West Bank	5.9	149
Fiji	18.3	800	Northern Marianas	0.48	2	Western Sahara	267	28
French Guiana	88.2	155	Palau	0.49	17	Western Samoa	2.83	17

SATELLITE IMAGERY AND REMOTE SENSING

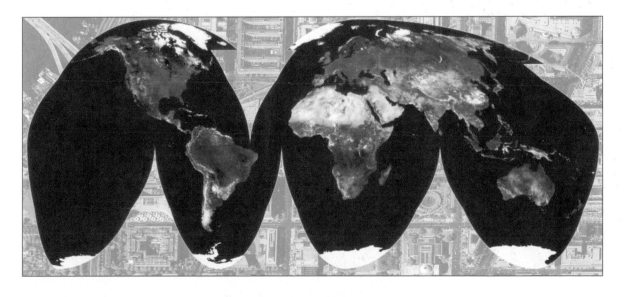

All satellite images in this section courtesy of NPA Group Limited, Edenbridge, Kent (www.satmaps.com)
Philip's would like to acknowledge the valuable assistance of Richard Chiles and the staff at NPA in the preparation of this section.

The first satellite to monitor our environment systematically was launched as long ago as April 1961. It was called TIROS-1 and was designed specifically to record atmospheric change. The first of the generation of Earth resources satellites was Landsat-1, launched in July 1972.

The succeeding two or three decades have seen a revolution in our ability to survey and map our global environment. Digital sensors mounted on satellites now scan vast areas of the Earth's surface day and night. They collect and relay back to Earth huge volumes of geographical data which is processed and stored by computers.

Satellite Imagery and Remote Sensing
Continuous development and refinement, and freedom from national access restrictions, have meant that sensors on these satellite platforms are increasingly replacing surface and airborne data-gathering techniques. Twenty-four hours a day, satellites are scanning and measuring the Earth's surface and atmosphere, adding to an ever-expanding range of geographic and geophysical data available to help us identify and manage the problems of our human and physical environments. Remote sensing is the science of extracting information from such images.

Satellite Orbits
Most Earth-observation satellites (such as the Landsat, SPOT and IRS series) are in a near-polar, Sun-synchronous orbit (*see diagram opposite*). At altitudes of around 700–900 km the satellites revolve around the Earth approximately every 100 minutes and on each orbit cross a particular line of latitude at the same local (solar) time. This ensures that the satellite can obtain coverage of most of the globe, replicating the coverage typically within 2–3 weeks. In more recent satellites, sensors can be pointed sideways from the orbital path, and 'revisit' times with high-resolution frames can thus be reduced to a few days.

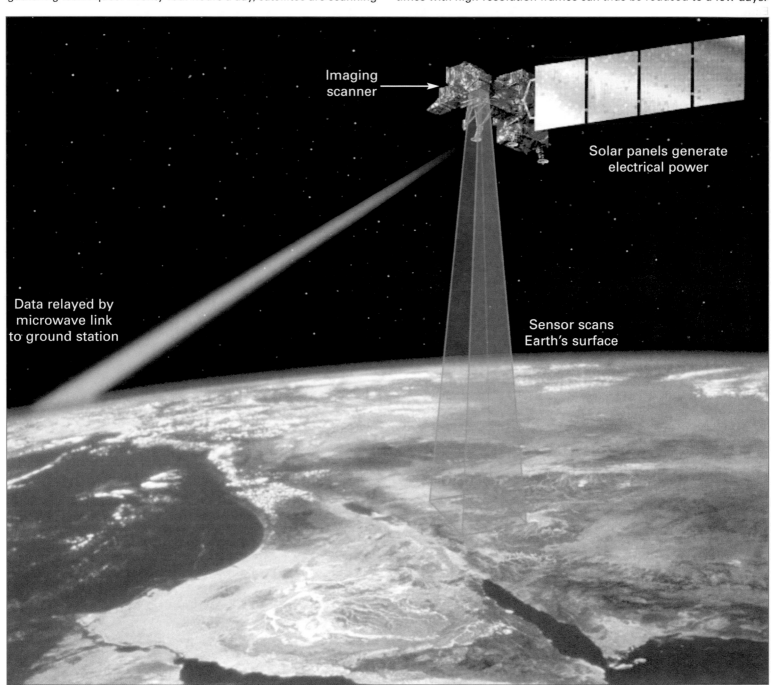

Imaging scanner

Solar panels generate electrical power

Data relayed by microwave link to ground station

Sensor scans Earth's surface

Landsat-7
This is the latest addition to the Landsat Earth-observation satellite programme, orbiting at 705 km above the Earth. With onboard recorders, the satellite can store data until it passes within range of a ground station. Basic geometric and radiometric corrections are then applied before distribution of the imagery to users.

Exceptions to these Sun-synchronous orbits include the geostationary meteorological satellites, such as Meteosat. These have a 36,000 km high orbit and rotate around the Earth every 24 hours, thus remaining above the same point on the equator. These satellites acquire frequent images showing cloud and atmospheric moisture movements for almost a full hemisphere.

In addition, there is the Global Positioning System (GPS) satellite 'constellation', which orbits at a height of 20,200 km, consisting of 24 satellites. These circle the Earth in six different orbital planes, enabling us to fix our position on the Earth's surface to an accuracy of a few centimetres. Although developed for military use, this system is now available to individuals through hand-held receivers and in-car navigation systems. The other principal commercial uses are for surveying and air and sea navigation.

Digital Sensors

Early satellite designs involved images being exposed to photographic film and returned to Earth by capsule for processing, a technique still sometimes used today. However, even the first commercial satellite imagery, from Landsat-1, used digital imaging sensors and transmitted the data back to ground stations (*see diagram opposite*).

Passive, or optical, sensors record the radiation reflected from the Earth for specific wavebands. Active sensors transmit their own microwave radiation, which is reflected from the Earth's surface back to the satellite and recorded. The SAR (synthetic aperture radar) Radarsat images on page 118 are examples of the latter.

Whichever scanning method is used, each satellite records image data of constant width but potentially several thousand kilometres in length. Once the data has been received on Earth, it is usually split into approximately square sections or 'scenes' for distribution.

Spectral Resolution, Wavebands and False-Colour Composites

Satellites can record data from many sections of the electromagnetic spectrum (wavebands) simultaneously. Since we can only see images made from the three primary colours (red, green and blue), a selection of any three wavebands needs to be made in order to form a picture that will enable visual interpretation of the scene to be made. When any combination other than the visible bands are used, such as near or middle infrared, the resulting image is termed a 'false colour composite'. An example of this is shown on page 109.

The selection of these wavebands depends on the purpose of the final image – geology, hydrology, agronomy and environmental

GEOGRAPHIC INFORMATION SYSTEMS

A Geographic Information System (GIS) enables any available geospatial data to be compiled, presented and analysed using specialized computer software.

Many aspects of our lives now benefit from the use of GIS – from the management and maintenance of the networks of pipelines and cables that supply our homes, to the exploitation or protection of the natural resources that we use. Much of this is at a regional or national scale and the data collected from satellites form an important part of our interpretation and understanding of the world around us.

GIS systems are used for many aspects of central planning and modern life, such as defence, land use, reclamation, telecommunications and the deployment of emergency services. Commercial companies can use demographic and infrastructure data within a GIS to plan marketing strategies, identifying where their services would be most needed, and thus decide where best to locate their businesses. Insurance companies use GIS to determine premiums based on population distribution, crime figures and the likelihood of natural disasters, such as flooding or subsidence.

Whatever the application, all the geographically related information that is available can be input and prepared in a GIS, so that a user can display the specific information of interest, or combine data to produce further information which might answer or help resolve a specific problem. From analysis of the data that has been acquired, it is often possible to use a GIS to generate a 'model' of possible future situations and to see what impact might result from decisions and actions taken. A GIS can also monitor change over time, to aid the observation and interpretation of long-term change.

A GIS can utilize a satellite image to extract useful information and map large areas, which would otherwise take many man-years of labour to achieve on the ground. For industrial applications, including hydrocarbon and mineral exploration, forestry, agriculture, environmental monitoring and urban development, such dramatic and beneficial increases in efficiency have made it possible to evaluate and undertake projects and studies in parts of the world that were previously considered inaccessible, and on a scale that would not have been possible before.

requirements each have their own optimum waveband combinations. The following pages give an indication of the variety and detail provided by satellite imagery.

SELECTED REMOTE SENSING SATELLITES

Year Launched	Satellite	Country	Repeat Cycle
Passive Sensors (Optical)			
1972	Landsat-1 MSS	USA	18 days
1975	Landsat-2 MSS	USA	18 days
1978	Landsat-3 MSS	USA	18 days
1978	NOAA AVHRR	USA	12 hours
1981	Cosmos TK-350	Russia	varied
1982	Landsat-4 TM	USA	16 days
1984	Landsat-5 TM	USA	16 days
1986	SPOT-1	France	26 days
1988	IRS-1A	India	22 days
1988	SPOT-2	France	26 days
1989	Cosmos KVR-1000	Russia	varied
1991	IRS-1B	India	22 days
1992	SPOT-3	France	26 days
1995	IRS-1C	India	24 days
1997	IRS-1D	India	24 days
1998	SPOT-4	France	26 days
1999	Landsat-7 ETM	USA	16 days
1999	UoSAT-12	UK	n/a
1999	IKONOS-2	USA	n/a
Active Sensors (Synthetic Aperture Radar)			
1991	ERS-1	Europe	up to 168 days
1992	JERS-1	Japan	44 days
1995	ERS-2	Europe	35 days
1995	Radarsat	Canada	16 days

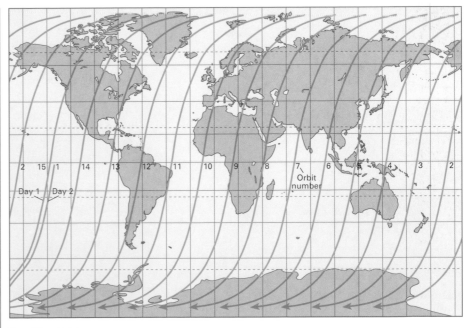

Satellite Orbits

Landsat-7 makes over 14 orbits per day in its Sun-synchronous orbit. During the full 16 days of a repeat cycle, coverage of the areas between those shown is achieved.

Natural-colour and false-colour composites

These images show the salt ponds at the southern end of San Francisco Bay, which now form the San Francisco Bay National Wildlife Refuge. They demonstrate the difference between 'natural colour' (*left*) and 'false colour' (*right*) composites.

The image on the left is made from visible red, green and blue

wavelengths. The colours correspond closely to those one would observe from an aircraft. The salt ponds appear green or orange-red due to the colour of the sediments they contain. The urban areas appear grey and vegetation is either dark green (trees) or light brown (dry grass).

The right-hand image is made up of near-infrared, visible red and

visible green wavelengths. These wavebands are represented here in red, green and blue, respectively. Since chlorophyll in healthy vegetation strongly reflects near-infrared light, this is clearly visible as red in the image.

 False-colour composite imagery is therefore very sensitive to the presence of healthy vegetation. The image above thus shows better discrimination between the 'leafy' residential urban areas, such as Palo Alto (south-west of the Bay) from other urban areas by the 'redness' of the trees. The high chlorophyll content of watered urban grass areas shows as bright red, contrasting with the dark red of trees and the brown of natural, dry grass. *(EROS)*

Europe at Night

This image was derived as part of the Defense Meteorological Satellite Program. The sensor recorded all the emissions of near-infrared radiation at night, mainly the lights from cities, towns and villages. Note also the 'lights' in the North Sea from the flares of the oil production platforms. This project was the first systematic attempt to record human settlement on a global scale using remote sensing. *(NOAA)*

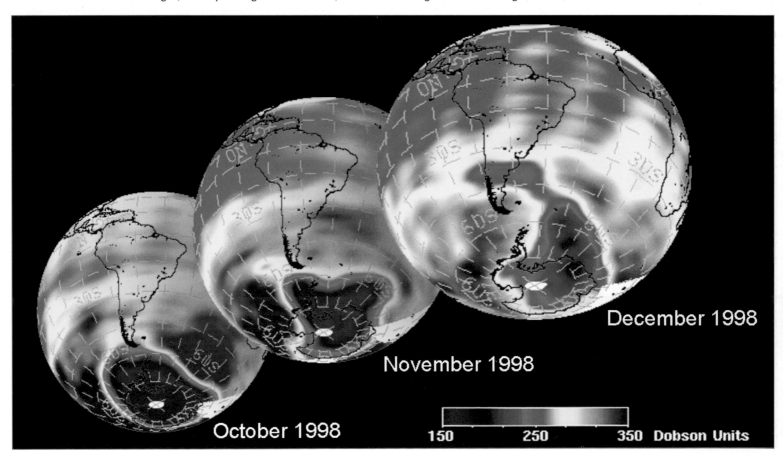

December 1998

November 1998

October 1998

150　　250　　350 **Dobson Units**

Ozone Distribution

The Global Ozone Monitoring Experiment (GOME) sensor was launched in April 1995. This instrument can measure a range of atmospheric trace constituents, in particular global ozone distributions. Environmental and public health authorities need this up-to-date information to alert people to health risks. Low ozone levels result in increased UV-B radiation, which is harmful and can cause cancers, cataracts and impact the human immune system. 'Dobson Units' indicate the level of ozone depletion (normal levels are around 280DU). *(DLR)*

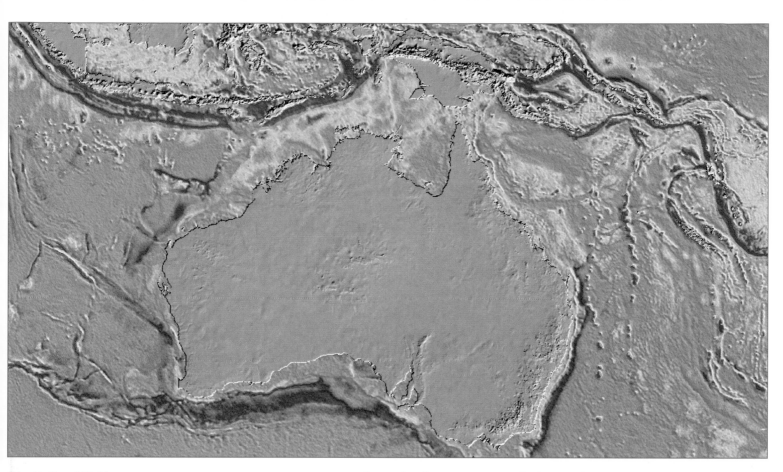

Gravitational Fields

The strength of the Earth's gravitational field at its surface varies according to the ocean depth and the density of local rocks. This causes local variations in the sea level. Satellites orbiting in precisely determined orbits are able to measure the sea level to an accuracy of a few centimetres. These variations give us a better understanding of the geological structure of the sea floor. Information from these sensors can also be used to determine ocean wave heights, which relate to surface wind speed, and are therefore useful in meteorological forecasting. *(NPA)*

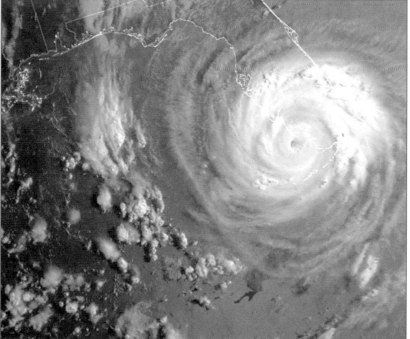

Weather Monitoring

Geostationary and polar orbiting satellites monitor the Earth's cloud and atmospheric moisture movements, giving us an insight into the global workings of the atmosphere and permitting us to predict weather change. *(J-2)*

Hurricane Andrew

Although Hurricane Andrew, which hit Florida on 23 August 1992, was the most expensive natural disaster ever to strike the USA, its effects would have been far more disastrous had its path not been precisely tracked by large scale satellite images such as this from the AVHRR sensor. *(NOAA)*

Western Grand Canyon, Arizona, USA
This false-colour image shows in red the sparse vegetation on the limestone plateau, including sage, mesquite and grasses. Imagery such as this is used to monitor this and similar fragile environments. The sediment-laden river, shown as blue-green, can be seen dispersing into Lake Mead to the north-west. Side canyons cross the main canyon in straight lines, showing where erosion along weakened fault lines has occurred. *(EROS)*

Niger Delta, West Africa
The River Niger is the third longest river in Africa after the Nile and Congo. Deltas are by nature constantly evolving sedimentary features and often contain many ecosystems within them. In the case of the Niger Delta, there are also vast hydrocarbon reserves beneath it with associated wells and pipelines. Satellite imagery helps to plan activity and monitor this fragile and changing environment. *(EROS)*

Ayers Rock and Mt Olga, Northern Territory, Australia
These two huge outliers are the remnants of Precambrian mountain ranges created some 500 million years ago and then eroded away. Ayers Rock (*right*) rises 345 m above the surrounding land and has been a part of Aboriginal life for over 10,000 years. Their dramatic coloration, caused by oxidized iron in the sandstone, attracts visitors from around the world. The Yulara tourist resort (shown in blue) and the airport can be made out to the north of Ayers Rock. *(EROS)*

Mount St Helens, Washington, USA
A massive volcanic eruption on 18 May 1980 killed 60 people and devastated around 400 sq km of forest within minutes. The blast reduced the mountain peak by 400 m to its current height of 2550 m, and volcanic ash rose some 25 km into the atmosphere. The image shows Mount St Helens eight years after the eruption in 1988. The characteristic volcanic cone has collapsed in the north, resulting in the devastating 'liquid' flow of mud and rock. *(EROS)*

Kuwait City, Kuwait

This image shows Kuwait after the war with Iraq, which took place in 1991. During this conflict, more than 600 oil wells were set on fire and over 300 oil lakes were formed (visible as dark areas to the south). Satellite imagery helped reduce the costs of mapping these oil spills and enabled the level of damage to be determined prior to clean-up operations. *(Space Imaging)*

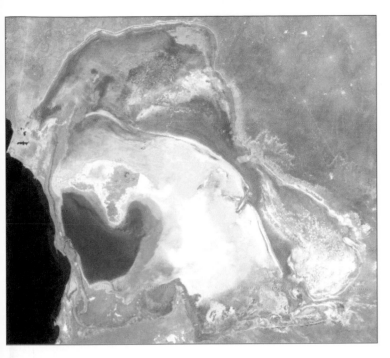

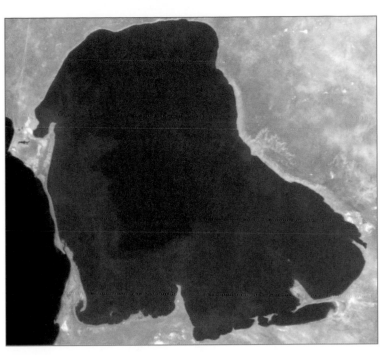

Kara-Bogaz-Gol, Turkmenistan

The Kara-Bogaz-Gol is a large, shallow lagoon joined by a narrow, steep-sided strait to the Caspian Sea. Evaporation makes it one of the most saline bodies of water in the world. Believing the Caspian sea level was falling, the straight was dammed by the USSR in 1980 with the intention of conserving the water to sustain the salt industry. However, by 1983 it had dried up completely (*left*), leading to widespread wind-blown salt, soil poisoning and health problems downwind to the east. In 1992 the Turkmenistan government began to demolish the dam to re-establish the flow of water from the Caspian Sea (*right*). Satellite imagery has helped monitor and map the Kara-Bogaz-Gol as it has fluctuated in size. *(EROS)*

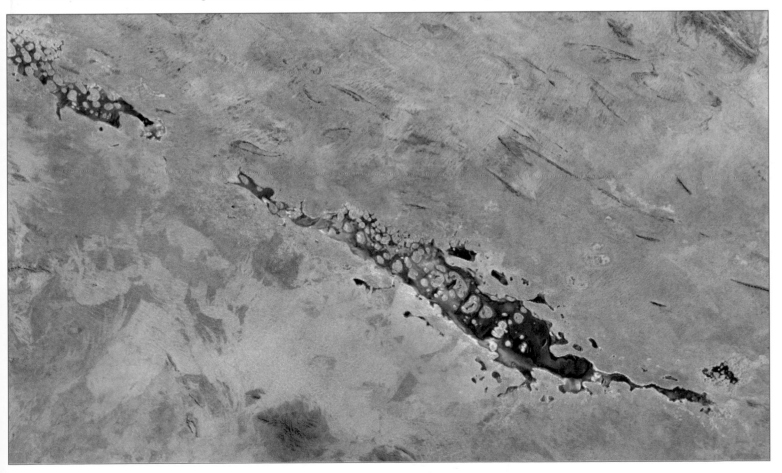

Lake Amadeus, Northern Territory, Australia

This is a saline lake system in the area between the Great Sandy Desert and Ayers Rock. An important wetland environment at the heart of one of the most arid areas in Australia, it supports a wide range of complex habitats and exists due to seepage from the central Australian groundwater system. Changes in its extent in an otherwise remote site can be monitored using satellite imagery such as this Landsat ETM scene. *(EROS)*

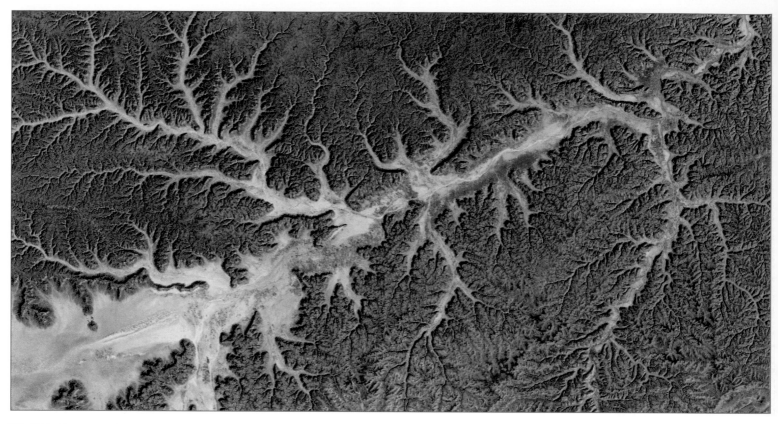

Wadi Hadhramaut, Yemen

Yemen is extremely arid – however, in the past it was more humid and wet, enabling large river systems to carve out the deep and spectacular gorges and dried-out river beds (*wadis*) seen in this image. The erosion has revealed many contrasting rock types. The image has been processed to exaggerate this effect, producing many shades of red, pink and purple, which make geological mapping easier and more cost-effective. *(EROS)*

North Anatolian Fault, Turkey

The east–west trending valley that runs through the centre of the image is formed by the North Anatolian wrench fault. It is the result of Arabia colliding with southern Eurasia, forcing most of Turkey westwards towards Greece. The valley was created by the Kelkit river removing the loosened rock formed by the two tectonic plates grinding together. This active fault has recently caused considerable damage further east in the Gulf of Izmit (*see page 120*). *(EROS)*

Zagros Mountains, Iran
These mountains were formed as Arabia collided with Southern Eurasia. The centre of this colour-enhanced image shows an anticline that runs east–west. The dark grey features are called *diapirs*, which are bodies of viscous rock salt that are very buoyant and sometimes rise to the surface, spilling and spreading out like a glacier. The presence of salt in the region is important as it stops oil escaping to the surface. *(EROS)*

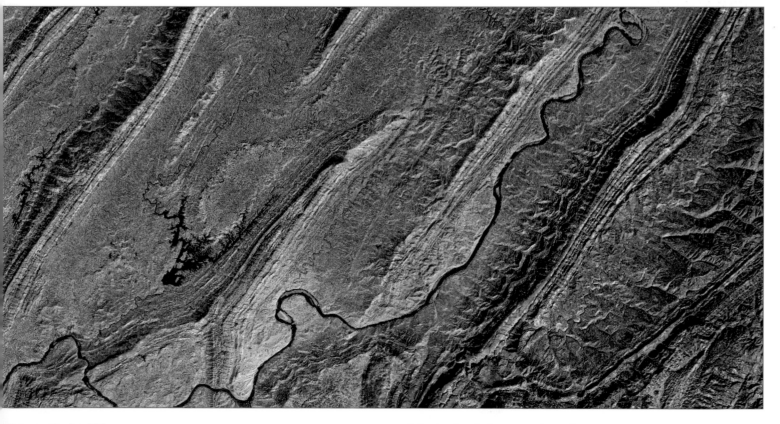

Sichuan Basin, China
The north-east/south-west trending ridges in this image are anticlinal folds developed in the Earth's crust as a result of plate collision and compression. Geologists map these folds and the lowlands between them formed by synclinal folds, as they are often the areas where oil or gas are found in commercial quantities. The river shown in this image is the Yangtze, near Chongqing. *(China RSGS)*

Montserrat, Caribbean Sea

Synthetic Aperture Radar (SAR) sensors send out a microwave signal and create an image from the radiation reflected back. The signal penetrates cloud cover and does not need any solar illumination. This image of Montserrat shows how the island can still be seen, despite clouds and the continuing eruption of the Soufrière volcano in the south. The delta visible in the sea to the east is being formed by lava flows pouring down the Tar River Valley. *(Radarsat)*

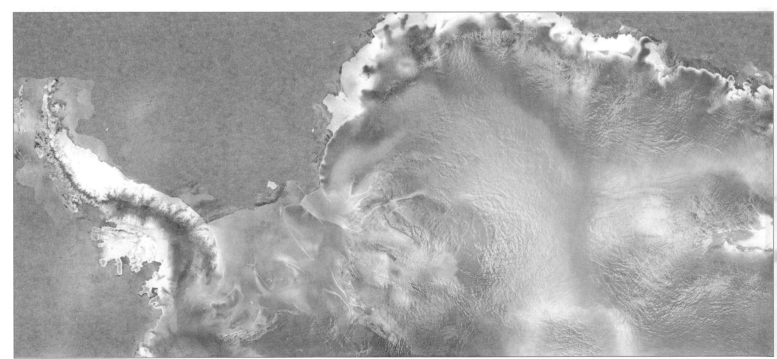

Antarctic Peninsula

SAR image brightness is dependent on surface texture. This image of part of Antarctica clearly shows the Antarctic ice tongues projecting from the Wilkins and George VI Ice Shelves at the south-west end of the peninsula as well as other coastal ice features. Images can be received, even during the winter 'night', and over a period of time form a valuable resource in our ability to monitor the recession of the ice and also the 'calving' of icebergs. *(Radarsat)*

Las Vegas, Nevada, USA

Two satellite images viewing the same area of ground from different orbits can be used to compile a Digital Elevation Model (DEM) of the Earth's surface. A computer compares the images and calculates the ground surface elevation to a vertical precision of 8–15 m, preparing this for thousands of square kilometres in just a few minutes. Overlaying a colour satellite image on to a DEM produced the picture of Las Vegas shown here. *(NPA)*

Legend:
- Urban (tall)
- Urban dense
- Urban
- Industrial
- Paved
- Urban / Tree mix
- Trees (coniferous)
- Trees (deciduous)
- Forest clearing
- Grass or crops
- Open
- Water

Seattle, Washington, USA

Image processing software can use the differing spectral properties of land cover to 'classify' a multispectral satellite image. This classification of the area around Seattle was used together with elevation data to model the transmission of mobile phone signals before installation of the network. Microwave signals are affected by the absorption, reflection and scattering of the signal from vegetation and urban structures as well as the topography. *(NPA)*

Gulf of Izmit, north-west Turkey

On 17 August 1999 an earthquake measuring 7.4 on the Richter scale caused extensive damage and loss of life around Izmit. This image is a composite of two black-and-white images, one recorded on 7 August 1999 and the other on 24 September 1999. The colours in the image indicate change: orange highlights severely damaged buildings and areas where debris has been deposited during the rescue operation; blue indicates areas submerged beneath sea level as a result of the Earth's movement during the earthquake and fire-damaged oil tanks in the north-west. *(NPA)*

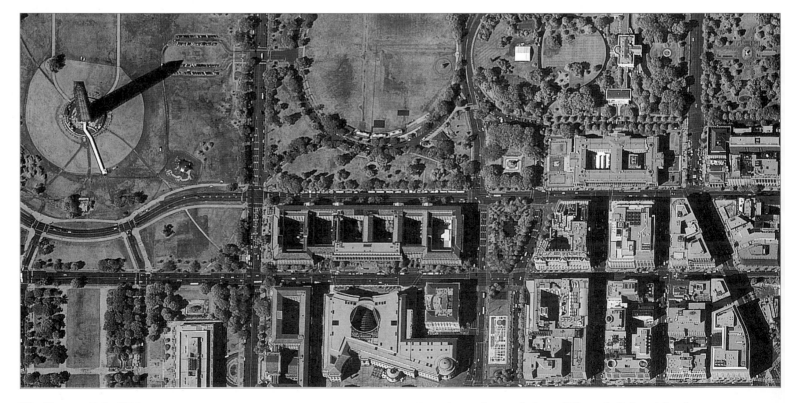

Washington D.C., USA

This image, with the White House seen at top right and the Washington Monument to the left, was recorded on 30 September 1999 by Space Imaging's IKONOS-2 satellite. It was the first satellite image to be commercially available with a ground-sampling interval (pixel size) of 1 m. With a directional sensor, image acquisition attempts can be made in as little as 1–3 days (cloud cover permitting). This level of resolution enables satellite imagery to be used as a data source for many applications that otherwise require expensive aerial surveys to be flown. In addition, data can readily be acquired for projects in remote regions of the world or areas where access is restricted. *(Space Imaging)*

INDEX TO
WORLD MAPS

The index contains the names of all the principal places and features shown on the World Maps. Each name is followed by an additional entry in italics giving the country or region within which it is located. The alphabetical order of names composed of two or more words is governed primarily by the first word and then by the second. This is an example of the rule:

New South Wales □, *Australia*..	**34 G8**	33 0S	146 0E
New York □, *U.S.A.*	**43 D10**	42 40N	76 0W
New York City, *U.S.A.*	**43 E11**	40 45N	74 0W
New Zealand ■, *Oceania*	**35 J13**	40 0S	176 0E
Newark, *U.S.A.*	**43 F10**	39 42N	75 45W

Physical features composed of a proper name (Erie) and a description (Lake) are positioned alphabetically by the proper name. The description is positioned after the proper name and is usually abbreviated:

Erie, L., *N. Amer.*	**42 D7**	42 15N	81 0W

Where a description forms part of a settlement or administrative name, however, it is always written in full and put in its true alphabetical position:

Mount Isa, *Australia*	**34 E6**	20 42S	139 26E

Names beginning with M' and Mc are indexed as if they were spelt Mac. Names beginning St. are alphabetized under Saint, but Santa and San are all spelt in full and are alphabetized accordingly. If the same placename occurs two or more times in the index and all are in the same country, each is followed by the name of the administrative subdivision in which it is located. The names are placed in the alphabetical order of the subdivision. For example:

Columbus, Ga., *U.S.A.*	**41 D10**	32 30N	84 58W
Columbus, Ind., *U.S.A.*	**42 F5**	39 14N	85 55W
Columbus, Ohio, *U.S.A.*	**42 F6**	39 57N	83 1W

The number in bold type which follows each name in the index refers to the number of the map page where that feature or place will be found. This is usually the largest scale at which the place or feature appears.

The letter and figure which are in bold type immediately after the page number give the grid square on the map page, within which the feature is situated. The letter represents the latitude and the figure the longitude. In some cases the feature itself may fall within the specified square, while the name is outside.

For a more precise location, the geographical co-ordinates which follow the letter-figure references give the latitude and the longitude of each place. The first set of figures represent the latitude, which is the distance north or south of the Equator measured as an angle at the centre of the Earth. The Equator is latitude 0°, the North Pole is 90°N, and the South Pole 90°S.

The second set of figures represent the longitude, which is the distance east or west of the prime meridian, which runs through Greenwich, England. Longitude is also measured as an angle at the centre of the Earth and is given east or west of the prime meridian, from 0° to 180° in either direction.

The unit of measurement for latitude and longitude is the degree, which is subdivided into 60 minutes. Each index entry states the position of a place in degrees and minutes, a space being left between the degrees and the minutes. The latitude is followed by N(orth) or S(outh) and the longitude by E(ast) or W(est).

Rivers are indexed to their mouths or confluences, and carry the symbol ⇝ after their names. A solid square ■ follows the name of a country, while an open square □ refers to a first order administrative area.

ABBREVIATIONS USED IN THE INDEX

Afghan. – Afghanistan	Conn. – Connecticut	Isla, Island, Isle(s)	Mo. – Missouri	Nebr. – Nebraska	Provincial	Sib. – Siberia
Ala. – Alabama	Cord. – Cordillera	Ill. – Illinois	Mont. – Montana	Neths. – Netherlands	Pt. – Point	St. – Saint, Sankt, Sint
Alta. – Alberta	Cr. – Creek	Ind. – Indiana	Mozam.– Mozambique	Nev. – Nevada	Pta. – Ponta, Punta	Str. – Strait, Stretto
Amer. – America(n)	D.C. – District of	Ind. Oc. – Indian Ocean	Mt.(s).– Mont, Monte,	Nfld. – Newfoundland	Pte. – Pointe	Switz. – Switzerland
Arch. – Archipelago	Columbia	Ivory C. – Ivory Coast	Monti, Montaña,	Nic. – Nicaragua	Qué. – Québec	Tas. – Tasmania
Ariz. – Arizona	Del. – Delaware	Kans. – Kansas	Mountain		Queens. – Queensland	Tenn. – Tennessee
Ark. – Arkansas	Domin. – Dominica	Ky. – Kentucky	N. – Nord, Norte, North,		R. – Rio, River	Tex. – Texas
Atl. Oc. – Atlantic Ocean	Dom. Rep. – Dominican	L. – Lac, Lacul, Lago,	Northern	Okla. – Oklahoma	R.I. – Rhode Island	Trin. & Tob. – Trinidad
B. – Baie, Bahia, Bay,	Republic	Lagoa, Lake, Limni,	N.B. – New Brunswick	Ont. – Ontario	Ra.(s). – Range(s)	& Tobago
Bucht, Bugt	E. – East	Loch, Lough	N.C. – North Carolina	Oreg. – Oregon	Reg. – Region	U.A.E. – United Arab
B.C. – British Columbia	El Salv. – El Salvador	La. – Louisiana	N. Cal. – New Caledonia	P.E.I. – Prince Edward	Rep. – Republic	Emirates
Bangla. – Bangladesh	Eq. Guin. – Equatorial	Lux. – Luxembourg	N. Dak. – North Dakota	Island	Res. – Reserve,	U.K. – United Kingdom
C. – Cabo, Cap, Cape,	Guinea	Madag. – Madagascar	N.H. – New Hampshire	Pa. – Pennsylvania	Reservoir	U.S.A. – United States
Coast	Fla. – Florida	Man. – Manitoba	N.J. – New Jersey	Pac. Oc. – Pacific Ocean	S. – San, South	of America
C.A.R. – Central African	Falk. Is. – Falkland Is.	Mass.– Massachusetts	N. Mex. – New Mexico	Papua N.G. – Papua	Si. Arabia – Saudi Arabia	Va. – Virginia
Republic	G. – Golfe, Golfo, Gulf	Md. – Maryland	N.S. – Nova Scotia	New Guinea	S.C. – South Carolina	Vic. – Victoria
C. Prov. – Cape	Ga. – Georgia	Me. – Maine	N.S.W. – New South	Pen. – Peninsula,	S. Dak. – South Dakota	Vol. – Volcano
Province	Guinea-Biss. –	Medit. S. –	Wales	Peninsule	S. Leone – Sierra Leone	Vt. – Vermont
Calif. – California	Guinea–Bissau	Mediterranean Sea	N.W.T. – North West	Phil. – Philippines	Sa. – Serra, Sierra	W. – West
Cent. – Central	Hd. – Head	Mich. – Michigan	Territory	Pk. – Park, Peak	Sask. – Saskatchewan	W. Va. – West Virginia
Chan. – Channel	Hts. – Heights	Minn. – Minnesota	N.Y. – New York	Plat. – Plateau	Scot. – Scotland	Wash. – Washington
Colo. – Colorado	I.(s). – Ile, Ilha, Insel,	Miss. – Mississippi	N.Z. – New Zealand	Prov. – Province,	Sd. – Sound	Wis. – Wisconsin

Place names on the yellow-coded large scale map section are to be found in the index at the end of that section

Place names on the yellow-coded large scale map section are to be found in the index at the end of that section

INDEX TO WORLD MAPS

C

Place names on the yellow-coded large scale map section are to be found in the index at the end of that section

INDEX TO WORLD MAPS

Erie — Greenville

Erie, U.S.A. 42 D7 42 8N 80 5W
Erie, L., N. Amer. 42 D7 42 15N 81 0W
Eritrea ■, Africa 29 F12 14 0N 38 30 E
Erlangen, Germany 10 D6 49 36N 11 0 E
Ermelo, S. Africa 31 B4 26 31S 29 59 E
Erode, India 25 D6 11 24N 77 45 E
Erzgebirge, Germany 10 C7 50 27N 12 55 E
Erzurum, Turkey 15 G7 39 57N 41 15 E
Esbjerg, Denmark 6 G9 55 29N 8 29 E
Escanaba, U.S.A. 42 C4 45 45N 87 4W
Esch-sur-Alzette, Lux. 10 D3 49 32N 6 0 E
Esfahan, Iran 24 B4 32 39N 51 43 E
Eskilstuna, Sweden 6 G11 59 22N 16 32 E
Eskimo Pt. = Arviat, Canada 38 B10 61 10N 94 15W
Eskişehir, Turkey 15 G5 39 50N 30 35 E
Esperance, Australia 34 G3 33 45S 121 55 E
Essen, Germany 10 C4 51 28N 7 0 E
Estcourt, S. Africa 31 B4 29 0S 29 53 E
Estonia ■, Europe 14 C4 58 30N 25 30 E
Etawah, India 23 F7 26 48N 79 6 E
Ethiopia ■, Africa 32 C7 8 0N 40 0 E
Ethiopian Highlands, Ethiopia 26 E7 10 0N 37 0 E
Etna, Italy 12 F6 37 50N 14 55 E
Euclid, U.S.A. 42 E7 41 34N 81 32W
Eugene, U.S.A. 40 B2 44 5N 123 4W
Euphrates →, Asia 24 B3 31 0N 47 25 E
Evanston, U.S.A. 42 D4 42 3N 87 41W
Evansville, U.S.A. 42 G4 37 58N 87 35W
Everest, Mt., Nepal 23 E11 28 5N 86 58 E
Évora, Portugal 9 C2 38 33N 7 57W
Évreux, France 8 B4 49 3N 1 8 E
Évvoia, Greece 13 E11 38 30N 24 0 E
Exeter, U.K. 7 F5 50 43N 3 31W
Extremadura □, Spain 9 C2 39 30N 6 5W
Eyre, L., Australia 34 F6 29 30S 137 26 E

F

Færoe Is., Atl. Oc. 5 C4 62 0N 7 0W
Fairbanks, U.S.A. 38 B5 64 51N 147 43W
Fairfield, U.S.A. 42 F3 38 23N 88 22W
Fairmont, U.S.A. 42 F7 39 29N 80 9W
Faisalabad, Pakistan 23 D4 31 30N 73 5 E
Faizabad, India 23 F9 26 45N 82 10 E
Fakfak, Indonesia 22 D5 3 0S 132 15 E
Falkland Is. □, Atl. Oc. 47 H4 51 30S 59 0W
Fall River, U.S.A. 43 E12 41 43N 71 10W
Falmouth, U.S.A. 42 F5 38 41N 84 20W
Falun, Sweden 6 F11 60 37N 15 37 E
Farah, Afghan. 24 B5 32 20N 62 7 E
Farmville, U.S.A. 42 G8 37 18N 78 24W
Fatehgarh, India 23 F7 27 25N 79 35 E
Fatehpur, India 23 G8 25 56N 81 13 E
Faya-Largeau, Chad 29 E8 17 58N 19 6 E
Fayetteville, U.S.A. 41 C11 35 3N 78 53W
Fazilka, India 23 D5 30 27N 74 2 E
Fdérik, Mauritania 28 D2 22 40N 12 45W
Fécamp, France 8 B4 49 45N 0 22 E
Fehmarn, Germany 10 A6 54 27N 11 7 E
Feira de Santana, Brazil 46 D6 12 15S 38 57W
Fernando Póo = Bioko, Eq. Guin. 30 D3 3 30N 8 40 E
Ferrara, Italy 12 B4 44 50N 11 35 E
Ferret, C., France 8 D3 44 38N 1 15W
Fès, Morocco 28 B4 34 0N 5 0W
Fianarantsoa, Madag. 33 J9 21 26S 47 5 E
Ficksburg, S. Africa 31 B4 28 51S 27 53 E
Figeac, France 8 D5 44 37N 2 2 E
Fiji ■, Pac. Oc. 35 D14 17 20S 179 0 E
Findlay, U.S.A. 42 E6 41 2N 83 39W
Finisterre, C., Spain 9 A1 42 50N 9 19W
Finland ■, Europe 6 F13 63 0N 27 0 E
Finland, G. of, Europe 6 G12 60 0N 26 0 E
Firozabad, India 23 F7 27 10N 78 25 E
Firozpur, India 23 D5 30 55N 74 40 E
Fish →, Namibia 31 B2 28 7S 17 10 E
Fitchburg, U.S.A. 43 D12 42 35N 71 48W
Flandre, Europe 10 C2 51 0N 3 0 E
Flensburg, Germany 10 A5 54 47N 9 27 E
Flers, France 8 B3 48 47N 0 33W
Flinders →, Australia 34 D7 17 36S 140 36 E
Flinders Ras., Australia 34 G6 31 30S 138 30 E
Flint, U.S.A. 42 D6 43 1N 83 41W
Flint →, U.S.A. 41 D10 30 57N 84 34W
Flora, U.S.A. 42 F3 38 40N 88 29W
Florence, Italy 12 C4 43 46N 11 15 E
Flores, Indonesia 22 D4 8 35S 121 0 E
Florianópolis, Brazil 47 E5 27 30S 48 30W
Florida □, U.S.A. 41 E10 28 0N 82 0W
Florida, Straits of, U.S.A. 45 C9 25 0N 80 0W
Florida Keys, U.S.A. 41 F10 24 40N 81 0W
Florø, Norway 6 F9 61 35N 5 1 E
Focşani, Romania 11 F14 45 41N 27 15 E
Fóggia, Italy 12 D6 41 27N 15 34 E
Foix, France 8 E4 42 58N 1 38 E
Fontainebleau, France 8 B5 48 24N 2 40 E
Fontenay-le-Comte, France 8 C3 46 28N 0 48W
Forlì, Italy 12 B5 44 13N 12 3 E
Fort Beaufort, S. Africa 31 C4 32 46S 26 40 E
Fort Collins, U.S.A. 40 B5 40 35N 105 5W
Fort-Coulonge, Canada 42 C9 45 50N 76 45W
Fort-de-France, Martinique 44 N20 14 36N 61 2W
Fort Kent, U.S.A. 43 B13 47 15N 68 36W
Fort Lauderdale, U.S.A. 41 E10 26 7N 80 8W
Fort McMurray, Canada 38 C8 56 44N 111 7W
Fort Sandeman, Pakistan 23 D2 31 20N 69 31 E
Fort Smith, U.S.A. 41 C8 35 23N 94 25W
Fort Wayne, U.S.A. 42 E5 41 4N 85 9W
Fort Worth, U.S.A. 41 D7 32 45N 97 18W
Fortaleza, Brazil 46 C6 3 45S 38 35W
Foshan, China 21 D6 23 4N 113 5 E
Fostoria, U.S.A. 42 E6 41 10N 83 25W
Fougères, France 8 B3 48 21N 1 14W
Foxe Chan., Canada 39 B11 65 0N 80 0W
France ■, Europe 8 C5 47 0N 3 0 E
Franche-Comté, France 8 C6 46 50N 5 55 E
Francistown, Botswana 31 A4 21 7S 27 33 E
Frankfort, S. Africa 31 B4 27 17S 28 30 E
Frankfort, Ind., U.S.A. 42 E4 40 17N 86 31W
Frankfort, Ky., U.S.A. 42 F5 38 12N 84 52W
Frankfort, Mich., U.S.A. 42 C4 44 38N 86 14W
Frankfurt, Brandenburg, Germany 10 B8 52 20N 14 32 E
Frankfurt, Hessen, Germany 10 C5 50 7N 8 41 E
Franklin, N.H., U.S.A. 43 D12 43 27N 71 39W
Franklin, Pa., U.S.A. 42 E8 41 24N 79 50W
Franz Josef Land, Russia 18 A7 82 0N 55 0 E
Fraser →, Canada 38 D7 49 7N 123 11W
Fraserburg, S. Africa 31 C3 31 55S 21 30 E
Frederick, U.S.A. 42 F9 39 25N 77 25W
Fredericksburg, U.S.A. 42 F9 38 18N 77 28W
Fredericton, Canada 43 C14 45 57N 66 40W
Fredonia, U.S.A. 42 D8 42 26N 79 20W
Fredrikstad, Norway 6 G10 59 13N 10 57 E
Free State □, S. Africa 31 B4 28 30S 27 0 E
Freetown, S. Leone 28 G2 8 30N 13 17W
Freiburg, Germany 10 E4 47 59N 7 51 E
Fremont, U.S.A. 42 E6 41 21N 83 7W
French Creek →, U.S.A. 42 E8 41 24N 79 50W
French Guiana □, S. Amer. 46 B4 4 0N 53 0W
French Polynesia □, Pac. Oc. 37 J13 20 0S 145 0W
Fresnillo, Mexico 44 C4 23 10N 103 0W
Fresno, U.S.A. 40 C3 36 44N 119 47W
Frobisher B., Canada 39 B13 62 30N 66 0W
Front Royal, U.S.A. 42 F8 38 55N 78 12W
Frunze = Bishkek, Kyrgyzstan 18 E9 42 54N 74 46 E
Frýdek-Místek, Czech Rep. 11 D10 49 40N 18 20 E
Fuji-San, Japan 19 B6 35 22N 138 44 E
Fujian □, China 21 D6 26 0N 118 0 E
Fukui, Japan 19 A5 36 5N 136 10 E
Fukuoka, Japan 19 C2 33 39N 130 21 E
Fukushima, Japan 19 A7 37 44N 140 28 E
Fukuyama, Japan 19 B3 34 35N 133 20 E
Fulda, Germany 10 C5 50 32N 9 40 E
Fulda →, Germany 10 C5 51 25N 9 39 E
Fulton, U.S.A. 42 D9 43 19N 76 25W
Funafuti, Pac. Oc. 35 B14 8 30S 179 0 E
Fundy, B. of, Canada 43 C15 45 0N 66 0W
Furneaux Group, Australia 34 J8 40 10S 147 50 E
Fürth, Germany 10 D6 49 28N 10 59 E
Fury and Hecla Str., Canada 39 B11 69 56N 84 0W
Fushun, China 21 B7 41 50N 123 56 E
Fuxin, China 21 B7 42 5N 121 48 E
Fuzhou, China 21 D6 26 5N 119 16 E
Fyn, Denmark 6 G10 55 20N 10 30 E

G

Gabès, Tunisia 28 B7 33 53N 10 2 E
Gabon ■, Africa 32 E2 0 10S 10 0 E
Gaborone, Botswana 31 A4 24 45S 25 57 E
Gabrovo, Bulgaria 13 C11 42 52N 25 19 E
Gadag, India 25 D6 15 30N 75 45 E
Gadarwara, India 23 H7 22 50N 78 50 E
Gainesville, U.S.A. 41 E10 29 40N 82 20W
Galápagos, Pac. Oc. 37 H18 0 0 91 0W
Galaţi, Romania 11 F15 45 27N 28 2 E
Galdhøpiggen, Norway 6 F9 61 38N 8 18 E
Galicia □, Spain 9 A2 42 43N 7 45W
Galle, Sri Lanka 25 E7 6 5N 80 10 E
Gallipoli, Turkey 13 D12 40 28N 26 43 E
Gallipolis, U.S.A. 42 F6 38 49N 82 12W
Gällivare, Sweden 6 E12 67 9N 20 40 E
Galveston, U.S.A. 41 E8 29 18N 94 48W
Galway, Ireland 7 E2 53 17N 9 3W
Gambia ■, W. Afr. 28 F1 13 25N 16 0W
Gan Jiang →, China 21 D6 29 15N 116 0 E
Gananoque, Canada 43 C9 44 20N 76 10W
Gandak →, India 23 G10 25 39N 85 13 E
Gandhi Sagar Dam, India 23 G5 24 40N 75 40 E
Ganganagar, India 23 E4 29 56N 73 56 E
Gangdisê Shan, China 23 D8 31 20N 81 0 E
Ganges →, India 23 H13 23 20N 90 30 E
Gangtok, India 23 F12 27 20N 88 37 E
Gansu □, China 20 C5 36 0N 104 0 E
Gap, France 8 D7 44 33N 6 5 E
Garda, L. di, Italy 12 B4 45 40N 10 41 E
Gardēz, Afghan. 23 C2 33 37N 69 9 E
Garies, S. Africa 31 C2 30 32S 17 59 E
Garonne →, France 8 D3 45 2N 0 36W
Garoua, Cameroon 30 C4 9 19N 13 21 E
Gary, U.S.A. 42 E4 41 36N 87 20W
Garzê, China 20 C5 31 38N 100 1 E
Gascogne, France 8 E4 43 45N 0 20 E
Gascogne, G. de, Europe 8 D2 44 0N 2 0W
Gaspé, Canada 43 A15 48 52N 64 30W
Gaspé, C., Canada 43 A15 48 48N 64 7W
Gaspé Pen., Canada 43 A15 48 45N 65 40W
Gatineau →, Canada 43 C10 45 27N 75 42W
Gatun, Panama 44 H14 9 16N 79 55W
Gatun, L., Panama 44 H14 9 7N 79 56W
Gauhati, India 23 F13 26 10N 91 45 E
Gävle, Sweden 6 F11 60 40N 17 9 E
Gawilgarh Hills, India 23 J6 21 15N 76 45 E
Gaya, India 23 G10 24 47N 85 4 E
Gaylord, U.S.A. 42 C5 45 2N 84 41W
Gaziantep, Turkey 15 G6 37 6N 37 23 E
Gcuwa, S. Africa 31 C4 32 20S 28 11 E
Gdańsk, Poland 11 A10 54 22N 18 40 E
Gdynia, Poland 11 A10 54 35N 18 33 E
Gebe, Indonesia 22 C4 0 5N 129 25 E
Gedser, Denmark 6 H10 54 35N 11 55 E
Geelong, Australia 34 H7 38 10S 144 22 E
Gejiu, China 20 D5 23 20N 103 10 E
Gelsenkirchen, Germany 10 C4 51 32N 7 1 E
Geneva, Switz. 10 E4 46 12N 6 9 E
Geneva, U.S.A. 42 D9 42 52N 76 59W
Geneva, L. = Léman, L., Europe 10 E4 46 26N 6 30 E
Gennargentu, Mti. del, Italy 12 D3 40 1N 9 19 E
Genoa, Italy 12 B3 44 25N 8 57 E
Gent, Belgium 10 C2 51 2N 3 42 E
George, S. Africa 31 C3 33 58S 22 29 E
George Town, Malaysia 22 C2 5 25N 100 15 E
Georgetown, Guyana 46 B4 6 50N 58 12W
Georgetown, U.S.A. 42 F5 38 13N 84 33W
Georgia □, U.S.A. 41 D10 32 50N 83 15W
Georgia ■, Asia 15 F7 42 0N 43 0 E
Georgian B., Canada 42 C7 45 15N 81 0W
Gera, Germany 10 C7 50 53N 12 4 E
Geraldton, Australia 34 F1 28 48S 114 32 E
Geraldton, Canada 42 A4 49 44N 86 59W
Germany ■, Europe 10 C6 51 0N 10 0 E
Germiston, S. Africa 31 B4 26 15S 28 10 E
Gerona, Spain 9 B7 41 58N 2 46 E
Getafe, Spain 9 B4 40 18N 3 44W
Ghaghara →, India 23 G10 25 45N 84 40 E
Ghana ■, W. Afr. 30 C1 8 0N 1 0W
Ghanzi, Botswana 31 A3 21 50S 21 34 E
Ghazâl, Bahr el →, Sudan 32 C6 9 31N 30 25 E
Ghaziabad, India 23 E6 28 42N 77 26 E
Ghazipur, India 23 G9 25 38N 83 35 E
Ghazni, Afghan. 23 C2 33 30N 68 28 E
Ghent = Gent, Belgium 10 C2 51 2N 3 42 E
Gibraltar □, Europe 9 D3 36 7N 5 22W
Gibraltar, Str. of, Medit. S. 9 E3 35 55N 5 40W
Gibson Desert, Australia 34 E4 24 0S 126 0 E
Gifu, Japan 19 B5 35 30N 136 45 E
Gijón, Spain 9 A3 43 32N 5 42W
Gilgit, India 23 B5 35 50N 74 15 E
Giridih, India 23 G11 24 10N 86 21 E
Gironde →, France 8 D3 45 32N 1 7W
Gisborne, N.Z. 35 H14 38 39S 178 5 E
Giza, Egypt 29 C11 30 0N 31 10 E
Gizhiga, Russia 18 C18 62 3N 160 30 E
Glace Bay, Canada 43 B18 46 11N 59 58W
Gladstone, Australia 34 E9 23 52S 151 16 E
Gladstone, U.S.A. 42 C4 45 51N 87 1W
Gladwin, U.S.A. 42 D5 43 59N 84 29W
Glasgow, U.K. 7 D4 55 51N 4 15W
Glasgow, U.S.A. 42 G5 37 0N 85 55W
Glencoe, S. Africa 31 B5 28 11S 30 11 E
Glendale, U.S.A. 40 D3 34 9N 118 15W
Glens Falls, U.S.A. 43 D11 43 19N 73 39W
Gliwice, Poland 11 C10 50 22N 18 41 E
Głogów, Poland 10 C9 51 37N 16 5 E
Glomma →, Norway 6 G10 59 12N 10 57 E
Gloversville, U.S.A. 43 D10 43 3N 74 21W
Gniezno, Poland 11 B9 52 30N 17 35 E
Go Cong, Vietnam 22 B2 10 22N 106 40 E
Goa □, India 25 D6 15 33N 73 59 E
Gobabis, Namibia 31 A2 22 30S 19 0 E
Gobi, Asia 21 B6 44 0N 111 0 E
Godavari →, India 25 D7 16 25N 82 18 E
Goderich, Canada 42 D7 43 45N 81 41W
Godhra, India 23 H4 22 49N 73 40 E
Godthåb = Nuuk, Greenland 48 C4 64 10N 51 35W
Gogama, Canada 42 B7 47 35N 81 43W
Goiânia, Brazil 46 D5 16 43S 49 20W
Gold Coast, Australia 34 F9 28 0S 153 25 E
Gomel, Belarus 11 B16 52 28N 31 0 E
Gómez Palacio, Mexico 44 B4 25 40N 104 0W
Gonabad, Iran 24 B4 34 15N 58 45 E
Gonda, India 23 F8 27 9N 81 58 E
Gonder, Ethiopia 29 F12 12 39N 37 30 E
Gondia, India 23 J8 21 23N 80 10 E
Good Hope, C. of, S. Africa 31 C2 34 24S 18 30 E
Gorakhpur, India 23 F9 26 47N 83 23 E
Gorkiy = Nizhniy Novgorod, Russia 14 C7 56 20N 44 0 E
Görlitz, Germany 10 C8 51 9N 14 58 E
Gorontalo, Indonesia 22 C4 0 35N 123 5 E
Gorzów Wielkopolski, Poland 10 B8 52 43N 15 15 E
Gota Canal, Sweden 6 G11 58 30N 15 58 E
Gotha, Germany 10 C6 50 56N 10 42 E
Gothenburg, Sweden 6 G10 57 43N 11 59 E
Gotland, Sweden 6 G11 57 30N 18 33 E
Göttingen, Germany 10 C5 51 31N 9 55 E
Gouda, Neths. 10 B3 52 1N 4 42 E
Gouin Res., Canada 43 A10 48 35N 74 40W
Goulburn, Australia 34 G8 34 44S 149 44 E
Governador Valadares, Brazil 46 D5 18 15S 41 57W
Gozo, Malta 12 F6 36 3N 14 13 E
Graaff-Reinet, S. Africa 31 C3 32 13S 24 32 E
Grahamstown, S. Africa 31 C4 33 19S 26 31 E
Grampian Mts., U.K. 7 C4 56 50N 4 0W
Gran Canaria, Canary Is. 28 C1 27 55N 15 35W
Gran Chaco, S. Amer. 47 E3 25 0S 61 0W
Granada, Spain 9 D4 37 10N 3 35W
Granby, Canada 43 C11 45 25N 72 45W
Grand Bahama I., Bahamas 45 B9 26 40N 78 30W
Grand Canyon, U.S.A. 40 C4 36 3N 112 9W
Grand Canyon National Park, U.S.A. 40 C4 36 15N 112 30W
Grand Cayman, Cayman Is. 45 D8 19 20N 81 20W
Grand Haven, U.S.A. 42 D4 43 4N 86 13W
Grand L., Canada 43 C14 45 57N 66 7W
Grand Manan I., Canada 43 C14 44 45N 66 52W
Grand-Mère, Canada 43 B11 46 36N 72 40W
Grand Rapids, U.S.A. 42 D4 42 58N 85 40W
Grand St.-Bernard, Col du, Europe 10 F4 45 50N 7 10 E
Grande, Rio →, U.S.A. 41 E7 25 58N 97 9W
Grande de Santiago →, Mexico 44 C3 21 36N 105 26W
Grande Prairie, Canada 38 C8 55 10N 118 50W
Granville, U.S.A. 43 D11 43 24N 73 16W
Grasse, France 8 E7 43 38N 6 56 E
Graulhet, France 8 E4 43 45N 1 59 E
Grayling, U.S.A. 42 C5 44 40N 84 43W
Graz, Austria 10 E8 47 4N 15 27 E
Great Abaco I., Bahamas 45 B9 26 25N 77 10W
Great Australian Bight, Australia 34 G4 33 30S 130 0 E
Great Barrier Reef, Australia 34 D8 18 0S 146 50 E
Great Basin, U.S.A. 40 B3 40 0N 117 0W
Great Bear L., Canada 38 B7 65 30N 120 0W
Great Belt, Denmark 6 G10 55 20N 11 0 E
Great Dividing Ra., Australia 34 E8 23 0S 146 0 E
Great Falls, U.S.A. 40 A4 47 30N 111 17W
Great Inagua I., Bahamas 45 C10 21 0N 73 20W
Great Karoo, S. Africa 31 C3 31 55S 21 0 E
Great Plains, N. Amer. 40 A6 47 0N 105 0W
Great Salt L., U.S.A. 40 B4 41 15N 112 40W
Great Sandy Desert, Australia 34 E3 21 0S 124 0 E
Great Sangi, Indonesia 22 C4 3 45N 125 30 E
Great Slave L., Canada 38 B8 61 23N 115 38W
Great Victoria Desert, Australia 34 F4 29 30S 126 30 E
Greater Antilles, W. Indies 45 D10 17 40N 74 0W
Greece ■, Europe 13 E9 40 0N 23 0 E
Greeley, U.S.A. 40 B6 40 25N 104 42W
Green →, U.S.A. 42 G4 37 54N 87 30W
Green B., U.S.A. 42 C4 45 0N 87 30W
Green Bay, U.S.A. 42 C4 44 31N 88 0W
Greencastle, U.S.A. 42 F4 39 38N 86 52W
Greenfield, Ind., U.S.A. 42 F5 39 47N 85 46W
Greenfield, Mass., U.S.A. 43 D11 42 35N 72 36W
Greenland □, N. Amer. 48 C4 66 0N 45 0W
Greensboro, U.S.A. 41 C11 36 4N 79 48W
Greensburg, Ind., U.S.A. 42 F5 39 20N 85 29W
Greensburg, Pa., U.S.A. 42 E8 40 18N 79 33W
Greenville, Maine, U.S.A. 43 C13 45 28N 69 35W
Greenville, Mich., U.S.A. 42 D5 43 11N 85 15W

Place names on the yellow-coded large scale map section are to be found in the index at the end of that section

INDEX TO WORLD MAPS

Greenville **Jakarta**

Greenville, *Ohio, U.S.A.* **42 E5** 40 6N 84 38W
Grenada ■, *W. Indies* **44 Q20** 12 10N 61 40W
Grenoble, *France* **8 D6** 45 12N 5 42 E
Grey Ra., *Australia* **34 F7** 27 0S 143 30 E
Greymouth, *N.Z.* **35 J13** 42 29S 171 13 E
Greytown, *S. Africa* **31 B5** 29 1S 30 36 E
Gris-Nez, C., *France* **8 A4** 50 52N 1 35 E
Grodno, *Belarus* **11 B12** 53 42N 23 52 E
Groningen, *Neths.* **10 B4** 53 15N 6 35 E
Groot →, *S. Africa* **31 C3** 33 45S 24 36 E
Groot Vis →, *S. Africa* **31 C4** 33 28S 27 5 E
Gross Glockner, *Austria* **10 E7** 47 5N 12 40 E
Groundhog →, *Canada* **42 A6** 48 45N 82 58W
Groznyy, *Russia* **15 F8** 43 20N 45 45 E
Grudziądz, *Poland* **11 B10** 53 30N 18 47 E
Guadalajara, *Mexico* **44 C4** 20 40N 103 20W
Guadalajara, *Spain* **9 B4** 40 37N 3 12W
Guadalete →, *Spain* **9 D2** 36 35N 6 13W
Guadalquivir →, *Spain* **9 D2** 36 47N 6 22W
Guadarrama, Sierra de, *Spain* **9 B4** 41 0N 4 0W
Guadeloupe □, *W. Indies* **44 L20** 16 20N 61 40W
Guadiana →, *Portugal* **9 D2** 37 14N 7 22W
Guadix, *Spain* **9 D4** 37 18N 3 11W
Guam ■, *Pac. Oc.* **36 F6** 13 27N 144 45 E
Guangdong □, *China* **21 D6** 23 0N 113 0 E
Guangxi Zhuangzu Zizhiqu □, *China* **21 D5** 24 0N 109 0 E
Guangzhou, *China* **21 D6** 23 5N 113 10 E
Guantánamo, *Cuba* **45 C9** 20 10N 75 14W
Guaporé →, *Brazil* **46 D3** 11 55S 65 4W
Guatemala, *Guatemala* **44 E6** 14 40N 90 22W
Guatemala ■, *Cent. Amer.* **44 D6** 15 40N 90 30W
Guayaquil, *Ecuador* **46 C2** 2 15S 79 52W
Guaymas, *Mexico* **44 B2** 27 59N 110 54W
Guelph, *Canada* **42 D7** 43 35N 80 20W
Guéret, *France* **8 C4** 46 11N 1 51 E
Guilin, *China* **21 D6** 25 18N 110 15 E
Guinea ■, *W. Afr.* **28 F2** 10 20N 11 30W
Guinea, Gulf of, *Atl. Oc.* **26 F3** 3 0N 2 30 E
Guinea-Bissau ■, *Africa* **28 F2** 12 0N 15 0W
Guingamp, *France* **8 B2** 48 34N 3 10W
Guiyang, *China* **20 D5** 26 32N 106 40 E
Guizhou □, *China* **20 D5** 27 0N 107 0 E
Gujarat □, *India* **23 H3** 23 20N 71 0 E
Gujranwala, *Pakistan* **23 C5** 32 10N 74 12 E
Gujrat, *Pakistan* **23 C5** 32 40N 74 2 E
Gulbarga, *India* **25 D6** 17 20N 76 50 E
Gulf, The, *Asia* **24 C4** 27 0N 50 0 E
Guna, *India* **23 G6** 24 40N 77 19 E
Guntur, *India* **25 D7** 16 23N 80 30 E
Gurgaon, *India* **23 E6** 28 27N 77 1 E
Gurkha, *Nepal* **23 E10** 28 5N 84 40 E
Guyana ■, *S. Amer.* **46 B4** 5 0N 59 0W
Guyenne, *France* **8 D4** 44 30N 0 40 E
Gwadar, *Pakistan* **24 C5** 25 10N 62 18 E
Gwalior, *India* **23 F7** 26 12N 78 10 E
Gweru, *Zimbabwe* **33 H6** 19 28S 29 45 E
Gyandzha, *Azerbaijan* **15 F8** 40 45N 46 20 E
Gympie, *Australia* **34 F9** 26 11S 152 38 E
Györ, *Hungary* **11 E9** 47 41N 17 40 E
Gyumri, *Armenia* **15 F7** 40 47N 43 50 E

H

Haarlem, *Neths.* **10 B3** 52 23N 4 39 E
Hachinohe, *Japan* **19 F12** 40 30N 141 29 E
Hadd, Ras al, *Oman* **24 C4** 22 35N 59 50 E
Haeju, *N. Korea* **21 C7** 38 3N 125 45 E
Hafizabad, *Pakistan* **23 C4** 32 5N 73 40 E
Hafnarfjörður, *Iceland* **6 B3** 64 4N 21 57W
Hagen, *Germany* **10 C4** 51 21N 7 27 E
Hagerstown, *U.S.A.* **42 F9** 39 39N 77 43W
Hague, C. de la, *France* **8 B3** 49 44N 1 56W
Haguenau, *France* **8 B7** 48 49N 7 47 E
Haifa, *Israel* **24 B2** 32 46N 35 0 E
Haikou, *China* **21 D6** 20 1N 110 16 E
Hail, *Si. Arabia* **24 C3** 27 28N 41 45 E
Hailar, *China* **21 B6** 49 10N 119 38 E
Haileybury, *Canada* **42 B8** 47 30N 79 38W
Hainan □, *China* **21 E5** 19 0N 109 30 E
Haiphong, *Vietnam* **20 D5** 20 47N 106 41 E
Haiti ■, *W. Indies* **45 D10** 19 0N 72 30W
Hakodate, *Japan* **19 F12** 41 45N 140 44 E
Ḥalab, *Syria* **24 B2** 36 10N 37 15 E
Halberstadt, *Germany* **10 C6** 51 54N 11 3 E
Halden, *Norway* **6 G10** 59 9N 11 23 E
Haldwani, *India* **23 E7** 29 31N 79 30 E
Halifax, *Canada* **43 C16** 44 38N 63 35W
Halle, *Germany* **10 C6** 51 30N 11 56 E
Halmahera, *Indonesia* **22 C4** 0 40N 128 0 E
Halmstad, *Sweden* **6 G10** 56 41N 12 52 E
Hama, *Syria* **24 B2** 35 5N 36 40 E
Hamadan, *Iran* **24 B3** 34 52N 48 32 E
Hamamatsu, *Japan* **19 B5** 34 45N 137 45 E
Hamar, *Norway* **6 F10** 60 48N 11 7 E
Hamburg, *Germany* **10 B5** 53 33N 9 59 E
Hämeenlinna, *Finland* **6 F12** 61 0N 24 28 E
Hameln, *Germany* **10 B5** 52 6N 9 21 E
Hamersley Ra., *Australia* **34 E2** 22 0S 117 45 E
Hamilton, *Bermuda* **45 A12** 32 15N 64 45W
Hamilton, *Canada* **42 D8** 43 15N 79 50W
Hamilton, *N.Z.* **35 H14** 37 47S 175 19 E
Hamilton, *U.S.A.* **42 F5** 39 24N 84 34W
Hamm, *Germany* **10 C4** 51 40N 7 50 E
Hammerfest, *Norway* **6 D12** 70 39N 23 41 E
Hammond, *U.S.A.* **42 E4** 41 38N 87 30W
Hammonton, *U.S.A.* **43 F10** 39 39N 74 48W
Hancock, *U.S.A.* **42 B3** 47 8N 88 35W
Hangzhou, *China* **21 C7** 30 18N 120 11 E
Hannover, *Germany* **10 B5** 52 22N 9 46 E
Hanoi, *Vietnam* **20 D5** 21 5N 105 55 E
Hanover, *U.S.A.* **42 F9** 39 48N 76 59W
Haora, *India* **23 H12** 22 37N 88 20 E
Haparanda, *Sweden* **6 E12** 65 52N 24 8 E
Happy Valley-Goose Bay, *Canada* **39 C13** 53 15N 60 20W
Hapur, *India* **23 E6** 28 45N 77 45 E
Harare, *Zimbabwe* **33 H6** 17 43S 31 2 E
Harbin, *China* **21 B7** 45 48N 126 40 E
Harbor Beach, *U.S.A.* **42 D6** 43 51N 82 39W
Hardanger Fjord, *Norway* **6 F9** 60 5N 6 0 E
Harding, *S. Africa* **31 C4** 30 35S 29 55 E
Hari →, *Indonesia* **22 D2** 1 16S 104 5 E
Haridwar, *India* **23 E7** 29 58N 78 9 E
Haringhata →, *Bangla.* **23 J12** 22 0N 89 58 E
Härnösand, *Sweden* **6 F11** 62 38N 17 55 E
Harrisburg, *U.S.A.* **42 E9** 40 16N 76 53W
Harrismith, *S. Africa* **31 B4** 28 15S 29 8 E
Harrisonburg, *U.S.A.* **42 F8** 38 27N 78 52W
Harrisville, *U.S.A.* **42 C6** 44 39N 83 17W
Hart, *U.S.A.* **42 D4** 43 42N 86 22W
Hartford, *Conn., U.S.A.* **43 E11** 41 46N 72 41W
Hartford, *Ky., U.S.A.* **42 G4** 37 27N 86 55W
Harts →, *S. Africa* **31 B3** 28 24S 24 17 E
Harvey, *U.S.A.* **42 E4** 41 36N 87 50W
Haryana □, *India* **23 E6** 29 0N 76 10 E
Harz, *Germany* **10 C6** 51 38N 10 44 E
Hasa, *Si. Arabia* **24 C3** 26 0N 49 0 E
Hastings, *U.S.A.* **42 D5** 42 39N 85 17W
Hathras, *India* **23 F7** 27 36N 78 6 E
Hatteras, C., *U.S.A.* **41 C11** 35 14N 75 32W
Haugesund, *Norway* **6 G9** 59 23N 5 13 E
Havana, *Cuba* **45 C8** 23 8N 82 22W
Havel →, *Germany* **10 B7** 52 50N 12 3 E
Haverhill, *U.S.A.* **43 D12** 42 47N 71 5W
Hawaiian Is., *Pac. Oc.* **40 H17** 20 30N 156 0W
Hawkesbury, *Canada* **43 C10** 45 37N 74 37W
Hay River, *Canada* **38 B8** 60 51N 115 44W
Hazard, *U.S.A.* **42 G6** 37 15N 83 12W
Hazaribag, *India* **23 H10** 23 58N 85 26 E
Hazleton, *U.S.A.* **42 E10** 40 57N 75 59W
Hearst, *Canada* **42 A6** 49 40N 83 41W
Heath Pt., *Canada* **43 A17** 49 8N 61 40W
Hebei □, *China* **21 C6** 39 0N 116 0 E
Hechuan, *China* **20 C5** 30 2N 106 12 E
Heerlen, *Neths.* **10 C3** 50 55N 5 58 E
Hefei, *China* **21 C6** 31 52N 117 18 E
Hegang, *China* **21 B8** 47 20N 130 19 E
Heidelberg, *Germany* **10 D5** 49 24N 8 42 E
Heilbron, *S. Africa* **31 B4** 27 16S 27 59 E
Heilbronn, *Germany* **10 D5** 49 9N 9 13 E
Heilongjiang □, *China* **21 B7** 48 0N 126 0 E
Hejaz, *Si. Arabia* **24 C2** 26 0N 37 30 E
Helgoland, *Germany* **10 A4** 54 10N 7 53 E
Helmand →, *Afghan.* **24 B5** 31 12N 61 34 E
Helsingborg, *Sweden* **6 G10** 56 3N 12 42 E
Helsinki, *Finland* **6 F13** 60 15N 25 3 E
Henan □, *China* **21 C6** 34 0N 114 0 E
Henderson, *U.S.A.* **42 G4** 37 50N 87 35W
Hengyang, *China* **21 D6** 26 52N 112 33 E
Henlopen, C., *U.S.A.* **43 F10** 38 48N 75 6W
Herat, *Afghan.* **24 B5** 34 20N 62 7 E
Herford, *Germany* **10 B5** 52 7N 8 39 E
Hermanus, *S. Africa* **31 C2** 34 27S 19 12 E
Hermosillo, *Mexico* **44 B2** 29 10N 111 0W
Hernád →, *Hungary* **11 D11** 47 56N 21 8 E
's-Hertogenbosch, *Neths.* **10 C3** 51 42N 5 17 E
Hessen □, *Germany* **10 C5** 50 30N 9 0 E
High Atlas, *Morocco* **28 B3** 32 30N 5 0W
Hildesheim, *Germany* **10 B5** 52 9N 9 56 E
Hillsdale, *U.S.A.* **42 E5** 41 56N 84 38W
Hilo, *U.S.A.* **40 J17** 19 44N 155 5W
Hilversum, *Neths.* **10 B3** 52 14N 5 10 E
Himachal Pradesh □, *India* **23 D6** 31 30N 77 0 E
Himalaya, *Asia* **23 E10** 29 0N 84 0 E
Himeji, *Japan* **19 B4** 34 50N 134 40 E
Hindu Kush, *Asia* **23 B2** 36 0N 71 0 E
Hingoli, *India* **23 K6** 19 41N 77 15 E
Hinton, *U.S.A.* **42 G7** 37 40N 80 54W
Hiroshima, *Japan* **19 B3** 34 24N 132 30 E
Hisar, *India* **23 E5** 29 12N 75 45 E
Hispaniola, *W. Indies* **45 D10** 19 0N 71 0W
Hjälmaren, *Sweden* **6 G11** 59 18N 15 40 E
Ho Chi Minh City, *Vietnam* **22 B2** 10 58N 106 40 E
Hobart, *Australia* **34 J8** 42 50S 147 21 E
Hódmezövásárhely, *Hungary* **11 E11** 46 28N 20 22 E
Hoggar, *Algeria* **28 D6** 23 0N 6 30 E
Hohhot, *China* **21 B6** 40 52N 111 40 E
Hokkaidō □, *Japan* **19 F12** 43 30N 143 0 E
Holguín, *Cuba* **45 C9** 20 50N 76 20W
Hollams Bird I., *Namibia* **31 A1** 24 40S 14 30 E
Holland, *U.S.A.* **42 D4** 42 47N 86 7W
Homs, *Syria* **24 B2** 34 40N 36 45 E
Honduras ■, *Cent. Amer.* **44 E7** 14 40N 86 30W
Honduras, G. de, *Caribbean* **44 D7** 16 50N 87 0W
Hong Kong, *China* **21 D6** 22 11N 114 14 E
Hongha →, *Vietnam* **20 D5** 22 0N 104 0 E
Honiara, *Solomon Is.* **35 B10** 9 27S 159 57 E
Honolulu, *U.S.A.* **40 H16** 21 19N 157 52W
Honshū, *Japan* **19 B6** 36 0N 138 0 E
Hooghly →, *India* **23 J12** 21 56N 88 4 E
Hoopeston, *U.S.A.* **42 E4** 40 28N 87 40W
Hoorn, *Neths.* **10 B3** 52 38N 5 4 E
Hopetown, *S. Africa* **31 B3** 29 34S 24 3 E
Hopkinsville, *U.S.A.* **42 G4** 36 52N 87 29W
Hormuz, Str. of, *The Gulf* **24 C4** 26 30N 56 30 E
Horn, C., *Chile* **47 H3** 55 50S 67 30W
Hornavan, *Sweden* **6 E11** 66 15N 17 30 E
Hornell, *U.S.A.* **42 D9** 42 20N 77 40W
Hornepayne, *Canada* **42 A5** 49 14N 84 48W
Horsham, *Australia* **34 H7** 36 44S 142 13 E
Hospitalet de Llobregat, *Spain* **9 B7** 41 21N 2 6 E
Hotan, *China* **20 C2** 37 25N 79 55 E
Houghton, *U.S.A.* **42 B3** 47 7N 88 34W
Houghton L., *U.S.A.* **42 C5** 44 21N 84 44W
Houlton, *U.S.A.* **43 B14** 46 8N 67 51W
Houston, *U.S.A.* **41 E7** 29 46N 95 22W
Hovd, *Mongolia* **20 B4** 48 2N 91 37 E
Hövsgöl Nuur, *Mongolia* **20 A5** 51 0N 100 30 E
Howell, *U.S.A.* **42 D6** 42 36N 83 56W
Howick, *S. Africa* **31 B5** 29 28S 30 14 E
Howrah = Haora, *India* **23 H12** 22 37N 88 20 E
Høyanger, *Norway* **6 F9** 61 13N 6 4 E
Hradec Králové, *Czech Rep.* **10 C8** 50 15N 15 50 E
Hron →, *Slovak Rep.* **11 E10** 47 49N 18 45 E
Huainan, *China* **21 C6** 32 38N 116 58 E
Huambo, *Angola* **33 G3** 12 42S 15 54 E
Huancayo, *Peru* **46 D2** 12 5S 75 12W
Huangshi, *China* **21 C6** 30 10N 115 3 E
Hubei □, *China* **21 C6** 31 0N 112 0 E
Hudiksvall, *Sweden* **6 F11** 61 43N 17 10 E
Hudson →, *U.S.A.* **43 E10** 40 42N 74 2W
Hudson Bay, *Canada* **39 C11** 60 0N 86 0W
Hudson Falls, *U.S.A.* **43 D11** 43 18N 73 35W
Hudson Str., *Canada* **39 B13** 62 0N 70 0W
Hue, *Vietnam* **22 B2** 16 30N 107 35 E
Huelva, *Spain* **9 D2** 37 18N 6 57W
Huesca, *Spain* **9 A5** 42 8N 0 25W
Hughenden, *Australia* **34 E7** 20 52S 144 10 E
Hull = Kingston upon Hull, *U.K.* **7 E6** 53 45N 0 21W
Hull, *Canada* **43 C10** 45 25N 75 44W
Humboldt →, *U.S.A.* **40 B3** 39 59N 118 36W
Húnaflói, *Iceland* **6 B3** 65 50N 20 50W
Hunan □, *China* **21 D6** 27 30N 112 0 E
Hungary ■, *Europe* **11 E10** 47 20N 19 20 E
Hungnam, *N. Korea* **21 C7** 39 49N 127 45 E
Hunsrück, *Germany* **10 D4** 49 56N 7 27 E
Huntington, *Ind., U.S.A.* **42 E5** 40 53N 85 30W
Huntington, *W. Va., U.S.A.* **42 F6** 38 25N 82 27W
Huntsville, *Canada* **42 C8** 45 20N 79 14W
Huntsville, *U.S.A.* **41 D9** 34 44N 86 35W
Huron, L., *U.S.A.* **42 C6** 44 30N 82 40W
Húsavík, *Iceland* **6 A5** 66 3N 17 21W
Hwang-ho →, *China* **21 C6** 37 55N 118 50 E
Hyderabad, *India* **25 D6** 17 22N 78 29 E
Hyderabad, *Pakistan* **23 G2** 25 23N 68 24 E
Hyères, *France* **8 E7** 43 8N 6 9 E
Hyères, Is. d', *France* **8 E7** 43 0N 6 20 E

I

Ialomiţa →, *Romania* **11 F14** 44 42N 27 51 E
Iaşi, *Romania* **11 E14** 47 10N 27 40 E
Ibadan, *Nigeria* **30 C2** 7 22N 3 58 E
Ibagué, *Colombia* **46 B2** 4 20N 75 20W
Iberian Peninsula, *Europe* **4 H5** 40 0N 5 0W
Ibiza, *Spain* **9 C6** 38 54N 1 26 E
Iceland ■, *Europe* **6 B4** 64 45N 19 0W
Ichinomiya, *Japan* **19 B5** 35 18N 136 48 E
Idaho □, *U.S.A.* **40 B4** 45 0N 115 0W
Idar-Oberstein, *Germany* **10 D4** 49 43N 7 16 E
Ife, *Nigeria* **30 C2** 7 30N 4 31 E
Iglésias, *Italy* **12 E3** 39 19N 8 32 E
Igluligaarjuk, *Canada* **38 B10** 63 30N 90 45W
Ignace, *Canada* **42 A2** 49 30N 91 40W
Iguaçu Falls, *Brazil* **47 E4** 25 41S 54 26W
Iisalmi, *Finland* **6 F13** 63 32N 27 10 E
IJsselmeer, *Neths.* **10 B3** 52 45N 5 20 E
Ikaluktutiak, *Canada* **38 B9** 69 10N 105 0W
Ikerre-Ekiti, *Nigeria* **30 C3** 7 25N 5 19 E
Ila, *Nigeria* **30 C2** 8 0N 4 39 E
Île-de-France, *France* **8 B5** 49 0N 2 20 E
Ilesha, *Nigeria* **30 C2** 7 37N 4 40 E
Ilhéus, *Brazil* **46 D6** 14 49S 39 2W
Ili →, *Kazakstan* **18 E9** 45 53N 77 10 E
Iller →, *Germany* **10 D6** 48 23N 9 58 E
Illinois □, *U.S.A.* **41 C9** 40 15N 89 30W
Iloilo, *Phil.* **22 B4** 10 45N 122 33 E
Ilorin, *Nigeria* **30 C2** 8 30N 4 35 E
Imperatriz, *Brazil* **46 C5** 5 30S 47 29W
Imphal, *India* **25 C8** 24 48N 93 56 E
Inari, L., *Finland* **6 E13** 69 0N 28 0 E
Inchon, *S. Korea* **21 C7** 37 27N 126 40 E
Incomáti →, *Mozam.* **31 B5** 25 46S 32 43 E
Indals →, *Sweden* **6 F11** 62 36N 17 30 E
India ■, *Asia* **23 K7** 20 0N 78 0 E
Indiana, *U.S.A.* **42 E8** 40 37N 79 9W
Indiana □, *U.S.A.* **42 E4** 40 0N 86 0W
Indianapolis, *U.S.A.* **42 F4** 39 46N 86 9W
Indigirka →, *Russia* **18 B16** 70 48N 148 54 E
Indonesia ■, *Asia* **22 D3** 5 0S 115 0 E
Indore, *India* **23 H5** 22 42N 75 53 E
Indre →, *France* **8 C4** 47 16N 0 11 E
Indus →, *Pakistan* **23 G1** 24 20N 67 47 E
Ingolstadt, *Germany* **10 D6** 48 46N 11 26 E
Inn →, *Austria* **10 D7** 48 35N 13 28 E
Inner Mongolia □, *China* **21 B6** 42 0N 112 0 E
Innsbruck, *Austria* **10 E6** 47 16N 11 23 E
Inowrocław, *Poland* **11 B10** 52 50N 18 12 E
Insein, *Burma* **25 D8** 16 50N 96 5 E
Interlaken, *Switz.* **10 E4** 46 41N 7 50 E
Inuvik, *Canada* **38 B6** 68 16N 133 40W
Invercargill, *N.Z.* **35 K12** 46 24S 168 24 E
Inverness, *U.K.* **7 C4** 57 29N 4 13W
Ionia, *U.S.A.* **42 D5** 42 59N 85 4W
Ionian Is., *Greece* **13 E9** 38 40N 20 0 E
Ionian Sea, *Medit. S.* **13 E7** 37 30N 17 30 E
Iowa □, *U.S.A.* **41 B8** 42 18N 93 30W
Iowa City, *U.S.A.* **41 B8** 41 40N 91 32W
Ipoh, *Malaysia* **22 C2** 4 35N 101 5 E
Ipswich, *U.K.* **7 E7** 52 4N 1 10 E
Iquique, *Chile* **46 E2** 20 19S 70 5W
Iquitos, *Peru* **46 C2** 3 45S 73 10W
Iráklion, *Greece* **13 G11** 35 20N 25 12 E
Iran ■, *Asia* **24 B4** 33 0N 53 0 E
Iran Ra., *Malaysia* **22 C3** 2 20N 114 50 E
Irapuato, *Mexico* **44 C4** 20 40N 101 30W
Iraq ■, *Asia* **24 B3** 33 0N 44 0 E
Ireland ■, *Europe* **7 E2** 53 50N 7 52W
Irian Jaya □, *Indonesia* **22 D5** 4 0S 137 0 E
Iringa, *Tanzania* **32 F7** 7 48S 35 43 E
Irish Sea, *U.K.* **7 E4** 53 38N 4 48W
Irkutsk, *Russia* **18 D12** 52 18N 104 20 E
Iron Gate, *Europe* **11 F12** 44 42N 22 30 E
Iron Mountain, *U.S.A.* **42 C3** 45 49N 88 4W
Ironton, *U.S.A.* **42 F6** 38 32N 82 41W
Irrawaddy →, *Burma* **25 D8** 15 50N 95 6 E
Irtysh →, *Russia* **18 C8** 61 4N 68 52 E
Ísafjörður, *Iceland* **6 A2** 66 5N 23 9W
Isar →, *Germany* **10 D7** 48 48N 12 57 E
Isère →, *France* **8 D6** 44 59N 4 51 E
Iseyin, *Nigeria* **30 C2** 8 0N 3 36 E
Ishpeming, *U.S.A.* **42 B4** 46 29N 87 40W
İskenderun, *Turkey* **15 G6** 36 32N 36 10 E
Islamabad, *Pakistan* **23 C4** 33 40N 73 10 E
Island Pond, *U.S.A.* **43 C12** 44 49N 71 53W
Ismâ'ilîya, *Egypt* **29 B11** 30 37N 32 18 E
Israel ■, *Asia* **24 B2** 32 0N 34 50 E
Issoire, *France* **8 D5** 45 32N 3 15 E
İstanbul, *Turkey* **13 D13** 41 0N 29 0 E
Istres, *France* **8 E6** 43 31N 4 59 E
Istria, *Croatia* **10 F7** 45 10N 14 0 E
Itaipu Dam, *Brazil* **47 E4** 25 30S 54 30W
Italy ■, *Europe* **12 C5** 42 0N 13 0 E
Ithaca, *U.S.A.* **42 D9** 42 27N 76 30W
Ivanava, *Belarus* **11 B13** 52 7N 25 29 E
Ivano-Frankovsk, *Ukraine* **11 D13** 48 40N 24 40 E
Ivanovo, *Russia* **14 C7** 57 5N 41 0 E
Ivory Coast ■, *Africa* **28 G3** 7 30N 5 0W
Ivujivik, *Canada* **39 B12** 62 24N 77 55W
Iwaki, *Japan* **19 A7** 37 3N 140 55 E
Iwo, *Nigeria* **30 C2** 7 39N 4 9 E
Ixopo, *S. Africa* **31 C5** 30 11S 30 5 E
Izhevsk, *Russia* **14 C9** 56 51N 53 14 E
İzmir, *Turkey* **13 E12** 38 25N 27 8 E

J

Jabalpur, *India* **23 H7** 23 9N 79 58 E
Jackson, *Ky., U.S.A.* **42 G6** 37 33N 83 23W
Jackson, *Mich., U.S.A.* **42 D5** 42 15N 84 24W
Jackson, *Miss., U.S.A.* **41 D8** 32 18N 90 12W
Jacksonville, *U.S.A.* **41 D10** 30 20N 81 39W
Jacobabad, *Pakistan* **23 E2** 28 20N 68 29 E
Jaén, *Spain* **9 D4** 37 44N 3 43W
Jaffna, *Sri Lanka* **25 E7** 9 45N 80 2 E
Jagersfontein, *S. Africa* **31 B4** 29 44S 25 27 E
Jahrom, *Iran* **24 C4** 28 30N 53 31 E
Jaipur, *India* **23 F5** 27 0N 75 50 E
Jakarta, *Indonesia* **22 D2** 6 9S 106 49 E

Place names on the yellow-coded large scale map section are to be found in the index at the end of that section

Place names on the yellow-coded large scale map section are to be found in the index at the end of that section

Place names on the yellow-coded large scale map section are to be found in the index at the end of that section

Place names on the yellow-coded large scale map section are to be found in the index at the end of that section

INDEX TO WORLD MAPS

Place names on the yellow-coded large scale map section are to be found in the index at the end of that section

Place names on the yellow-coded large scale map section are to be found in the index at the end of that section

Place names on the yellow-coded large scale map section are to be found in the index at the end of that section

Place names on the yellow-coded large scale map section are to be found in the index at the end of that section

Vanino

Zwolle

Place names on the yellow-coded large scale map section are to be found in the index at the end of that section